THE RUSSIANS AND PRUSSIANS DURING THE SEVEN YEARS' WAR

By
Alfred Rambaud

**Translated and Annotated
by G.F. Nafziger**

Original work:

PARIS
Berger-Levrault
5, Rue des Beaux-Arts

. . . .

1895

The Russians and Prussian During the Seven Years' War by Alfred Rambaud
Translated by G. F. Nafziger
Cover by Carl Röchling – *The Battle of Leuthen*
This edition published in 2022

Winged Hussar is an imprint of

Winged Hussar Publishing, LLC
1525 Hulse Rd, Unit 1
Point Pleasant, NJ 08742

Copyright © Winged Hussar Publishing
ISBN 978-1-945430-70-1 HC
ISBN 978-1-950423-96-5 EB
LCN 2022944123

Bibliographical References and Index
1. History. 2. Military. 3. Seven Years War

Winged Hussar Publishing, LLC All rights reserved
For more information
visit us at www.whpsupplyroom.com

Twitter: WingHusPubLLC
Facebook: Winged Hussar Publishing LLC

Table of Contents

PREFACE

Since the existence of the Russian Empire and the State of Prussia, these two powerful monarchies, neighbors, have frequently had cause for conflict, but there was only one war between the two states.[1] This war lasted from 1756 to 1761. It was marked by several bloody battles, Gross Jägersdorf, Zorndorf, Paltzig, and Kunersdorf, and included the Russian entry into Berlin and has left a durable memory in both nations. In the Winter Palace, at St. Petersburg, one sees with pleasure paintings representing the great events of the Seven Years War; and it was not long ago that the young German Emperor gave a toast in which he made a bellicose reference to the battle of Zorndorf, but for which there is no official transcript.

In this war, Russia operated in coordination with France, with the sworn goal "to break the forces of the King of Prussia". However, we will restrain ourselves, in this work, from seeking allusions to time present. The Seven Years War occurred under the most particular conditions; the combinations of alliances were so unforeseen and so strange, that the Europe of that time little resembles that of today. I will, as a result, restrict myself to discussing the role of Russia in the Coalition formed against Frederick II; how its armies were composed and how they behaved on the battlefields. Despite all the differences that the art of warfare presents in the 18th century and the 19th century, regarding the characteristics of recruitment, armament, tactics and the strategy of the reign of Elisabeth, we find traits that are common to the Russian Army in both centuries, which have something of a durable and permanent nature, something that is ingrained in the character of the nation and serves as a pledge of hope for the future.

In writing this work I have relied heavily on the recent work of Staff Colonel (subsequently General Major Masslovski, *Rousskaia Armia v Semilieinouiou Voinou. [The Russian Army in the Seven Years War.]* This is an enormous work of three volumes, containing a total of 2,500 pages in Russian, with a number of army returns, maps, and operational plans. The author, quite up to date in all that was published in every language, has in addition pillaged the Russian Archives of War and of the General Staff. His work is entirely military. For the five years of this war, he gives us each march and counter march, the end of each day's march, every council of war, and the

---

[1] In this, we are disregarding the armed co-operation that Prussia was forced to bring to Napoleon for the 1812 campaign. Napoleon required a Prussian contingent of 20,000 men under the General Yorck von Wartenberg. Moreover, none of the Prussian regiments followed it to Moscow and camped in the Kremlin. The support lent by Yorck von Wartenburg was always very precarious and eventually the Prussians defected at the beginning of the reverses suffered by the Grande Armée and a convention was signed at Tauroggen with the Russians as a prelude to the German uprising.

state of provisions in the Russian Army. After each operation, each fight, each battle, he criticizes that operation in detail, to seek out what is interesting to the specialists of the profession, be it positive or negative. The work is not easy reading, but it can be extremely instructive to soldiers, especially for students of the military, for whom it is especially intended. For the historian, it is invaluable, in the sense that it is a clear representation of the Russian Army of the Seven Years War. Said army cannot be confused with that of Peter the Great and Anna Ivanova, which it succeeded, nor with those of Catherine II, Paul I, or Alexander I, which it preceded. If we persist in depicting it as regiment or fantasy battles, it is not the Masslovski's fault: it is that we have forgotten the regulation of 1755 or 1756 which created the dragoons commanded by Apraxin or Fermor from all the other dragoons which had been commanded by Münich or later by Potemkin.[2]

It is regrettable that a work of this importance, precisely because it is too large to be translated, will remain unknown to French readers. I have edited a few parts of it for inclusion in the *Nouvelle Revue*, which I thought useful to make it more widely known.

However, in this book one will find I have made use of other sources than Masslovski. He is very sober on all that does not touch on the technique of the art of warfare. He neglects all anecdotes, even those which would be most instructive on the spirit and manners of the army. He did not do any research on the picturesque, even in his accounts of battles. In the approach he takes, he ignores memoirs and correspondence, which he supposes is known by the Russian reader; but, as they will perhaps be new for the French reader, I have used this material. Finally, I found with the Archives of the French Department of Foreign Affairs the reports of French and Austrian military attachés assigned to the Russian Army.

This book still differs from Masslovski's book in that, on the same depth, we have proposed different goals, since we did not have in mind the same readership.

However, like Masslovski, I did not wish to recount the history of either Russian policy or of Russian or European diplomacy. This history has frequently been examined. It is enough for me to reference, among the Russian works, that of Soloviev; among the German writers, those of Schœfer and Arneth; among the French works, *Louis XV et Élisabeth* by Albert Vandal, and with two volumes that I published in the collection of the *Instructions pour les ambassadeurs et agents français à l'étranger*. I will speak about the diplomatic history only as far as it will be useful to render comprehensible military operations.

August 1894.
A. RIMBAUD.

[2] Apraxin is sometimes rendered as Apraksin.

Frederick the Great by Anna Therbusch, 1772

CHAPTER I

RUSSIAN COURT AND EUROPEAN DIPLOMACY

The Tsarina Elisabeth Petrovna, daughter of Peter the Great, had long been isolated from the throne, initially by her cousin Anna Ivanovna, widow of a Duke of Courland, then by Anna Leopoldovna, of Mecklenburg, Duchess of Brunswick-Bevern, regent in the name of a child still in the cradle, which was the unfortunate Ivan VI. The government of the two Annas had delivered Russia to the Germans. One had seen Biren, son of a stableman of Courland, lover of Ivanovna, reign under the name of his mistress. Then, it was a German emperor who, in his swaddling clothes, gained the succession, under the supervision of his mother, Mecklenburg, and of his father, Brunswick.

Under Anna Ivanovna, the Westphalian Ostermann directed the foreign affairs; Münich, from Oldenburg, was the Grand General; Korff, Lœwenwold, Keyserling, and Bevern, occupied the major embassies; the armies were commanded by Bismarck and three Biren generals; the great servants of the court were held by another Lœwenwold, the Lievens, Brevera, and Eichler. The court was entirely German; its language, manners, the kitchen, policy, theater, modes, and its taste, were that of the small towns of Westphalia or Saxony. The leaders of the Russian aristocracy, the most eminent members of the clergy, were in disgrace, in the exile, or in prison. The daughter of the reforming Tsar, who the people, the soldiers and the priests venerated as "the spark of Peter the Great", was held far from the business of the court, was subjected to the most rigorous monitoring, and was always one day away from being thrown into a convent.

The coup d'état of December 1741, where Elisabeth took the initiative with the support of the French ambassador, La Chétardie, had briskly changed everything, placed the Brunswick Emperor and his relatives in prison, placed the daughter of Peter the Great on the throne, dispersed the German governors, and raised to command and some of the embassies their creatures.

This coup de main, supported by the Russian Guard regiments, acclaimed by the clergy and the people, greeted by the Archbishop of Novgorod as a triumph over "Beelzebub and his angles," sung about by the poet Lomonossov as the act of liberation of Russia from the "foreign flood" and tore from it "the night of Egyptian servitude," was the reaction of the national party against the "German domination," against their customs, their language, and their politics.

Elisabeth reigned as an absolute sovereign, with all the czarist absolutism. She had a sharp, natural intelligence, but was entirely devoid of education; she had the will of a ruler but did not have the facilities. The French ambassador, La Chétardie, wrote of this in his secret correspondence, which was intercepted, decrypted, and read. This correspondence presents a very unflattering portrait of the Tsarina, and shows her uniting the most outraged and intolerant devotion to the coarsest superstition; a sluggish mind and a naiveté that put her at the discretion of those around her; frightened and startled at the least business and smaller intellectual efforts; having a taste only for the festivals, the toilet, domestic intrigues, subjugated to ministers who betrayed her confidence, so badly served that one can buy her confessor and chambermaids. The secret correspondence of the other foreign ministers is hardly more favorable to her. In fact, her manners were always irresponsible. Before the coup d'état, as much by policy as by taste, she chose her favorites from the ranks of the regiments of her Guard. The secret marriage, by which she chose, in 1742, to marry one of her lovers, Razumovski, was not a brake for her; it only appeared to add spice to her adultery. Since 1749, the favorite who held this title was Ivan Shuvalov, whose elevation raised all his friends.

The empress was aged: born in 1709, she was 32 years old on her advent; she was 47 when the Seven Years War began. Catherine II, at that age, remained young; but Elisabeth was no longer a young woman, because infirmities had struck her. Her flaws did nothing but worsen, especially her loathing to occupy herself seriously with the business of the state.

The physical and moral weakness of the Empress supported the intrigues around her. The direction of foreign affairs as well as the direction of military operations would suffer accordingly.

Elisabeth, by the coup d'état of 1741, had been able to overthrow the Brunswick dynasty and to destroy the "domination of the Germans;" but she had been able to very little modify the international situation of Russia, whose characteristic feature was a narrow union with Austria.   Saint Simon tells us that her father had passionately sought an alliance with France, initially under Louis XIV, then under the regency of the Duke of Orléans. He had succeeded in obtaining a treaty of friendship and trade signed in 1717 in Amsterdam. Elisabeth's mother, Catherine I, had pursued the same policy, and at one point hoped to marry her daughter with the young Louis XV. The haughtiness of the Duke de Bourbon, successor of the Duke d'Orléans, had forced the empress Cahterine I to throw herself into an Austrian alliance. The Austro-Russian treaty, signed in Vienna, on 6 August 1726, fixed for the remainder of the century the direction of the Tsarina's policy. The German Anna Ivanovna and her advisers had hastened to give their support to the Court of Vienna in the War of the Polish Succession. The government of Louis XV had taken its revenge by provoking a war between the two united powers and Turkey, which they could end only by requesting the mediation of the King in the conferences for the Peace of Belgrade (1739).

With the advent of Elisabeth, Louis XV hoped that he would break with this tradition and that he would find her on his side in the War of the Austrian Succession. The new empress, indeed, had refused the troops provided for in the treaty of 1726 and the treaties which had renewed and confirmed it. But the very sharp concern of the Court of Versailles for Swedish interests, the excessive requests by La Chétardie in his first embassy, allowed Alexey Bestuchev-Ryumin, Elisabeth's new chancellor, to hold in check the pro-French sentiments of the Tsarina.

Chétardie was sent again on an embassy to Petersburg, and he sought to reconquer all his influence on the sovereign and to overthrow the Chancellor, however, his imprudent behavior, especially the discovery of his secret correspondence, caused an explosion. He was expelled from Russia. Two years later, in 1746, Bestuchev signed with the Tsarina a new offensive and defensive alliance with Austria; then, in 1747, treaties of subsidies were signed with England and Holland. This same year, a task force of 30,000 Russians marched through Germany, under the command of Prince Repnine, to operate in the Netherlands; but it arrived on the Rhine when the preliminaries of the Peace of Aachen were about to be signed (1748).

Russia had intervened in the War of Austrian Succession only as an auxiliary power of Austria, and not as a belligerent power. In the concepts of the time, the diplomatic relations between the Courts of Versailles and St. Petersburg should not have been broken. However, they were broken at the time when the Peace of Aachen was about to be concluded. They were so difficult to rebuild during the eight years that elapsed before new ambassadors were accredited. This period was almost entirely occupied by a raging fight between the two diplomacies on their traditional areas of competition: Sweden, Poland, and Turkey. In a report to the Tsarina, Bestuchev was pleased with results, which he regarded as glorious for Russian policy and the Army. "As long as Her Imperial Majesty had condescended to consider with an indifferent eye the interferences (those of France and Prussia) which tended to tear Europe apart, the flame of the war had done nothing but grow. On the contrary, as soon as she had expressed her will to intervene with an imposing force, at once, the situation of all European affairs assumed a quite different aspect... The Russian Observation Corps is not further advanced than is necessary to propagate in all of Europe the glory of the imperial arms, to gain for the sovereign the flattering title of "pacifier of the Continent," and moreover to bring back considerable sums, by the payment of subsidies as well as by the relief that the absence of the troops on the Treasury. " Bestuchev calculated that the net benefit on subsidies, in cash, over two years, had given the Treasury nearly a million rubles. This precision in calculation and the satisfaction expressed by the Grand Chancellor of Russia were worthier of a commercial prince, such as that of Hesse-Cassel, that of the minister charged with directing the diplomacy of a great empire. This mercantile interest would influence more than once Bestuchev's political maneuvers. The army and the nation felt humiliated. The provision of mercenaries would not arouse the military energies of such people. He had the instinct of another policy, where the size of the country, its national and religious aspirations, would have held more place.

There was a power that Russia hated and feared more still than France: it was the Prussia of Frederick II. During the War of the Austria Succession, in 1744, Bestuchev had already declared that the King of Prussia was more to be feared than France, "because of his proximity and the increase in his forces... It is naturally so, even if he were not so inconstant, avid, anxious and turbulent... Our dangers increase with the forces of the King of Prussia." It was against him much more than Louis XV in 1746 that the Austro-Russian alliance had been renewed. One was indignant with St. Petersburg for its "bravados" at "the overconfident neighbor." One did not forgive him for having drawn Russia aside in the conferences for the Peace of Aachen, under the pretext of which it had appeared a "mercenary" power in war. The reports that were received on his actions and movements betrayed his extreme liberty, with regards to the Tsarina, by his table talk; he did not cease mock her devotion, her penchant for drink, the easiness of her manners. Just as much for France, one found it everywhere blocking the interests of Russia. Louis had not dared to offer to Maurice of Saxony the hand of his sister with Courland for a dowry: this Courland that the Tsarina regarded as one of her future provinces! When Russia had tried to provoke a revolution in Sweden, it had pushed its rearming and had spoken in a threatening manner; he did not cease exciting the Poles and the Turks against her. In 1750, Elisabeth enjoined all the officers originating from her Baltic provinces and engaged in the foreign service to return without delay to Russia. It was especially the service of Prussia that this *oukaze* had in mind: the King of Prussia showed himself as being extremely irritated. One of these officers, the Estonian Collonge, had gone to the Russian Ambassador in Berlin, and was immediately arrested. The ambassador suffered, on this occasion, many affronts: one day, he was prohibited from visiting the new palace that the King was constructing, Sans-Souci; another day, after a convocation of the diplomatic corps, he was the only one of foreign ministers who was not invited to dine. One affected to invite him only at the balls. When he ceased appearing at court, the King seemed to take no notice. The ambassador had tried to recruit for the academy of St. Petersburg the Prussian astronomer Grichau: he was stopped at once by the order of the King. The same constraint prevented the illustrious Euler from going to Russia.

Frederick II, who would not suffer anyone from recruiting in his states and hung a Saxon recruiter, forcefully pressganged Saxons and Poles. He grabbed Russian subjects as they passed through his territories. It was thus that the *raskolnik* Zubarov was seized during his passage through Russia.

However, Frederick II, with regards to this man, did something even graver. He decided that this man would be more useful to him, not in a regiment, but as a dissident sent back to Russia with the mission of provoking a revolt among his co-religionists, exasperated by the bigoted persecutions of Elisabeth. And, in effect, Zubarov recrossed the frontier with a sum of 2,000 ducats and two soldiers.

Ismailovski Grenadiers   Line Grenadiers   Officer of the Foot Guard Grenadiers

Elisabeth did not hide her hatred for Frederic II: "The King of Prussia," she said to Lord Hyndford, "is certainly a malicious prince who does not have the fear of God before his eyes; he ridicules holy things; he never goes to the church; he is the Nadir-Shah of Persia." Thus, the scandalmonger spirit of the King and his bad comments had formed a frightening coalition of three women against him: Tsarina Elisabeth, Empress Marie-Therese and Marchioness de Pompadour, a queen of the left hand.[3] Gross, the Russian minister that had been recalled from Paris in 1748 and who had been transferred to the Berlin station, was, after the affronts mentioned above, also recalled from Berlin.

[3] Translator: "Une reine de la main gauche"[or queen of the left hand] means this was a "morganatic marriage" : The partner is of a lower social rank: During the wedding ceremony, the bridegroom holds his fiancée's right hand with her left hand instead of the right hand.

In addition, Bestuchev, who had decrypted the correspondence of Mardefeldt, the Prussian Minister to St. Petersburg, with as much of care as that of the representatives of France, made it possible to get rid of an agent who, in his eyes, was a spy. And thus, in 1749, diplomatic relations were broken with both Prussia and France.

Consequently, Bestuchev's obsession was to seize the first opportunity to cut down the power of Frederick II. On 7 May 1753 he read with his sovereign a celebrated report that recalled all the territorial increases of this dangerous neighbor, the conquest of Silesia and the plundering of Saxony, and the millions that had been used by him to increase his army from 80,000 to 200,000 men: his covetousness of Hanover, Courland, and Polish Prussia. "His grandfather and his great-grandfather, who did not have excessive forces, restrained themselves, because of the vicinity of Russia, from making themselves proud and difficult; they were constrained to seek an alliance with Russia; today what a difference!" His conclusion was that it was important for Russia to defend the states threatened by Frederick II and "to break his forces". In 1756, Bestuchev said again that it was necessary "to make of this proud prince a prince who is contemptible to the Turks, with the Poles, even with the Swedes."

In the general situation of Europe, it appeared obvious that one would have to fight Prussia at the same time as one fought France and the other sovereigns of the House of Bourbon; the alliance on which one could count was thus that of Austria and England. France, indeed, seemed inseparable from King of Prussia and, moreover, the relations between it and the Tsarina became more hostile every day. It was France which, in 1751, had forced Russia to evacuate Sweden, which it momentarily occupied, and in Constantinople, in 1755, his envoy Des Alleurs vigorously worked to encourage the Turks.

If it was difficult to bring together the Courts of Versailles and St. Petersburg, it is not that Elisabeth was opposed to it. On the contrary, since she had hoped to become queen of France, she had always preserved a sharp sympathy to France and the French King; she seemed to have inherited the French tendencies of her father and mother. Her favorite at the time, Ivan Guvalov, liked the French language, its arts, manners, modes, and furniture. "It is French to burn," he wrote to Frederick in 1760.

On the other hand, the Grand-Chancellor Bestuchev did not hide his dislke of the French. His hatred for Frederick II was for him a new reason to hate France, Prussia's ally. A French representative to the court of Russia had obstructed him a great deal: he did not worry about having to defend his position against the intrigues of another Chétardie. By his police force, by his black cabinet, he blocked any attempt at a rapprochement. In 1754, a certain Chevalier de Valcroissant, who came from France to Russia, probably with a secret mission, at once was arrested and locked up in the Schlüsselburg

Fortress.

Vice-Chancellor Vorontsov, Bestuchev's assistant and under the supervision of Grand-Chancellor, was the confidant to the most intimate feelings of the Tsarina. He was, like her, hostile in Frederick II and well-disposed towards France; but he was too careful to openly thwart the views of his superior; he was satisfied to take good note of his political faults.

Thus, the governments and the diplomats of the two countries persisted in their hostility. But Louis XV already had a policy distinct from that of his government: since 1747 his secret diplomacy had come into play. Elisabeth, on her side, kept her personal feelings to herself and started to find the supervision of her Grand-Chancellor at odds with her views. In spite of the official diplomacy, the police forces in the pay of the two chancelleries of the black cabinets and the decryption offices, the two sovereigns found means to communicate their feelings. While the Chevalier de Valcroissant groaned in the Schlüsselburg's dungeons, a certain Michel de Rouen, a French merchant established in St. Petersburg and who made buying trips to Paris, carried and reported with his notes their political messages. The Scot Mackenzie Douglas left for St. Petersburg, in June 1755, with instructions on the secret diplomacy of the King. He was introduced to Vorontsov, who did not dare to present him to the Tsarina but was given the responsibility of transmitting the proposals to her. Then Douglas, who, in spite of this first success, greatly feared Bestuchev, suddenly left St. Petersburg. He reappeared there the following year, this time with a letter from the French Minister of Foreign Affairs, and at the same time, was charged with both secret diplomacy and official diplomacy. Bestuchev attempted, one said, to get rid of him by assassination. Douglas succeed in being received by the Tsarina and had a signed treaty that would later be questionable (accession of Russia to the first Treaty of Versailles). What there was of ambiguity in the conduct in the policy of these two great countries was further accentuated by the role played by the mixed character of the Chevalier d'Éon, who was then attached to Douglas as his secretary. It was only in July 1757 that an ambassador of the King, the Marquis de L'Hôpital, made his entry with great pomp into St. Petersburg, while an ambassador of the Tsarina, Michel Bestuchev, the proper brother of the Grand-Chancellor, had gone to Paris to take possession of the station given to him for eight years.

An unforeseen crisis, which had just upset diplomatic Europe, had precipitated this bringing together of France and Russia. It is what one called the inversion of alliances. France and England, the two ancient enemies, were again at war; but this time the ally of England was Prussia, and the ally of France was Austria.[4]

With this alliance, Austria was to bring Russia into alliance with France. The most singular imbroglio of treaties had prepared this singular

---

[4]Modern sources refer to his inversion of alliances as the Diplomatic Reovlution.

combination of the European forces.

On 30 September 1755, at St. Petersburg, Bestuchev had concluded with Williams, the English Minister, a treaty by which Russia would furnish a contingent of 80,000 men in exchange for a sum of £500,000 and an annual subsidy of £100,000.

In their negotiations, Williams believed that British gold would be spent for Austria's benefit against France and Bestuchev counted that the Russian soldiers would be employed against Prussia. On both sides, they had not considered it useful to clear up and specify the obligations. The warnings had however not missed by Bestuchev: Vorontsov begged him to assure that the Tsarina's troops were not used against her intentions and her interests; he advised his colleague to at least defer the ratification of the treaty. Bestuchev unquestionably believed that English subsidies would only enable him to make a not very dangerous war against Prussia, "in the name of and with the money of another power;" he estimated that the military action of Russia could be limited to a simple "diversion", of a kind of exercise or of military promenade, which would increase the reputation of the Tsarina, would offer the occasion to her generals to show their bravery and their talents, her officers the opportunity to prove their devotion, and to allow the soldiers to give themselves over to "these noble occupations, suitable with their profession, and in which they could not be exerted too much." Again, he calculated the sums that would flow into the Treasury. Personally, he was avid and corruptible; Williams had found irresistible arguments to deaden his perspicacity. Vorontsov's merit was to have designed the policy in the form of a treaty for the sale or hiring of Russian soldiers to a foreign power.

With the news of the Treaty of St. Petersburg, great terror spread throughout Berlin. Berlin had always had and there was particularly on that day a fear of Russia. It was so close and by an invasion from the east could bring with it most catastrophic results. Frederick II's father had already said: "I know the means well of detaching the Russian bear; but who then will be given the responsibility to replace the chain?" And the King-Philosopher would write, in 1769, to Prince Henry: "It is a terrible power, which in one century will make Europe tremble." He saw only one expedient to draw Prussia from this danger, and that was to conclude a treaty of alliance and subsidies with England. It was signed in Westminster, on 16 January 1756: in return for financial assistance, Frederick committed himself to taking uparms "against any power that would violate Germanic territory." He had no scruples about denouncing his old alliance with the Court of Versailles and to be put in the pay of a power that had begun the war with France with the assassination of Jumonville and the piracies of Boscawen. He rejected the advances of Louis XV, who had sent the Count de Nivernais to him to renew the treaty of alliance and who had offered the Prussian envoy Knyphausen the rich prize of Hanover, by telling him: "The treasury of the King George II is well furnished; what your King can grab [is his]; it will be a good catch." The fear of the Russians had caused Frederick not to listen.

What is no less surprising, is the indifference that England showed in passing from an Austrian alliance to a Prussian alliance, to mobilize its forces and its subsidies against this Marie-Therese who had been so devoted to them during the last war; it is the peace of conscience with which it engaged itself to subsidize, at the same time, Russia and Prussia, even though it was certain that these two powers awaited only English money to throw themselves on each other; this was its absolute misunderstanding of the feelings and the most obvious interests of these continental powers. That Marie-Theresa looked on retaking Silesia as a sacred duty, Frederick II sought to preserve it against all comers, Elisabeth sought "to break the forces" of a dangerous neighbor, nothing of which interested England; she wanted to know nothing; she knew nothing of it. It was enough for England to maintain a mercenary power on the continent: that this power was called Austria, Prussia or Russia, mattered little; that these three states had divergent interests, that the only fact of the treaties of subsidies had as their result the arming Prussia against Austria, Russia against Prussia, and set fire to the four corners of Europe, was a deep policy which did not trouble William Pitt for a moment.

The first consequence of the Treaty of Westminster was the cancellation of the treaty of St. Petersburg: Williams appeared not to have initially understood that one was the destruction of the other. He fought, begged, lavished promises, and even cried, declaring that "England was lost." He left St. Petersburg with the hope of returning there soon.

Frederick II was also completely mistaken about the situation. He initially believed that the Treaty of Westminster would turn to his advantage the stipulations of the Treaty of St. Petersburg, which would place at his disposal the Russian troops bought by England: "I have 100,000 men, he said; "if one could add 30,000 Russians to it! " In May, he took measures to facilitate the landing of them in Pomerania, in order to hold the Swedes in check, who were necessarily the allies of France.

But already, on 25 March, a large government council had been held, in the presence of Elisabeth. The following resolutions were taken: 1° to urge Austria to attack Frederick II, by promising the assistance of 80,000 Russians; 2° to try to obtain, in the Continental war, the neutrality of France, whose war against the English appeared already to sufficient occupy them; 3° to prepare Poland to accept the passage of Russian troops on its territory; 4° to determine the means of holding Sweden and Turkey in check; 5° to break the forces of Frederick II, by obliging them to restore Silesia to Austria and to deliver East Prussia to Russia (Russia proposed to yield this province to Poland, which in exchange would yield its rights to Courland to Russia and would grant a correction of its border in the Ukraine).

It was on 19 February that Esterhazy, the Austrian ambassador to the Court of St. Petersburg, had revealed to them the Treaty of Westminster. Russia was already tied to Austria by the treaties of 1726 and 1746. However preliminary articles were ordered in March, in the greatest secrecy, and given to Esterhazy in April. They were to lead to a new offensive and defensive treaty, that of 2 February 1757, in virtue of which each of the two Imperial courts was to arm 80,000 men against Frederick II; Russia committed itself to not terminating hostilities before Austria had recovered Silesia and the County of Glatz. It received from Austria an annual subsidy of a million rubles.

The Treaty of Westminster had other consequences. It confirmed the Court of Versailles in its projects of conciliation with Austria, hastening the conclusion of an alliance which the traditional diplomats regarded as unrealizable and against nature. On 1 May 1756, there was signed in Versailles the first treaty between France and the House of Hapsburg. However, Louis XV only put 24,000 men at the disposal of Austria. Then, after the invasion of Saxony by Frederick II, the Treaty of Stockholm, of 21 March 1757, concluded by France and Austria with Sweden, ensured them, by means of subsidies, the help of a Swedish army of 20,000 men. Then the Second Treaty of Versailles, dated 1 May 1757, raised the French forces in Germany to 105,000 men. Finally, the Third Treaty of Versailles, dated 30 December 1758, maintained them at 100,000 men. France threw itself with all its forces into the continental war.

At St. Petersburg, where they had restricted themselves to hoping for the neutrality of France and where they had decided on the means of holding a tight rein on Sweden and Turkey, the joy was great when they learned of the conclusion of the first Austro-Russian treaty. It was no longer the neutrality of France, it was its co-operation; of its two clients, Sweden and Turkey, one became an ally; the peace of the other was assured. Russia successively acceded to the First Treaty of Versailles, the Treaty of Stockholm, and the Third Treaty of Versailles.

However, Russia was not precisely the ally of France; it was only the ally of its ally, Austria. Though Louis XV had an ambassador at St. Petersburg and military attachés with the armies of the Tsarina, he did not agree to enter direct negotiations with Russia, but only for the negotiation of a commercial treaty. He never wanted to grant to him indispensable subsidies to a country that was still poor to be maintained on the war footing: he preferred to give money to Austria and that Austria then give money to Russia. Thus, Russia seems to have entered the Coalition only under the terms of the Austro-Russian treaties of 1726 and 1746, which had been directed against France. France entered the war not as a belligerent power, but as an auxiliary power of the one of the allies; it was forced, as much as one could, to subordinate its politics and even its military operations to those of Austria; and, like the policy of Austria is primarily egotistic and its operations badly directed, this was one of the main causes of the failure of the Coalition.

The government of Elisabeth saw the situation much more clearly than that of Louis XV; it was distressed to see France subordinating itself to Austria and forcing Russia to subordinate itself to Austria as well. It would have liked to free itself and see the French freed of a touchy and suspect supervision. On several occasions, by official channels, by the secret correspondence, again in December 1760, the Tsarina proposed to Louis XV a new treaty of alliance, wider and more explicit than the simple Treaties of Accession, directly concluded between France and Russia. Louis XV always refused these propositions.

Louis XV had an ulterior motive. If the rapprochement between France and Russia put an end to the fight between their diplomacy in Stockholm, in Warsaw, in Constantinople, the germs of conflict were not eliminated. The King always feared Russia's ambitions. He feared them for his traditional allies, Sweden, Turkey, and Poland, especially for Poland. On several occasions, during the Seven Years War, Russia had sacrificed the interests of the Coalition, even the interests of France, for those of Poland. And how does he view the interests of Poland? In the narrowest manner, he was passionate, as an absolute prince, for the maintenance of what he called "Polish freedoms," which was actually for the maintenance of the noble anarchy by which Poland was to die. More still than Russia's official diplomacy, its secret diplomacy was to be alert to anything that involved this country. Not a Russian unit, marching to fight the common enemy, did not traverse the territory of the Republic without the agents of the King in Warsaw and St. Petersburg hearing reservations and protests. Louis XV did not want to hear of the acquisition of East Prussia by Tsarina, or the replacement of this province against the Polish rights on Courland, or of an unspecified correction of border, in the remote Ukraine, between the Republic and Russia.

Would one believe that this monarch, who was so scrupulous with regards to the integrity of the Polish territory was the same who would one day, with crossed arms, participate in the partitioning of Poland?

Louis XV felt reluctant regarding a sincere friendship with Russia. Unceasingly in the instructions he sent to his ambassadors, he told them to be on guard against this Utopia: "The distance between the two empires is too great for there ever to be formed an alliance between them." Because of this frame of mind, just as he feared Russia becoming more powerful, he did not wish that it become victorious, even over the common enemy. If they beat Frederick II, the Russians would become "too demanding and arrogant." One comforted oneself of their failures, because "the Russian Ministry could no longer form such claims that could embarrass it."

Otherwise, the Austrians did not wish that the Russians were too victorious either. More than once we will see them blocking the Russians' operations, trying to limit their successes and, so to speak, setting traps for their generals.

These ulterior motives in an obvious union, the fears and the rivalries otherwise surviving everywhere in the alliance, the jealousies that the ally's successes inspired, the fear that it might be too victorious, is what made impotent this great effort of the allied continent against the smallest of the military monarchies.

Musketeer, Drummer, Senior Officer, and Grenadiers of the Semenovski Regiment

Other causes of weakness are unique to Russia. One would have thought it could act with all the focus of an autocratic government. But it did not. If one wanted to find, during this war, unity in its actions, the continuation in its ideas, a unity in its efforts, it is not in the absolutist courts of the Coalition, no more in Petersburg that in Vienna or Versailles. It was initially in Frederick II's camp; it was then in London, despite the competition between the parties and the noisy discussions in Parliament. The Russian autocracy showed itself less unified than the British oligarchy. We are misled by appearances: actually, there were more parties, more divisions, and more irreconcilable issues between them, in the Winter Palace than at Westminster Palace. The war against Frederick II was not seen with the same eye by all of Elisabeth's courtiers. The alliance with France, unlike that of the time of the writing of this work, was not national; the people were unaware of it, the army was unconcerned, as was the Russian aristocracy, about what to think, regarding what occurred in the Winter Palace or at Tsarskoe-Selo.

Not enough time had passed since an ambassador of France complained about seeing the Russian society avoiding his salons as long as he had not received the explicit order to attend them, since this same ambassador had seen himself expelled from the capital, since the Russians had felt the hand of France in Sweden and Constantinople. These French, against which they had fought at Gdansk and which one had provoked twice on the Rhine, were after all, for many Russians, only a variety of Niemisi, i.e., Germans, foreigners, infidels. A new alliance had begun as an intrigue, by a merchant of courteousness, a Scottish adventurer and a knight who passed as being a Chevalier. This was only a half-alliance, an under-alliance, subordinated to that which France maintained with Austria. By itself, it offered Russia no advantage, and seemed to refuse it everything. France had not ceased being the friend of the Turks; the Swedes and continued protecting the Poles. This alliance was fragile; it was held together with a single string, the life of a morbid woman who was physically older than her age.

It had not yet been strongly determined to continue the alliance with France and the war with Prussia by the Empress Elisabeth, and with her favorite Shuvalov, and all the Shuvalovs, his vice-chancellor Vorontsov, and consequently most of the Vorontsov family. Let us remember that, 50 years later, in 1807, there were not, in Russia, many decided partisans of a Franco-Russian alliance beyond Emperor Alexander and his Rumyantsev minister. As for Elisabeth's Grand-Chancellor, Alexis Bestuchev, he saw himself thrown into this alliance as a result of an error in his calculations. This error, which had made him the dupe of England, had decreased him in the eyes of his sovereign as with his own people. His credit had dropped as that of his rival Vorontsov rose. Bestuchev had intended to fight France and now found he was about to fight on France's side. He had ceased appearing infallible. This did not act to reconcile him with France. He was at least hesitant and tepid, even admitting that he did not remain hostile at the bottom of his heart. Others were resolutely hostile. It is necessary for us to speak here about the Young Court, because there had been a Young Court since Elisabeth had aged.

Elisabeth, as of her advent, appeared to be determined not to marry, at least officially. However, one needed an heir to the throne. To this end, she brought a young prince from Holstein, the progeny of the marriage of one of her sisters to the duke of that country. He was called Peter, but when baptized into the Orthodox Religion in Russia, he was called Peter Feodorovich, though the name of his father was Charles-Frederick. He was the grandson of Peter the Great, but even though he was brought to Russia at the age of 14, he remained a German. His tutor, another German, was named, Brummer, or as a contemporary commented, a trainer of horses, who beat and tied Peter to the foot of his bed but was incapable of teaching him anything. Few heirs to a throne were ever so badly treated. Peter was small, weak, almost deformed, and marked by smallpox; he appeared to be completely stripped of intelligence, courage, or kindness. Married at age 18, he neglected his wife to continue to waste his time in the most puerile recreations. He played with tin soldiers, maneuvered his servants, played with his dogs, and scraped at the violin. He detested books and any application of the mind.

His wife was also a German, the Princess Sophia von Anhalt-Zerbst-Dornberg, who, when baptized in the Orthodox Faith, became the Grand Duchess Catherine Alexievna, even though her father called her Christiana-Augusta. Her father was from a cadet branch of the House of Dornberg, as well of that of Anhalt-Zerbst. He had been obliged to seek service in Prussia and had become a general. He commanded the garrison of Stettin with his wife and daughter there when Frederick II caught wind of the project of a Saxon marriage for Elisabeth's heir. "Nothing was more contrary," he tells us, "to the State of Prussia than an alliance between Saxony and Russia, and nothing would have appeared more denatured than to sacrifice a royal princess of Prussia to flush out the Saxon woman." But it was not unnatural to offer the girl of a lesser prince who had become a general. Without consulting him, Frederick offered and caused the young girl to be accepted. Elisabeth accommodated most readily the proposal. Her mother was from Holstein: the future couple were distant cousins. Catherine II told us herself, in her *Memoirs* published by Hertzen, which described her life as a grand duchess in a court full of intrigue and traps, between an empress who treated her as a poor relationship; a husband whose first aspect had struck her with horror; the Grand-Chancellor Bestuchev who supervised her and hated her as a creature of his enemy the King of Prussia; a mother with an anxious and agitated character who compromised her in her intrigues, of Young Courtiers who only sought to lose her, and of the old men, like Shuvalov, who spied on her and who only sought to find fault in her. What humiliations devoured her; what tears she poured out! She was forbidden to cry when her father died: "It is not appropriate for grand duchess to cry for a father who was not a king."[5]

However, the future Catherine II had been well armed for the battles of life. She was born a "struggle-for-lifer." She had an elegant, imperial beauty, with the apparent softness of the blondes; the tears that poured from her blue eyes, if they remained without effect on her husband, had the gift of touching the defiant Empress and even softened her enemies. She had a sharp intelligence which was to make her a great woman, Catherine the Great. She arrived in Russia already steeped in French culture, which she owed to a teacher in Stettin, Miss Cardel. In the insipid leisure of her life as grand duchess, she devoured books. She read books by Racine, Molière, Montesquieu, even Boileau, and Brantôme. While her husband played with puppets, she wrote in her diary's profound thoughts. She took care not to parade her knowledge and her freedom of thought. Surrounded, like she said, by excessively pious people and hypocrites, she affected the greatest zeal for the Orthodox Faith to which she had become so recently the follower; competing with the piety of her Aunt Elisabeth, she rigorously observed the fasts, never finding the rites too long. Born German, but arrived at St. Petersburg at the age of 14, she knew the language of the country better than the natives of the court and affected to be more Russian than the descendants of Rurik. She especially had a very clear sight of her situation, distinguished her goal perfectly and did not fear to look at future opposition. As of the first interview with her fiancée, she summarized her impressions thus: "The heart did not predict great happiness for me, but my ambition supported me. At the bottom of my heart, I knew what would never let me doubt for a moment that I would manage to become the Empress of Russia, to be my own boss." To become her own boss if needs be, by removing her husband. Perhaps the dreams of young girl made her foresee, without being frightened, the catastrophe that would occur years later.

Ambition did not change her heart, or her manner of speaking. They did not speak for Peter Feodorovitch. Catherine was surrounded by a rough supervision, but also by all the bad examples of a corrupt court. Several times her supervisors had been able to prevent amorous intrigues: bold young men, whose advances had not been rejected by her, suddenly disappeared. Her aunt, who hoped for her to produce an heir to her throne, would have preferred that such a child was by her husband. When it was seen that there was nothing to hope for on this side, the monitoring was slackened. The influence which the "beautiful Soltykov could exert" on the grand duchess seems not to have had any political character. Moreover, he was almost immediately sent to announce in Sweden the birth of an imperial prince (the Paul I). He was then named minister in Hamburg and never reappeared at the court. Then the favorite Stanislaus Poniatowski appeared who Catherine II would one day make King

---

[5] A. Rambaud, *L'impératrice Catherine II dans sa famillie*, in the *Revue des Deux-Mondes*, of 1 February 1874.

of Poland. Soltykov did not make policy, and the diplomatic corps near the Court of Russia appears to have been generally unaware of him. Poniatowski made some policy, and we will see what that was. The French Court was moved some: its representative from Warsaw worked to have him recalled and succeeded.

But, not long afterwards, Poniatowski reappeared in St. Petersburg, more in favor than ever, and his name often appears in the correspondence of de Broglie and Durand, the French ministers in Warsaw, of the Marquis de L'Hôpital and the Count de Breteuil, the French ambassadors with St. Petersburg, and even in the secret correspondence between Louis XV and Elisabeth. The new liaison of the Grand Duchess had become the business of the State; it concerned the European balance of power.

In the crisis that tore Europe, what were the feelings of the Grand Duke and the Grand Duchess? The first was not of a complicated nature. On the contrary it was very simple. Initially he remained German, a Holsteiner; despite his Orthodox baptism, he did not lose any occasion to deride the ceremonies of national worship; the future Emperor of Russia completely misunderstood his future subjects. He regretted his throne in Holstein, which he had, in the meantime, inherited. He readily admitted: "One dragged me into this cursed Russia... I would be now on the throne of a civilized nation." His Germanism was otherwise summarized in a fanatic, unreasoned, unintelligent admiration for his German hero Frederick II. As soon as he ceased playing with tin soldiers and he began to play with real soldiers, i.e. initially he had rigged out his stablemen in uniform, he began to be, and remained thereafter, "the monkey of the King of Prussia." He did not appear with the Conference at the government council chaired by Elisabeth, other than under protest by his words or his silence. In 1756, he refused to give his signature for the resumption of diplomatic relations with France. The decisions against Prussia inspired a deep sorrow and a violent anger in him. Later he was afflicted with the Russian victories and was delighted by its reverses. His aunt was obliged to exclude him from the conferences because one suspected him of delivering to his hero Russian diplomatic and military secrets. Austria, to attenuate his hostility a little, took advantage of his weakness: she agrees to sign with him, in his capacity as Duke of Holstein, a treaty, by which he placed at his disposal, in return for a rather large subsidy, his Holstein army, that is to say, some poor battalions.

More complex were the spirit and the policy of the Grand Duchess. She owed the marriage that had placed her on the steps of an imperial throne to Frederick II. The King of Prussia hoped to have an ally in her, an ally whose influence would stop this torrent of the Russian invasion, Cossacks, Tatars, which threatened to overflow onto his States. However, she did not love Frederick II. In 1755, she said to the British envoy: "He is the natural enemy of Russia, and the worst man in the world." At this time, she was very English just as her husband was very Prussian. It was the house of the English consul Wroughton who had sheltered her first rendezvous with Poniatowski; the Envoy Williams had also supported this intrigue; it was he who had brought Poniatowski to St. Petersburg and had presented him as being one of his secretaries. On the contrary, the French diplomacy had denounced and cursed the liaison. That greatly influenced the choice that the Grand Duchess made between the political parties. Moreover, Catherine had need of money: her aunt held the purse strings; England had an open hand. Williams encouraged her to shake the heavy yoke, "while ceasing to constrain herself, by declaring highly for those that she would honor with her kindness, while showing that she would be personally offended of all that would dare be against them." On the other hand, she "never spoke to him about the King of England other than in the terms of the deepest respect and the highest regard," regarded him as "the best and the greatest ally of the Empress," was entirely persuaded of "the utility of a close union between England and Russia," flattered herself that "the King will grant also his friendship to the Grand Duke and to herself."[6] In April 1756 she declared that "whoever would try to destroy the union between England, Austria, and Russia was not a friend of this empire." In July of the same year, she charged Williams with affirming the "devotion of the Grand Duchess to the King of England," showing herself "very concerned about the rumors that speak of an alliance with France and the arrival of a French ambassador." She entrusted her needs for money, considering that she "was obliged to pay to the chambermaids of the Empress." Williams could give "his word of honor to the King that all, to the last penny, would be employed in what she believed to be the common cause and for the advantage of the two nations." She asked for 20,000 ducats and she obtained them. It is true that Bestuchev received much more, - £2,500,000 - from this same England, and that he took from any source: 10,000 ducats from France, even Prussian money and Austrian money. This was the custom of the time. When Williams was forced, after his failure, to leave Petersburg, Catherine still wrote to him: "I will seize all the conceivable occasions to bring back Russia to what I believe is its true interests, that is to say to be closely united with England." If such a correspondence had been discovered, it had been enough to justify charges of high treason against the Grand Duchess. But her confidences with Williams had been much more and touched on otherwise delicate subjects. She dared to say to him what she proposed to do in the case where the Tsarina would die and at the very instant when she would die: "I will go straight to the room of my son... At the same moment, I will send a confidential agent to inform five officers of the Guard, of whom each one will bring me 50 soldiers....

---

[6]Extracts from Williams' correspondence *In the Court of Russia there are One Hundred Years* (Anonymous), Paris and Leipzig, 1860.

Myself I will enter the room of dying Empress, where I will receive the oath of the Captain of the Guard and I will take this one with me." She believed she could count on the support of Generals Apraxine, Löwen, Buturline, and of Chancellors Bestuchev and Vorontsov. She added: "I am determined to reign or perish."

As long as the Empress enjoyed a robust health, her will was all-powerful. Ministers, courtiers, and diplomats did not have to take account of what the Grand Duke and the Grand Duchess might think. But at the beginning of the Seven Years War, Elisabeth grew weak and had blackouts. Shuvalov and Vorontsov, the two families that were most entirely devoted to her, were in anguish and terror. The favorites of the day started to fear a new reign, and others hoped for it. Europe was in agitation. There was fear in Versailles, in Vienna, and in Dresden. There was hope in London and in the camp of Frederick. The Empress' blackouts were a political and diplomatic fact of the highest degree; the world had its neck turned towards the bed of Elisabeth. Most dangerous for Elisabeth was that the favorites would maintain her condition secretly and did not let any doctor approach her, fearing indiscretions more than hope in the remedies. At the end the Marquis de L'Hôpital, with all the conceivable precautions of language, however explained to the favorites how their interests were linked to the interests of France, speaking to them about a certain Doctor Poissonnier, both a celebrated surgeon and a distinguished physician of the diseases of women. He caused them to ask that he make the voyage to Russia to visit the Empress. Of course, secrecy would be strictly kept, and they would find some pretext, for example a trip of scientific curiosity, to explain this voyage. L'Hôpital hoped that the Poissonnier mission would be at the same time both political and medical ; that it would strengthen Elisabeth's so invaluable health for the anti-Prussian coalition, and also that it would exert on the spirit of his imperial customer an influence favorable to the French interests. Poissonnier came to St. Petersburg, but it was several months before he was able to diagnose his majestic patient. Elisabeth had already a Greek doctor, Coudoidi, who saw with displeasure the arrival of his French fellow doctor. Holding the rank of lieutenant-general in the army, he refused to consult with a rival who was not even "doctor of the King" and State Counselor. It was only when Poissonnier obtained the honorary title of Associate of the Academy of St. Petersburg that the lieutenant-general-doctor became humanized. He allowed Poissonnier to see his patient. The French doctor noted in Elisabeth several serious afflictions; but he believed he could reassure the Versailles Cabinet that there was no immediate danger. He did not answer for the future. However, it is this future that the Young Court discounted.

There were thus at least four parties in Russia: that of the family of Brunswick, which watched from the fortress of Schlüsselburg and dreamed of revenge for the coup d'état of 1741; that of the Empress herself, who had an absolute confidence only in the families of her three favorites, Razumovski, Shuvalov and Vorontsov; that of the Grand Duke, which was very small, because most had perceived his being a nullity; and that of the Grand Duchess who, without worrying about Holsteiners, wanted to make Catherine an empress, either associated with her son, or of her chief. This is the party that grew daily, as the health of the Tsarina failed, and the Grand Duke became more hateful to the Russians. And already Bestuchev, who had long been the enemy and the persecutor of Catherine, approached her and worked out a plan where the Grand Duke would have another role, only that of a sacrifice. It was understood that the intrigues of the court could influence the operations of the army.

Thus, the Coalition which was formed against Frederick II was a coalition divided against itself, with the divergent interests of France, of Austria, of Russia, of Sweden, of Saxony, and other Germanic states. And Russia itself had an uncertain will, being torn in opposite directions by the Old Court and the Young Court.

And which enemy did one have to fight? Undoubtedly the state of Frederick II was one of the smallest among the great powers; but it could make any Prussian a soldier; it had the best organized army in Europe, and no one knew how to command an army like Frederick; finally, it could count on an inflexible Gallophobia [hatred of France], on immense financial resources, and on the powerful maritime diversions of Great Britain. This was precisely the ally that Prussia needed: to its poverty England brought the support of the riches; to its purely Continental armies, the support of the most formidable fleet. England had at its head an aristocracy which, amidst the discussions and the storms of the Parliament, had more continuity in its ideas and more power to force its subjects than any despot. In charge of Prussia was a despot who thought as a citizen and a philosopher. Frederick II, before a Europe divided, concentrated in himself alone all the powers of his state, all the resources of his nation, being at the same time an absolute king, and his own generalissimo, and his own Prime Minister. He was the greatest of the sovereigns of the epoch, and one of the first among the captains of all times. His spirit, if it were sullied by a blemish, was most open and freest; his heart, if it was inflexible and hard, was animated by a heroic virtue. What could Louis XV, Adolph-Frederick of Sweden, Elisabeth of Russia, and even Marie-Therese of Austria, hope for in the presence the most brilliant king of the 18th century, the King of the men of war, and a king who merged the absolute monarch with the citizen so devoted to his fatherland in the Roman sense and in the modern sense of this word?

It was for all these reasons that Prussia and England would have the last word, that Frederick II would hold all his provinces against his enemies' attacks and the St. James Cabinet would annex all the colonies of France and

Spain.

This Seven Years War had its adventures: against the French, against the Austrians, the Swedes, Prussia was overcome in turn or was victorious. It was by the Russians that it suffered the most overpowering defeats. They beat its regiments three times and entered its capital; only once, at Zorndorf, could Frederick II be victorious; we will see that even Frederick, at the time, was not so sure that he had won. This Russian army, with its thundering victories, with tough resistance, which, only among Allies, withdrew from the battlefield with glory, was better than its government, than its diplomacy, sometimes even its generals. It is now our task to study its organization.

CHAPTER II

THE RUSSIAN ARMY BEFORE AND DURING
THE SEVEN YEARS WAR

The Russian Army, at the death of Peter the Great (1725) contained about 200,000 men; the Tsarina Anna Ivanova brought it to 210,000 men; the Tsarina Elisabeth, in 1747, brought it to 270,000 men. It appeared that it must have been the most powerful in Europe, because, in 1756, Bestuchev estimated that of France at 211,000 men, that of Austria at 139,000 men, that of Prussia at 145,000, while the English Army had only 10,000 men, Saxony 18,000, and Poland 16,000. However, while the other states, except for Poland, had troops that had been promised to them and the King of Prussia could mobilize a much larger force, there was a large discrepancy in the figures that Russia inscribed on paper and the actual effective numbers in its barracks.

This enormous total consisted of 172,240 men of the regular army, also called the active or field army; there were 74,548 garrison troops, 27,758 territorial militia, 12,937 men in the artillery and engineering corps, and 43,739 irregulars. Upon eliminating the Imperial Guard, — which remained in St. Petersburg to protect the person of the Tsarina and maintain public order, — the troops maintained in the garrisons, those that were with the territorial militia, who watched the Finnish and Tartar peoples, the forces which were never organized or that would have to march incredibly long distances, the typical vacancies in the ranks of nearly all regiments, this immense empire had at its disposition no more than 130,000 men for offensive operations in Europe.

The regular troops, both infantry and cavalry, recruited uniquely in the ten governments of Great Russia. The other regions of Russia were exempted from this heavy load; that is to say: the Baltic provinces, with their German nobility and bourgeoisie superimposed on the rural classes of the Finnish races to the north and the Letts in the south; Little Russia, which, for barely 100 years, had suffered Polish domination; the territories of Iaik, Lower Volga, the Don, with their populations of Cossacks; and finally the Basin of the Middle Volga, with its Finnish or Finnish-Turkish peoples, as well as the Tartars, Mordves, Tchouvaches, Tcheremisses, Mechtcheraks, Bashkirs, Kalmuks, and others.

The pouring out of blood weighed, therefore, on only one race, that same race that had created the Empire. It was, with them, most unequally distributed. Initially, as in ancient France, the nobility and the clergy of all orders were exempted; then the merchants, artisans, clockmakers, and most of the people of the cities escaped service by paying a special tax or providing replacements. Even the *odnodvorisy*, or free peasants, who escaped service by paying a fee, entering the territorial militia, or serving as suppliers to the army or orderlies to the officers, etc.

Thus, the load of providing men for the ranks fell on the serfs, who belonged to the nobles, to the crown, to the monasteries, or the guilds. The serf paid with his body, but the serf's owner was stripped of his possession. This was totally unlike the conscription process of the late 19th century, nor even the French drafting of the 18th century militia. It was not the fate which, with the blind impartiality of chance, designated the men of the army. The law was restricted to determine the size and the age required of the recruits; it did not distinguish if the man was married or unmarried, father or breadwinner. It fell to the arbitrary decision of the landowner. An *oukaze* from the sovereign ordered the raising of so many soldiers per thousand souls; it was left to the owners to provide this quota. Nobody asked the landowners for the reasons for their choices; they delivered the peasants whose face displeased them, or who were thought lazy, or finally those against whom they had an unspecified objection; it did not matter if he had elderly parents, a fiancée, a wife, or children. Recruitment was one of the penalties which the master used against his slaves. Often the recruit was led away tied to a cart, shackles on his hands, and irons on his feet. The man who wore a uniform had no chance of ever returning to his village: the duration of his service was determined by no law. There were in this army very old and very young men. Masslovski cites for us the case of three cuirassiers that were taken to a court-martial for a rather serious offense: one was 30 years old, one was 36, and the third, Mezentsef, was 60. When the soldiers were no longer useful, even in the garrison regiments, they were retired; they then received small pensions or rations; one placed them in some monastery or sent them to colonize some distant province. There was nothing in Russia that resembled the splendid hospitality that Louis XIV reserved to his veterans in his Hôtel des Invalids. However, it was not very different from the French system of the 16th century, where the soldier was discharged and housed in some monestary or became a robber or a beggar.

Recruitment operations were, for many reasons, slow. It was necessary for some recruits to cover the immense distances of the empire to join the depot battalions or the field battalions. The recruits of the 1754 *oukase* did not reach their regiments until the end of 1756. It was the same for subsequent years. In addition, many recruits perished on the way due to fatigue, privations, homesickness, stress at having their hair and beards cut, as they believed without them man ceased being "made in the image of God." To "be shaven" became an idiomatic expression for becoming a soldier.

Unlike the French Army and those of many other armies at the time, the Russian Army did not recruit volunteers and did not count on volunteers to fill its ranks. The city dwellers had no taste for the army; as for those of the fields, they were slaves. Peter the Great had issued a law that one could accept volunteers from among the serfs, but this had been repealed at the insistence of the landowners. Elisabeth had not restored this law. What clearly shows that the government did not depend on recruitment was that the vagabonds were not incorporated into field regiments, but only into garrison regiments. In addition, it did not accept foreign volunteers. There were some who came forward at the beginning of the Seven Years War, but Elisabeth was only willing to grant them the pay and rations of Russian soldiers, "not expecting to treat foreigners better than her own subjects." However, as it stood, the pay and rations of her regiments were not sufficient to attract Poles, Germans or French volunteers. The ranks of Russian Regular Army, at least, were purely Russian. This was in great contrast to that of Prussia. Frederick filled his ranks by taking recruits from Poland and Saxony, accepting deserters and adventurers, forcibly enlisting travelers, couriers, and Saxon, French, Austrian and Russian prisoners of war. His army, according to the words of Michelet, became a true "Harlequin suit." It was a traveling army where an iron discipline was the only means of maintaining the men to their duty. As a result, after each defeat the Prussian Army suffered heavily from desertion. [7]

The astonishment that this system of recruitment caused the Russian soldiers can be found in the popular songs that were sung in the Russian Army until the late 19th century: "With the cruel king — there are foreign troops, who are not his, — rented troops, made captive."[8]

The Russian Regular Army recruited almost entirely of peasants, that is to say, the most robust elements of the nation and the morally healthiest, presented an image of patience, obedience, and endurance. The soldiers' songs are melancholic; they tell us the regrets "of the little soldiers, of the unhappy heads of soldiers," snatched from their villages, their warm *isba* in winter, with the enormous brick stove on which one slept so many good naps, of their fiancées who were afflicted at their departure and who perhaps would too quickly seek comfort in the arms of another. But this soldier, who does not like the military trade, was quickly well-trained at the depot.

Accustomed to a hard and poor life, there was nothing too repugnant for him in the ordinary life in the army and to sleep in a barracks. Trained in obedience to orders, even to the whims of his lord, he did not find it difficult to obey his officer; and often was his lord who he finds as his officer. He has, though negligible, the pride of the name "Russian;" he worships the Tsarina; he brings under the flags the feelings of burning piety and strong beliefs,

[7] Editor's note: Recent schoolarsip challenges this view of the Prussian Army of the Seven Years' War. In particular, see

[8] A. Ramboud, *La Russie épique,* Paris, 1874.

mixed with a bit of superstition, that his priest and his parents inculcated into him. There are many holds on him that his leaders will have if they also have "a Russian heart." In a battle or an attack, his priests came to bless him and walk at the front of the army, among the singing of psalms and floods of incense, the banners, the crosses, the miraculous icons. He confessed himself, communicated, slept peacefully while dreaming of the place reserved in Paradise for brave men who sacrificed themselves for the cause of God and the Tsarina. Then he dressed himself in a white shirt if one remained in his haversack, made the sign of cross and picked up his arms. As much from conviction as because the Church, he had ordered it thus, he observed, even in the field, the very rigorous fasts and prolonged abstinences of the Orthodox Faith. These deprivations were added to those produced by a defective logistical system. The generals sometimes complained that their soldiers, on marches and in combat, were exhausted. Even the excessively pious Elisabeth

Officer of the Horse Grenadiers

raised the question in front of the Holy Synod and requested a relaxation of fasts, etc.

In general, the clothing of the soldier, if not very luxurious, was quite appropriate with the country and the climate. In 1802 during Elisabeth's reign, in opposition to the Prussian innovations instituted under Paul I, there seemed a golden age, — Semen Vorontsov, then Ambassador in London, greatly praised the military of the former regime: "Peter the Great, by imitating what was good among foreigners, did not imitate their clothing. He saw that in Prussia, two thirds of the soldiers being foreign, one had more regard for the management of money than for the conservation of the men. He gave to his army boots and coats, that the Prussians did not have, because they would have cost too much." However, it was these good boots and warm coats, with loose-fitting pants, not as much later, but full and convenient, wearing uniforms that were loose, but making the movements of the soldier much easier, which Elisabeth's soldiers wore.

The cut of clothing was that of almost all the European armies at that time: one can add that French military modes dominated. The uniform of the Russian dragoon, for example, was almost that of the French cavalry at Fontenoy: a blue jacket, with yellow facings and turnbacks, chamois leather breeches, white belts, and large boots like those of the Postilion of Longjumeau. The infantry, like the cavalry, wore a tricorn rather than a bicorn, worn "in line," very broad from one edge to another. Certain units wore a strange headpiece, which resembled a miter or a *sanbenito*, bearing a dazzling gilded copper front plate. The hussars, like those in France, were distinguished from the rest of the army by certain traditional details borrowed from the Hungarian style of dress. They wore a high cylindrical bonnet [a mirleton], the small jacket with brandenburgs [braid], a dolman [jacket] with fur trim that was worn thrown over one shoulder, skin-tight breeches, soft half-boots, and a sabretache.

The same Semen Vorontsov noticed that the old regiments, which had fought at Poltava, in the wars with Sweden, those against Persia and Turkey, had a powerful esprit de corps, pride in their flag and pride in their regiment.

The regimental names never changed; they were those of the provinces; and the famous actions of the aforesaid regiments were preserved by tradition in the army and served to motivate the soldiers. Who does not know that the Astrakhan and Igremanland Regiments distinguished themselves under Peter the Great? All the Russian Army knows that the 1st Grenadier Regiment decided the outcome of the battle of Gross Jägersdorf; that this same regiment and that of the 3rd Grenadiers were distinguished more than any other at the battle of Zorndorf; that the Rostov Regiment performed wonders of valor at the battle of Paltzig; that the 1st Grenadiers decided the outcome of the battles of Frankfurt (Kunersdorf) and Kagul. All these regiments knew by tradition the glory that was attached to their names, and they were jealous to preserve it. I witnessed that after an action below Silistrie, where the 1st Grenadiers distinguished themselves, Marshal Rumyantsev went the following day, before the regiment, thanking the grenadiers for their heroic courage. They shouted to him: "Why are you astonished? When were we different?"

Unfortunately, Paul I had the idea of replacing the old, permanent names, with the names of their colonels, colonels who were often Germans, which would strip the regiments of one of their moral supports.

Semen Vorontsov, who saw Russian soldiers wounded at the battle of Bergen, then in the hospital at Portsmouth, noted that they no longer knew what unit to which they belonged. The common answer was, "Before I was of such regiment (and said the old provincial name); now I no longer know if the Tsar gave the regiment to some German."

Another difference between the armies of Peter the Great, of Elisabeth, of Catherine II, and the armies of Paul I and Alexander I, was that in the first one, a soldier, was able to rise from the lower ranks, which stimulated the zeal and the courage of the humblest men. A private could become a corporal, farrier, sergeant, color-bearer, and master-at-arms; while, under Paul I many of these ranks were eliminated, thus removing any hope of advancement and reward. Under Elisabeth, this hierarchy was intact, the cadres were solid, and ambitions, if modest, motivated the men. Also, in the Seven Years War, with the bloody business at Zorndorf and Kunersdorf, one saw, with almost all the officers having been killed or wounded, a lieutenant commanding a whole regiment and companies were led into battle by their sergeants.

Discipline was severe. In truth Tsarina Elisabeth, in an élan of piety, at the critical day of her advent, had sworn to never authorize a death sentence. Sometimes the generals complained, asking that she restore this penalty in the military code, asserting that without it they would be impotent to repress excesses. However, with soldiers as with civilians, the abolition of capital punishment was more specious than real. There remained the knout, with which a single blow, properly applied, could break the spinal column; there was the stick which no one in Russia did not know; there remained the gauntlet. In the case, mentioned earlier, Cuirassier Mezentsev and his two accomplices, were initially condemned to be broken on the wheel. This torture was commuted. They were to run a gauntlet of thousand men armed with rods, one twelve times, the others ten times: overall, ten to twelve thousand blows of rod.

Undoubtedly the Russian armies, during the Seven Years War, committed excesses. They were especially ascribable to the irregular troops. They had as their excuse that they were famished. After all, East Prussia appeared to have suffered less from the Russians than Saxony did at the hands of the Prussians. There were acts of indiscipline, of petty thieving, appalling drunkenness, even in the regular troops. What, however, gives a rather high idea of the moral and national valor of this army, is the very the small number of deserters, while it was enormous in the Prussian army and even in French Army of this time. In 1756, though the Russian Army had a strength of 128,000 mens there were only 185 desertions.

Under the Empress Anna Ivanovna (1730-1740) there were many generals foreign origin and especially Germans: Münich was from Oldenburg; the Birens, from Courland; Bismarck, from Pomerania; and Lascy, from Ireland. The Revolution of 1741 had pushed them aside. Under Elisabeth, Fermor was of English origin, but he was born in Pskov. Löwen and many of the other leaders had German names, but were Russian subjects, born in the Baltic provinces. Villebois was of a French family, but his family had come to Russia during the reign of Peter the Great. Neither then, nor later was any effort made to remove foreigners of merit; but the vast majority, almost the totality of the body of officers was of Russian nationality.

The nobility, which was not subjected to the draft, was no less obliged "to serve the Tsar." Peter the Great had made it a strict obligation for the nobility to serve, which he regarded as the corollary of the recognized rights of the landowners, any land holding being supposed a fief of the crown. Under Anna Ivanovna, the years of instruction and service were rigorously determined for the young nobleman. From ages seven to 20 years, he was to study. From 20 with 45 he was to be useful in the administration of the state or the army. There had been instituted for him two periods of examination: at 12 and 16 years, he appeared in front of a jury. Whoever, after the second examination, was uneducated in the catechism, arithmetic or geometry was made a sailor. It is seen, by the *Memoirs* of Bolotov, a gentleman of poor fortune, whose parents took care that their sons received instruction. The teaching methods were not always advisable; Bolotov's first instructor inserted science into his head with blows of rods on another part of his person. He was a German instructor.

The young nobleman entered the Army, either entering the Corps des Cadets, founded by Münich, or enrolled in a regiment; the most favored, very naturally a small number, could choose the Guard Regiments. The apprentice officer learned and performed all the exercises of the soldier: he was distinguished from the private only by rank insignia; he carried a musket and a haversack, until he was promoted color-bearer; he became, then, sub-lieutenant, then lieutenant. Almost all knew mathematics, history, drawing, the elements of fortification and the other arts of warfare. The noble class was, with the black clergy, the only literate class of the empire.[9] Many spoke, read and wrote German; some knew French which, since the advent of Elisabeth, tended to supplant German. Bolotov, around 1755, read *Gil Blas* in the original French.[10] This body of officers, less cultivated and undoubtedly less refined

---

[9] Monks, among whom were chosen the prelates, with the exclusion of the white clergy (secular and married.)

[10] Translator: *L'Histoire de Gil Blas de Santillane,* by Alain-René Lesage, is a novel published between 1715 and 1735. Some consider it the last masterpiece of the picaresque genre.

than those of France, did not lack instruction. They had the national qualities: bravery, endurance, the military view of honors, and, more than the privates, the concept of personal honor. Officer ranks were not as rigorously closed to the commoners as those of France at the same time: undoubtedly the *oukaze* of Peter the Great, prescribing to hold an officer's post open for one sergeant in eight, had been abolished by his daughter; rare were those of the lowest rank who rose to the higher ranks; but finally, even that was seen.

The nobility of the Baltic provinces, under the terms of the privileges recognized at the time of their conquest, were not subjugated with the obligation "to serve the Tsar." However, when it was useful, they served under the same conditions as the Russian nobility. However, they showed much eagerness for this, filling the administration and the regiments, because they were poor, prolific, and warlike. They brought with them the qualities of the Germanic race of the North, energy, tenacity, exactitude, meticulousness, and the advantages of a very Western culture. The defect of these officers, in their capacity of Germans and Protestants, was that they did not well understand the virtues and the weaknesses of the Russian peasant transformed into a soldier; but, although they kept German sympathies, their fidelity was in general unassailable.

The regular infantry consisted of the three Guard Regiments, Preobrajenski, Semenovski, Ismailovski, and 41-line regiments. The Guard did not leave St. Petersburg. Of the line, only 32 were, in 1756, put on a wartime footing. The 12 others, very incomplete, were held back for service in the interior. Each regiment, when complete, contained three battalions of musketeers (each battalion having 4 companies of 144 men and 6 non-commissioned officers) and two companies of grenadiers (each with 200 men). The musketeers were armed with muskets. The grenadiers, in addition, carried grenades in their giberne.[11] The line regiments carried the names of provinces, regions, or cities: Mourmon, Riazan, Tchernigov, Kazan, Apcheron, Siberia, Nevsky (of the Neva), and Ladoga. There were the 1st and 2nd Moscow Regiments. Only four carried simple numbers: the 1st, 2nd, 3rd, and 4th Grenadiers, which were formed at the beginning of 1756. At the same time a third company of grenadiers had been added to the other regiments destined to enter Prussia. The grenade was, at this time, in great favor.[12]

Picaresque, coming from the Spanish "picaro" or a thief, about a roguish hero who passes through a series of humorous or satiric episodes depicting the life of the common man.

[11]Giberne was French forcatridge box.

[12]The history of some of these corps gave rise, in the literature, gave rise to some important works: for example, *Histoire du regiment Apchéron (1700-1892)*, by Captain Boguslavski, 3 Vol. St. Petersburg, 1892; *Essai d'histoire du regiment des grenadiers de Pétersbourg Roi Frédéric-Guillaume III (1726-1880)*, by F. Orlof, St. Petersburg, 1881; *Histoire du 13e regiment des Leib-Grenadiers Erivanski (1642-1892)*, old Butyrski Regiment, St. Petersburg, 1892; *Histoire du regiment Pavlovski (1790-1890)*, by Voronsov, Butovski, Waldberg, and Karepov, St. Petersburg, 1890. In the *Rousskais Starina* of 1883 one finds the histories of the other Guard

To complete these regiments, then to form the Corps of Observation that Peter Shuvalov commanded in Poland, the necessary men were drawn from the regiments that remained in the interior of Russia. They were rebuilt as best one could, by drawing men from the territorial militia, garrison troops, and dismounted dragoons, even officers were brought forward and replaced by the Little Russians, who were not otherwise familiar with military service.

The armament of the infantryman consisted of a sword and a musket with a bayonet, which weighed 14 pounds. Each of the 32 regiments of the operational army were to have a total strength of 4,000 men, but, they contained 1,500 to 1,800 men each.

The regular cavalry consisted of two Guard Regiments, the Leib-Cuirassiers and the Horse Guards, plus 32-line regiments, including 3 cuirassier regiments and 29 dragoons. They should have had an effective strength of 39,546 men. In March 1756, "in order to put the Russian cavalry in a state, not only to fight against all the other European cavalry, but to even surpass them," they underwent a radical reform. The number of cuirassier regiments was augmented, and the horse grenadier regiments were created.

In reality, the operational army of 1757 contained no more than 7,000 regular cavalry in 14 regiments. There were five cuirassier regiments: Imperial Highness, Kiev, Kiazan, Novotroitsa, and the 3rd Cuirassier Regiment; five horse grenadier regiments: Kargopol, Riga, St. Petersburg, Riazan, and Narva; four dragoon regiments: Tobolsk, Nijni-Novgorod, Archangel, and Tver. All the rest were left in the interior to protect the lines of communication.

It was also necessary to reform their armament. Instead of the epee it was proposed to give to the cuirassiers a straight sword and the sabers to the dragoons and horse grenadiers, the commission said, "that they can, in the combat, slash as well as thrust, because one knows the natural aptitude of the Russian nation to strike and cross: also, of a weapon appropriate to these provisions, one can hope for the best effects." Let us notice that the substitution of the saber for the epee, a weapon for fencing rather than combat, had taken place in the French Army at the time of Louvois. Moreover, the dragoons and horse grenadiers of Elisabeth had muskets with a bayonet; the cuirassiers had a musket without a bayonet. A new cavalry regulation was worked out: the squadrons were drawn up to make coordinated maneuvers and to execute changes of face. They even performed target practice from their horses, a practice that had fallen into disuse since 1706. This transformation, executed in the field, was not without disadvantages. Only a few of the regiments could operate according to the prescribed method. The virtues of the old regulation and the new regulation were long disputed in the Russian cavalry. What remained especially defective were the horses. The type of the horse used by the heavy and the medium cavalry was rare in Russia. The state

Regiments, Preobrajenski and Semenovski.

had not allocated sufficient sums and what was provided was wasted or badly employed. One saw tall men on small, old, and weak horses. One of Frederick II's spies, was thought to be a certain Captain Lambert, and who historians identify as the "Voyager from Riga" because he wrote from that city a report on the Russian Army that severely criticized the Tsarina's cavalry. The cuirassiers had just been mounted on German horses, which one had requisitioned from the cities of the Baltic provinces and for which one had paid an average of 60 rubles apiece, without the officers in charge of the purchases being overly concerned with the age, blemishes or their degree of training; many of these animals, hitherto employed to drawing the carriages of the bourgeois, were not mountable: some were blind. The squadrons were not able to put themselves in rank: exercises with live fire threw them into disarray.[13] One saw horsemen emptying their stirrups. Three of the five cuirassier regiments had not received their armored breastplates yet. As for the dragoons, "they do not even deserve to be called cavalry." The men were as badly trained as the horses. Detached for a long time at the Turkish and Tartar borders, the squadrons had rarely operated together. Their officers were so simple that the officers of the other cavalry units used the expression: "Stupid as a dragoon officer."

The regular cavalry was certainly, during this war, the weak side of the Russian Army, while the King of Prussia was formidable by the number of his squadrons, the beauty and the strength of their horses, the instruction, and the solidity their men, and the wild spirit of the chiefs. With this cavalry he did not hesitate to charge squares of intact infantry; to carry positions crowned with artillery. Frederick II made the same bold and successful use of his cavalry as Napoleon would later do with his. Even, unlike the Russians, Frederick II readily sacrificed this weapon out of preference for his infantry and especially his artillery. His infantry was never superior to that of the Russians; his artillery was always inferior to that of the Tsarina.

The criticisms of the "Voyager from Riga" speak mostly about the Russian regular cavalry. There remains for us to speak of the irregular cavalry. What characterized this arm is that every cavalier had two horses, one of which served to carry his baggage, provisions, and booty. It is curious to see classed in this category the hussars. There were six regiments of hussars, four of which were old: Serbia, Hungary, Moldavia, and Georgia, and two were recently raised: Slavo-Serbia and New Serbia. One can consider these as the only foreign troops in the Russian Army, as they were recruited from outside the

---

[13] Translator: Horses are naturally skittish. In order to prepare them for combat the French used an extensive training method to make them accustomed to the sounds of battle, starting with line of soldiers banging pots and pans as the horses were walked across a parade ground towards them. Upon reaching that line, they were petted and fed. This progressed to the sound of pistol and musket shots, bugles, flapping flags, and even cannon shots and after advancing towards the sources of those sounds, they were again petted and fed. This process took several weeks. Taking a carriage horse and expecting it to react calmly to a musket shot is little short of insanity.

borders of Russia, in the lands whose names they bore, be it from the military colonies that Elisabeth had created in the south of the Empire, like New Serbia. At least they were races connected to Moscow or practitioners the Orthodox religion. "The Traveler from Riga" finds them much superior to the Russian regular cavalry, but less well mounted than the Prussian hussars; less educated; less sharp in their evolutions; less lively on patrols and reconnaissances. They had a very particular organization: they were to be assembled and armed at their own expense, with the help of a pay of 120 rubles per annum. Each of the six regiments contained five squadrons, that is to say, 1,000 men. It cost 40,000 rubles to maintain them: almost all were armed as Cossacks. However, as the hussars were in no way superior to them, one explains this preference with difficulty. It undoubtedly held that the hussars had a permanent organization which, even in times of peace, was not present among the Cossacks;[14] and if they were not braver, at least they were disciplined.

Among the armed Cossacks, only two corps approached the organization of the hussars. Those were the Tchuguiev and Slobode Cossacks. The latter unit was frequently qualified as a hussar formation. They were cantoned in the marks of the Ukraine, whose possession was still disputed with the Tartars of the Crimea. They formed a type of military colony. The men of the Tchuguiev Cossacks were formed by Field Marshal Münich as a corps of 500 horsemen: 300 being Little Russians and 200 being baptized Kalmucks. They were not given any land, because it was not desired that agricultural trades interfere with their military education. They drew pay and rations. By the way of non-combatants, they had only one drummer, a kettle drummer, and two wagon drivers. The Slobode Cossacks had about the same organization. They formed five pulks or regiments, each one of a thousand men with 2,000 horses. Their armament consisted of a musket, a saber and a lance. Their uniform was that of the hussars, but almost all in blue. They had close-cropped hair, except two long locks that hung from the temples and a very long, elegantly frayed moustache. They were as well disciplined as the hussars but were lower to them in military virtue. Manstein, the aide-de-camp to Münich, assures us in his *Memoirs* that, in the eyes of the Turks, they passed for the poorest of the Cossack "armies." They rendered little service in Seven Years War. Of the 5,000 that set out to join the army only 3,000 arrived. The 1757 autumn campaign so exhausted them only 2,000 remained to return to their homes and these had lost half of their horses. They did not appear in the following campaigns.

The other Cossack "armies" were those of the Urals, which had approximately 8,600 men; those from the Volga, 1,060 men; the Caucasus with 500 men; the Azov with 400 men, and finally the Don, with nearly 15,000 men. The latter was the only one which took part in this war.

[14]Kosaks, or more precisely Kazaks, a name of Turkish-Tartar origin, is the origin of the word "Cossacks." It was used in the original text, but we will use "Cossack."

There were 15,003 inscribed Cossacks, but only 9,000 were registered in the pulks. Each pulk had 500 riders with 1,000 horses. They were subdivided into sotnias or "hundreds." The head of the sotnia was a *sotnik* or an *essaoul*. The pulk was commanded by a *unpollinovnik* or colonel. The other officers consisted of the quartermaster, *pisars* or scribes, *khorongji* or standard bearers. In peacetime the *Dontsy*[15] (men of the Don) were divided into two commands: the "ancient" under Krasnochtchokov, and the "new" one, under Stephan Efremov. These two chiefs were brigadiers. In the field, the Don Cossacks were distributed between the various infantry corps, two or three pulks per corps.

The Tsarina did not spend more than 18,000 rubles per annum for the Don army. In peacetime they received neither pay nor rations and were not required to maintain any organization. On the campaign they were frequently left to maintain themselves. At times it was they who fed the regulars with the requisitions and what they pillaged from the countryside.

The Don Cossacks were an undisciplined element of the Russian Army. Each year they elected their polkovniks, sotniks, and all their other officers except for the brigadiers. They felt themselves barely required to obey them and they treated their leaders not as commanders, but as equals and comrades. A Don pulk was a moving republic, or rather a moving anarchy. It obeyed only the laws of the steppe. It was driven with an extraordinary speed, being never encumbered with wagons, because the second horse could carry food for 21 days. The Don Cossacks were the terror of the peasants, and even of the Tsarina's generals, who did not dare too employ them, and had them supervised and contained by the dragoons, for fear of them spreading plundering and devastation, starving the army and the country in which one operated, and to pushing the inhabitants to despair and insurrection.

The Don Cossacks were armed with a musket or a bow, a saber and an inordinately long lance. They followed their own tactics, which resembled that of the old Scythians, which consisted of skirmishes, sudden attacks, simulated flight, and unexpected returns. Unable to resist the charges of the Prussian cavalry, they harassed, blocked, and demoralized an enemy army. When they charged with wild cries, "Ghi! Ghi!" at the gallop on their small, disheveled horses that were as hot-blooded as their masters, in the odor of their fawn-colored leathers and their furs, the Prussian infantry lost its head. This tactic disconcerted all the European generals. Indeed, it was not always well understood by the Russian regulars. Bolotov, who saw them at work, continued to see them as "contemptible warriors," good for the escape, not for the attack. They were marvelous scouts. Because of them the Russian Army often surprised the enemy and was almost never surprised, able to rest in its camps while the adversary was exhausted with constant alarms. One

---

[15] Translator: Henceforth "Dontsy" will be translated as "Don Cossacks" in this work.

wondered, however, if the services that they returned were not outweighed by their Asian way of war.

The "Traveler of Riga," while noting that they are the bravest of the Cossacks, criticized them still more severely than Bolotov. "They go," he tells us, "without order, they are like a herd, so that a column of 800 Don Cossacks can hold a quarter of mile. They have a very primitive way of loading their musket, carrying their powder in a horn and their balls in a small bag. Their generals think so little of them that they little worry about them or even if they might be massacred." The same witness, who remained some time within the district of Apraxine and dined at the generals' table, gives us a curious portrait of Krasnochtchokov, the most popular of the Cossack chiefs:

> "All his [military] science consists of striking the enemy from afar with his lance or his arrow. He claims to have never given quarter. He never took part in other action, but that of Otchakov. I know that there he was unable to direct the reconnaissances. He would not listen to talk of night actions, saying that they could easily prove unfortunate, because the devil could mislead them at night.... He owes his rise to his relationship with Razumovski... The Russians say that he is wizard. General Lopukhin assured me of it, and as I said to him that in Germany one does not believe in the wizards, he said to me: "Is it possible that one does not believe in a thing so certain?"

It is curious to find, in 1758, in the account of the skeptical "Traveler" the first indication of this legend of Krasnochtchokov that was so largely developed in the popular songs of Russia. In those songs he is the brave and astute hero, par excellence, the Achilles and Ulysses of the Slavic people. He took Berlin, and, in some versions, it was he who carried off *la Prussienne*, Frederick II's wife or daughter[16], which had become here the personification of the city of Berlin. It was he who, disguised as a merchant, penetrated near to the King. He poured the King vodka while Frederick questioned him about the hero Krasnochtchokov, and the Cossack chief, and after allowing himself to be identified, sprang out of a window and escaped all pursuit. Moreover, for the Russian people, Frederick II was also a wizard: he could, at his liking, take the shape of a blue pigeon, a gray cat, a brilliant falcon, a black corbel [crow], a fish, a duck, and thus thwart all the efforts and all the traps of his enemies. The cruel king, for these naive imaginations, is a type of enchanter and werewolf. It was Krasnochtchokov, alone, who had the force to compete with him.

---

[16]Translator: Frederick II did marry but had no children.

Guard Cuirassiers   Hussars

The qualities and the defects of Don Cossacks, a population very mixed with Asian elements, are still the most curious of the irregular corps, those of the various nations, or the heterogeneous nations. These heterogeneous or alien elements came from Finnish, Finno-Turk, Tartar, and Mongolian races and included the Kalmuks of the Volga, Tatars of Kazan, Mechtchéraks, Bashkirs, and Kalmuks baptized at Stavropol. In their country, one knew neither the servile mode of the peasants of Great Russian, nor the quasi-republican organization of Cossacks. At the head of their tribes there were *starchines* or notables, at the same time great landowners and natural leaders of the military units.

Bravest of these riders were unbaptized Kalmuks from the Volga, half Moslems, and half Chamanists, one of the most authentic residues of the old Mongol invasions. At the beginning of the Seven Years War, there had been the intention bringing into the army 8,000 of them. The army was satisfied then with half that number, by giving to other half the order to stand ready. This was reduced to only 2,000. They distinguished themselves in the wars against Kuban Tatars; but, in spite of their warlike virtues, one hesitated to employ them. In the same way one asked only for 500 riders, always with the two horses, like the four other groups. These heterogeneous pulks appeared so frightening by their independent spirit (they recognized only their national chiefs as having the right to punish them), by their practices of plundering and their brutality, which required the Russians to always observe their encampments with detachments of regular cavalry. When Kalmuks of the Dunduk Dacha chief had to cross Russian territory, the Russians had to escort them with Don Cossacks and the dragoons, to prevent them sacking Russian villages. The Russians looked at them as deer that were dangerous to unchain.

Marvelous horsemen, they fought on foot as well as on horseback. There was no uniformity in their armament. In a detachment of 286 Mechtcheraks, one found 72 muskets, 242 bows, and 63 sabers. The Russian State gave to them a uniform in their national taste, very Asian. It provided them with cloth for their fur bonnets and their kaftans: red cloth for Kalmuks, green for Mechtchoraks and Bashkirs, and blue for the Tatars from Kazan. These yellow tinted warriors, with their high cheekbones, Oriental eyes, close-cropped heads, and the rare beard, their quivers were covered with fur, they carried a half-moon saber; their boots had a re-curved point., screaming their war cry in unknown languages, they mixed in their coarse beliefs several religions and all the Asian superstitions, and were, in the Russian Army, like scarecrows. On the borders of a terrified Germany, they revived the memory of the ancient invasions, resembling the followers of Attila the Hun and the Mongols of Genghis Khan.

The artillery of the Russian Army came in four categories: that of regimental artillery, field batteries, position batteries, and siege batteries.

In 1755, each regiment of infantry was to have attached to it six regimental guns - two 3pdr cannons and four 6pdr "mortars". Up to this period the guns were badly served because the infantry officers barely understood this service. The *oukase* of September 1756 designated an artillery officer to serve with every infantry regiment, who was to wear the uniform of the infantry regiment to which he was assigned. As these guns were dispersed along the front, this officer could barely hold them in hand. Despite the regulations, most of the regiments, instead of having six guns, only had four: two cannons and two "mortars". The dragoon pulks, which were to have a cannon and two "mortars,"[17] barely had two pieces. The Slobode Cossacks had two cannons per pulk. As a result, the Russian Army's regimental guns came to 522 "mortars" and 257 cannon. Despite that, the Russians only sent 350 regimental guns with their army against Prussia. In addition, in 1756, a certain number of *blisniats* were constructed. These were small, 3pdr "mortars" with two of them on each carriage. They rendered little service and the regiments, that found themselves burdened with them, abandoned them alongside the roads.

The field batteries, at the beginning of the war, consisted of 233 guns, all in bronze, of which 107 were cannon, 91 were "mortars", and 35 were howitzers, in eight different calibers.

Around this time important reforms were implemented in the artillery by Peter Shuvalov, who was Grand Master of Artillery.[18] On certain points these changes moved them beyond the weapons used by France and

---

[17] These "mortars," as the Russians called them, were actually a type of howitzer.
[18] Sometimes given as Shuvalov.

Russia. Shuvalov created artillery troops, reducing the weight of the guns and carriages by half, reducing the number of calibers to five, developing the use of explosive projectiles and canister, and augmenting the accuracy and range of the guns. We are assured that the Russian projectiles could carry 500 and 1,000 meters. This was quite superior to the range of French guns of the time, but it is doubtful that Shuvalov actually achieved this.

Shuvalov's principal creation was the *edinorog* (licorne), a sort of howitzer that was smaller and lighter, which could throw a projectile 1,500 meters, which, against close targets, permitted very rapid canister fire.

As these reforms occurred at the beginning of operations, it was necessary that much of the regimental artillery or the field artillery had received the new, sophisticated guns. Unfortunately, the campaign started without them. However, the reputation of this "secret" artillery, of this "lately invented" artillery was great in the Russian Army; Bolotov spoke about it only with respect and mystery. Concerns were also great in Europe: Austria, to flatter the Tsarina, requested a copy of the new gun; on the contrary Louis XV, to whom the Russians offered to send one along with a Russian artillery officer, declined politely this courtesy. It was not advisable for him to encourage "the vanity of Mr. de Schwalow." This artillery, whose guns initially appeared in the battle of Gross Jägersdorf, played a paramount and murderous role in the following battles.

Another of Shuvalov's creations was the Corps of Military Engineers, something which, until Vauban, had not existed in France. This corps contained 3 generals, 10 staff officers, 66 officers, 192 drivers, 229 miners, some student engineers, and artisans of every sort. It eventually totaled 1,302 men. Some were dispersed to the various fortresses throughout the Empire, while others were grouped into an engineering pulk in St. Petersburg. In peacetime, they were employed not only on fortifications, but on topographical and surveying work, as well as construction projects of every sort. In wartime, it was not organized for a serious role in the campaign operations. They were used only for siege works. The army sent against Frederick II only received a small engineering detachment of 66 men, under the direction of General Bosquet, an officer of French origin. The Russians also owed Shuvalov for the creation of the Engineering Archives. They already knew how to construct boat bridges. They used canvas pontoons that appeared to be of their invention. The Prussians only had copper and iron pontoons.

The weakness of the Russian Army was its train. In Münich's campaigns against the Tatars of the Crimea and the Turks one could see that it was not very mobile. It was drowned in the vastness of its convoys. A simple sergeant had up to ten wagons; an officer up to thirty; general Gustav Biren had 300 beasts of burden. Some wagons were even provided the privates, casualties and the sick, and for the movement of ammunition. Undoubtedly there had been efforts to reduce these impedimenta; but Apraxine's army, during the 1757 campaign, had a train of 6,000 wagons. As no one tried to make a rational classification of it, each regiment, each company took care of their own wagons. With the soldiers employed to lead them and the 10 or 12 men that each captain employed as orderlies, more than one third of the manpower of every regiment was immobilized.

Another encumbrance was the chevaux de frise, often called "Spanish horsemen," that it persisted in carrying with it, because, at the beginning of the campaign, neither Russian infantry nor cavalry dared to face the Prussian cavalry without this barrier. Bolotov called them a "ridiculous defense" and slowly one began renouncing them.

For the provision of food there was an intendance having at its head a proviant-meister[19]; but it was sometimes faced by insoluble problems. The countries that one had to cross, Prussia, Poland, and Pomerania, were too poor not to be quickly exhausted by any passing army. The convoys coming from Russia encountered the obstacle of infinite distances, of the bad and ruined roads, of this sandy or clayey ground where later the Napoleon's *grognards* would be swallowed up[20], overflowing rivers, or taken by the winter, or carried away by ice floes. The Russians used every possible means, such as requisitions, vivandiers, and direct purchases. For the latter, there was rarely sufficient money. The question of obtaining food, especially fodder for an excessive multitude of horses and beasts of burden numerous magazines had to be established and defended, which more than once stopped the army and condemned it to standing fast or even withdrawing. The other supplies were provided with same slowness. Even so, for the 1758 winter campaign, the major part of the soldiers had still received neither tulupes (fur-lined sheepskin coats), nor fur gloves.

An Austrian officer, who saw Apraxine's camp at the end of 1757 said, without being unjust, "In the Russian Army they are not aware of the use and utility of food wagons, and ovens. They have no knowledge of the distribution of magazines, of policing an army, of forage regulations, of discipline, of the collection of contributions, and the considerations that one should have for the people of a conquered land, of the conservation of men, hospitals, etc., etc."[21]

What appears to have been most defective in the Russian Army was the service of hospitals and ambulances. Even in the French Army one

---

[19] There are many German words used in the Russian military language coming from the time of Peter the Great: provianat-meister, feldzeug-meister, rottmeister, landmiliz, etc.

[20] See the *Cahiers* of Captain Coignet (5th Notebook): "We sank up to the knees. It was necessary to take rope to tie our shoes to our feet, and when we tore our legs from this moving sand, the rope broke and the shoes remained... Sometimes it was necessary to grab the leg from behind tearing it out like a carrot, and carrying it ahead, then grabbing the other..."

[21] Archives of the Department of Foreign Affairs, Correspondence, Russia 1. LIV, Piece 131, November 1757.

complained about the too small number of able doctors and surgeons. The situation was far worse in the Russian Army! The patients and the casualties didn't have shelter in which they could simply die in peace. The memoirs of prince Jacob Chakovskoi, quoted by Soloviev, offer a distressing picture of this to us. Ghakovskoi saw rows of patients, that their comrades carried on stretchers, some already half dead, that had been returned from the great hospital, because it already overflowed with patients dying of contagious fevers. In the hospitals one was asphyxiated by the lack of air and miasmas; one did not dare to open the windows because the cold would have killed the convalescents and even the healthy. And this occurred in Moscow, in the center of the empire, only because approximately 20,000 recruits had passed through the city. It was worse in the field. An Austrian officer wrote in November 1757: "I saw with horror the patients who groaned on grass, without tents and covers. All the places were filled with these unhappy men abandoned without any help. Which impression would this make on their comrades?"

As for garrison and territorial militia regiments, I will say only a few words, since they did not take any part in the operations of Seven Years War, other than by the dispatch of men who were used to bring the active army corps up to strength. The garrison troops organized, in 1716, by an *oukaze* issued by Peter the Great, formed 49 regiments of infantry, 7 of dragoons, and 4 independent battalions and 4 squadrons. Each garrison infantry regiment contained two battalions with 4 companies, plus a grenadier company. This infantry was divided among the various fortresses, by regiments; in the unfortified cities, it was replaced by local troops formed of free peasants (*odnodvortsy*), discharged soldiers and some gentlemen.

Garrison regiments were recruited in the same manner as the active army. Also, the government had the right to select the best soldiers allocated for this purpose. Garrison regiments were constituted for the interior defense and to serve as training depots for recruits.

However, one was very surprised, in 1756, when the Russian Government attempted to draw men from the garrison regiments to form the Observation Corps, and they found that they could find no more than 7,000 to 8,000 good soldiers. It immediately became apparent that the instruction of these troops had been extremely neglected. As a means of saving money, they had been provided very low pay and limited rations. Thus, official eyes were closed to every abuse. The soldiers had married, and, because of the parsimony of the government, they had entered all sorts of trades, including highway robber. There was little training and no large-scale operations. These regiments had become a kind of national guard, and a very poor one at that. One could not even employ them to escort the convoys. As for manpower, which, on paper, came to 75,000 men, the reality was far lower. The dragoon squadrons and independent squadrons were no better. The pulks from Kazan,

Orenburg, and Siberia were suitable only to provide escorts, carry mail and serve as a constabulary. Only the Voronezh Pulk and the Roslavl Squadron were suitable for field use.

The territorial militia (landmiliz) was divided into two parts: that of the Ukraine, employed to observe the Crimean Tatars, and that called the "Beyond the Kama," which supervised the northeastern tribes. The first contained 28 pulks of dragoons, that is, men capable of operating on foot or on horseback; the second, 3 regiments of this type, plus 1 regiment of infantry. The total should have come to 28,000 men. Only the Ukraine pulks were capable of rendering, in this war, some services on the lines of communication and without almost leaving their territories. These troops were recruited among the Little Russians.

By all these details, one can see that if the empire, at this time, had a large defensive force, it could not, in spite of the enormous figures which we have presented, deploy a very large offensive force.

As Russia then had access to only one sea, it had only one fleet, that of the Baltic. This fleet was divided into two squadrons: that of Kronstadt and that of Revel. The first contained 14 ships-of-the-line carrying 954 guns, 5 frigates, a praam and two galiotes with mortars; the second had 6 ships-of-the-line carrying 372 guns, 2 frigates, 42 galleys. The Russian Navy played only one secondary role in Seven Years War. It did not have to make a junction with the allied fleets, or to fight the English Fleet. It had to be satisfied with contributing to the provisioning of the army and to assist in some operations on the coast of East Prussia and Pomerania.

Russia did not have a Minister of War or a Naval Minister. In the French system there was a single "agent" in charge of each department, but Peter the Great had preferred the collegial organization. It was in favor in most German States. In France, under the name of "polysynodie," it was operational for only a few months, at the time of the Regency, when one had substituted it for the ministries of Louis XIV an equal number of "courts of King Petaud." Otherwise, the collegial organization was attached to the oldest institutions of Muscovy: among the Tsars of the Kremlin, everything was decided by councils of boyars; in charge of each college of Peter the Great, there was a president assisted by a vice-president. Ever since the foundation of the ministries, under Alexander I, the minister was always assisted by a *tovarichtch*, his assistant or his colleague.

Under Tsarina Elisabeth, during all the campaigns against Frederick II, the Generalissimos of the Russian Army, Apraxine, Fermor, Soltykov, and Buturline, never took a decision of any significance without calling a war council. Moreover, they were overloaded with a daily and extensive correspondence with the War College. As if this were not enough to obstruct their actions, Grand-Chancellor Bestuchev, wanted to see and do everything himself, wanting to direct the Army and Navy in addition to internal order and diplomacy, he came up with the idea of the Conference. It is made up of generals and civil dignitaries sitting at St. Petersburg. It claimed to lay out with the Generalissimo his campaign plan, to prescribe his every march and countermarch, and to determine at which time he must avoid or fight a battle.

It is for this reason that the supreme leader had to address report after report, to ask the conference's opinion on all the possibilities, to submit all his projects, to explain all his acts, in a word, to ask for the permission of be victorious. As the army was 1,000-1,500 kilometers from the capital, before the permission could be asked of St. Petersburg and be given to the general headquarters, every aspect of the military chessboard would have changed. The enemy whom one could beat had time to escape, the place where one hoped to surprise had time to resupply itself; the bird sitting on a branch, flew away, and often the Russian Army found itself in the annoying situation that it did not have the authorization to move or crush the enemy without permission from St. Petersburg. In addition, the members of the Conference, deliberating at such a distance from the battlefield, strove to guess all the assumptions that might arise to the Generalissimo, forgetting that which would become reality, only afterwards knowing the true provision of the belligerent armies, the true manpower of the Russian forces, the state of the stores and the parks of ammunition. The plans that they sent to their military subordinate were full of contradictions, inconsistencies, forecasts contradicted in advance, impossibilities and dreams. The Generalissimo, placed between this Conference which deliberated from afar and this terrible King of Prussia who acted with lightning speed to execute his resolutions and his movements, was paralyzed. He does not dare to advance, out of fear that he might not be able to move back in time; he feared the occasions to attack. Nothing was more harmful to the Russian armies during this war; nothing contributed more to exhausting them than pointless marches and countermarches. These movements made sterile their successes and missed the opportunities for victories with inexplicable retreats. The Conference, the hybrid creation of Bestuchev, which subordinated the operations of war to the uncertainties of court politics, was the worthy predecessor of the Austrian Hof-Kriegsrath, which, during the Wars of the French Revolution, was for the Imperials an institution of reverses and an academy of defeats. In the face of a Frederick II or a Bonaparte, this was a huge handicap for the general who was tied to the apron strings of the Courts in St. Petersburg and Vienna.

The deaf divisions that worked the Coalition of 1756, the intrigues of the Winter Palace, the supervision exerted over the Generalissimo by the Conference, were what contributed more to making the victories of Gross Jägersdorf and Kunersdorf fruitless.

CHAPTER III

THE RUSSIAN ARMY ENTERS THE FIELD IN 1757

Russia had been caught off guard by the "inversion of alliances" in 1756. As long as Grand-Chancellor Bestuchev had believed that he could count on English subsidies and the military support of Austria, the war with Frederick II appeared to him to be nothing more than a simple "diversion" and he had given little attention to the reforms that the state of the Army demanded.

The defection of England, which gave Frederick II the support of English money and its fleet, abruptly ripped him from his bliss. The Colleges of War and the Navy deployed a feverish activity. Blow followed blow, accumulating and sometimes contradicting the *oukazes* that reformed the cavalry, the infantry, the artillery, the irregular forces, armament, tactics, the logistical system, in short, all the branches of the Army and Navy.

The news of the Treaty of Versailles (1 May 1756) which brought to the Coalition against Frederick II the support of France, Sweden, and their clients in the Germanic Empire, with the assurance that Poland would be passively flexible and Turkey completely quiet, reassured the St. Petersburg Cabinet.

However, in the autumn of 1755, one could still fear that Frederick II might start the war with Russia by a conquest of Courland. The armies of the Tsarina were extremely deep in the interior of Russia getting on a war footing. In September, St. Petersburg learned of the sudden invasion of Saxony by Frederick II. The hatred and the fear that the King of Prussia inspired increased further. Preparations were hastened. On 30 September[22], Field Marshal Apraxine was named Generalissimo and on 16 October he received the order to advance to the border. As for the war, it was declared for yet another year, by proclamation of 16 August 1757.

But what was the border? One remembers how much Eastern Europe, in 1756, was partitioned. Russia extended along the Baltic its provinces of Estonia and Livonia like an arm. It then extended further, along a narrow spit of land where Memel was located and before which the province of East Prussia ran. However, these two points of the territory of the two enemy monarchies projected did not unite at their top. Between them were Courland and Semigalia, vassal countries of Poland. Then, supposing that East Prussia could come completely under the power of the Russians, they could not leave there, to invade the other provinces of Frederick II, without crossing neutral

---

[22]The author uses the new style dates and not the old-style dates, generally employed by Masalovski. In the 18ᵗʰ century, the difference between the two calendars was 11 days; 9ᵗʰ century, the difference was 12 days.

territories. East Prussia, detached from the monarchy, was like a small island, limited to north by the Baltic, in the east by Courland, the south by Poland, on the west, by West Prussia or Polish Prussia, with her two almost independent, municipal republics of Danzig and Thorn, mistresses of the Lower Vistula. The theater of the war, at the end of 1757, was a strip of land without depth, enclosed between the Baltic and the mass of Polish territories. In this strip of land there were successively Russian Livonia, the autonomous Courland, Prussian Prussia, Prussian Poland, and Prussian Pomerania.

Thus, for the Russian Army to invade the easternmost provides of Frederick, it had to cross two frontiers and could only confront its enemies on the narrowest front. To fall on the flank of the central mass, the principal territories of Frederick II, - Prussian Pomerania, Brandenburg, and Silesia — it was move more than 500 kilometers into entirely Polish territory. In the late 19th century, the Russian and Prussian monarchies shared a common border, but at this point there were not in contact at any point. From the north to the south was a neutral territory, consisting of Courland, Lithuania, and Poland, which separated them. There was a great distance between their closest cities in the north, Riga and Memel. There was an enormous distance between the closest fortresses in the south, Mohilev on the Dnieper and Frankfort am Oder. It took three partitionings of Poland, the last in 1815, to bring these two great military states into contact, with one acquiring Posen and the other Warsaw, by which they reduced the distance between them to 500-600 kilometers.

Poland of 1756, formed with Polish, Lithuanian and Russian territories, did not offer any obstacle in the passage of Elisabeth's army. Its king was the Elector of Saxony, the ally of Austria and France. If the Polish Diet did not subordinate its policy to that of the Court of Saxony, it was, in fact, subordinate to it. There was no Polish Army, so to speak. What existed were 12,000 men, badly educated and badly disciplined. In addition, this army was neither national nor royal. Each *voievode*, each castellan, each powerful lord, being the master in his government, his castle, or his domain, was also the master of the forces stationed there. He used them according to his perception and private interests. The Army was not a public force. Even in the cities, especially those on the Vistula, each one provided for its own defense as it sought fit. Thorn, Warsaw, and Posen were occupied without difficulty by the Russians. Danzig succeeded in holding its gates closed. In all Poland, the humiliation of this invasion was not felt in the same way. The eastern populations spoke Russian and practiced the Orthodox Religion, and were sympathetic to the Russians, while the Catholics of the true Poland looked at them with indifference or hostility. The cities along the Vistula, which were colonies of Germans and Protestants in a Slavic country, were rather pro-Prussian. Except for some demonstrations torn from the Diet by the zeal of the French ministers, Poland, during all five years, passively allowed itself to be occupied and crossed by

Russian columns. Though Poland was an enormous country, it was totally disorganized and without any force.

This peaceful invasion was opposed only by Poland's forests, waterways, and marshes. The Russians found the ground more rebellious than its inhabitants.

In the war undertaken by the Coalition against Frederick II, the special objective of the Russian Army was to be naturally the province of East Prussia, then completely isolated, by Polish Prussia, from the rest of the Prussian Monarchy. On his side, Frederick II had understood that it was not there, in this eccentric province, that one could strike the decisive blow against him. The battlefields of Silesia, of Bohemia, of Saxony, and Westphalia, in the middle of Germany and the continent of Europe, were, in his eyes, far more important. Thus, he recalled his best troops from East Prussia.

However, Frederick II's kingdom was such a marvelous military power that even in this remote province, neglected and almost sacrificed, even in this theater of war which looked like a secondary theater, the Russians encountered generals and officers who would have been in the forefront of the other European armies, and troops that, though of a lower quality than Frederick's best were no less deserving of the name "Prussian." If the artillery was the "shameful part of this small army," if the infantry presented regiments of very unequal value, the cavalry showed itself, as it did elsewhere, well-mounted, well-equipped, well-trained, and full of spirit.

Field Marshal Hans von Lehwaldt governor and generalissimo had been born in East Prussia, of a family originating in Brandenburg. He had been trained at the school of the elder Dessau and had acquired his rank and gray hair under the royal flag. He was brave, honest, of severe manners, and had strong religious beliefs. In 1751 this old soldier of 61 years was rewarded for his services during the War of the Austrian Succession with a field-marshal's baton. As he appeared to have more the qualities of a subordinate than of a commander-in-chief, the King had entrusted to him the government of a province which, according to any appearance, had no reason to fear invasion, being far from Austria and close to Russia, then so peaceful. The government of East Prussia was to be, for Lehwaldt, a place of retirement and an honorable sinecure. When the King realized that his political forecasts were in error, he sent General von Goltz, one of his aide-de-camps, a well-trained officer and a good tactician, steeped in the maxims of the King-Captain,who was to compensate by his councils with the Marshal's inadequacies.

Lehwaldt counted among his lieutenants: Rüsch, a Transylvanian who, passed into Prussian service, brought with him the fire of Hungarian or Rumanian blood, and who, in charge of the Black Hussars, was made famous by the impetuosity and even the boldness of its charges; Schorlemer, Malachowski, Prince von Holstein, Plalen, Plettenberg, Finck von Finckenstein, and marvelous cavalry generals; Dohna, the intrepid chief of the advance guard; Manstein, Manteuffel, Below, Kanitz, Kalnein, Gohr, and others less famous, which directed the infantry.

The general with whom the Tsarina was going to confront Lehwaldt was the Field Marshal Stephan Feodorovitch Apraxine. He was not in favor at the court, was disliked by Shuvalov, the man of the moment, who prevented him from speaking with the Empress. He was, however, a courtier; but his successes came at the time of Catherine II then in the reign of Anna Ivanovna. He was accused of cowardice because one day he had received a slap from Razumovski, the morganatic husband of the Tsarina; but who thus, in his place, would have dared ask the reason for it? Undoubtedly, he did not have a Roman character. He was large, even to the point of deformity: Hasenkamp[23] described him as a kind of Falstaff. At 50 years of age he remained gallant, though a little debauched; he had become even friendlier to the pleasures of the table.

The "Traveler of Riga" claimed to have been with him for a long time and to have noted that he did not have the theoretical instruction necessary for such a high command. He had little concern about sparing his men or horses. He allowed himself to be directed by the councils of Major General Wymarn, who had previously been an aide-de-camp to Marshal Keith. It is true that we have here the testimony of a German who praises a German at the expense of a Russian.

Among Apraxine's lieutenants were, in addition to Krasnochtchokov and the Cossack chiefs, were Generals-in-Chief Lopukhin, Matvei Löwen, Femior, Brown; Lieutenants General Prince Golitzyn, the Löwens and the Tolstoys; Major Generals Rumyantsev, Villebois, and Prince Lubomirski.

Vassili Abrahamovitch Lopukhin, according to the "Traveler from Riga," was "by the way of war the most innocent man of the world," spending his days eating, drinking, and playing. We know already that he believed in sorcery. These defects, if he really had them, did not make him wrong to the eyes of his men. He was one of the most loved of the Army's leaders: very religious, devout and even superstitious, he was inclined to premonitions; we see this in the night that preceded the battle at Gross Jägersdorf, where he was to die, holding religious ceremonies in his tent and spending it in prayer.[24]

Matvei Löwen, of a Baltic family, was, along with Weymam, an adviser to the Generalissimo and "the oracle of the Russians." He was also "their idol." He was also a good soldier, good tactician, one of the rare chiefs who were concerned about sparing and preserving his men and the horses, celebrated by his successes against the Turks with Otchakov and the Swedes with Wilmanstrand, he suffered, by misfortune, from poor health. Under his

---

[23]*Ostpreussen unter dem Doppeladler,* Koenigsberg, 1806, a very precious work for everything that occurred in East Prussia.

[24] Bolotof.

hands were the principal masses of the Russian regular and irregular cavalry.

Wilhelm von Fermor, who was going to take the command of the right wing, was also from the Baltic, but of English origin. He had made his career under the orders of Field Marshal Münich and had been distinguished against the French in the siege of Danzig (1734), then against the Turks and the Swedes. We will examine him more thoroughly later.

Brown or Braun had the same origin as Fermor.

Among the young people, Villebois had only participated in the Swedish campaign. He showed talents but was inclined to disparage the Russians. The "Traveler from Riga" says of him: "The devil carries me off; one must affect here to be as stupid as them if one does not want to have them all as enemies."

Pierre Alexandrovitch Rumyantsev is future the Field Marshal of Catherine II, the future hero of the Danube (Zadunaiskt). "He is already one of their more skillful generals," wrote the "Traveler from Riga" in 1758, who only reproaches him for being too burning in his enterprises and unable to moderate himself. The battle of Gross Jägersdorf and the siege of Kolberg would clarify this.

Prince Lubomirski had initially served in the Austrian cavalry; he extolled power then, with only one regiment of Imperial cuirassiers, he broke three Prussian cuirassier regiments.

The order given to Apraxine, in October 1756, was to cross the border and to make a "diversion," which was easier to formulate than to carry out. The preparations for war were far from being completed. There were insufficient horses for artillery. Magazines were not yet organized. For a winter campaign, the men had received neither touloupes nor mittens. The army was still very dispersed. The 1st Corps, that of Lopukhin, containing 25,000 men, occupied Livonia and Courland, but had a notable part of its forces in Estonia and in the Provinces of Pskov, Novgorod, and even St. Petersburg. The 2nd Corps, that of Vassili Dolgorukov, containing 15,000 men, was barely formed and was not concentrated. The 3rd Corps, that of Matvei Löwen, which was completely composed of cavalry and contained 25,000 men, was in the same situation. His outposts had hardly reached the Polish border, parallel to the Niemen. 4th and 5th Corps, those of Brown and Fast, totaling almost 14,000 men, appeared in Estonia only in September.

It was necessary that the five corps had receive all their field and regimental artillery; in particular the Shuvalov howitzers required that they wait. Apraxine calculated that he only had available the 25,000 to 26,000 men of Lopukhin and believed that Frederick II could oppose him with 145,000 men. Russia had, at this time, a cordon of troops rather that an operational army.

The instructions that Apraxine received with the order to begin hostilities were full of uncertainties and contradictions. They prescribed almost at the same time, says Masslovski, "to advance and to stop." "In all the doubtful cases and especially if one were in the presence of superior forces, it was necessary, if possible, to avoid fighting battle."

Before leaving St. Petersburg, Apraxine had obtained an audience with the Empress. One can guess what the terms of this interview by the promptness of the reproaches that were made immediately afterwards, by the Tsarina to Peter Shuvalov: "You do nothing but exaggerate in my eyes the forces I have. You do not have the fear of God to mislead me thus?" Ivan the favorite, in his turn, reproached the Marshal "for frightening the sick Empress." After this Shuvalov took care to never see the Empress again.

What would prove that Apraxine had more character or perspicacity the "Traveler from Riga" did not recognize in him, was that, upon his arrival at the general headquarters, he was almost fighting with the Conference and Bestuchev, its creator and inspiration. A Russian officer, who had arrived in Danzig, disguised as lackey in the service of a lady, gave the Generalissimo precise information about Prussian forces. There had never been a question of the Prussians invading Courland. The rumors that abounded were false. Apraxine communicated this news, and other information which confirmed them, to the Conference. The conclusion that he drew from this was that as Courland was not being threatened, it was useless to undertake a winter campaign.

The Conference, in three consecutive rulings, continued to insist that the operations be opened immediately, to preempt any movements by the King of Prussia on Courland. Apraxine energetically resisted this. He demanded that he be given a strict order, after which, without discussing more, he was ready to act. The Conference did not dare to give this order. In this year 1756, which saw the invasion of Saxony, the defeat of the Austrians at Lobositz and the capitulation of the Saxon Army at Pirna, Russian troops, nor those of France and Sweden, appeared on enemy territory.

The Conference, forced to leave with the army a little rest and time to organize itself, started to work out plans for the following campaign. All these plans had the same defect of dividing, at the beginning of the campaign, the Russian forces. A principal army was to be employed to strike a decisive blow in East Prussia. A second army was to affect a junction with the Austrians in the main theater of operations. Apraxine answered, reasonably, that it was important "to concentrate the army, and not to break it up," adding that earlier one would find a favorable occasion to attack resolutely.

On 22 December, believing that Lehwaldt was prepared to launch his offensive, the war council, chaired by Apraxine decided, "without awaiting the enemy's attack, to attack the enemy; to attack him with all our forces."

This possibility was not carried out. The war council of 3 February 1757 then adopted a plan that consisted of marching on Königsberg and capturing it, while the fleet would operate against Pillau.

In March 1757, the Russian field army was concentrated on the right bank of Niemen. In April, Apraxine was informed by Russian General Schiringer, detached to the Austrian general headquarters, that the Austrians had not finished their preparations for the upcoming campaign. The Field Marshal then observed with the Conference that it was very difficult to cooperate with an army which was not ready: "If, to date, the Austrians have not started, though they are closer than us to the Prussians and in a much kinder climate, the Russian Army has good reason not to compromise themselves lightly in risky operations, because with an enemy like the King of Prussia one should not jest."

The sea was not yet free of ice. The roads were hateful, but the Russians worked to make them passable. Many of the irregular troops had not yet arrived. One could do nothing serious before May. Moreover, nothing was pressing: all the information collected showed that Lehwaldt was holding himself on the defensive.

While the invasion of East Prussia was still suspended, let us see what occurred in this province.

This country is bathed by the Baltic, which forms on its coasts two lagoons, like two small inland seas, separated from the Baltic by long and narrow spits of land. They are the *Kurisches Haff* in the north, and the *Frisches Haff* in the south. At the northern end of *Kurisches Haff* is the town of Memel, which, in 1807, was the last asylum of the King of Prussia. Close to the northern end of the *Frisches Haff* is the town of Königsberg, capital of all the province. Pillau commands the entrance to this *Haff*. The Niemen, which flows into the *Kurisches Haff*, waters Tilsit and Ragnit in East Prussia, and Kovno and Grodno in Lithuania. Pregel, which flows into the *Frisches Haff*, waters Königsberg, Tapiau, Wehlau, Insterburg, and Gumbinnen. It receives the Alle River, which passes to Bartenstein, Friedland (not very far from Eylau), Allenburg, and Bürgersdorf. The Niemen and Pregel form two parallel lines of defense; on the contrary the Alle is in general perpendicular to the Pregel, being on its left bank. All these famous names, Eylau, Friedland, and Tilsit, that we find on the 1757 battlefield would again appear as the fields of battles in 1807. The conquest of this province was most important for the Russians as they hoped that it would be given to them in a general peace. But the conservation of the province was no less important to Frederick II. This was the land of the *Pruss*, an old Lithuanian nation of the country, destroyed or absorbed by German colonization, which had given their name to all his monarchy (and even the name of these vanished people was to dominate one day the lands between the Nieman and the Moselle). Moreover, Frederick was king only because of this eccentric province of his empire. The title of his grandfather and his father was not "King of Prussia," - because the King of Poland, Master of West Prussia, had protested, - leaving him only as the "King in Prussia." It is the glory of Frederick II that allowed him to replace the article in this phrase; a little odd, the first being considered more honorable. This province was the cradle of his ancestors and the royal city of Königsberg. This province was properly "the Kingdom of Prussia!" It was the only province where his royalty was subordinated to no other, because in Brandenburg and elsewhere Frederick was subordinate to the Holy Roman Emperor. Finally, it was the most important of his two seaboard provinces.

The country of East Prussia was poor, sandy, and marshy, but was relatively well-populated. In 1757 it contained some 500,000 inhabitants. The German race mixed with formerly Lithuanian elements made it a hardy and strong race. It seemed to carry to its princes, heirs to the former Grand Masters of the Teutonic Order and the Hohenzollern dukes, a steadfast fidelity. Let us not forget that in 1813 it was from this old Lithuanian country, a remote colony of the Germanic race, that sent the signal that sparked the uprising of Germany against Napoleon.

Frederick II, although he was absorbed by the desperate fight in the battlefields of Bohemia, Saxony and Silesia, although he understood that the fate of providence would be decided, not on the Pregel or the Alle, but on the Elba and the Oder, had, however, provided for the defense of East Prussia. In doing so he counted on the resources of the country itself to organize its resistance. Initially he had called upon the devotion of his faithful "vassals and subjects" for a loan of 500,000 thalers.

The Grand Duchess Catherine informed the King of Prussia of all that occurred in the court and the Russian Army. The Englishmen Sir Williams and Minister Mitchell served as intermediaries. In December 1756, Frederick II was informed that the Tsarina, learning of the attack prepared on Cleves by the French, considered it "as an enemy less formidable than it appeared to be five weeks ago; that consequently one had decided to march to the assistance of the Empress-Queen [Maria Theresa] 80,000 regular troops and 30,000 to 40,000 irregular troops; but that nothing was ready. Every regiment was short 500 men, and the order had only just been given to recruit them."[25]

Frederick II passed that information on to Lehwaldt (26 December), communicating to him the alarming news and, at the same times, the reasons he had to reassure him. "The Russians will not be in a state to march before June; in the second place, the Tsarina is sick and it is doubted she will recover; in the third place, if she dies, I am certain we will have nothing to fear from the Young Court."[26] The same information is found in several letters from

---

[25] Frederick, II, *Politische Correspondenz*, Vol. XIV, p. 163.
[26] Ibid. Vol. XIV, p. 170. He wrote to Lehwaldt again, on 9 March 1757. "You can be assured that everything that Apraxine does, he will do it against his will, because he supports the Grand

January 1757. They are full of conjectures on the state of Elisabeth's health and the consequences that might follow her death. The other hope is that in France Mme. de Pompadour, following Damien's attempt on Louis XV's life and the entrance of repentance and devotion into Louis XV's heart, would be dismissed. This would give a "furious shock to the Austrian clique."

Thus, Frederick II always hoped that the friends that he counted in Winter Palace would manage to suspend the attack. He hoped that Apraxine, who was said to be devoted to the Grand Duchess, would make only a courteous and pure form of war. Moreover, though he greatly feared Russia, he had a certain contempt for its troops, which he rather regarded as a mob than an army. His information on its military organization, drawn from his discussions with the old man Field Marshal Keith, who had formerly commanded in the Russian Army, was extremely outdated. He was not current with either the 1756 reforms or the new manpower. He had shared this confidence, which was a little imprudent, not only with his entourage, but with the inhabitants and the authorities of East Prussia. He had left Lehwaldt only 19,400 regular troops, and the corps of the Prince of Hesse-Darmstadt, which contained 9,400 men and was cantoned in Prussian Pomerania, which Lehwaldt used as a reserve, but which at the same time had to observe the Swedes. However, the needs of the war in central Europe soon obliged the King to withdraw the Prince of Hesse and his small army. He abandoned Pomerania as he had already abandoned East Prussia, his two Baltic provinces! Lehwaldt was left work with what resources he could obtain from the land. Beginning in 1756 he had called all recruits to Königsberg, incorporating them into the garrison regiments, forming their cadres from retired officers, and exercising them with muskets sent by Berlin.

The Soldier-King, father of Frederick II, for remote and vague needs, and, in the state of his relations with Russia, had ordered that the garrison regiments should be prepared for service in the field. There were three of them in East Prussia, but the men were untrained, and the officers could pass for invalids. In the furious drain of soldiers by which Frederick II exhausted his States, a major part of these garrison troops had been directed to the battlefields of central Europe, where, determining their limited tactical value, he employed them only in the reserve or second line.

In addition to the garrison regiments, there was the landmiliz.

The landmiliz, this ancestor of the Landwehr of 1813, was older than the royalty. Frederick I had projected transforming it into a levy en masse of all the population; but the agricultural classes were in majority, so it was necessary to limit it to the townsmen and those of the large boroughs. This force was formed into a militia of middle-class man and peasants, all in

---

Duchess; however, he may receive from his court positive orders. *Politische Correspondenz*, Vol. XIV, p. 351.

infantry, with very little cavalry. The Soldier-King found that it cut a poor figure beside his beautiful line regiments. The institution fell into disuse, but in the ten last years of his reign, he tried to reorganize it. All in all, in the entire monarchy, there existed only the four regiments of landmiliz, those of the Mark, Magdeburg, Pomerania, and East Prussia. The last two were to render some services in Seven Years War, one against the Swedes, the other against the Russians. However, they hardly existed except on paper. They were, at most, trained two weeks per year, and more when there appeared rumors of war. Only officers, the non-commissioned officers and the drummers were permanents, for most were on half-pay or were invalided out of the regular army. The Land Regiment of East Prussia carried the title of its colonel: von Hülsen. This regiment, having only a single battalion, was made the garrison in the Memel Fortress. Lehwaldt worked on reforming the provincial militia, while raising in the border districts five or six companies. He attached to them the Land Hussars and a corps of jägers. The jägers were recruited among the foresters of any rank, their sons, and the disciples of Saint-Hubert. It is not known if the jägers contained both infantry and mounted men, if they formed a military unit or if they were distributed, as marksmen, in the other provincial companies.

Through perseverance, Lehwaldt managed to raise 2,214 militiamen. He hoped to employ them to hold the borders against the irregular troops and the petty thieves of the Russian Army, and also against the criminals of every type, who would benefit from the disorder to plunder the Prussian or Polish countryside. This militia was not even permanent. It was only called-up on certain occasions when the tocsin sounded. In the absence of officers, which even the garrison regiments lacked, elderly gentlemen, gentlemen farmers, and invalided non-commissioned officers were given commissions. The commander-in-chief of all the new militia was a retired major, Katarzynski von Gutteck. As the province was divided into two nationalities, Lithuanians in the south and Germans in the rest, the uniform was not very different: white for the Lithuanians with blue facings, blue or gray for the Germans with white facings. A uniform was necessary; because, in the ideas of that time as today, every combatant who did not wear a uniform was an insurgent, a "schnapan," as they were called in the 17th century. The use of non-soldiers against regular armies had constituted a violation of the law of nations, and provoked severe responses by the enemy.

The militia had as an arrière-ban something very similar to the Landstürm, and what Lehwaldt, as opposed to the mobilizable militia, described as a sedentary guard. The inhabitants of the border districts, upon the approach of the enemy, were to rise in mass, under the control of the foresters. It is probable that these peasants did not have uniforms, because it was prescribed to them to arm themselves not only with rifles or muskets, but with scythes and pitchforks. They were to be called out by the sound of the church bells, by messengers on horseback, and various signals, such as barrels of tar and bales of straw impaled on the end of a pole and lit. Otherwise, the role of this insurrection was limited as far as military operations go. It was only used to exasperate the regular Russian army, and its irregular auxiliaries.

Of some more utility was the bourgeois guard in certain cities. In Königsberg, the bourgeois guard was divided into two bans: one regular and the other a reserve. The first was formed into ten companies, with its staff, it came to 3,000 men, plus a squadron of 150 men. The infantrymen carried muskets. The riders, recruited among the butchers, brewers, market-gardeners, and wagon drivers, were provided with a saber and pistols. These weapons were provided by the State arsenals or the city or by the requisitions among the inhabitants. As for the reserve, consisting of "all those who could move," it had to be satisfied with swords, scythes, pitchforks, even of poles and pokers to stir up the embers in the fireplaces. It was thus a completely inorganic force. Let us add that the pleasure of playing soldier did not have the same allure to all the inhabitants of the city. The University and all the University's employees, printers, booksellers, masters of the dance, the urban nobility, the royal employees, the clergy, the lawyers, in a word all the privileged people, objected. These were received with suitable reserve while the others were answered by threats of fines or prison. In certain open cities, such as Tilsit, Schippenbeil, and Gerdauen, as well as in the fortified towns, weapons were also distributed to the inhabitants.

For the province, in addition to the fortified bridge at Marienwerder over the Vistula, two old iron guns and two invalids were its total defense, not counting the three fortresses of Pillau, Memel, and Königsberg. Only the last had some importance as it presented a continuous enclosure with a ditch and 32 bastions, plus a citadel and the detached fort of Friedrichsburg. Lehwaldt barely had time to make repairs to this fortress and could hardly deal with both others.

They had good wooden arrows, but the situation was hardly reassuring. The King could send him, as reinforcement, only sound advice. He conferred to him full civil and military powers over the province and the army, which made him a kind of a dictator. Frederick also enjoined him never to call together a war council.

Lastly, on 5 February 1757, awakened from all his illusions, the King ordered Lehwaldt to mobilize his troops, waiting until he was informed, "by a hand as sure as possible," of the imminent invasion of the Russians. He added: "I rely on your prudence, your experience, and your wise provisions; but my will is that you do not spare the Russians, and that you do not haggle with them (nickt schonen, noch marchandiren).... If they enter Prussia, fall on them at once on the nape of their neck and give them such good blows that they will well feel them… I recall having heard Marshal Keith say that, to give them a good slap, one must initially, with the cavalry, to collapse their wings; then, as their infantry is formed in a square, break them at once on one point, and they are finished, because they are in total confusion, then one only has then to make as many prisoners as possible, then to dispatch a trumpet to the enemy chief, an invitation to send agents and money, so that in the future they will take care of the prisoners…."[27]

Thus, Lehwaldt only had to think of handling his future prisoners. With the remainder, when, based on the injunctions of the King, he started towards the border, the dispatches which he left to Colonel Puttkammer, Governor of Königsberg, were written with this same feeling, both wise prudence and contempt for the Russian Army, especially for the Russian irregular troops: "Although, according to any appearance, only the Kalmuks, Cossacks and others of the same quality will arrive before Königsberg, the Lord Colonel will make all his arrangements as if they were indeed people who would have enough courage to assault the place…. He will inform the officers to be constantly on their guard, so that twenty men should not fear of a thousand Cossacks, because if these twenty do their duty, they are not thousand of this type will reach this goal." At the same time, he charged some of these Courland officers, who were useful under the Prussian flags, *inter alia* Count Dohna or General von Lottum, to go in disguise to the quarters of the Russians and to inform him of their movements.

In April 1757, Apraxine affected a passage of the Duna, and, at his general headquarters at Riga, held a review of his army. He had invited to this festival the ladies and the notables of Riga. The walls of the city, the windows, and even the roofs of the houses abounded with spectators. All applauded the procession of the regiments, which followed one another in good order, preceded by their quartermasters carrying standards, followed by the horses in hand, whose caparisons of oil-cloth seemed like silk. The officers saluted with their swords upon passing the review stand, their flags dipped. All the soldiers had clean uniforms, and well-polished weapons and packs. They carried sprigs of foliage to their hats; on the grenadier's miter, which recalled ancient helmets, there were tufts of feathers."Splendid Spectacle," assures the eyewitness Lieutenant Bolotov, of the Archangel Regiment, which was then going into battle for the first time.

In May, Apraxine, "to cover his magazines," occupied Kovno on the Niemen. Brown, with the advance guard of 15,000 men, was in Mittau. Lopukhin, with the main body of the army, 32,000 men, camped around Riga. Rumyantsev, with 4,000 horsemen, had passed the Duna at Dunaburg. Soltykov commanded at Revel, the "landing corps," 10,000 men, that the Navy was to transport to the Prussian coast. Approximately 17,500 men were delayed

[27] Frederick II, *Politische Correspondenz*, Vol. XIV, pp. 245-246.

around Dorpat and Pskov. Major General Kastiurine, with 3,000 Slobode Cossacks, Krasnochtchokov with 2,000 Don Cossacks, Majors Hake and Suvorov, with 2,000 Kalmuks, approached only Vilna. Except for the irregular forces, all this force, considering the mass of the impedimenta, moved rather slowly, barely 10 or 12 kilometers per day. All the difficulties concerning the supply of such an army in such a country were already being felt. The region produced few cattle. The cattle coming from the Ukraine did not arrive until September. It was the time of Lent, and the abstinence prescribed by the Church exhausted the troops in its marches. Apraxine wrote to the Conference: "It is true that a *oukaze* issued by Peter the Great, this Emperor of happy and immortal memory, authorizes the soldier in the field to eat meat even during times of fast; but I do not dare to take on me to put this *oukaze* into effect in the current circumstances. It is necessary, however, to take recourse to this for the re-establishment of the health of the army; because in this country one can find neither garlic nor onions, and it is, however, with this that the soldiers would nourish themselves in the days of abstinence." Thus, even for this detail, it was necessary for the Generalissimo to refer the decision to the Conference. The Conference referred the question to the Empress, who referred to the Holy Synod about it. The Synod granted authorization, but it only arrived after the fast of Saint Peter, at the end of June 1757.

It was only on 23 June that the left wing of the Russian Army, forming the advance guard and commanded by Fermor, left Poland, and crossed the border of Prussia. On the 30th, it was concentrated under Memel. The naval squadron, commanded by Valronde, arrived almost at the same time. It was composed of six vessels provided with guns suitable for the bombardment of a city.

Already the appearance of the long lances of the Don Cossacks had thrown panic into the Prussian countryside. Despite the recommendations Apraxine made in favor of the peaceful inhabitants, the Don Cossacks everywhere carried off cattle, horses, and even people. The peasants fled their village with their herds into the depths of the woods. The employees of the flatlands took refuge, with their archives, in Memel. The fortress, whose fortifications had not been repaired, had 80 guns of various calibers. The garrison was formed only of the Polenz Battalion, the best unit of the local organized landmiliz. The fortress was commanded by an elderly, though still energetic officer, Lieutenant Colonel von Rummel.

The first operation that Apraxine wished to undertake was an attack against Memel. He was encouraged there by what he knew of the limited resistance that this small fortress could present, and by the purely defensive attitude that Lehwaldt affected. Only contrary winds kept Lewis' squadron out of the port of Memel, which carried Soltykov's corps and the siege artillery. Fermor, who was to take the command of the extreme left, was forced to wait.

There was even a question of replacing him by Brown.

However, on 8 June, Apraxine addressed this instruction to Fermor: "As soon as he is in front of Memel, he will summon the fortress, informing [the governor] that if he refuses quarter will be given to no one. If he meets too serious a resistance there, he must limit himself to taking position and waiting for the siege artillery, order the galleys to land the Cossacks on the shore, at the most favorable points, and to have them push to the vicinity of Königsberg. After the arrival of the siege, he will begin a regular attack." Fermor had then his general headquarters at Libau (Courland). He answered that he had only 7 regiments of infantry with a total staff complement of 321 officers and 8,281 combatants of the 27,000 men that Apraxine had assigned to him. It was still necessary to wait.

On 13 June, Soltykov landed at Libau, with a corps very tested by storms. It had lost two galleys. The following day it landed the siege artillery. This same day Krasnochtchokov arrived with some 1,800 Cossacks and 3,765 horses. The infantry still awaited its regimental artillery and baggage, which the fleet delivered on 21 June. The Russians thought that they had the power to fix the day when the attack would begin. On 20 June, Fermor's advance guard began its movement. Behind him came the main body, divided into three brigades. However, it totaled 16,000 men instead of desired 27,000.[28] Romanius, who preceded the advance guard, with a flying corps of 700 Cossacks or hussars, was to spread proclamations to the population everywhere. The proclamation promised that "those who presented no resistance, but would submit peacefully, would be the objects of Imperial favor and protection and that one would do them no evil". It was recommended to the leaders of these scouts to take hostages among the notables, but to leave the others in peace; if the population resisted, they were to seize the cattle and the goods, but without burning the villages. They were to try to insinuate themselves inside the country by "some reliable language."

At 6:00 a.m., on 30 June, the hostilities were initiated by Valronde's squadron. They were the first shots of the Russo-Prussian War. The Russians bombarded the city and the citadel. Some fires ignited in the fortress, but the garrison quickly extinguished them.

During this time, Generals Fermor and Soltykov proceeded on a reconnaissance. They concluded that it was impossible to take the fortress by assault and that it was advisable to proceed with a regular siege.

The cannonade of the Russian fleet had continued for a few hours when Fermor sent a summons to the Prussian commander, von Rummel. Von Rummel refused to enter into negotiations for a capitulation and burned the suburbs.

---

[28] Hasenkamp estimates that 21,000 Russians advanced cross country and that 9,000 were transported by Soltykof on ships. The figures provided by Masslovski are based on documents.

With the gleam of this fire the Russian generals were able to determine where to establish their batteries. The Russians spent the entire night constructing their batteries. At 6:00 a.m., on 1 July, the ground batteries joined the fire of the Russian fleet.

By the morning of 2 July, Memel had already received 982 projectiles. The garrison answered rather actively, but without causing great damage to either the squadron or the army's batteries. The Russians entrenched themselves and pushed forward their approaches. On the 3rd, Rummel asked for the authorization to send a courier to Lehwaldt, in order to receive instructions and authorization to surrender, if he thought it appropriate. Fermor refused. At 4:00 a.m. on the 4th, as the Russian works were already extremely advanced and the bombardment had continued with the same intensity, Rummel raised the white flag. The conditions that he proposed were, in the estimate of Masslovski, "impertinent." He asked for the free exit of the garrison with the honors of war, with the civil authorities, the treasury and, in a word, all State-owned property. Fermor granted only the free exit of the garrison, with their weapons in hand, without the honors of war. He refused everything else. Rummel, after the evacuation of the place, went to Labiau.

On 5 July Fermor made his entry into Memel and, the following day, he sent his report to Apraxine. The Generalissimo testified his dissatisfaction at the too advantageous conditions that his subordinate had granted. Indeed, Memel, with 800 men against 16,000, crushed by the combined fire of the fleet and the ground batteries, should have surrendered unconditionally. It greatly annoyed Apraxine that the Polenz Battalion, which was to form the core of the militia that Lehwaldt had endeavored to organize, was allowed to escape. Fermor's success brought no glory. The fortress had yielded only to the bombardment. The digging of the saps had been useless and had immobilized the whole corps of 16,000 men before an insignificant collection of hovels. Half that number would have sufficed to produce this result and the rest, especially the Cossacks, could have been more usefully employed elsewhere.[29]

Fermor had ordered, the day of his entry into Memel, the singing of a *Te Deum* in a Lutheran church. To Archpriest Wolf fell the unpleasant duty as a faithful subject of Frederick II, to speak from the pulpit. He took for the text of his sermon a verse from the lamentations of Jeremiah. His compatriots admired his courage, and Fermor did not make known to him his displeasure. Then the civil servants and the inhabitants were forced to take an oath of homage and subjection to the Empress Elisabeth. Elisabeth fully believed that she would retain this conquest. Fermor was then occupied returning to the

---

[29]Translator: Though this is surely true, that this force could have been better employed, it is necessary to note that the field commanders could make no decisions regarding the employment of their forces without consulting the Conference, so surely, Femor and Apraxine had specific orders from St. Petersburg as to the most miniscule details of this operation that were to be blindly followed.

city all its fugitive inhabitants, to sound the depths of the port, to repair its fortifications, to supply the place, and to requisition horses, which the Russian Army particularly needed. Then he received orders from the Generalissimo to leave a garrison in Memel, part of the squadron in its port, to send the rest of the fleet on a cruise along the coasts of Prussia, and then to march on Tilsit.

Fermor dispatched his advance guard on 21 July, but he did not leave Memel until the 26th. The heat was overpowering; this region suffered from very hot summers and cold winters. To spare his troops, Fermor limited their daily march to 20 kilometers, and that twice, only marching after 2:00 a.m., and 5:00 p.m. On 27 July, a Cossack patrol appeared before Tilsit and carried away a bourgeois who was delayed in the countryside. On the 29th, a lieutenant of the Vladimir Regiment delivered a summons to the city and citadel asking them to surrender. On the 30th, Fermor stood in sight of the city. Tilsit's fortifications were in a worse condition than those of Memel. Its garrison consisted of only four companies of militia. It made no effort to resist. A mile from Tilsit Fermor was met by the clergy and several members of the civilian authorities, who "very humbly begged him to take the city under its protection, and, in witness of their submission, allow them to immediately take the oath to the Tsarina." Fermor's report confirms the account of Hasenkamp, the local historian. This delegation was made up of the four principal pastors, Burgermeister Boltz and Vice-Burgermeister Rösenick, a member of the Rath [city council] and two of the prominent bourgeois. Fermor accepted them with an exquisite courtesy. The following day, 31 July, the Russian advance guard made its entry. The grenadiers occupied the important posts. The bourgeois guard of Tilsit marched out under arms in front of the Rathhaus and took the oath to the Tsarina. A *Te Deum* was celebrated in the church, with a sermon of thanksgiving. All the civil servants, all the pastors of the nearby parishes, all the male inhabitants above the age of 15 years, who spoke German or Lithuanian, also took the oath. Fermor spent several days organizing his conquest, to have the inhabitants rebuild the bridges over the Niemen, to establish furnaces, hospitals, and ambulances. The advance guard remained in Tilsit for several days and it was only on 9 August when the main body of the Russian Army could pass over the newly rebuilt bridges. In mid-August, the Prussian eagle was removed from the city's monuments and replaced by the Tsarina's coat of arms. Tilsit became a Russian city. The militia was obliged to surrender its weapons. An order was issued that prohibited gatherings or meetings.

While the right wing of the Russian Army conquered this spit of land, running from Memel to Tilsit, which forms the north-eastern end of East Prussia, the principal mass of the army, under Apraxine and Lopukhin, prepared itself to enter Prussian territory. The crossing of the Niemen lasted from 28 July to 1 August. The troops marched very slowly, encumbered with wagons and baggage, constantly suffering for the lack of supplies. The main army was divided into three corps: the 1ˢᵗ, under Fermor, the 2ⁿᵈ under Lopukhin, and the 3ʳᵈ, under Brown. Their advanced guards were formed of Cossacks, who were to precede their movement. The general direction of their march was on Gumbinnen, the principal town in the Lithuanian districts of East Prussia. On 1 August, they crossed the frontier near Wierzbolow (Wirballen). The cavalry began to spread out across the Prussian countryside.

> This entry into Prussia produced on us a very particular impression. We had under our feet the land of our enemies. And one said: "God blesses us! We have thus arrived here, finally, on the lands of Prussia. Will God want us to leave safe and sound? Who is intended to leave his head there? We found the localities of this Kingdom of Prussia very different from those of Poland; Everywhere was in a different order, another mode; the villages were clean, were distributed and built systematically; the roads were good, paved in the low places, sometimes raised up as roadways, and were planted trees on the sides. In a word, one could not look at all that without a feeling of satisfaction. Moreover, as no devastation had yet occurred here, all the inhabitants had remained in their houses and, without expressing any fear, were held on the threshold of their residences. The women and the young girls filled with fresh water some buckets and gave water to the soldiers who passed. In short, one would have believed oneself not on an enemy's land, but among a friendly people.

CHAPTER IV

THE BATTLE OF GROSS JÄGERSDORF (30 August 1757)

For a long time Lehwaldt had believed that the Russian invasion would not take place; that Russia would limit itself to demonstrations; that some friendly influence, acting in St. Petersburg, as Frederick II still hoped, would indefinitely suspend the irruption of the torrent. He had been able to count on the support of the Prussian Pomeranian Corps and on the protection of the British Fleet, which would surely move to oppose any enterprises by the Russian Revel and Kronstadt Squadrons.

Suddenly, however, Lehwaldt was in the presence of a formidable reality: approximately 90,000 men were going to descend on his small army; the Russian invasion proceeded like a kind of barbarian invasion, led by clouds of riders that seemed to be the sons of Attila. Blow followed blow as he learned of the fall of Memel, the occupation of Tilsit, the passage of the Niemen at many points, and Apraxine's entrance into Prussia. The Pomeranian Corps was lost to him, and there was no news of the British Fleet. He could not count on Frederick II, who had just suffered a terrible defeat at Kolin, under the walls of Prague (July). Threatened to his front and flaks by a numerically superior enemy, he had reason to fear seeing a Russian squadron forcing Pillau and making itself master of Frisches-Haff and throwing a force into his rear. He would then be obliged to evacuate half of the province and surrender the royal city of Königsberg. It was necessary to discuss, with the government of Berlin the possibility of a complete evacuation, which would leave to the province to deal with the enemy. Lieutenant von Humboldt, who arrived from Frederick's camp, and had covered nearly 1,800 kilometers in 14 days, brought to Lehwaldt a letter from the King (July 11th). This letter spoke only about confidence, defense to the last extremity, and an energetic offensive: "You cannot fail to defeat a Russian corps, whatever it may be." The King of Prussia, in his letters to the Field-Marshal, stuck to the tactic that it had already recommended in a dispatch of June 12th: "There is nothing more to do than to only fall on the first corps that will dare to approach you, to attack it and you will defeat it; and then, hit the others!" Lehwaldt thus acted to profit from the dispersion of the Russian forces, to attack them and to destroy them in detail.

Happily for Lehwaldt, though attacked by the Russians, Pillau was defended, and the siege was converted into a blockade. The Marshal had nothing more to fear, at least for the time, for his line of retreat.

The very same day of the entry into Prussia, 220 horse grenadiers and 180 Chuhuiv Cossacks, under the orders of the Major La Roa, had pushed to the villages of Kattenau and Kummeln. Reassured by the inhabitants, who affirmed that there were no Prussian troops in the vicinity, this officer stopped the horse grenadiers and had let the Cossacks advance to Nibutsin. La Roa had been misled by the inhabitants, and the Cossacks were surprised by the black Malachowski Hussars. After a short fray, they were thrown back on Kummeln, with the grenadiers. The grenadiers were, in their turn, beaten and thrown back on Kattenau. The Russians found safety only upon the arrival of some squadrons of Russian cavalry, which pushed back the Malachowski Hussars and pursued them until nightfall. The affair, thus finished, was to the advantage of the Russians; but it had begun with a nasty surprise, which produced accusations of negligence. Bolotov goes further. He says that this combat "spread in our army a high impression of the bravery of the Prussians, increasing in the hearts of many soldiers the fear that they already had of the enemy, inspiring in them timidity and cowardice." He adds:

> Finally, what was of more important and was more serious in its consequences, it was that not only the Prussian soldiers, but the inhabitants thought that we [the Russians] all were weaker than women and warriors who were good for nothing. Consequently, these inhabitants started to arm themselves against us, to do us every evil and worry us. Apraxine, who hitherto had been shown very soft on the inhabitants, was indignant at such a hostility among people to whom he had ensured "the Imperial favor and protection." He decided that in the future, if similar acts occurred, no quarter would be given, and the guilty villages would be destroyed.
>
> This order had barely left his mouth, when our Cossacks, Kalmuks, and other light troops abused it to make evil. Being everywhere to spy on the movements of the enemy, they spared neither the culprits nor the innocent; in many places, by greed for the spoils, they spread devastation, not only driving the inhabitants out of their villages, but plundering, killing, torturing, sacking and burning their houses, giving themselves over to the disorders, cruelties and excesses of which barbarians alone would have been capable. In this manner they inspired in all the inhabitants of Prussia an extreme hatred and animosity against us, covering us with dishonor and shame in front of the whole world... and, moreover, by the devastation of the country, they ensured the failure of all our enterprises in this year.

Thus, from their first steps on Prussian soil, the indiscipline of the irregulars caused the conquered to forget their peaceful dispositions and the good will that Bolotov have initially offered at the beginning and unleashed all the terrors and fury of a partisan war.

From 6 to 10 August, Apraxine rested at Gumbinnen, where he was received by the magistrate, and imposed the oath of loyalty on the inhabitants. A few days later, he ordered some executions of peasants caught with arms in hand. Some were hung, the others had the fingers of their right hand cut off. On the 8th, he held a council of war and decided to march on Insterburg, at the confluence of the Inster and the Pregel, where he planned to join with Fermor.

On his side, Lehwaldt, steeped in Frederick's consuls, proposed to anticipate this junction, and if he could, to first wipe out Apraxine and then Fermor. He had Insterburg occupied by the Malachowski Hussars. From Königsberg, he sent him reinforcements, by the right bank of the Pregel with the Prince of Holstein, by the left bank of the Dohna. He had taken care, to assure the communication along the two rivers, by throwing bridges over them at Taplacken and Bubainen.

The two armies were quite close to one another. On 7 August, Stoffeln, who formed the Russian advance guard, marched out. On the 8th, he engaged in skirmishes at Gerwischkemen and Pitckine, where Malachowski was supported by some insurgent peasants. Insterburg was captured, recaptured, and taken anew and on the 11th, Apraxine himself occupied the village as Malachowski vainly attempted to harass him.

Lehwaldt had seen his offensive projects disconcerted by this brisk Russian attack. His advance guard had already arrived at Saalau when Insterburg fell into their hands. He received the order to withdraw. On 13 August, Sibilsky's army corps finally arrived in that city. On the 18th, Fermor camped near it, at Georgenburg. All the Russian forces now found themselves united under Apraxine's hand. It was an imposing mass of 89,000 men. There was no longer any chance that Lehwaldt could surprise or destroy one part or another of it.

From that point on Lehwaldt found himself on the defensive, constantly occupying, along with Königsberg and the two banks of the Pregel. Beyond Königsberg, he established magazines at Wehlau, at the confluence at the Pregel and the Alle. His headquarters was on the Kalehnen heights, which were easy to defend. He had his advance posts at Saalau and Siemohnen on the right bank of the Pregel, at Norkitten, on the left bank. All the woods of the two banks were observed by his cavalry and filled with armed peasants, who the devastations of the Russian irregular troops had completely exasperated.

On several occasions, in order to test his adversary, Apraxine had used his superiority in light cavalry and moved strong reconnaissance forces down the two banks. On 18 August, for example, 5,000 to 6,000 irregulars, under the command of General Kastiurine, descended the Pregel by its left bank, as if they were going to Königsberg. An equal number, under Krasnochtchokov, moved on the right bank, as if to menace Kalehnen. Almost everywhere they were engaged by the Black Hussars and the peasants. They were well-aware of Lehwaldt's position, which had its center at Kalehnen, with the woods and marshes covering its two wings. The Russians made sure that all his army was on the right bank. As for the left bank, Kastiurine could traverse it with complete freedom, pass within sight of Wehlau and push as far as Allenburg. One reproached him for not having tried to burn the Wehlau magazines, and not to have tried a *coup de main* on Friedrichsburg and Königsberg.

The only thing that remained for the Russian Generalissimo to do was to descend the right bank and to force the Kalehnen position. It seemed that he wanted to do it: On 20 August he issued orders to march on Saalau. Then he abruptly changed his plan and line of attack. It would now be by Allenburg and from there on to Königsberg. The leading cause of this change, which required the displacement of the Russian Army, was always the difficulty in living off the land that the Russians occupied. However, the soldiers had no food shortage: Bolotov, quite to the contrary, shows us it was in abundance. The inhabitants of the Prussian villages had driven off their cattle but the villages still abounded in smaller livestock and all kinds of poultry. Cossacks, Kalmucks, hussars, even the dragoons, had a nearly endless supply available for sale to the infantry at a minimal price. However, the sheep, pigs and poultries were not inexhaustible. Bolotov states that the Russian Army was already short of corn and salt. Fodder was especially lacking. One can imagine what the 7,000 regular riders and the 12,000 irregular horsemen, each equipped with two horses, plus all the pack and draft animals would consume. The plague of the Russian Army was its mass of light cavalry, which its generals feared to employ, because it would produce further devastation. It was because of its horses and its pack animals that Apraxine found himself obliged to pass from right bank to the left bank of the Pregel. He hoped to attract his adversary there, because Lehwaldt would not accept finding himself threatened on his flank, by Wehlau, in his rear by Königsberg, and at the same time find his line of retreat cut by the occupation of Allenburg.

On 24 August, the Russian Army began its passage of the Pregel at Siemohnen. The passage required three days. When this was completed, the Russian Army found itself concentrated at Norkitten, in the angle formed by that river and its affluent, the Auxinne, which flowed in a deep valley, which Bolotov described as frightening. The Russian Army now had at its back the Pregel and the Auxinne. On its front was a small forest, known as Gross-Gross Jägersdorf, which could only be traversed by following two roads, but which one could move around on both sides. It encamped in this location, pitching its tents, and deploying its innumerable wagons as a sort of mobile entrenchment, which was called a "Wagenburg" ["wagon fort"].

Lehwaldt, disturbed by the movements of the Russian Army, without being able to get accurate information on them, thought it necessary to withdraw from Kalehnen and Taplacken on Wilkensdorf. To cover this operation, he threw on the Saalau the cavalry of Rüsch and Kanitz. On the 26th, this cavalry fell on that part of the Russian Army which had not yet crossed the Pregel but was driven back. The reconnaissance was badly handled, as Lehwaldt was still ignorant of the essential point: Apraxine's perilous situation, where his troops were on both sides of the river and could be surprised *en flagrant délit* in his passage. It was not until the 28th that he learned that the Russians were concentrated on the left bank. He thought that they were going to move on the Alle and attempted to turn them. He resolved on leaving nothing but a few fortified posts on the right bank and then to move, with the bulk of his forces, to the left bank. He crossed the Pregel at Piaten and moved to camp at Puschdorf. He occupied a position analogous to that of the Russians, having his back on the Pregel and the Alle, separated by the Wehlau Forest, and on his front the Norkitten Woods.[30]

If the Russians debouched from the Gross-Gross Jägersdorf Woods and the Prussians came out of their Norkitten Woods, they would encounter one another on a little plain, in the middle of which was the village of Gross-Gross Jägersdorf, with those of Metschullen to the west and Uderballen and Daupelken to the east. For the moment, the two armies were only 7 kilometers apart, and, a singular thing, each of them was ignorant of the presence of the other's proximity. The woods completely screened them from each other.

When Apraxine learned of the Prussian crossing of the Pregel, he was shocked. He had organized all his movements in the hope of turning the strong positions at Kalehnen and Taplacken, or to force Lehwaldt out of his position. And now he had abandoned it voluntarily.

Lehwaldt appeared to seek to move over to the offensive. Each morning strong reconnaissance forces of cavalry spread alarm in the Russian camp. On 29 August, Schorlemer, with 40 squadrons of hussars and dragoons, almost all the army's cavalry, pushed up to Gross-Gross Jägersdorf, driving back the Russian advance posts and piercing the curtain of Cossacks. Then, aggressively pressed, they fell back to Puschdorf. This was yet another less than perfect reconnaissance. Schorlemer had found the Gross Jägersdorf Woods entirely empty of Russian troops, but he had been unable to cross it and penetrate to their encampment. Above all, he had not been able to divine the role that the Sittenfeld heights, which ran to the southeast of this wood to the sources of the Auxinne, would play in a battle. Frederick II would later criticize Lehwaldt's timidity for not having attacked that very day, to have not turned this imposing

---

[30] By "Norkitten Woods" we are describing the mass of forest that extends to the west of Gross-Jägersdorf and the Gross-Jägersdorf Woods, which the Russians had to cross to move to that same village, although this forest was much closer to Norkitten than the forest of that name.

reconnaissance by his cavalry into a battle. "It is impossible," said Frederick, to "understand the reasons that caused him to postpone until the following day what could have been decided immediately."

During the evening of the 29th, each of the two armies had returned to their respective camps. It was on the morning of the next day that Lehwaldt had decided to attack the Russian Army, to surprise it, to destroy it in the angle of the Pregel and the Auxinne, and with a single blow end the campaign.

At about the same time, Apraxine conceived an equally bellicose plan. He could no longer live in the confined plain between the woods, the water, and the swamp, where he was confined. He had rations for only three days. Forage was lacking. Under the pressure of the same necessities of a nomadic horde, to seek new pasturage, the Russian Army was constantly obliged to move. Apraxine planned to move in two marches, by Eschenburg on Allenburg and the line of the Alle. It was, therefore, during the morning of 30 August that his troops set out, moving through the two roads through the Gross Jägersdorf Woods, and turning it along both of its flanks.

While Lehwaldt counted on surprising the Russians in their encampment, Apraxine hoped to conceal his first march from the Prussians. He did not believe there would be a battle on that day. The order that he had adopted was conceived not for battle but for the march. In the two roads through the Gross-Gross Jägersdorf Woods, veritable defiles, on the right marched the 1st Corps (Fermor), on the left the 2nd Corps (Lopukhin). The 3rd Corps (Brown) had divided itself and moved along both roads in the footsteps of the preceding corps. Each had its baggage and artillery move on its left, in order to protect them against an attack coming from the west.

The right column consisted of the following infantry regiments: Nijni-Novgorod, Mourmon, Tchernigov, Viatka, Rostov, and further to the right, destined to turn the edge of the wood, the other regiments of Fermor and Brown's corps, those of Siberia, Nevski, Vologda, Ouglitch, and the 1st Grenadiers or the Iazykov Grenadiers. It had as a rearguard or a reserve, under Rumyantsev, those of Troitsa, Voronezh, Novgorod, and the 4th Grenadiers. It was covered by part of the cavalry: Nijni-Novgorod Dragoons, 3rd Cuirassiers, Imperial Highness (Empress?) Cuirassiers, Riga Horse Grenadiers, Petersburg Horse Grenadiers, Tchougouiev Cossacks, Serbia Hussars, and the Hungarian Hussars.

The left column consisted of the following infantry regiments: 2nd Grenadiers, Narva, Kiev, 2nd Moscow, Vyborg, Ladoga, 3rd Grenadiers, Petersburg, Kazan, and Schüsselburg, supported by some cavalry squadrons.

Finally, turning into the woods by its extreme left, the advance guard, commanded by Sibilsky, was to march from Norkittenon Sittenfelde. His infantry consisted of the Pskov, Archangel, Bielozersk, Boutyrski, and Apcheron Regiments. His cavalry consisted of the Kargopol, Narva, and

Riazan Horse Grenadiers, the Serebriakov Don Cossacks, the Kapnist Slobode Cossacks, a field pulk of Ukrainian Cossacks, and the Volga Kalmuks.

The total army contained some 55,000 men[31], of which 10,000 to 12,000 were irregular cavalry, supported by 150 to 200 regimental and field guns.

To face them, Lehwaldt had 24,000 men, plus 50 squadrons of magnificent cavalry and 64 cannon of all calibers.

In order to avoid any surprise by the Prussians during the night of 29/30 August, Apraxine had occupied a height dominating the defile to the west with the Iazykov Grenadiers, the Vologda, Sousdal, and Ouglitch Infantry Regiments, and a few heavy cannons forming a battery position. At the mouth of the other defile, he posted the 2nd Moscow Infantry Regiment. Finally, Sibilsky occupied the Sittenfeld Heights with the Serebriakov Cossacks and his advance guard. Out of further precaution, he had begun his march early and nearly all of his forces had passed through the woods and were encamped at the foot of the heights.

The Russian Army rested under arms, ready to march the following day. Suddenly, towards 3:00 a.m., or 4:00 a.m., an alarm was given by a sentinel and the drums rolled bringing everyone to their feet.

In the face of the Russian Army, in three columns, came through the three defiles in the Norkitten Woods, there appeared the entire Prussian Army. The left column was very far from the other two and had made a long detour to move on Gross Jägersdorf. It consisted solely of cavalry: the Malachowski Hussars, Finckenstein Dragoons, Platen Dragoons, Plettenberg Dragoons, and Schorlemer Dragoons. The central column was formed solely of infantry: Kanitz, Below, Dohna Infantry Regiments, Polenz and Manstein Grenadiers, and the Manteuffel Garrison Regiment. The right-hand column, mixed infantry and cavalry, advanced in the following order: Rüsch Black Hussars, Kalnein Infantry Regiment, Lehwaldt Infantry Regiment, Gohr Grenadiers, Prinz von Holstein Dragoons, Lossow Grenadiers, and the Sydow Garrison Regiment.

The cavalry column did not appear on the battlefield until the other two had already arrived. The infantry had cleared the woods at 2:00 a.m., but their lines were not yet formed until about 4:00 a.m. The army now presented itself in the following manner: a first line of infantry, under the orders of von Dohna, was formed from left to right: Dohna, Below, Kanitz, Kalnein, Lehwaldt, Gohr and Lossow Regiments. This line, which was longer than the other, extended from Gross Jägersdorf to Daupelken, with Uderballen on its front. The second infantry line, under the orders of Kalnein, consisted of the Polenz and Manstein Grenadiers, with the Manteuffel and Sydow Garrison Regiments. The Prussian

---

[31]In his report to Frederick II, Lehwaldt swears that the Russians had 100,000 men, and more than 100 cannon. —From the camp at Peterswalde, 1 September 1757, *Politische Correspondenz*, Vol. VI. pp. 330 and following.

cavalry squadrons formed on the flanks of the infantry.

At this time a fog covered the plain surrounded by woods that would serve as a battlefield. The heads of the hotilecolumns found themselves 1,200 meters from each other. Though the Russians could not see the Prussians, they heard them coming. Lehwaldt, to give heart to his men, or as a point of honor, had his trumpets sounding and his drums beating at the heads of his regiments. Bolotov, who was on the Sittenfelde heights with the Archangel Regiment, declared that he had seen nothing and did not comprehend how the two Prussians columns closest to him could cross the 1,000-1,200 meters that separated them from the woods occupied by the Russians.

Apraxine's army was completely surprised. It is evident that Apraxine had done nothing to scout any distance. He should have sent patrols to the edge and even into the interior woods through which the Prussians advanced. The order he adopted for his march was very defective for battle. Each regiment was stretched out in the narrow defiles, encumbered with its artillery and baggage, while if attached the lead elements would have been driven back on the tail of the columns. When the Prussian trumpets were heard and the first shots woke up the army with a start, the Russians found themselves embarrassed, pell-mell with wagons and caissons. It was almost impossible to separate themselves from the baggage wagons and move through the thick and inextricable woods, to array themselves in line along the edge of them. The moment of agony that seized the Russians at this time is clearly stated in Bolotov's *Mémoirs:*

> Oh, my God! What confusion in all our army and its baggage! What cries, what clamors, what galloping horses and what disorder. Here one heard the cry: "By here, by here, the artillery!" There: "Cavalry! Send us cavalry quickly!" Then there: "To the devil with the baggage! To the rear, to the rear!" Everywhere echoed the cries of the pickets and the leaders, and, what was even worse, was the escorts and wagoneers. They only knew to cry: "Go! Go!" and push the horses that pulled the wagons. That said, there was already a great clutter! However, at this unexpected alert, everything became utterly indescribable. Everyone was agitated; nobody knew what to do or undertake. Even our commanders and our guides had lost their heads and run here and there, not knowing what to do. Never had I seen them so flabbergasted in one minute. One galloped passionately, with a very pale face, and shouted, ordered, but without knowing what. Another was occupied with moving the wagons, insulting and beating the drivers. A third seized a gun, galloped at its side full out with his horse. Yet another grabbed a regiment, pushed a passage through the wagons and caissons, without

knowing where he led it.

Apraxine agrees with this in his report, talking of the disorder of ideas into which this unforeseen attack threw them: "I was initially in the grip of an inexpressible sorrow when I saw that the enemy was attacking us, moving at full speed, with such a fury and in such good order. From behind my convoy, I was unable to act at all points successfully; I was in a situation so perilous that around me I had to have an escort from which two grenadiers were killed, a post orderly and several officers and hussars were wounded."

However, the orders that he gave were appropriate for the situation. He directed Sibilsky to strongly occupy the Sittenfelde heights, aligned perpendicular to the front that the other regiments were going in kind so that the attackers would be taken at a right angle, in a square of fire. Consequently, Sibilsky laid out his infantry regiments from north to south. On his left was the regular cavalry and behind him the irregular cavalry.

The 2nd Corps (Lopukhin) accepted orders to form for battle on the edge of a wood, supporting, at a right angle, its left on Sibilsky's line. The 1st Corps (Fermor) was to be formed in the same way while trying to support its left on Lopukhin's line. The reserve (Rumyantsev) would remain with the baggage guard, while waiting for new orders.

Lehwaldt should have recognized the new disposition of the Russian Army and especially the dangers that the placement of Sibilsky's corps posed to him. It had prolonged some distance along the flank against the Prussian attack and threatened to envelope him. It is probable that the fog prevented him from seeing this.

Around 5:00 a.m., without waiting for the arrival of the large cavalry column, Prince von Holstein charged, with his dragoons, the hussars, and the Cossacks opposite him. He crushed them. Then, passing between Uderballen and Daupelken, he collided with the 2nd Moscow and Vyborg Regiments, which held the east defile. Received by a rolling musketry fire and canister, he was forced to fall back on Uderballen. At least, by sweeping the plain, he had supported the formation of the Prussian lines and their forward march.

As the eastern defile was the least encumbered, it was there that the first regiments of Lopukhin's corps were formed: Petersburg, Kazan, and Schlüsselburg, extending to the north of Sibilsky's line; the others, Vyborg, 2nd Moscow, Kiev, Narva, and the 2nd Grenadiers, were at right angles to these; Ladoga and 3rd Grenadiers being a little behind.

Then, by the other defile, emerging in their turn and lining up, from the east to the west, on the edge of wood, were the regiments of Rostov, Viatka, Tchernigov, Mourom, and Nijni-Novgorod.

Unfortunately, there remained between the 2nd Grenadiers and Rostov a great vacuum. It was at this weak point that all the effort of the

Prussian infantry was directed. Lehwaldt had not been able to put into practice Frederick II's precepts: to begin the battle with a cannonade, then execute a cavalry charge, and only after that sending in the infantry. His artillery was inferior to that of the Russians. His great cavalry column was still not at hand and Prince von Holstein had been repulsed. He had to engage his infantry immediately. It advanced on the Russians vigorously. The Lossow, Gohr, Lehwaldt, Kalnein, and Kaunitz Regiments, struck the face of Lopukhin's infantry, while the Below, Manstein, and Polenz Regiments, moving through the gap in the Russian line, tried to turn it. It could be destroyed before the remainder of the Russian line could complete its forming up. Sibilsky, laid out perpendicular to Lopukhin, could only help him extremely indirectly; because in front Sibilsky's line extended a marshy ground on which he did not dare to risk himself. Moreover, he had not received an order. Sibilsky's five regiments and the three of Lopukhin's regiments, which extended to the north thus remained simple spectators to this first engagement. Bolotov, who served in the Archangel Regiment, gives us this moving account of the action:

We saw all the spectacle. The Prussians advanced, in the greatest order and of the proudest appearance, in their attack on our army, which extended along the wood. Arriving within musket shot, they fired a well-sustained salvo on our [troops]. It was the first time that I saw enemy fire on our compatriots. Our hearts pounded; and we were all very astonished that, from our side, not a musket shot was fired, as if the Prussian salvo had destroyed them to the last man. The Prussians, after having fired, continued to advance while reloading their muskets, coming even closer to our [troops] and of all their first line fired a new salvo. Our astonishment was still larger, and we could only think when we saw that not a shot was fired in response. "Lord, have pity on us! What does that mean?" we said moving closer to each other and contemplating from the top of our hill this spectacle. "Are ours still alive? What do they do? Is anybody there truly alive?" Some of the timorous were ready to conclude that everyone had been killed: "How would be it possible that after these two terrible salvos, at such a short range, could a single man escape from it?" However, our eyes showed us quite the opposite. As soon as the wind had dissipated the smoke a little, we once again saw our line of battle upright in front of the Prussians; but from which such a silence came, that nobody could understand it. Some old men, of a superstitious spirit, insinuated that our soldiers' muskets had been bewitched; but this idea was mocked as ridiculous. Continuing to observe, we saw that the Prussians, after their second salvo, continued to advance, reloading their muskets while marching, and, coming even closer, fired a third and more terrible salvo. This time, we shouted, "It is well done. They are surely all killed!" We had barely uttered these words when to our satisfaction we could see that all ours had not died, that there were still many of them alive; because instantaneously after the enemy's salvo, our muskets and artillery answered, not by salvos, and though greatly disordered, it was more violent than that of the enemy. As from this moment, the Prussians ceased firing by salvos. The fire of the two sides did not stop for a moment, and we could not distinguish the enemy's shooting from ours. Only the cannon shots were recognized as were the discharges of Shuvalov's secret howitzers, which were easily recognizable in the thick smoke.

At this time the fog, the smoke of the battle, and the smoke from the burning villages concealed the attacks from the spectators. "One could not see ten paces in front of oneself," assured Lehwaldt. The cannonade continued, and the musketry was at nearly point-blank range while one fought in the shadows. It was, in short, a battle like Eylau. The Russians of 's corps defended themselves with a desperate energy, dispalying, in this disorder, the stoic bravery of their race. The bayonet was put to work. Narva and the 2nd Grenadiers lost half their strength in a few moments. General Zybine was killed. General-in-Chief Lopukhin, fatally wounded, fell into the Prussian hands. Finally, these two regiments folded and were thrown back into the woods.

It is at this time that Rumyantsev, "one does not know on whose orders," according to Masslowski, cut a path through the thickets and wagons, and brought into the gap between the 1st and the 2nd Russian Corps, the four regiments Troitsa, Voronezh, Novgorod and 4th Grenadiers. They fell on the flanks of the Manstein and Polenz Grenadiers, their blood up with the destruction of 2nd Grenadiers and Narva. They fired a salvo and charged with bayonets. The Prussians were ejected onto the plain. The Russians were now formed and closed up in line, and a new hope revived their courage.

On the right wing of the Russians, the Iazykov Grenadiers, protected by a battery, even before Fermor's division had been put into line, had pushed back the charges of the Schorlemer Dragoons. It is to them that Apraxine owed the conservation of that most important point. Despairing of breaking them, the Prussian cavalry, Finckenstein Dragoons and Malachowski Hussars, were thrown on the left. These two regiments charged with such a fury that everything they encountered, regular and irregular cavalry, horse grenadiers, cuirassiers, hussars, and the Tchougouiev Cossacks, collapsed, pursuing them to the Russian Army's baggage, to the Norkitten camp. But then the Iazykov Grenadiers turned about and directed on this Prussian cavalry salvo fire. The Shuvalov howitzers, though few in number, showered projectiles on them. This most brilliant charge had the double result of driving the Russian cavalry from the field for the rest of the day, but it also put the Prussian cavalry out of the fight for the next few hours preventing them from again resuming the offensive.

The Russian infantry of this same wing, freed from its fear of the Prussian squadrons, could now take the offensive against the Prussian battalions which were opposite it. It moved around the flank of Lehwaldt's first line and started to fire into its rear.

It was 9:00 a.m., Lehwaldt threw into action his last reserve, advancing his second line; it consisted only of the Manteuffel and Sydow Garrison Regiments. A battalion of the Sydow Regiment, shaken by the terrible Russian fire, lost in the darkness that enveloped it, fired on the Prussian first line: "by a fatal blunder," as Lehwaldt observed in his report to Frederick II. Then all this infantry started to fold and collapse: a part disbanded in the plain and was pursued to the edge of the Norkitten Wood.

The right wing, like the center, swung back to the Russians. Only Sibilsky's corps remained inactive. Because the infantry's weapons were so mediocre, they hesitated to move onto the plain in the presence of Prussian cavalry. The Prince von Holstein and Schorlemer Regiments, and Platen Dragoons, and the Black Rüsch Hussars, concentrated near Uderballen, which covered their infantry and watched Sibilsky's movements. It was necessary to remove the threat of this cavalry. Then an incident occurred, which Bolotov describes as follows:

> The left wing of our corps was covered by the Don Cossacks. From the beginning of the battle, they had run on the enemy cavalry, which stood behind a swamp. Though we could see them, we were quite humiliated by the mediocre success of these mediocre warriors. At first, they showed much ardor. The action occurred more than a verst from us. We thought that with their long lances, they would run everyone through, but we were to quickly witness the opposite. All their bravery consisted of crying "Ghi! Ghi!" and firing with their carbines. As the Prussians remained immobile and prepared to receive them, the Cossacks saw that this would not be their victory, and immediately rode off. And how they ran! This we saw well, but what then

happened, we saw badly, because the Cossacks, galloping around the swamp, disappeared from our sight. We saw, however, that the Prussian cuirassiers[32] and dragoons, riding in their pursuit, had also turned the swamp, chasing them towards our front like a flock of sheep. The Cossacks did not know where to flee. They ran wildly straight at our front. The Prussian cavalry, galloping on their heels, sabered them without mercy. Our infantry, seeing these unfortunate Cossacks fleeing and about to perish, judged it necessary to open gaps so that the Cossacks could find refuge behind them. However, this quickly became serious. The Prussian cavalry, continuing to pursue by squadrons, and in the best order possible, arrived in a torrent and, the Cossacks concealing them, they now fell on our infantry. The infantry opened fire on this cavalry. Yet it was difficult to stop the terrible shock of this cavalry. The first squadron passed like an arrow, always in pursuit of the Cossacks, and, scattering, put to the sword everyone they found behind our lines. We had to turn about and face to the rear. This did little, as the Prussian cavalry now charged our flank, and would have cut us to pieces and would have fixed to its advantage the dubious victory, if one had not found the means of containing their impetuosity. Our heavy battery had, happily, time to turn its guns, and its discharges of canister were very successful. It took in enfilade this cavalry that galloped past squadron by squadron, destroying one of them almost entirely, and not only broke the élan of the others, but forced them to flee wildly. As for those who galloped behind our line, they were taken like rats in a trap. Our infantry closed up and the Prussian cavalry perished in the most miserable way. Our cavalry charged them and sabered them to the last man.

We know that Bolotov did not like the Cossacks. He considered them as half-savages and uncivilized. On all the pages of his writing, he related, with pleasure, their excesses. In the present case, he demeans them by calling them "mediocre warriors" and "soldiers without courage." His excuse is that they did not understand. The Cossacks were not made to charge regular cavalry, but to badger the enemy, to make him lose patience, and, if possible, to draw it into some trap. At Gross Jägersdorf, quite simply, they tested on the Prussians their old, national tactic like the Scythians of Herodotus, which had often succeeded for them against the Turks and Tatars. This time it had the same success with

---

[32] This is an error. The Prussians had no cuirassiers in this battle.

the Germans: the Schorlemer and Prince von Holstein Dragoons, after having resisted their provocations for a long time, had the imprudence to charge them. In the fog and smoke, they did not see that they were being drawn under the fire of 18 battalions of 40 regimental guns, several batteries of heavy caliber guns, under the sabers of the dragoons, horse grenadiers, and the Sibilsky Kalmuks. It was certainly coordinated between this general and Serebriakov, the Ataman of the Cossacks. The beautiful Prussian cavalry fell into the trap, and the best part of it perished.

As a result, the obstacle that had held Sibilsky in inaction disappeared; the ground was cleared in front of him. Immediately his army corps went over to the offensive: infantry, regular cavalry, squadrons of hussars, Cossacks and Kalmuks shook out and advanced. The Prussian infantry, which had marched and fought since daybreak, then stood for five hours under the fatal fire of the Russian guns were famished and exhausted. The Kalnein Regiment had lost two fifths of its manpower. The Prussians saw almost all artillery reduced to silence, its cavalry driven back by the Russian right wing, crushed by their left wing. They were already worried about the offensive movement of Fermor's corps, but outright fear swept its ranks when Sibilsky's corps, formed by fresh troops, made its appearance on stage. Initially its retreat was executed in good order, but it soon became a rout. In 15 minutes, the battlefield was evacuated and Lehwaldt's army disappeared into the wood out of which it had marched that morning.

It was 10:00 p.m., and the battle was won for the Russians, all along their line. They occupied the abandoned Prussian positions. The sky was filled with their hats as they threw them up in joy and one heard their "hourrahs" of victory. They fired salvos with the muskets and cannon taken from the Prussians. It was the first victory that the Russians had ever taken over a truly European army. The Russian infantry had just revealed itself to the world.[33]

It was not beautiful to contemplate, this battlefield, and the impression that Bolotov gives us of it is truly compelling:

As soon as the ranks were broken, our first care was
to ride up and examine the battlefield. What a spectacle was
offered to us, the like of which we have never seen before!
On climbing the hill, on which the Prussian line had drawn

---

[33] Translator: It is with difficulty that I translate this last sentence. Yes, the Russian infantry was an unknown quantity in the West, but it outnumbered the Prussians by a huge quantity and not only were the Prussian troops not the cream of the Prussian army; the best ones having been taken to the south to face the Austrians, but these were absolutely the best troops in the Russian Army. True, Apraxine's incompetence came close to losing the battle and the steadfastness of the Russian infantry saved it, much to the common soldier's credit, the deck was clearly stacked against the Prussians. Had Lehwaldt not advanced with drums and trumpets sounding but taken the Russians by the surprise that was in his grasp, this would have most likely been a complete slaughter of the Russians.

up and had fought, was covered with enemy corpses; and the astonishing thing which was offered to us, it is that all were lying naked as at the moment of their birth. They had been stripped not only of their socks and shoes, but even of their shirts; but by whom and when they had been so completely stripped, we did not know; the battle hardly finished and little time had passed! We were astonished at the dexterity with which the escorts, ordinances and other people had stripped them. Near each man, one saw nothing but the wood of the cartridge pouch which had been used to contain the cartridges and the blue paper which covered them. These objects had obviously not seemed useful to anybody; as to the other objects, they were gone. Even the soldier's hair ribbons, which was not worth three deniers, had been untied and carried...

The Russian victory was incontestable. They had driven back the Prussians at every point. They had captured 29 cannons, nearly half of Lehwaldt's artillery. If they had not captured any flags, declared Apraxine in his report, it was because, "so prompt had been the Prussian flight, that they had time to assemble their flags in a safe place and carry them to security: which the proximity of the woods made easy." However, the Russian losses seem to have been greater than those of the Prussians, which can be explained by the Russians being caught by surprise. The Russians lost 1,818 killed and 2,237 wounded. The Prussians lost 1,449 dead and 4,494 wounded. These are the figures given by Masslowski. Apraxine, in his report, states that the Prussians lost 4,600 men, not including 600 prisoners. Schaefer has used this figure.

On both sides the leaders were not spared. Of the Russian generals, three had been killed: Lopukhin, Zybine, and Kapnist, who commanded the Slobode Cossacks. Seven had been wounded: Weymarn, Chief of Staff, Tolstoy, Chief of Artillery, du Bosquet, Engineering Commander, and Generals Löwen, Manteuffel, Villebois, and Plemiannikof. In the entire officer corps the Russians lost 38 dead and 232 wounded. On the Prussian side, Lehwaldt had two horses killed under him, but received no other wound. Von Goltz, the precious councilor, who had been sent to him by Frederick II, had died at his side. Dohna and seven other generals were wounded.

Apraxine, in his report, described the brilliant actions of his subordinates: "Your Imperial Majesty, based on the casualty listings, can see how well the officers have done their duty. None scorned it; they scorned only their lives. Not one of the wounded officers left his station, nor allowed himself to be bandaged before the action was finished and victory assured. Those of the generals who were not wounded had at least a horse, sometimes two horses killed under them." Of 31 generals serving in the line, nearly a third had been wounded!

It is to the soldiers also that homage must be paid: the Russian artillery had been exceptionally well served; the infantry overcame so many difficulties, dealing with the absence of orders, accepting isolated and hand-to-hand combat. Without the tenacity of the 1st Grenadiers on the right wing, without the heroic sacrifice of 2nd Moscow and Vyborg in the center, the action would have been lost at the beginning. The victory of Gross Jägersdorf was a soldiers' victory.

Masslowski attempted to defend Apraxine against the criticisms of Bolotov, who accused him of making an inadequate use of scouts, and the absence of all dispositions for battle, in a word, his lack of command. He shows that Apraxine's plan contained many good ideas. It appears to us that the points on which he justified the Generalissimo were secondary. The errors committed were those of consequence. One of these was his initial choice of the camp at Norkitten, with two rivers at his back, so close to the Prussians that one could hear them sounding their drums in their camp, and the almost impossibility of decamping without risking an encounter with them. Since, so near them, this flank march by three or four separate columns separated from each other by so many obstacles; the encumbrance of the artillery and wagons in the narrow defiles; and the immobility of Sibilsky's corps until the end of the battle were all major errors. There was only a single general in this army who showed himself to be a true tactician – General Rumyantsev. Frederick II did not hesitate to give him the honor of winning this battle, because in leading his 20 battalions against the flank and rear of the Prussian infantry had repaired the errors of his commander and decided the victory. The inadequacy of the dispositions taken by Apraxine caused the Russian Army to lose all the advantages of its numerical superiority. Because of his decisions, a large part of the Russian artillery and infantry remained in the woods, inactive; and, in reality, the Russians fought with an army of only 55,000 men.

If Apraxine had brought all of his forces into action, the Prussians would not have just been defeated, they would have been annihilated. One was victorious without being there; this is the impression of Bolotov, and after him of the historian Soloviev. The same was believed by the Russian Army and people. The *byline* or popular song about this battle is quite curious: "Ours start to fire, the clouds of dust and of smoke rise, we see absolutely nothing… One fought, one massacred oneself, for 14 hours. One started to raise the bodies; one collected colonels up to five, the generals up to ten." It is a strange thing that this battle, so well won, did not leave in the memory of the masses the recollection of a victory. The *byline* has the dying Lopukhin say: "I will write to the Tsarina that it was Apraxine, the general, who was not at his station and who lost all the army."

Lehwaldt had not shown himself a great tactician. He attacked the Russian Army frontally, without taking account of the second army, that of Sibilsky, which was on his flank. In claiming to force the entrance of the wood, he condemned his soldiers to scatter like the Russians. He lost the advantages that were assured him by his well-trained and well-drilled troops. He restored to the enemy his advantage of numbers. He had every opportunity for victory, and yet it was impossible for him to gain a decisive victory. On the contrary, by turning the position of the Russians, and launching his formidable cavalry into their flank or rear, he could have thrown the Russian Army into an irrevocable disorder. He was in a position at Norkitten extremely similar to that of that Napoleon, in 1807, when he met the Russians at Friedland. In short, the principal fault of Lehwaldt was to have sought a battle against Apraxine as events would prove that he could have, without a battle, obliged Apraxine to evacuate the province.

Frederick II, with the receipt of Lehwaldt's report on the battle, showed himself less severe in his appreciations than one might have feared. He assured the old general of his whole satisfaction for the bravery that he had shown, blaming the loss on the chances of war. He refused the resignation that Lehwaldt offered him.[34] At the bottom, however, Frederick was humiliated at this defeat. For a long time, he could not forgive the Prussian "bearskins" for being defeated by the "barbarians." At that time, Frederick did not yet personally know the Russian Army. He would meet it at Zorndorf and Kunersdorf. It is only after having seen it in action that he ceased scorning it, because then he had the experience that someone other than Lehwaldt could be beaten by it.

At 4:00 a.m., on 8 September, the inhabitants of St. Petersburg were awaked by the sound of 101 cannon shots announcing the victory over the Prussians. Great was the joy of Elisabeth when she received Apraxine's report. She liberally rewarded the commanders that the Marshal indicated to her, such as Panine, who had brought the news. On the contrary the Grand Duke, as the French Ambassador wrote, "publicly showed his sorrow at the [Russians] winning of the battle; he cannot hide sorrow that he feels. This makes a bad impression on the Russians, who see all that they have to fear if ever this prince suddenly reigns over them." The Grand Duchess occupied herself with comforting and reassuring the British Agent Williams, who was obliged to leave St. Petersburg. The Young Court thus remained very pro-Prussian or pro-English.

Otherwise, Louis XV did nothing to rally to Catherine. It was at this time that he succeeded in getting the Saxon Court to recall Poniatowski. What made the dispositions of the Young Court more worrying for alliance, was that

[34] De Roetha, 6 September 1757, *Politische Correspondenz*, Vol. XV, p. 332.

Elisabeth in September suffered a rather serious relapse of her health. At least she held firm for the Coalition. Speaking about her nephew the Grand Duke, she said: "Oh that he does not have a brother!" It was actively discussed that she not leave the throne to the Grand Duke, but to his very young son. As for Grand-Chancellor Bestuchev, he had still not regained the confidence of the Allied courts. The Ambassadors of France and Austria did not cease denouncing him to Elisabeth. She agreed with Esterhazy that he was "malicious and a bad servant," but that she did not know what to do with him until she had removed the chancellery from him. "Give him a pension of 100,000 rubles," retorted the Austrian ambassador; "you will gain a thousand percent more there." It is on Bestuchev that they laid all of Apraxine's slowness. The Allied courts were convinced that Apraxine was devoted not only to Bestuchev, but to Grand Duchess Catherine. They took little joy in his victory of 30 August and his subsequent operations provided them with new reasons for complaint.

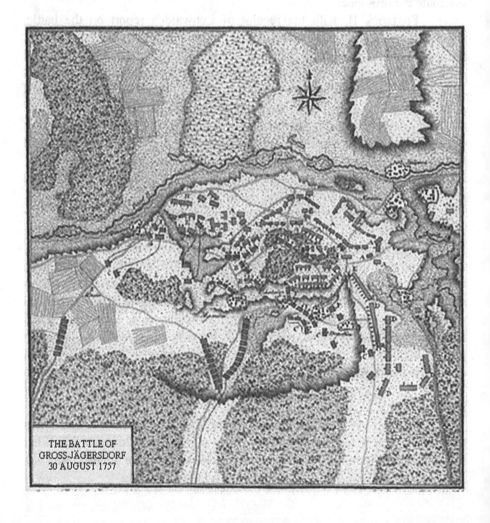

THE BATTLE OF
GROSS-JÄGERSDORF
30 AUGUST 1757

Ural Cossack on vedette.

CHAPTER V

APXARINE'S RETREAT

Why is it that the victory of 30 August, which brought joy to Russia's friends and afflicted its enemies, had no result? How could it provoke a precipitous retreat and the almost total evacuation of the conquered territory? How could Lehwaldt, defeated at Gross Jägersdorf, appear to be the victor? This is what we will now attempt to explain.

After the victory, Apraxine had not pursued the Prussians, although it was only 10:00 a.m., and Sibilsky's corps was intact. He could plead that a pursuit through marshes and woods was the riskiest of operations. He addressed to Lehwaldt a courteous letter to inform him of the good treatment received by Prussian prisoners in his camp and to propose an exchange [of prisoners?] to him. During this time Lehwaldt crossed the Pregel and reappeared in Wilkensdorf, which was a very strong position. Bolotov was astonished that Apraxine did not take the offensive against him: "We had been, however, delighted with the idea of soon revisiting, the famous city of Königsberg …. Here we are the third day after the battle; and each morning it is the *diane* [reveille] that is beaten [on the drums], and not the *général* [a long drum roll that was an alarm].… What do we do here? And why did we dawdle for such a long time?" Apraxine pushed out a strong reconnaissance, on 2 September. It was necessary to attack the Prussians or to turn their line. Apraxine did not dare to attempt it. He was satisfied to take up a position on the Alle, between Allenburg and Burgersdorf, which was burning. He did not try to take Wehlau, where Lehwaldt's magazines were located, and which commanded the confluence of the Alle with the Pregel. He had Krasnochtchokov cross the Alle as other Cossacks, under Serebriakov advanced as far as Friedland; still others blocked Wehlau. Apraxine understood that he could not attack Königsberg before he defeated the Prussians a second time. However, he refused to seek this battle as too many of his regiments had been decimated by the action of 30 August. He could not count on the prompt arrival of recruits to fill the holes in his regiments' ranks made by combat and disease.

On 8 September, Lehwaldt withdrew from Wilkensdorf and Wehlau on Tapiau, as if he wanted to allow the Russian Army an open line of retreat, and Apraxine to resolve to withdraw. The Russians were going to withdraw on Tilsit and the line of the Niemen. In the council of war that Apraxine held on this occasion, two projects were examined: one, risky, was to attack Lehwaldt; the other, strictly calculated, was the withdrawal on Tilsit. The council decided almost unanimously for the latter. They comforted themselves by thinking that by re-establishing communications with Russia, they could rebuild the army and assume the offensive, and, for example, take the port of Labau on the Kurisches Haff. In his report of 14 September, Apraxine explained his resolution thus: "I do not retreat, since I beat the enemy and put them into subjection to Your Imperial Majesty; it is in honor and glory that I move on Tilsit, with the only thought of not exposing to some misfortune an army fatigued by so many marches and which finds here only a desolated country. I am assured that the enemy will not be able to praise himself as having, by some skill at war, constrained my victorious army to withdraw on Tilsit.... The allied courts could not reproach me it." And he recalled that neither Frederick II after his victory of Lobositz nor the Austrians after that of Kollin had pursued the enemy.

On 9 September, after having ordered the Cossack leaders Demoline, Krasnochtchokov, and Serebriakov to contain the enemy by demonstrations on the Alle, Apraxine ordered them to march Astrawischken, Judlauken, and Jaenischken, with the most stage being that to Ilmsdorf. For the first three days the Russians marched from the west to the east, because they had to move around the large Astrawischken Forest. From Judlauken to Insterburg, the Russians marched due north.

The withdrawal announced itself as being extremely difficult: choking heat, the dusty days in this sandy country, were suddenly succeeded by overpowering rains. The bodies of dead horses littered the road: Apraxine ordered most of the carriages to be burned to be able to harness his artillery. Food started to become as rare as fodder. Diseases, some contagious, prevailed among the men and included typhus, smallpox, scurvy, and dysentery.

Lehwaldt, who the Cossacks left by Apraxine wrapped in a curtain of cavalry, went several days without knowing that Apraxine had evacuated Allenburg. As soon as he learned it, he quickly marched on his flank and harassed him with his cavalry. On 19 September, the Russians were charged by Rüsch and Prince von Holstein, who gathered up the stragglers and made some prisoners. Apraxine had to precipitate the evacuation of Gumbinnen, where he burned his magazines. At the same time, the armed peasants again resumed their partisan war against the invader. The Russian troops committed excesses, having as an excuse that they were being attacked by the inhabitants.

As the Russians approached Tilsit, the roads became increasingly bad. It was necessary to sacrifice even more of the army's wagons. Nonetheless, the Russian Army still required four days, from the 16th to the 19th to cross the Inster at Sesslacken. On the 19th, Lehwaldt's advance guard occupied Insterburg, almost on the heels of the retreating Russians and the inhabitants renounced their oaths to the Tsarina.

Rüsch attacked the Russian convoys and captured many cattle and much flour. Consequently, Apraxine believed he could not maintain himself in the country, believing that he should desolate the land so as to at least slow down the Prussian pursuit. In truth this victorious army was, less than 20 days after its victory, a pursued army. Malachowski, Rüsch and Prince von Holstein, on his flanks, made the same war as the Cossacks of 1812 on the flanks of Napoleon's Grande Armée. Apraxine would have liked Removed space to have given his troops a little rest in his camp at Sesslacken: but the very same day he was driven out by Lehwaldt's approach. The Prussians immediately occupied the town. Lehwaldt now began to escort his adversary. He arrived almost as soon as Apraxine in the vicinity of Tilsit. On 23 September Apraxine attempted to make an "entry" into this city. He was received by the magistrate with the sound of ringing alarm bells and artillery salvos. In order to enter he had to impose on the population.

At the bottom, Apraxine was devoured by concerns. It was in Tilsit that he fixed the term of its "evolution"; he had promised to his government that he would stop there only to prepare for a new offensive. However, to remain there, a battle would have to be fought. Then shortly after his arrival, Prince von Holstein and Lehwaldt occupied the villages close to the city. In Ragnit, a small, nearby borough, the bourgeois united with the Malachowski Hussars to drive out the Russian garrison.

The situation of Elisabeth's army was truly lamentable: she counted 8,996 sick and in the hospital at this time. She was demoralized. As a result of the disorganization of the logistical system, petty thieving and plundering had grown dramatically. We need to point out that in such a country, under similar conditions, the Grande Armée of 1812 had already started to melt even before entering to Russia. The petty thieving exasperated the population, and their reprisals justified in their turn crueler reprisals by the Russians.

The town of Ragnit had just been delivered to the Cossacks and the Volga barbarians plundered and burned. About 20 inhabitants were murdered. All this resulted in the Russians, then in Tilsit, finding the surrounding country rising up against them. And, also, in a famished country: by the Niemen, neither upstream, nor downstream, nothing could come. As for the tactical conditions, they were equally bad. It was necessary to fight a battle with the river at their backs and two cities on the edge of open revolt, Tilsit and Ragnit, on their flanks. The impetuous general of light cavalry, Demoline, declared that the ground in front of Tilsit was impracticable for cavalry and artillery, being muddy, and filled with undergrowth and marshes; that it provided every advantage for the local insurgent local population. On 24 September, after a council of war it was decided to hold in the city until they were able to ensure the passage of the river. They hoped that they would benefit from the respite to dispatch to Courland all the useless horses and to return to Russia two thirds of the irregular cavalry. They decided to keep only the 4,000 Don Cossacks. All the others were not good, as to that point all they had done was to bring the inhabitants to revolt, and to starve the country and the army.

Affecting a crossing of the river was not an easy thing. No one had envisioned all the circumstances which now made this a critical situation for the army. Lehwaldt's bold offensive after such a defeat, the rains that had delayed and harassed the troops, their moral and medical state, and finally the uprising of the civilians had changed everything. The Russians repaired the fortifications of Tilsit and placed guns on its ramparts. At the same time, they established two additional bridges over the Niemen. On 24 September, the cavalry passed over the bridge constructed on piles. The following day, the infantry started to pass. Two days later, the two new bridges were finished. All of the 27th the army continued to flow across the river. Lastly, on the 28th, the rearguard evacuated Tilsit and Ragnit, destroying all the provisions and ammunition which it could not carry, and burning the bridges behind it. To contain the inhabitants, the Russians had placed bales of pitch on the roofs of the houses; but they were not ignited. The operation was supported by a rather sharp cannonade, which the Prussians were not long in answering. The two following days, the two armies fired at each other across the river. On the 29th, Lehwaldt had occupied Tilsit, and Malachowski set out on a reconnaissance on the footsteps of the retreating Russian army. The last shots of the cannon on the ramparts of Tilsit were the last shots of the campaign.

It was obvious that the Russians would not restrict themselves to simply recrossing the Niemen. The Russians would also recross the Prussian frontier, abandoning their conquests and losing all the fruits of Gross Jägersdorf, abandoning to those defeated on August 30th their total revenge. As of 9 October, the situation of the Russian Army had worsened. In its wake traveled 15,000 sick and wounded. There were not enough horses to draw all the baggage wagons, so multitudes of wagons were abandoned along the roads. The Russian rearguard was in constant action with the Prussian cavalry, which constantly harassed their retreat. The Russian Army now moved in two columns, Apraxine traveled with the larger column that moved on Memel, while a second column moved further to the east, along a shorter road that would take it off Prussian territory more quickly. On 16 October, Apraxine reached Memel.

Apraxine resolved to at least keep this first and this last trophy of his successes, this city over whose ramparts the flag of the Tsarina still floated. He installed a garrison of 10,000 to 12,000 men in it and gave command of the garrison to Fermor. Then, with the remainder of his forces, he crossed Semigalia[1] and took up winter quarters in Courland.

In St. Petersburg, if one had been enthusiastic for the victory of 30 August, they were surprised to see Apraxine, instead of continuing his offensive, executing a retreat. The ambassadors from France, Austria and

---

[1] Translator: Semigalia is the Latinized form of "Zemgale" a province of Latvia.

Saxony complained loudly. Esterhazy was still excited by the reports which he received from Saint-Andrew; the Austrian military attaché assigned to the Russian Army. This army and its leader were judged with equal rigor by this officer sent to observe them by Count Esterhazy. Here a fragment of this correspondence:[2]

> ...When one considers the little order that reigns in this army, everything that goes wrong here should astonish no one...
>
> When Marshal Apraxine found so many obstacles to the march of his army, which had the air of the migration of some barbarian people, he should have taken the step to return the excess of his crews and horses [to Russia] before entering Prussia, as General von Saint-Andrew had advised to him; he should have gotten rid of most of the Tartars, who only served to devastate the country. He should have reduced the multitude of the carriages with which the soldiers are encumbered. He could have replaced these useless embarrassments by carriages led with order, which Courland and Livonia could have easily provided him; but any remonstrance was useless.
>
> Upon learning the news of the battle of Cochenitz in Bohemia[3], Marshal Apraxine, having very precise orders, took the resolution to enter Prussia. This he undertook without the least precaution. He believed it sufficient to send ahead the Cossacks and Kalmuks, who plundered and ruined all. As a result, the army that followed them found nothing. This general gave to the inhabitants of Prussia the strongest assurances of protection and the re-establishment of good order and discipline. One saw them coming on all sides to give the oath of fidelity and assuming docility what was required of them. But they barely had devoted themselves to this confidence, that one started to mistreat them, to burn their villages, to massacre, rape, break in the doors of the churches, to plunder them, dig up the dead, and finally to reduce, by amazing horrors, to true desert a country so well cultivated and so fertile that any other army would have found there what was necessary to remain for a long time; an abundance of everything. So many cruelties determined

---

[2] Account of an officer that the Count of Esterhazy had sent to the Russian army in Prussia. – November 1757. Foreign Affairs of France, Correspondence, Russia, Vol. LIV, piece 131.
[3] This is the battle of Kolin, fought in July 1757.

these unhappy people to give up their land and flee from the hands of the barbarians by seeking asylum and the weapons to avenge themselves and fight for their King in the Prussian Army....

The misfortunes of the campaign must be allotted to: 1° the lack of military skill of the general, who allowed himself to be led by ill-disposed people; 2° his ambition, his cupidity, his ill-will...

Though, according to the common opinion, the Russian soldier can endure fatigues, it has been shown, by the experience and the testimony even from their generals, that these men, seemingly robust, but badly nourished, support them less well than ours, and, which still proves this, that for three years, Russia has provided more than 120,000 recruits and that the Russian infantry was reduced from 50,000 men to 25,000, at the end of the campaign; that, during only one summer, the number of sick had risen to 10,000 and there were as many deaths. It is to be concluded from all this that one should not expect great assistance from a power which, though having great resources, so slightly fills its engagements and which cannot, by its current administration, undertake anything against well- disciplined troops.

Nothing has me surprised so much, as upon approaching the Russian Army, to see an advance guard made up of two regiments of cavalry and five regiments of infantry, when it crossed a small river: the cavalry was mounted on small horses that could barely carry them, and these men had the worst appearance. The infantry, which barely comes to 20,000 men, is in a piteous state. I never saw troops so dilapidated. At two miles from there, I met the baggage that traveled in two columns, without it appearing as if the army intended to follow them. A quantity of sick who followed and fell dead on both sides of the road, a multitude of marauders dispersed [across the countryside], at least three men escorted each ox or cow, caused me to believe that all the army was mixed with the baggage and the cattle. I found, however, the army camped two miles from there. I sought the two lines, without being able to find one according to regulations. One tells me that it was not the habit, in the Russian armies, to camp in two lines, but *en potence*, at an angle, while growing into a square; the headquarters and the train of the army were always in the center....

The daily service of the army resembles everything else. Marshal Apraxine has never attempted to reconnoiter the enemy position, and the generals imitate him very religiously. One never had but false news of the situation and movements of the Prussians. To have detachments and guards in front of the army is unknown. One [trusts this task to] the Cossacks and Kalmuks, who usually are occupied only with plunder. The Marshal never made use of spies, and von Lehwaldt had near the general a sergeant who daily went to the Prussian camp to report what had occurred and was said to be in the Russian Army as well as the general's cabinet. This unfortunate man found the means to save himself when he was discovered.

The French and Austrian Ambassadors, irritated by all these reports, complained less about Generalissimo Apraxine than of the Grand Chancellor Bestuchev who they accused of duplicity and treason. They suspected that there was an arrangement between the Marshal and the Young Court.

It was the moment that Bestuchev had approached Catherine and seeing the decline of the Tsarina's health and the nullity of the Grand Duke, when he developed a plan to ensure the Grand Duchess, either as associated with her husband, or like the tutor of her son, the imperial succession. Catherine acknowledges, in her *Memoirs*, that the Grand-Chancellor communicated this plan to her, but that she had not attached any importance to "this species of drivel" and that she had burned the compromising note. But already she held herself ready for any event; she went so far as to say at a full table, in front of all the foreign ministers, with L'Hôpital himself: "There is not a woman as bold as me; I am of an unrestrained temerity." But, however bold the plans of Catherine and Bestuchev, they had no interest in the 1757 campaign ending in a kind of humiliating disaster. If they counted on the army, if Apraxine were, as Williams ensured her, "entirely at the disposal of the Grand Duchess," they had no interest that this army appeared to be beaten, or that the Generalissimo was completely discredited! It is certain that to the contrary Bestuchev did not cease pressing Apraxine to stop this despairing retreat: Catherine also wrote to him in the same sense, and if her notes might have been used to charge her with a crime against the State, it is not because she gave bad council to the Marshal, but because she had permitted herself, a simple grand duchess, to maintain a correspondence with a general.

The considerations of interior policy thus had no impact on Apraxine's retreat; it was the result of purely military considerations; Masslowski, thanks to papers taken from the military archives, has been able to show us the evidence.

The Conference, upon the first news of the retrograde movement, was attacked by the complaints of the ambassadors; it did not initially know how to answer them. On 24 September, it was only due to the lack of fodder that the army was retreating. As a result, it wrote to Apraxine enjoining him to resume the offensive and to at least make an effort on Labiau. The College of Foreign Affairs accepted the order to positively verify that operations were continued. However, on 25 September, Apraxine announced his retirement on Courland. On 3 October, he declared that it was impossible for him to resume active operations. On the 5th, a new *oukaze* was sent from the Tsarina to the College of Foreign Affairs: The allied courts were informed that, considering the state of affairs, "our field marshal can correctly judge, not only in our interest, but in that of the Allies, that it was incomparably more useful to conserve, in light of the upcoming campaign, a good army than to pointlessly expose it to the dangers that neither bravery, nor courage, nor human forces could save them." They promised a new offensive. It was this offensive that the army was not in a condition to begin. The council of war, held on 9 October, declared that it could not undertake the offensive. Then a letter from Tsarina arrived at the general headquarters, enjoining Marshal Apraxine: 1° to keep Memel; 2° to attack Labiau; 3° to threaten Königsberg; and 4° to beat Lehwaldt if he crossed the Niemen. During the night of 16/17 October, the council of war met. He declared that he could keep Memel and even beat Lehwaldt if he ventured to attack him; but that to re-occupy Prussia, to threaten Labiau or Königsberg, was impossible. The generals who took part in this council were at the same time soldiers and courtiers: they showed a very sharp sense of duty and even a certain courage in resisting an order signed by Elisabeth. They were unanimous and Fermor, who would replace Apraxine, voted as did Apraxine. One could not carry out the order, declared the generals, "without exposing to total destruction the men and horses by hunger... They would only act on one new and formal order from the Empress who enjoined not to take any account of the evidence of a total destruction of the army without any possible result." The Tsarina could not give this order. However, as she needed to satisfy the allied ambassadors, a scapegoat, an expiatory victim was needed. This would be Apraxine. On 28 October, he was relieved and criminally charged. Fermor was designated to replace him. The council of war charged with judging Apraxine was very embarrassed to find him guilty as it would have been necessary to condemn, as accomplices, all the generals. His chief of staff, Weymarn, was also caught up in Apraxine's disgrace.

Apraxine's recall provoked sharp regrets in the army. Though it had cruelly suffered under his orders, it honored him as the general who had given it its first victory over the Germans. Here is what its secretary, Vesselitski, wrote on 20 November to Bestuchev:

14 Nov. (V. 8t.) 1757.

... The departure of His Excellency, the General Field Marshal, for St. Petersburg gave place to various conjectures among the soldiers. Their compassion for him was great. They regard it as an extreme misfortune for them to be deprived of such a generalissimo, that they like and greatly esteem. Amongst them they spoke in the following words: "At the same time when God has done us the honor of giving us a Field Marshal [who is a] man of piety, here it is, for our sins, he is taken from us. As for these irreligious people, the Germans, can one expect any good of them? They all are co-religionists: does the crow pierce the eyes of the crow? Can they have the same zeal and the same constancy as the men of our country? And then, when in the battle all our Orthodox generals, those who with honesty and faith served our mother Elisabeth Petrovna, were killed," - and other similar remarks. In a word, it was easy to see, the major dissatisfaction that they felt at seeing that the people directing the army were strangers. As for me, the humblest slave of Her Imperial Majesty, such remarks, if universal, in the present situation, appeared very important to me, and, including how much damage and danger can be borne from this distrust with regard to the main leaders, and to the contrary, how much profit and advantage can one hope for feelings of love and confidence, — considering my zeal and my jealousy to safeguard the interests of Her Imperial Majesty, — I believed it absolutely necessary, as soon as these rumors reached me, to refer to Your Highness very humbly and to give the care to relieve here your deep foresight of it...

But already the trial begun against Apraxine had suddenly taken a new development with unforeseen repercussions. In his papers one had found the letters from Bestuchev and the three letters from the Grand Duchess.

The Grand Duke, who hated his wife and who believed he had complaints about the Chancellor, had the singular idea to carry his complaints to Esterhazy. Esterhazy advised him to trust the Tsarina. Peter took this advice: he excused himself for what he had said or the bad things he had done in the past, blaming it all on the bad council of Bestuchev and his wife. Elisabeth was touched, forgave her nephew, and then directed her anger on the bad adviser. The Coalition formed against Bestuchev by Vice-Chancellor Vorontsov, Secretary Volkov and Shuvalov could thus triumph. On 25 February 1758, in full Conference, Bestuchev was arrested. He had had time to destroy his papers and to inform Catherine that she had nothing to fear on this side. Catherine was hardly more in safety, between the ire of her aunt and the hostility of her husband. Poniatowski found the means to send her a letter, informing her that they sought to return her to Germany. Almost at the same time, her most intimate confidants Elaghine, Adadourof, and the goldsmith Bemhardi, were arrested; the minister from Holstein, Stambke, was expelled. A special subcommittee, formed of Nikita Troubetskoi, Buturline, Alexis and Shuvalov, with Volkov as secretary, began the preliminary investigation against Bestuchev. A series of questions were asked of him: To what end had he sought the good graces of the Grand Duchess? Why hadn't he revealed her correspondence with Apraxine? What did the conferences with Stambke and Poniatowski cover? — "You said to His Highness the Grand Duke that if he continued to be such as he was, you would take certain steps regarding him. You have to explain clearly which changes you wished to make regarding the Grand Duke, and what were these measures that you wanted to take in his connection." - Then, they ordered him to explain "why Apraxine had come into such favor with the Grand Duchess, and who arranged this favor for him?" Fortunately for the defendants the essential documents relating to this had been destroyed in advance. The commission guessed as much but was not able to prove anything. Besides, they hesitated to push their investigations too far, out of fear of identifying too many people to be punished that were too highly placed. They considered Bestuchev guilty: to have slandered the Empress; to have sown division between Their Highnesses and Her Majesty; to have taken it upon himself not to carry out her orders or to oppose their execution; that, to correct Apraxine's slowness, to have preferred to employ an "illicit correspondence by a person who did not agree to take part in the political matters"; to have, at the time of his arrest, delivered in writing state secrets. The commission condemned him to death, but recommended leniency to the Tsarina. He was detained until April 1759, and then exiled to his lands. Apraxine died during the trial.

The Grand Duchess was not taken before the commission. She underwent a kind of house arrest, and a disgrace which lasted until 1759. At least she was not returned to Germany. Deprived of her exiled or imprisoned friends, of Poniatowski and the minister from Holstein, her advisers, and subjected to the most rigorous police surveillance, languid in sorrow and tears, she sought the means to recover. She won over Elisabeth's confessor; she even addressed to the confessor the most humble letters,[4] humbler than she acknowledges it in her *Memoirs*; she ended up obtaining from her two interviews where she partially justified herself. She did not have this "indomitable heart" that her recent historians give her and that "nothing could make her fold." Bestuchev had fallen, Vorontsov was triumphant, the Young Court was in disgrace, put

---

[4] See *Papiers de Catherine II* in the collection of the *Soc. Imp. d'hist. de Russie*, Vol VIII, p. 74.

out of the fight until the spring of 1759; it seemed to the allied courts that they had won, at least in the Winter Palace. Cardinal de Bernis wrote on 24 March 1758: "The events in Russia can save the fatherland." L'Hôpital was less enthusiastic. Initially he was comforted rather quickly with the sad outcome of Apraxine's campaign: "I do not know if one must consider these failed operations as unfortunate for peace, since the Russian ministry will not be able to form any more such claims that might be embarrassing." He did not believe that Apraxine's disgrace and his replacement by Fermor would raise up the Russian Army: "It does not have a chief, the one being just named barely being better than General Apraxine. As a result of the indiscipline, cowardice and plundering of these troops, not only they will be able to undertake nothing this year, but it will not be possible to form another army next year."

L'Hôpital and the Austrians were unjust in this criticism. The plundering and indiscipline with which they reproached the Russian Army, only occurred among the irregular troops. And they are the only ones who could be accused of cowardice. What proves that the French Ambassador was ill-informed, is that in the year the 1758 the Russian Army reappeared and was more frightening than ever.

He had the bad grace to be so severe on the Russians. All in all, in the year 1757, the Austrians, initially defeated in Prague, victorious at Kolin, finished the campaign with the crushing defeat at Lissa (Leuthen). The easy successes of Richelieu in Hanover, at Hastembeck and Clostersevern led to the disaster of Rossbach. The Russians had begun with a bright victory and finished by a laborious retreat. None of confederates had had room to throw stones at the others. The assessment of the Russian Army supports its comparison to the other allied armies.

Russian Dragoons

CHAPTER VI

THE CONQUEST OF EAST PRUSSIA

When it was a question of replacing Apraxine as Commander-in-Chief of the Russian Army, it was not according to the seniority list that Fermor was chosen. He was junior to Buturline, the two Shuvalovs, George Löwen and Peter Soltykov. He was the seventh most senior general officer. But it seems that the two Shuvalovs were challenged; Soltykov and Buturline were too far away, one occupied creating the "Observation Corps," the other with supplementing the third battalions of the regiments of regular army. Fermor, on the other hand, had remained at the general headquarters. Fermor had defended Apraxine against those who claimed he had, for political considerations, precipitated the army's retreat; it would thus appear odd that one entrusted him to succeed Apraxine. But it was obvious also that nobody was more up to date with the situation of the army than him. Besides, it was he who had taken Memel and Tilsit, and he had distinguished at the battle of Gross-Gross Jägersdorf.

One could consider it regrettable that he was a German, a Protestant, and even a convinced Protestant. He was one of those "irreligious German people," who the Orthodox Vesselitski was unhappy with being in the army, recalling the Russian proverb: "Does the crow pierce the eyes of the crow?" However, none of the generals, except for Soltykov, gained over Frederick II such a brilliant success as Fermor. At the Russian Court, nobody doubted his loyalty and his fidelity; all agreed to recognize his capacity; finally, he passed not only for a good general, but also for distinguished engineer. He had around Elisabeth powerful protectors and advocates; because, even before Bestuchev had fallen into disgrace, as if he had envisaged his pending fall, it was not with him, but instead with the favorite Ivan Guvalov and Vice-Chancellor Vorontsov, that he was in correspondence (several of his letters were subsequently published in the *Vorontsov Archive*). One could not charge him with having relations with the Young Court. He was rather of the Shuvalov and Vorontsov Party, that is, the party of the Empress. Also, the ambassadors of France, Austria and Saxony did not hesitate to recommend him, although L'Hôpital estimated that he would do no better than his predecessor.

The historians of our century variously appreciated him. Hasenkamp cannot praise enough his humanity, his courtesy, his politeness, and his concern for the conquered populations of East Prussia. For the contrary reasons, Masslovski, believing that he too greatly spared the defeated, was willing to judge him severely. If Fermor had sympathies for the German people and the things of Germany, Masslovski claimed him to be "antipathetic" to Russian nature. He reproached him for badly misunderstanding the national character of the troops that he commanded. On several points, he furnished proof of his contentions, but one sometimes found him excessive in his bias against Fermor.

Weymarn, having become enveloped in Apraxine's disgrace, Fermor found himself deprived of the services of the excellent Chief of Staff who had experience in the preceding campaign. All the labor necessary for the reorganization of the army now fell almost entirely on Fermor. Also let us note that Brown, who commanded one of the two army corps, always affected a certain independence with regard to the new Generalissimo. It was the same for Peter Soltykov who, so far from the principal army, commanded the "Observation Corps." Other generals, the "Orthodox ones," bowed only begrudgingly to his authority. Lastly, more narrowly still than his predecessor Apraxine, Fermor was going to be closely controlled by the Conference, which made him less of a generalissimo than the executor of its deliberations. The Conference of St. Petersburg, on the one hand, and the Hof-Kriegsrath of Vienna, on the other hand, would continue to influence in the most annoying way the operations of Fermor and Daun. Between these two generals held under close supervision, the King of Prussia, who was his own Conference and Hof-Kriegsrath, would keep the monopoly of timely decisions, fast movements and striking thunderous blows.

From the moment Fermor assumed command, the principal Russian army was dispersed in its winter quarters, where Apraxin had taken it; that is to say, in Semigalia and Courland. The 1st Corps, that of Brown, was cantoned around Telchi; the 2nd Corps, that of Ivan Soltykov, extended from Memel, which was occupied by Riazanov's brigade at Libau; the 3rd Corps, that of Golitzyn, was at Fraunburg; the field artillery, under Tolstoy, was at Libau. The entire army was reduced to 72,000 men, and to bring to full strength all the regiments, one calculated that it lacked 8,641 horses and 21,915 soldiers. In what concerned the men, this enormous "deficit" could not be imputed solely to the losses of the battle of Gross-Gross Jägersdorf, nor to desertions, which were above 852 men, but to the privations and sicknesses that had decimated the army during the retreat. There were also many men in the hospital.

In this army one had reduced greatly the figure of the irregular forces. Apraxine and Fermor had seen the devastation and the dangerous aggravation they spread in the occupied territories, and how much their service "with two horses" complicated the question of fodder, by encumbering the columns with an enormous mass of animals. Apraxine had closed his eyes to their depredations. Then the army had sent the Slobode Cossacks and most of the heterogeneous irregular forces back to their homes. Only the Tchougouiev and Don Cossacks, 500 Volga Kalmuks and the hussar pulks were retained.

Fermor had proposed to the Conference a certain number of reforms. He proposed a permanent organization of the corps and brigades; completing all the infantry regiments to two battalions, plus two grenadier companies; decreasing the dispatching of officers from the ranks on various missions; a better distribution of the wagons so that the regiments and companies would no longer be encumbered by them; to reduce the load carried by each soldier; to modify his uniform and his equipment which had become too inconvenient; to oblige the irregular cavalry to one horse per man and two pack horses for every ten men.

The Conference approved this plan of reforms, but time made it possible to carry out only a small portion of it. The load of the soldier was decreased; the powdered queue was eliminated; shoes and warm clothing were provided for the winter campaign, but the irregular troops continued the two-horse system and the army's baggage train remained a huge, disorderly mass.

Most urgent had been the provision of recruits to the principal army and filling in the vacancies in the officer corps. It was decided to raise 43,000 men, but none would reach the depots before the end of the year. The solution was to draw replacements from the line and garrison regiments still inside Russia. In spite of these expedients, the regiments in Prussia did not reach the desired 1,552 men. For the officers, it was quite as difficult. In vain one put at the disposal of the Generalissimo the promotion of the Cadet Corps, to give promotions to the noble non-commissioned officers of the Guard Regiments and to require this service of the sons of gentlemen. The army required nearly 500 officers and barely half were available. What further complicated the task of the War College, was the necessity to find men and officers to form the "Observation Corps" created by Shuvalov and commanded by Peter Soltykov, because it had been decided to form a new body of 40,000 men, which would be commanded by Bourtourline, which would be put at the disposal of the Austrians to assist them in Silesia. Bourtourline's corps existed only on paper and as for the Observation Corps, it retained its original defects, poor soldiers, poor horses, and an absolute lack of cohesion, and that its cooperation with the principal army was the essential cause of these delays as were its reverses.

While waiting, Fermor's army, which had to preserve the conquests of 1757, the city and the district of Memel, were covered, on the side of Prussia, initially by the Memel River, then by a cord of cavalry which observed the banks of the Niemen. The irregular cavalry had even formed a camp at Prökuls.

Lehwaldt, after his successes in the autumn campaign, had not pushed the Russians much further than the Niemen. In addition, Frederick II was not man to be left without an occupation in a crisis as terrible as that which had occurred to one of his army corps. Immediately after this almost total delivery of East Prussia, on 7 October, Lehwaldt received the order to report with his troops to Prussian Pomerania and to drive out the Swedes. The Field Marshal left some hope to his administrators in East Prussia that he would soon return; but he acted as if he would not return. He freed the state prisoners kept in the fortresses. He emptied all the public treasuries, except for those of the University and of some benevolent foundations. He took along all his forces, even the Sydow and Manteuffel Garrison Regiments, in all 30,000 men. He also took that year's recruits, at a rate of 60-70 per regiment. He took the guns from the fortresses, except for some badly cast guns, and emptied their arsenals and magazines. To defend the province, he left only four companies of the Puttkammer Garrison Regiment. Two companies were placed in Pillau, under the orders of Unruh, and two were in Königsberg, under Hünert von Wuthenow. A detachment of 60 to 70 hussars, under Lieutenant von Faye, were posted in observation close to Gumbinnen. Also, there were the civil guards of the cities and the landmiliz, which was reorganized a little; two companies of infantry, under Captains Plewe and Kortzfleisch, were stationed in Russ; some squadrons of Landhusaren, recruited among the foresters, hunters and poachers, were formed. One of the chiefs of this improvised cavalry, the forester Eckert, was distinguished for having supported, from October to January, the partisan war beyond the Nieman against the Russian irregular cavalry. Hasenkamp ensured that he was feared by the Don Cossacks and the Kalmuks.

The province of Prussia was not abandoned. Frederick II thought that, even with Lehwaldt's army, he could not stop a new invasion of East Prussia. Perhaps he hoped that his friends in St. Petersburg would manage to prevent it. However, in any case, Lehwaldt's 30,000 men were too necessary for him in the principal theater of operations so he could not expose them to being destroyed in East Prussia. He felt that it would be on the battlefields of Bohemia, Saxony or Silesia that the fate of this province as well as that of the monarchy would be decided. He felt that a victory or a defeat between the Elbe and Oder would save or definitively lose the war. And finally, he had done a sufficient job for the honor of the land from which he drew his royal title, since for the first time he had refused to abandon it without a battle to its northern neighbors and he had succeeded in chasing them from it.

The inhabitants of the province necessarily had a different perspective on this than their king. They saw with concern the withdrawal of Lehwaldt's regiments, almost all of which were recruited amongst them, and thought with terror of an army of 80,000 Russians, Cossacks or Tatars, a storm hanging over their heads. The memories of the last occupation and the excesses of the irregular cavalry, the disaster at Ragnit and the ashes of so many villages, did not reassure them.

However, Lehwaldt's departure took place under favorable auspices. One had just received in Königsberg the news of the great victory gained by Frederick II, on 5 November 1757, over the French army, under Soubise, at Rossbach. Prior to this battle Frederick had only defeated Saxon and Austrian armies, but this victory, crushing the army that Louis XV had inherited from the Great King was of major importance. Rossbach had a moral scope well beyond the victories at Molwitz, Pirna or Lobositz. Hitherto confined within the limits of German wars, Frederick II's glory now became European, universal. What military power could, from then on, compete with his, and who could he not defeat after having overcome the French? It is this day that Frederick appeared in Germany not as the hero of what were almost civil wars, but as the champion of the German race against all foreign races. All Germany, even that which fought against him, gloried in his victory over the French. He appeared like another Arminius and the god of war. It is the military glory of Frederick II which, from a collection of principalities and seigniories, connected between them by feudal bonds or a network of bureaucracies, created the Prussian nation, and of the Prussian nation would become the leaven of German nationalism. On 25 November, the news of this victory was greeted in the province with a great patriotic festival. The German Society of Königsberg held a solemn meeting: its president Flottwell made a speech "on the glory by which the Muses accompany the heroes on the battlefields;" an honorary member named von Liedert spoke on "the love of humanity for war." One sees from these allusions to these heroes who were wonderful spirits under enemy cannister, was the favorite of Apollo as well as of Mars, and, among the carnage, remained a Philosopher-King and a king philanthropist. Eight days after the news of another great victory occurred, that of Smoothed (Leuthen), gained on 5 December 1757 over the Austrians. It was celebrated in Königsberg by a large parade of the civic guard, which then formed 7 battalions and 35 companies, and by artillery salvos fired by the cannon of the fortress.

However, the French at Rosbach and the Austrians at Lissa were far away. The Russians were nearby. They were the imminent danger, from whom the victorious King, also far away, could not preserve his royal city. They were properly what Hasenkamp calls the *landfeind*, "the enemy of the land". Would Rosbach and Lissa prevent the invasion of the victors of Gross Jägersdorf? One was divided between patriotic pride and a quite legitimate fear. The government in Berlin assured that there was nothing to fear from Fermor; but constantly, with each movement of the Cossacks between the Memel and Niemen Rivers, there were alarms. Then the inhabitants who had taken asylum in Königsberg fled to Danzig and those of the lowland flowed back into Königsberg. Excursions of Russian cavalry became more frequent, more important, and took on the appearance of reconnaissances. In December, Riazanov left Memel, Brown's squadrons left Telchi, and those of Sloffeln advanced from Vorony. In front of all of them were Krasnochtchokov's Don Cossacks.

In December, Fermor had received from St. Petersburg the most pressing instructions to undertake a winter campaign. He was pressed to conquer the province of which his predecessor had occupied only the smallest portion. He assured that all the necessary preparations had been made and as soon as the Nieman was frozen, he would begin his offensive. On 17 December, he communicated to the Conference his plan of attack and received Imperial approval for it. The army was to advance in two columns: one from Memel and the other by Tilsit. One column would occupy the port of Labiau on the Kurisches Haff. The other would advance on Königsberg. If the fortress resisted, it would be bombarded, then it would be taken by storm. Fermor, overcoming his loathing for the use of irregular cavalry, was resigned to give the Cossacks a freer hand. However, he had them commanded and supervised by officers of the regular army. For this purpose, he appears to have chosen officers of the German race. The right-hand column, under Soltykov, contained two brigades of infantry (Riazanov and Leontiev) and part of the cavalry, having Krasnochtchokov commanding the advance guard. It had a total of 20,000 men with 36 guns. The left column, containing 10,000 men, would be commanded by the energetic Rumyantsev. The remainder of the army would move brigade by brigade, and, considering the rigorous season, sleeping either in villages or forests, so the men could always have heat.

On 31 December, Rumyantsev began his movement. On 5 January, he was in Popelian, on the 9th he was in Tauroggen, which became famous in 1813 for the patriotic *pronunciamento* by Yorck von Wartenburg. There he was met by 1,000 Don Cossacks under Serebriakov, which had just run upon, not far from Tilsit, the Land-husaren of the forester Eckert. The Russians sent forward Colonel Zoritch, with his hussars, to examine if the ice on the Niemen, between Tilsit and Ragnit, would support the movement of the army. Hostages were taken from among the principal citizens of the region to ensure the peaceful behavior of the population and to obtain information on the state of the country. The manner in which they operated clearly indicated that Elisabeth's generals expected resistance. At the same time a proclamation, from the Tsarina, was distributed to the inhabitants of Prussia. Here are some of its passages:

> ... We have seen with an extreme dissatisfaction that, contrary to Our orders, this province was evacuated when Field Marshal Lehwaldt was defeated with his army and that the inhabitants had gone back voluntarily to Our protection; with an even sharper dissatisfaction and sorrow We learned that, during the evacuation of the province by Our armies, some localities were burned and devastated. At the moment when Our armies will enter the Kingdom of Prussia, We believe it Our duty to promise Our benevolence and favor to all the inhabitants who will gladly place themselves under our protection, who remain in their residences and will

continue to be engaged in their occupations, and to assure to those who suffered from the devastations inflicted in the last campaign, that those excesses occurred entirely against Our intentions.

Thus, the Tsarina, once more, repudiated Apraxine's retreat. She recognized that this withdrawal had been accompanied by deplorable excesses. She assured the interested parties that those who had acted, on these two points, had done so against her intentions and those similar things would not be repeated. Apraxine's evacuation was regarded by her null and void, thus the second occupation would be only a continuation of the first and would revive all the rights that the first had conferred to her. We must draw this conclusion from it that the oaths that one had given to Elisabeth in 1757 remained in full strength. Those of the inhabitants who had not so sworn, like the others, were to swear allegiance and fidelity to her. This is how Fermor understood it and as a result, along all the road to the Niemen he demanded the oath.

Rumyantsev advanced now rather quickly. He knew the military situation of the province and that there would be no resistance. On 13 January, he occupied Tilsit without a blow. He was greeted at its gates by the Magistrate, the clergy, and the principal citizens, who requested the protection of the Tsarina and swore the oath. Rumyantsev remained in the city for four days.

The right column took a little longer to reach the Niemen. Riazanov's brigade, on 13 January, had only reached Prökuls. Not far from this locality a party of Prussian landmiliz camped, which was withdrawn in all haste on Königsberg. On the 14th, Riazanov occupied Russ, and thus the heads of the two columns had advanced about the same depth into East Prussia.

As soon as the Russian movement was clearly an invasion, all of the remaining Prussian troops in the province hastened to evacuate it. The four Puttkammer companies left Pillau and Königsberg; the hussars of Lieutenant von Faye withdrew so as to not be cut off from Gumbinnen by Rumyantsev's squadrons. All these troops were withdrawn by forced marches on the Lower Vistula and Marienwerder, in order to join Lehwaldt's army there. Before evacuating these places, they had removed all their guns, except some castings that were useless, then had emptied the magazines and destroyed all the gunpowder.

As for the civil population, a part had begun to flee, while the remainder submitted. The villagers brought fodder and oats to the Russian outposts. The landmiliz, infantry and cavalry, disappeared as if by magic.

On 16 January, Riazanov arrived at Rautenberg, where Fermor joined him. It is also at Rautenberg that Rumyantsev joined them, coming from Lappienen. Detachments of cavalry were directed on points considered to be most important. Stoffeln, the brilliant commander of the vanguard, entered

Tapiau on the 17th and Labiau on the 19th. There the *Amtsrath* Kuwert and his Rachow colleague informed Stoffeln that they had received from the government sitting in Königsberg the order to present no resistance to the Imperial Army and to accommodate its needs.

It was obvious that if Königsberg was giving such advice to smaller localities, that Königsberg was not prepared to defend itself. If they had been inclined to defend themselves, the march of the Russian columns had been so fast, that any defense would have been disconcerted. On 5 January the first detachment crossed the border. By the 20th, Königsberg was enveloped by Stoffeln's cavalry, which encamped in Lauth, by the main body of Riazanov and Rumyantsev's forces, which arrived at Kerymen. These two localities were in the immediate surroundings of the capital. The columns had had to overcome great difficulties, all the roads being covered with snow. The speed of advance produced what Masslovski calls "the panicked submission of the land." On the 14th, the Königsberg Government Council met and the five provincial ministers assisted: von Lesgewang, von Wallenrodt, von Tettau, von Rhod, and von Gröben. This was the same day that the two Puttkammer companies evacuated the city, with all the material which could be transported. The council had nothing better to do than to develop a plan for the capitulation of the city. On 18 January, in another meeting, the five ministers signed the capitulation project and appointed three commissioners to discuss the capitulation with the Russians. The men so designated were von Grabowski, vice president of the tribunal; von Auer, Counselor of the Domain and War; and Hindersin, the Burgermeister. Thus, they represented the three orders: nobility, functionaries of the state, and the bourgeoisie. They wrote to the King and Lehwaldt to excuse themselves for having surrendered, based on the too evident necessities of the situation. But suddenly a disagreement arose among the assistants. Was it necessary to evacuate the land already conquered by the enemy and to escape the obligations of the oaths given to the Tsarina or to undergo this humiliation and to remain at one's station, where they could try to defend the interests of the province and the State? The major part of the ministers were especially moved by the disapproval of the King for the taking of such an oath, even when "extorted." Wallenrodt, Tettau, Rhod, Grabowski, and many of the civil servants, hastily withdrew to Danzig, a free city of the Kingdom of Poland. There remained only Lesgewang, a blind old man, and Marwitz, president of the chamber of finances, nailed to his bed with gout.

On the 20th, Fermor arrived at Keymen, a staged stop on the road to Königsberg. It was there that the following day that he received the three commissioners appointed by the Königsberg government, and the main local officials from nearby communities who accompanied them. The commissioners had begun their trip to intercept the Generalissimo, but they had not expected to find him so close to the city. The conditions which they proposed were those that one expected from an impregnable fortress, while Königsberg was essentially surrendering unconditionally. They asked that the city, the orders of the State, the University, the pious churches and foundations, the *zünfte* or corporations of craftsmen [i.e. guilds], all the colleges in a word, be confirmed in all their "privileges, franchises, rights, prerogatives; that employment, treatments, pensions, and revenues be respected, that the trade was free outside as it was inside the city; that the Prussian officers, who remained in the hospital, continued to draw their pay; that the postal service was ensured, and freedom of the worship guaranteed; that "the light troops (read: irregular. i.e., the Cossacks), not placed in the city, unless necessary.

In short, the Russians could put their hands only on the material and the incomes belonging at the Prussian State, and after what had been withdrawn upon the Russian invasion, these were very thin spoils.

Fermor received the delegates with the most perfect courtesy. Being of the German culture, a Protestant in his beliefs, he could have only sympathy for the vanquished, their University, their religion, all their institutions and contracts. From another perspective, especially after the excesses of the last campaign, it was important to reassure the populations with a great act of benevolence, to move the opinion in Germany and Europe in a direction favorable to Russia. He granted all the articles of this singular capitulation. Hasenkamp admired that he also conceded them to the people, over whose heads he held a sword. Masslovski, however, was somewhat indignant about what he saw as an act of weakness and almost of treason.

However, the result of this policy was more satisfactory. Fermor's leniency completed "the panicked submission of the country," which the force of the weapons had begun.

At the Russian Court, when one has experienced such a favorable system from a conquered province, when it was seen that one could not draw from it a recruit, or a war contribution, nor a sum of taxes higher than that which was obtained under the Prussian domination, they began with being astonished and ended up being irritated. We found strange that the province was infinitely better handled under the two-headed eagle than under the one-headed eagle of the Hohenzollerns; that it did not contribute at all to the so crushing responsibilities as the war imposed on the taxpayers and on the recruitable men of the empire. We also compared the mild conduct of Fermor with the behavior of Frederick in Saxony, which he crushed with contributions and requisitions; where he forcibly recruited against the legitimate prince, where the populations were pillaged and decimated. The effect of this comparison was later turned against Fermor and greatly entered his disgrace. Nonetheless, the province continued to be no less well treated.

The capitulation was signed on the 21st. The following day, at daybreak, Stoffeln, with all the cavalry of Rumyantsev's column, left Keymen. At 11:00

a.m., it occupied the suburbs of Königsberg. Jakovlev, who had started out at the crack of dawn with eight companies of grenadiers and eight regimental guns, occupied the posts of the bourgeois guard. At 4:00 pm., Fermor made his entry with the 4th Grenadiers and the Troitski Regiment, accompanied by Soltykov and the Russian and Foreign Volunteer Gentlemen. The old royal city had taken on a festive air. The bells rang and on the city's towers drums beat and trumpets sounded. Fermor went straight to the castle, where Lesgewang, one of the five ministers, spoke to him and gave the city's keys to him. Two hours later, Nottelfeld's brigade artillery and the remainder of Riazanov's division occupied the city and deployed their guns on the public places. In his letter to Vice-Chancellor Vorontsov, Fermor declared that he put three pulks of hussars, nine squadrons of dragoons, 2,500 Cossacks and four regiments of infantry, with their artillery, in districts of the city; but the major part of the army camped outside, in the snow. Many inhabitants hastened to invite the Russian officers into their homes.[5]

The day of his triumph in the Holy City of the Hohenzollerns, Fermor dispatched Bruce, lieutenant of the Preobrajenski Regiment, carrying his report to the Tsarina and the keys of the fortress.

Lastly, this same day, Fermor sent detachments to occupy Pillau and Fischhausen, and took possession of Friedrichsburg. There were found a large quantity of cannon. The army corps were put into winter quarters, in order to occupy all the province. Brown, delayed with his corps in Semigalia, received the order to press his march, brigade by brigade.

Fermor stated that the Prussian civil servants and the other subjects who had escaped taking the oath were summoned to return, at the cost of losing their employment and seeing their goods sequestered. The execution of his threat against the recalcitrant individuals followed closely the threat.[6]

As of 23 January, the pastors had received the order to substitute, in the public prayers, the names of Frederick II and of the Crown Prince, with those of the Empress Elisabeth Potrovna, the Orthodox Grand Duke and the Grand Duchess.

All the acts were to be written and all the judgments given in the name of the Tsarina. In the official parts, Königsberg from now on was indicated as a "Russian imperial city". The coins of the currency were changed: ducats, thalers and gulders carried the effigy of Elisabeth with this Latin legend: ELISABETHA I.D.G. IMP. TOT. RUSS., and on the the the reverse the two-headed eagles.

One of the last concerns that had occupied Lehwaldt had been to know how one was to proceed with regard to the inhabitants of the province who, during the first Russian invasion, had been obliged to take the oath of

[5] *Vorontsof's Archive*, Vol VI, p. 337.
[6] In this article we will borrow much from Hasenkamp, *Ostpreussen unter dem Doppeladler*, Königsberg, 1866.

fidelity to Tsarina Elisabeth. In the Prussia of that time, and for those with a Protestant conscience like of Lehwaldt, it was serious thing to take an oath. The Field Marshal had thought that the pastors alone had the quality to raise up their flocks. But many of the pastors had also sworn the oath. In addition, the civil government of the province estimated that this would be to expose to possible reprisals by the enemy the ministers of the Gospel who might give their blessing to this type of perjury. Frederick II did not have such refined scruples. By an order of cabinet dated from Magdeburg, he declared that that "the oath given to the Empress of Russia was an oath extorted by violence and was therefore null and void… in his full sovereign authority, the King relieved his subjects from them." Thus, says Hasenkamp, "this delicate business of conscience was solved, not by the authority of the Church, but by a process of pure bureaucracy." Many Prussian subjects, especially among the pastors, felt their conscience only half appeased. And they were going to be subjected to new tests!

On 24 January, the very same day that the East Prussians formerly celebrated the birthday of Frederick II, all of the inhabitants of the province took the oath of subjection and fidelity to the Empress of Russia. In Königsberg, the ceremony was done with great pomp, even in the church of the castle, at the foot of the altar. The Chambers of War and the Domain, the Colleges of Justice, the municipality, the delegates of the bourgeois, heard the reading of the proclamation in which Elisabeth assured her people of her "benevolence and favor." Then each one, according to the formula read by a pastor, pronounced the oath aloud and confirmed it by his signature at the bottom of the act. In the following days, it was the turn of the university, the College of Trade, the indirect tax authorities, etc. Russian General Rothhelfer received the oath, having beside him Pastor Arnoldt, Aulic preacher and professor at the university. The civil servants, who because of illness, were prevented from going to the church had to take the oath in their homes. In all the cities and localities of the province, the same formality was completed. One does not find a single civil servant who refused the oath. Domhardt himself was subjected. He declared thereafter that it had been "the bitterest moment of its life". Here is the formula of the oath:

> I, the undersigned, by God Almighty and his Holy
> Gospel, swear fidelity and obedience to the very glorious
> and very powerful Empress and Sovereign Autocrat of all the
> Russias, Elisabeth Petrovna… and to His Imperial Highness
> the Grand Duke Heir Peter Feodorovitch, committing myself
> to support with all of my efforts the majestic interests of Her
> Imperial Majesty, and, if I am informed of some infidelity
> against these interests, as soon as I shall be informed of it,

not only to reveal it promptly, but to endeavor in every case to fight it; finally, to act in accordance with what I swore above, as I must answer for it before God and His rigorous judgment. And that thus God has my body and my heart in His protection!

It is seen that the formula demanded not only fidelity and obedience but contained an obligation to reveal and prevent any attempt of infidelity and disobedience.

On 29 February 29th, seven days after the capitulation, Fermor caused to be celebrated in Königsberg, the "Russian imperial city," a "festival for the re-establishment of peace." In all the churches they sang a *Te Deum*, to the accompaniment of drums and trumpets.

Everywhere the blazon of Hohenzollerns was removed from monuments, and the two-headed eagle took the place of the Prussian eagle. Many inhabitants, seeking to place themselves under the direct protection of the Empress, raised these badges on the doors of their houses or on their cupboards. The portraits of Elisabeth and the Grand Duke decorated the living rooms of the nobility.

Thus, the Tsarina had taken possession of the land and the fortresses by arms, the consciences by the swearing of an oath and the prayer called on her behalf, of the public property deprived of Frederick II's seal and his coat of arms. Elisabeth sought to be regarded as the legitimate and definitive sovereign of the country, mistress of the ground and its inhabitants, Empress and Autocrat in Königsberg as in Moscow. Let us see the nature of the Russian domination during the five years that this occupation lasted.

Fermor was almost immediately appointed General Governor of Prussia, with the same treatment and all the advantages that had been enjoyed by his predecessor, Lehwaldt. He had as a successor, the next year, another German, Baron von Korff, who was succeeded by Lieutenant General Suvorov, father of the hero of the campaigns in Turkey, Poland, Italy, and Switzerland; then Lieutenant General Panine; and finally, with the same rank, Feodor Voieikov.

Apart from the director of the general government, nothing seemed changed in the administration of the province. This administration was very complicated, as it arrives in the countries where the feudal forms remain beside a more modern regime, it contained no less than 32 colleges, offices, courts or chambers. The principal ones were the Königsberg Chamber for the German land and that of Gumbinnen for the Lithuanian land. Above them stood the Provincial Government Chamber, seated at Königsberg. The attributions of these various bodies were quite tangled. It took the Russians very long time to recognize this and before they could exert some form of surveillance.

Domhardt, President of the Gumbinnen Chamber, could with impunity, until the end, group many civil servants in a league of passive resistance against Russian domination, that extended over the country like a network of patriotic associations, to form a kind of Tugendbund intended to maintain the Prussian spirit, to divert part of the provincial income and pass large sums of money to Frederick II. Soon Russian generals were placed in charge of the Königsberg and Gumbinnen Chambers. Near each administrative college, there were Russian officers who acted as supervisors. Nonetheless, the German employees succeeded in concealing part of the business from them, amusing them with unimportant duties, reducing them to the role of simple forwarding officials. Bolotov, who spent long hours attempting to penetrate the style of the Prussian Chancellery and making translations of its parts, understood something of its trade. One translated, one copied, and that was about all.

Except for Domhardt and some civil servants of truly Prussian spirit, one can say that the country did not present any resistance to Russian domination. The effort was made, and the province gently slipped into becoming a Russian province, just like Estonia or Livonia, where the equestrian order and the bourgeois were also German, but that Peter the Great had welded them forever into his monarchy. Provided that the Russians respected the Protestant religion, the privileges of the knighthood, the bourgeoisie, the university, and the guilds, it was not impossible that the province of East Prussia would have followed the example of the other Baltic provinces.

Hitherto appeals from the provincial courts had been carried to the Court in Berlin: it was decided that in the future the Faculty of Law the University would act as a Court of Appeals.

On 30 January, General Riazanov, appointed Senior Commander of Königsberg, enjoined the Bourgeois Guards, as well as the various local militia, to deposit their arms and ammunition in the closest arsenal. In March, this injunction had to be renewed. It was then extended to ordinary persons and the arms manufacturers. Even the shotguns, arquebuses and collectable weapons were surrendered. Grocers had to give up their gunpowder. The country squires, the peasants, and the foresters, then complained that they could not defend themselves against wolves and the petty thieves from Poland and from Lithuania. The postilions [mail carriers] feared being attacked on the roads. The forest agents could no longer stop poaching. The Russian authorities were thus obliged to admit some exceptions to the rule. In addition, it had become necessary to search the houses of recalcitrant people to stop the smuggling of weapons and ammunition brought by sea.

Disarmament was not the only measure of the Russian distrust of the population. From time to time the military authorities closed the gates of Königsberg; police regulations prohibited the inhabitants from circulating in the city at night without lanterns; the access to the belltowers was severely limited; even for the fires, instead of alarm bells, drums and the trumpets were to give the alarm. One had to prevail against the members of this Tugendbund of Domhardt, whose leader and members were not known, but whose existence the Russians suspected. On 13 February 1758, Judge Grabowski was stopped and transported to Russia. It was the same for the Postmaster Koslowski. The Russians censored the mail and letters were to be given to the post office unsealed.

The newspapers, if not very important at that time, were also watched. Hitherto the censure of *Königsberger Zeitung* was entrusted to the university. The military authorities reserved it. Fermor undoubtedly had good reasons to act thus. In a letter to Vorontsov, he complained about the "impudent Berliner lies which appear in the Königsberg newspapers;" It would have been announced, for example, that the Russian guns had fallen into the river during the passage of the Vistula. Fermor transformed it into an official journal, a certain "gazette of the State, of peace and of war" which had already existed under the Prussian domination. He had the two-headed eagle engraved on its top. This *Official* newspaper of the conquest was charged with expressing sympathies of the inhabitants for the Russian garrison, "to which each one highly prefers over the the former Prussian garrison," and to praise "the exquisite taste which governs the richness and exquisite uniforms of the Russian officers." The well-read men of Königsberg could read with stupor in their gazette's tirades on the brutality that Frederick II exerted in Saxony, on the humanity of the Tsarina who did not think of exerting such reprisals on the provinces conquered by her arms. The victories of the King of Prussia were questioned, the successes of the Coalition singularly exaggerated. Hasenkamp found all that ridiculous and odious; but he was not able to make comparisons to the *Moniteurs* of Lorraine, of Versailles, etc., when the conquerors of 1870 insulted the French populations. In 1758, there appeared in Königsberg a weekly French language newspaper.

The new government of East Prussia required of the pastors much more than just prayers for Elisabeth and the Grand-Ducal couple. The church was to celebrate all the official festivals of the Russians: the day of the birth of Elisabeth, that of her crowning, and the birth of the children of the Grand Duke. These festivals, together, cost the town of Königsberg 5000 thalers. At each of them some member of the university was to pronounce, in the hall, a *Festrede*: it was usually Professor Werner who provided prose, Professors Bock and Watson who read pieces of poetry. Werner occasionally showed himself humiliated: one day he declared himself sick and paid 8 thalers with his colleague Hahn to speak in his place; on the contrary Bock, in his *Memoirs*, years later, had all the vanity of a poet and pride in the success his poetry gained from the foreign governor.

What the Russian authority could have saved its constituents, was the celebration of the victories obtained over their king and an army where many of their brothers fought and died. Here the winners certainly had a heavy hand. The battle of Zorndorf, in 1758, the defeat of Frederick II in Kunersdorf, in 1759, were celebrated in Königsberg by salvos from the citadel, a *Te Deum* in the churches, an official dinner, and an illumination of streets. For Kunersdorf, the Russians imposed on Pastor and Professor Arnoldt, the "Aulic preacher" (Hofprediger) of the preceding regime, the obligation of giving a sermon in the church of the castle. From this unpleasant drudgery he withdrew not without honor; because he preached on "the duties of the victors and those of the defeated," warning the first against insolence, the second against discouragement. The affair produced some rumors. Arnoldt was put under close arrest in his house, under the guard of a picket of soldiers, and one spoke of transporting him to Russia. However, he contracted a serious illness, which, with the requests of the consistory and the clergy, saved him from this misfortune. He was released after a few weeks, but Governor Korff prohibited him from preaching for a whole year. Some wished to impose on him a public retraction, but this was limited, in a palinode sermon, to a declaration that he had not intended to offend the Imperial Court.

The service of the oath, the festivals of Königsberg, especially the rejoicings for his defeats, ate at Frederick II's heart. He refused to grant his subjects the benefit of mitigating circumstances which resulted from the *force majeure* and necessity. He refused to distinguish between those who had yielded spontaneously or by force. He held a deep resentment against the province, and, on the day that he recovered it until the end of his reign, no requests could decide him to visit East Prussia.

Separate from the pressure on its political and religious conscience, the country had nothing about which to complain regarding the Russian administration. It probably underwent requisitions in kind and corvées for cartage but were the peasants of the Russian Empire not also subject to that? And what were these inconveniences in comparison to the situation of Saxony under Frederick II's yoke? The taxes do not appear have been increased. In truth, when Russian authorities did not ask for recruits for Elisabeth's army from East Prussia, those who might have been subjected to being drafted instead paid a military tax. By comparison, the demands made on it were light in comparison to the other provinces of the Prussian Monarchy. The excesses that had marked the invasion and the retreat of Apraxine's army, in 1757, did not reoccur during the years of occupation. Hasenkamp took the pain to collect in the archives and document facts of violence or marauding to regulars or to irregulars of the Russian Army, officers, or soldiers. He identifies 40 such incidents. These were trifles, and the armies of the 18th century committed others well, even in friendly countries. The historian of East Prussia also provides an account of forest offenses: the cutting of trees, which was not very serious. It would be necessary to put into the balance the whole profit gained by the country during the Russian occupation, for its agriculture and trade, since for five years, it was not the theater of military operations. The ports remained free. Some individuals grew wealthy working as suppliers to the Imperial Army. The university continued its courses, and Emmanuel Kant became chair in its math department.

So as to not discuss it later, let us finish here what we have to say about the fate of the province under the Russian regime. The inhabitants of East Prussia had little hatred for their Russian occupiers. The best society of Königsberg welcomed Russian officers into its salons, while the Governor's soirées included them as well. An unexpected thing, but Hasenkamp quite frankly confesses, it was the Russians who civilized the Germans of the East Prussia. A lot of their officers belonged to wealthy families and were of a more refined culture than those of the conquered province. They spoke French, which was at that time the mark of a well-educated individual. They had a taste for well-cut clothes, the best food, choice wines, and an elegant and luxurious table service. The natives of Prussia were, on the contrary, the most backward of the Germans. Paris fashions arrived there only after they were long in the western parts of Germany. Their food was coarse. It was the Russians who spread the use of tea by their conquest, which was nearly unknown, and coffee, which was exceedingly rare, and punch, which astonished and charmed. They also introduced the Prussians to the use of theaters for numerous meetings, by throwing on the ground a movable floor, in order to create one large room. Here they gave balls and masquerades. In brief, nobody was bored in Königsberg, neither the winners nor the losers, while the rest of Europe was prey to the curses of the war.

East Prussian society had kept its Gothic forms and customs; there was an abyss between the least country squire and the most cultivated or richest of the commoners. They never met in the same salons. Every class was held with regard to the other in a rigid hierarchy. The noble looked with arrogance on the magistrate and the academic. There was more egalitarian mindset among the Russians. The noble class was not closed, and it constantly grew with those of wealth and education, with those who gained the favor of the Empress, whom she elevated to the first rank. It was in the Governor's salon that gentlemen and German bourgeois met for the first time. It was there that they learned not to despise each other.

Even better, it was the Russian conquest that emancipated Prussian women. Prior to the arrival of the Russians, they lived as recluses in the manor or family home, where they were fed the most austere precepts of Protestantism, infatuated with her nobility or her bourgeoisie, clothed sumptuously and austerely in the frocks of her grandmother, rarely attending a dance, never in the theater, rarely leaving her lodgings except to go to church, and always under the escort of some chaperon. It was unbecoming for a woman to lean out her window. The Governor gave to the ladies of Königsberg the example to follow, attending public acts and the university; it became of fashion in Königsberg, as in France to attend the functions of the *Académie française*. The governor invited the ladies to his soirées, inviting the bourgeois as well as the Baroness. His officers won them by the charm of their conversation, by their invitations to the dance, by all flexible elegances of the Slav. A great many romances occurred. Hasenkamp shed many tears over the decadence of the domestic morals; note, however that the ladies didn't complain.

As for the reproaches that Hasenkamp makes against the Russian soldiers that they had given to the good Prussian people the habits of drunkenness and to the civil servants of the Tsarina to have taught with their German colleagues the processes of administrative corruption, one can ask if the court of the King Sergeant had been so sober, and if the Russian word *vziatki* (misappropriations, bribes) did not have its double in the German dictionary.

The last year of Seven Years War, for the inhabitants of East Prussia, was the most agitated of all, for over the period of a few months the province found itself under the rule of four different sovereigns: Elisabeth, Peter III, Frederick II, Catherine II, then Frederick II again.

Upon receipt of the news of the death of Elisabeth, the patriotic party, in the province, had raised its head and the people demonstrated greater audacity. Domhardt had collected 300,000 ducats and personally went to the camp of Frederick so as to place it in his hands. Even before the publication of the Russo-Prussian Peace, he had sent Frederick large quantities of grain. He also maintained, almost without concealing it, an active correspondence with the King.

General Panine, who the Germans saw as malevolent and treacherous, was replaced by Lieutenant General Feodor Voieikov, who they saw as more humane and open. On 5 July 1762 he issued the peace proclamation. The evacuation of East Prussia by the Russian troops appeared to be only a question of days. It was only delayed by the insufficiency of the means of transportation. While waiting, the Russian authorities handed over to the Prussian civil authorities the administration of the province. The military bureaucrats, such as Bolotov, received orders to rejoin their regiments, or were called to other jobs. As they had spent so long pushing paper in the Königsberg Chancellery they felt some distress at this change; and as their German hosts were very accustomed to them there were touching scenes of farewell. Bolotov's hosts, were an old man and an old woman, who had accepted nothing from him for food, laundering and lodging for several years. Bolotov noted that they were Swiss and not Prussians, but the Prussians barely behaved differently. His

German teacher, Weimann, also refused all payment for his lessons and cried when hugging his student good-bye.

As of 25 June, the King of Prussia had addressed instructions to the civil servants and to the population of the province, to determine the conduct that they were to observe with regard to the Russian troops, as long as they should occupy the country: above all, one had to provide for their maintenance and means of transport.

The King already made changes in the administrative staff, as if he had been the master. He accepted the resignation of Count Finckenstein, considered to be unable or too docile to the Russians, and, in charge of the reorganized government, placed the faithful and energetic Domhardt.

The publication of peace had been an occasion for rejoicings, which with a good heart the population joined. This day, 5 July, the *Königsberg Gazette* had appeared with its former title, the Prussia eagle re-occupying the place usurped by the Russian eagle. Colonel Heyden resumed his functions of 1758, as commander of Königsberg. The stations of the Russian troops were given over to the reorganized civic guard. The bourgeois companies of foot and horse escorted the two heralds charged with proclaiming with his trumpets the *notifactorium* of peace. The Prussian coats of arms were again placed on public monuments, to the sound of music and bells, among the acclamations of people in a festival, which linked in its cheers the name of the Emperor of Russia to that of the King of Prussia. All Königsberg was decorated with draperies and flowers, and the ships in the port were dressed. On 8 July, Voieikov issued a proclamation which relieved the Prussian subjects of their oaths of fidelity that they had had given a few weeks earlier, at the time of the advent of the new Tsar. On 9 July, the members of the government, who had left the city in 1758, made their re-entry. One saw again, four years older, Ministers Wallenrodt, Rhod, Tettau, and the other refugees who had gone to Danzig. The last Russian official festival which was celebrated in Königsberg was, on 10 July, that of Peter III. On that occasion there were religious offices, a military parade, and an illumination. On the 11th, there occurred the formal handing-over of the administration to the Prussian authorities. It was solemnized by an academic act, with a program in Latin and a piece of poetry in Latin. Other festivals followed, for the peace concluded with Sweden. On 14 July, there was a sermon in the cathedral, on a text from Isaiah, where it is question about the Babylonian Captivity, and again one read out publically the peace treaty with Russia and Sweden. The evening, a large banquet, offered by the municipality, brought together in Junckerhof the officers of the two armies; while the generals feasted in the castle, the Russian soldiers improved their ordinary rations, thanks to an amount of money voted by the municipality. The wounded of the ambulances, the families of the invalids, the patients, the poor, had their share in these liberalities.

It was in the middle of these feasts, of the *Te Deum,* of the academic acts, the official reception, the lanterns and bouquets, there came like a bolt of lightning, the news of the fall of Peter III. A proclamation from Voieikov, dated 16 July, announced to the people of Königsberg the advent of Catherine II. The treaty of peace became deciduous. The new empress took possession of East Prussia.

"Consequently," the proclamation said, "whoever holds for invaluable his terrestrial happiness has only to show submissiveness and obedience." We will see, indeed, that Catherine II had, at the beginning, some hesitation on the action to be taken with regard to Frederick II. Moreover, feeling how much his Army of Silesia was at the discretion of the King, she saw in East Prussia a pledge and a hostage of which she did not wish to deprive herself before any final adjustment. The province answered him for its army. Voieikov again resumed his functions of governor general and again, the Russian soldiers re-occupied the citadel and the various posts. The Russian Imperial eagle reappeared on the public monuments and on the head of the *Königsberg Gazette.* Public cases were placed under the Russian sequestration. The Prussian officers who had come for purposes of recruitment, were retained as prisoners of war, and their victims returned to their hearths.

Then, upon the death of Peter III, when the return of her Army of Silesia had reassured the Tsarina on all the possibilities which she had feared, new orders were dispatched to East Prussia. A new proclamation by Voieikov, dated 6 August, announced that the province was definitively given over to the disposal of the King. Again, the Prussian coat of arms reappeared on the monuments and on the head of the gazette; again, the stations and the citadel were occupied by Prussian soldiers. That same day, Field Marshal Lehwaldt made his entry into Königsberg, in the capacity as governor of the province. The academic acts, the official reception, the public readings of proclamations became more beautiful.

Three times in six years, the province had been declared Russian and for the third time, it again became a royal land. The reaction that followed the advent of Catherine II had lasted only 20 days. This time, the evacuation was pushed forward aggressively, and the abandoning of its conquest by the Russian Empire became final. It had well escaped it! Without the passion of Peter III for Frederick II, it probably would have remained a part of the Russian Empire.

CHAPTER VII

THE FIRST RUSSIAN INVASION OF BRANDENBURG
THE BOMBARDMENT OF KUSTRIN (AUGUST 1758)

The occupation of East Prussia by the Russian Army and administration had to have a great influence, first on the diplomacy of the Coalition, then on the conduct of military operations. Elisabeth pondered if she would reserve or to keep this province or yield it to Poland in return for its rights to Courland and a rectification of the border on the side of the Ukraine. Austria had initially agreed to this arrangement; but, on the one hand, she dreaded any enlargement of Russia in Europe; on the other hand, she feared that Elisabeth's persistence in maintaining her conquest would one day make the general peace impossible: this peace that had to return to Marie-Theresa Silesia! The bad will of the Court of Vienna to sustain its ally's interests was so visible that bitter notes were exchanged between the two courts. There came the time when the Tsarina threatened to make a separate peace with Frederick II, not hesitating to return Königsberg to him so as to fall again with all her strength on the other members of the Coalition.

The reluctances and the fears of Austria were no less strongly felt by Louis XV. He dreaded, also, an enlargement of Russia in Europe. The idea of an exchange of the Prussian territory for Polish territory was even more unpleasant to him than the perspective of seeing the Tsarina annexing the province herself. He held above all, more than Frederick's victories, to the integrity of the territories of Poland and to the maintenance of that which he called, "its liberties." The proximity of the Russians caused him to worry for Thorn and especially Danzig. France's diplomatic agents, in Warsaw, in Vienna, and in St. Petersburg, were fully occupied with protesting against all projects that one lent to Russia, against these perpetual passages of troops through Poland, against the abuses or unavoidable excesses that came with them. When Choiseul reproached the Russians for the management of East Prussia, it was less from the interest in resources that the Tsarina could have pulled from it, less by the animosity against the subjects of Frederick II or by the resentment for which the subjects of the Elector of Saxony had endured, than out of spite to seeing Elisabeth treating his province as if it was already part of her patrimony.

From the military point of view, the fact of the occupation of East Prussia directed, to some extent, all the movements of the Russian troops. This province became their general headquarters, their base of operations, and their center of provisioning, in a word their redoubt. They could neither evacuate it to move into Posnania or Silesia, nor to move too far from it, out of fear of being attacked in their rear. They were held by their conquest.

When Austria claimed to draw in the Russian Army, to make it an auxiliary and a wing of its own army, to bring all of it to the principal theater of war, the St. Petersburg Cabinet pled this could not be done without abandoning the defense of East Prussia. It was on this point that all the attempts of Chancellor Kaunitz, over the period of two years, to produce a junction on an unspecified point in Silesia were to fail.

This East Prussia, which held the Russian Army, moved it away from Austria. It was East Prussia which gave the St. Petersburg Court the idea of acting independent of its ally, extinguishing its ambition to transform its role as an auxiliary power into that of a belligerent power for its own account, suggested that Russia should become emancipated from Austria by a narrower and more direct alliance with France.

As Elisabeth was rejected by Louis XV, she had to approach Vienna, and to seek a transaction between these two contradictory facts: the need to be maintained in East Prussia, and an obligation to help Austria.

This search for a transaction gave rise to projects that we see appearing, disappearing, and returning obstinately in the political and military correspondence of these five years. Sometimes it was question of forming this new army of 40,000 men, which never existed but on paper, but that Russia absolutely had to put at the disposal of Austria; sometimes one spoke of dismembering the principal army and detaching about 20,000 men from it that would then join that of Daun. But always the Russian generalissimo, either Fermor, Soltykov or Buturline, protested against this weakening, which would have reduced it to impotence, and which would have broken up the Russian forces so completely that the Tsarina's flag would have, so to speak, disappeared from the theater of the European war. One enemy alone could have given to the Tsarina a council so harmful her interests and to the glory of her arms. Such projects added a new series of conflicts to those, of every kind, that already weakened the Coalition. This was the dissension that occurred between Elisabeth's diplomacy and the control of her generals. A third test of the alliance resulted from forcing a deviation from the line followed by the Russian Army by making it incline towards Daun's army followed, without, however, making the two lines completely parallel or convergent.

The Russians, having East Prussia for a base of operations, could, indeed, choose between three principal lines of operations: they could follow the shores of the Baltic and occupy Danzig to secure the Lower Vistula, push straight forward and invade Prussian Pomerania, affect their junction with the small Swedish army, cut Frederick II off from any communication with the sea; or, by Küstrin or Frankfurt-am-Oder, then move directly on Berlin, seize the capital and the principal province of the Prussian monarchy; or, by Posen, where they could cooperate with the reconquest of Silesia or Saxony.

Any of these three lines, followed with constancy, could lead to a great result: the conquest of a province from the common enemy. The evil was that the Russians could never hold resolutely with any of these three plans. In the 1758 campaign, the Russians could have made Danzig capitulate, occupied West Prussia, conquered Pomerania, and destroyed Lehwaldt's army. Consequently, the following year, they could have invaded Brandenburg; then, in a third campaign, crushed Frederick II between them and the Austrians.

However, this was not done. Until the end of the war, the Russian Army, even when it most definitely marched on Küstrin and Frankfurt, was constantly pulled by two contrary influences. Sometimes it was necessary for it to deviate towards the north, because on its right side the Prussian Army of Pomerania acted against it, threatening its lines of communication, even threatening Königsberg; sometimes it was necessary for it to deviate towards the south, because Chancellor Kaunitz assailed with complaints Chancellor Vorontsov, and Daun complained that the Russians refused to help him in Silesia and Saxony. The Russian Army was like a planet drawn at the same time by two opposing forces, which, instead of advancing in straight line, moved by a series of zigzags. There flowed so many orders and counter-orders, so many marches and countermarches, all of which exhausted the army, marking its path with dead horses and abandoned wagons, and exposed it to suffering from hunger, because it was impossible for the logistical system to modify its supply lines and the sites of the magazines as quickly as required by the vicissitudes of policy. The Russian Army seemed rather a crowd of vagabonds wandering through Poland and Germany rather than an army following a reasoned plan of operations.

Diplomacy acted in the most disastrous way on the army's command. It was out of consideration for France that the Conference refused to authorize Fermor the authority to occupy Danzig, whose magistrates were animated by very Prussian feelings, which, by the mistress of the sea and the Vistula, blocked the provisioning of the Russian troops, stopped the convoys of boats on the Vistula, and the convoys of carts over its bridges, which put the hardest test to Russian patience. It was out of consideration for Austria that the Conference unceasingly modified the plans of its generals, diverted them from the two lines of operations that seemed best indicated, that which led to Pomerania and that on to Berlin, forcing them to move closer to the Imperials, without however wanting to completely deliver the Russian Army to them. Because to deliver it over to the Austrians, would be to almost sacrifice it. With Daun's slowness, the erudite pedantry of his marching operations, his tactics, which seemed a rebirth of those of Montecuculli, and the meticulous interference of the Hof-Kriegsrath, it was impossible to establish a junction point, where the Russians would not find Frederick instead of Daun. One could never be sure of Daun's plan, even if he had received one from Vienna, and his words were in contradiction to the assurances of Kaunitz. Did the generals of the Tsarina slander Austria when they claimed that Austria only aimed at bringing the Russian Army under the fire of the Prussian batteries, and to throw in front of Frederick II as one opposes to the furious bull with a picador, to burn off the power of the enemy before facing it oneself? The Austrians undoubtedly did not make these unpleasant calculations; but 40 years later Suvorov found himself abandoned by the Austrians when the decisive moment arrived. All in all, during the Seven Years War, the most sterile of the campaigns were those the Russians made. The 1761 campaign showed Russia's greatest cooperation with the Viennese Court and when the Russian Generalissimo placed himself completely at the disposition of his Austrian colleague.

Fermor, agreeably surprised of the readiness by which the inhabitants of East Prussia had accommodated him, enchanted to be appointed governor general of the province, would have been easily delayed by the delights of Königsberg. The Conference pressed him to put himself in a condition to begin a new campaign in the spring. The Russian forces were extremely dispersed. Fermor had under his hand only the corps of Soltykov and Golitzyn. The 3rd Corps, under Brown, was still distributed around Telchi. The Observation Corps, or Shuvalov's corps, was forming in Pskov, Smolensk, Torjek, Veliki-Luki, Volmar, and Dorpat. Plans said he was to have 20,000 men; however, he did not have more than 7,000, and his forces had never been more than 10,000 to 12,000. Fermor had immense spaces, nearly 1,000 kilometers to be crossed, to join the principal army. It was as much with these interminable marches as with the poor choice of its components that one owed its premature exhaustion. And then one should speak about the corps that was to be formed for operations in Silesia, which drained the third battalions, the depots, and the soldiers of the garrison regiments. This force was never established.

In February, the principal army, that is, the corps of Soltykov, Golitzyn, and Brown, started to move towards the Lower Vistula. On the 10th, Stoffeln, with the Tchougouiev Cossacks, 300 hussars and some cuirassiers, arrived before Marienwerder. He was accepted by the magistrate, the civil servants, and the inhabitants, who presented the keys of the city to him and begged him to allow them to take the oath of loyalty. He found in the fortress large quantities of supplies and 38 pontoons, which were very useful for him to establish a bridge over the Vistula. He moved by Graudenz, and Kulm, and entered, on the 17th, into Thorn. Unlike Danzig, the Russians always had the friendliest relations with the citizens of Thorn. On 23 February, Stoffeln returned to Marienwerder; from there, he moved on Danzigwerder, and sent a detachment of cavalry to Riesenburg. Everywhere he was well greeted, received the oaths of the authorities, and of the notable citizens, though one was in Polish territory, he collected military information, and asked the Poles to provide provisions. Elbing made a little more resistance. The magistrate would have liked to save the city from the inconveniences of the passage of the Russian troops. He had even started to build a bridge over the Elbing River, which would have made it possible for the columns to circumvent the city. He was told that this work was useless and that he had to open the city's gates. Riazanov made his entry on 3 March, called up and dismissed the Polish garrison, granting it a civil capitulation, but under conditions that were much less advantageous than those given to Königsberg. Fermor arrived in the city on 5 March and was accepted there with the honors due to his rank.

Frederick II was very irritated by this occupation. He had his emissary, Secretary Benoit, made the sharpest complaints to Warsaw. He declared that he would regard himself as free to occupy any Polish city as might appear appropriate to him. In response Augustus III then wrote the Russian generalissimo asking him to evacuate Elbing. Fermor answered with a refusal wrapped in the most courteous forms, informing the Conference, at the same time, of the importance that he attached to this strategic point, which was so invaluable to maintaining secure communications with East Prussia. However, after the advance guards, Russian units occupied the principal cities of the Vistula. Riazanov was established in Munsterberg; Demicou, Stoffeln, and Krasnochtchokov's cavalry were in Marienwerder; the Treiden brigade was in Graudenz, where Brown arrived in his turn, after having crossed 412 versts[7] in 14 days, in spite of the depth of the snow. Thorn accepted a garrison of 400 grenadiers, and the Russians worked to restore its fortifications. Fermor would have agreed to seize Danzig, at least Weichselmünde, and the fort at the mouth of the Vistula, by which all entrance to the river was blocked. He even proposed to the Conference a plan to encircle, isolate, and blockade the city. However, the Conference didn't dare to give him the authorization to do it, for fear of protests by Benoit and most probably those of the French agents.

From the points that he occupied on the Lower Vistula; Fermor could extend an information network into the adjoining countries. He received some information thanks to the reconnaissances carried out by the Serebriakov and Krasnochtchokov Cossacks, the Tekeli Hussars, and Stoffeln's cavalry. He also received some members of the Catholic clergy and Polish minor nobility. One Jesuit priest was a source of abundant and accurate information. Fermor knew that Count Dohna, Lehwaldt's successor, was occupied blocking the Swedes below Stralsund; that Frederick II was closely watching Daun. The closest Prussian troops were stationed in Bütow. Further away the squadrons of Platen beat the countryside around the fortress of Kolberg. All in all, the roads were free, either to enter Pomerania, or to invade Brandenburg. As a result, it was astonishing to see Fermor spending April and May inactive. We know that he was waiting for the recruits and the officers whom he had requested.

---

[7] A verst is 3,500 feet, so 412 versts is 273.1 statute miles or 443.7 kilometers.

It was only on 6 June that he decided for Pomerania. The army moved in three columns: Panine went by Dirschau, on Preussisch-Stargard; Soltykov, by Münsterwald, on Tuchel; Rumyantsev's cavalry, by Neuburg, on the same point; Krasnochtchokov's Cossacks, followed by Stoffeln's squadrons, on Konitz. When they had arrived at Konitz and Tuchel, the army stopped. Then it changed direction, turning towards the south, in the direction of Bromberg. Fermor had ordered Demicou's cavalry to leave for Driesen, an important point on the Netze, from where he could raise contributions and collect information on both Pomerania and Brandenburg; but the roads were found to be too bad and the country too marshy. Demicou was satisfied to make raids into Pomerania: on Neu-Stettin, where, on 20 June, he defeated a force of Prussian hussars, killed 28 of them and took 32 prisoners, capturing 2,000 cattle and as many sheep. Then he moved on Tempelburg, on the Draheim, where he captured a colonel and 19 men, then destroyed five cast iron cannon. On 2 July, he was in Posen, and deposited his spoils there. Then he set out again and joined Rumyantsev, in Wronke, and received from him the order to move on Driesen. During this time, the main body of the army, continuing its march by Bromberg, arrived at Posen. From 1-3 July, the main body completed its concentration. From Tuchel to Posen, he marched 228 versts in 12 days.[8]

It was obvious that Fermor had returned to his initial idea, which was to take from Frederick II one of his most important fortresses on the Oder, Küstrin or Frankfurt, where large quantities of supplies and ammunition had been accumulated, which the King of Prussia regarded as one of his secure retreats in case of misfortune. For an operation on Küstrin, the point of Driesen was of great strategic importance. It gave the occupant the ability to move along the two banks of the Wartha. Driesen was defended by Colonel Gordt with 1,000 men. When Demicou appeared, with a reinforcement of ten squadrons of horse grenadiers and two howitzers, Gordt answered his summons with the fire of a cannon. Demicou had to be reinforced by Eropkine, who took command of the operation. In front of this new attacker, Gordt decided to retreat. Eropkine pursued him. The Prussians tried to hold a position at Friedberg, on 15 July; but were driven out, the Prussians withdrew across a plain where all their men, enveloped by hussars and Cossacks, were killed or captured.

The path to Brandenburg was definitively opened. Frederick II hastened to pull Dohna out of Pomerania, where he had driven back the Swedes everywhere. Leaving Platen's cavalry at Belgard to cover Kolberg, Dohna rushed to Brandenburg. On 6 July, he arrived in Schwedt, on the Oder. From there, he directed the Malachowski Hussars on Frankfurt, and his advance guard, commanded by Kanitz, on Landsberg, only two marches from Driesen, which was occupied by the Russians. On 24 July, Dohna took up a position at Lebus, on the Oder, equidistant from Küstrin and Frankfurt, holding himself to

---

[8] Translator: 151 miles or 245 kilometers.

march to the relief of whichever city was threatened.

Fermor would have readily attacked Dohna. A few marches would have taken him from Posen on the Oder. But at this time Brown was quite far away. The Observation corps was even further. Fermor moved slowly, painfully, spending five months covering 850 versts, barely 170 versts per month.[9] Word already arrived of the exhaustion of his horses and even of his men. Its creator, Peter Shuvalov, grew aware of this weakness as well. He wrote: "This body can fight and gain the victory only through artillery; its regiments must be placed in a situation such that they are only used to cover the guns." This corps was overloaded, being overburdended with artillery. In addition to the regimental guns, it contained 110 heavy caliber cannon, large numbers of caissons, a bridging train, and engineering material down to sandbags. When he arrived at Thorn, he considered it necessary to leave 50 of his heavy cannons and most of his impedimenta there. He kept with him only sufficient cannon to support his forces, ranging from 8,000 to 10,000 combatants. This corps was a barely organized mass of men, the regiments being very reduced in their strength and no longer grouped in brigades and corps. Officers were lacking, especially senior officers. Before appearing on a battlefield its general-in-chief had changed four times: after Shuvalov, came Soltykov; after Soltykov, Brown; and after Brown, Zacharie Tchernychef. Soldiers, non-commissioned officers, officers, generals, barely knew each other. If attacked, and the artillery failed to do its duty, this heterogeneous force would have collapsed. Finally, after a long series of marches, it rejoined the principal body. Fermor had now almost all of his forces concentrated at Betsche (or Pszczewo), not far from the Obra, at the confluence of the Wartha. This occurred on 26 July, the day before Dohna occupied Lebus.

It was at this time that the Conference intervened again. Yielding to the pressure of the Austrians, it decided that the Observation Corps, reinforced by 8,000 men drawn from Fermor, would be placed under the orders of Brown and directed on Glogau, to cooperate with Daun's operations in Silesia. Fermor had protested vigorously.

The day of the meeting with Betsche, Fermor sent cavalry reconnaissance forces in all directions. By this means and his "particular confidants," he learned that a great panic had appeared in Berlin, as a result of a renewed attack by the Swedes on Peene, and that the authorities were prepared to flee to Magdeburg; that Dohna was concentrated between Küstrin and Frankfurt; that Frederick II and Prince Henry did not cease sending reinforcements to him; that the King himself, with part of his army, had left his positions at Olmütz and had left in an unknown direction. The Russian cavalry in Landsberg announced the appearance of a Prussian advance guard of very great size.

---

[9] Translator: 563.5 miles, 112 miles; 900 kilometers, 180 kilometers.

Fermor called his council of war. It estimated that the Prussians intended to dispute their proposed crossing of the Oder, then threaten the Russian Army's flanks so as to cut off its communications with East Prussia. He spoke energetically against any dispatch of troops for Glogau. He decided that they would move in mass on Frankfurt and after having forced the passage he would execute a diversion against Berlin.

On 26 July, the main body advanced from Betsche on Mezeritz, where one crossed Obra. The following day, Stoffeln occupied Landsberg, which the Prussians gave up without a fight.

The Russians then received news of the Austrian army from General Springer, Russian military attaché to Daun's headquarters. According to a conversation that Springer had with Daun, the Field Marshal stated he had received no orders, no plan of operation, and nothing about the Russian Army. A letter from Kaunitz to Fermor ensured on the contrary that Daun had the most precise instructions; that besides Fermor would not go to Silesia, because there were too many fortresses; that instead he would move towards the west, on Lusace, in order to try to lock up and encircle Frederick II between the two imperial armies. Fermor could have demanded to know who was being misled. The difference in opinion was sharp between Daun, Kaunitz and Ambassador Esterhazy, who pushed on the Conference to send 20,000 Russians into Silesia. If the Austrians found that there were too many fortresses in Silesia for them to tackle, why send Brown into it? And how was one to explain Daun's movement on Lusace, this escape towards the west, as Fermor sought to approach him?

Throughout the end of July there occurred, in the Russian Army, long deliberations in a council of war, followed by long halts and reconnaissances being sent in every direction. The objective of the army's operations changed constantly. It was successively Frankfurt, then Küstrin, then, after it was known that Daun was moving away, it became Stargard, where the Russians hoped to link-up with the Swedes. Finally, it swung back to Küstrin. The army received conflicting information on the Austrian army and contradictory directions from the Conference, which obliged Fermor to mark time. In his reports, he complained about the "hot summer days," the lack of fodder, and the bad condition of the Observation Corps. The corps was seen as incapable of movement. Its horses could barely stand, and the 8,000 reinforcements added to his 12,000-man force destroyed more than they added to its combat capability. Its new commanding officer, Brown, fell ill. He was replaced by Zachary Tchernychef. Even though its new commanding officer vigorously pushed it, the rearguard, overloaded with a heavy artillery train was always a march or two to the rear, causing Fermor to constantly fear it might be captured by the Prussians before he could move to its support.

During the first days of August, the Russian advance guards occupied Zielenzig, Königswalde, Sonnenburg, and Drossen. On 5 August, Stoyanov, with a strong cavalry reconnaissance, fell on 6,000 Prussians at Kunersdorf, which Dohna, now established at Frankfurt, had encamped before its cantonments. The Prussians were driven back with a loss of 44 men. Fermor, whose headquarters were at Königswalde, understood that he was a bit too far advanced. From Frankfurt, Dohna could fall on his right flank, defeat his dispersed corps, and throw them into the Wartha Swamp. Fortunately, for the Russians, the Prussians did not recognize the perilous situation where the Russians found themselves. The Russians were able to conceal their movement and withdraw on Landsberg. The Russian light cavalry rendered Fermor invaluable services, forming a mobile screen between his main body and the Prussians. The Prussians, constantly harassed and unable to conceal their least movements, let the best opportunities escape.

The Russian Army moved, by Landsberg, to the far bank of the Wartha. Though they had marched many miles, they had not acted and could still not decide on an energetic offensive on either Frankfurt or Küstrin, or to make an offensive into Silesia, or to link-up with the Swedes. The only effort that could be made from its position north of the Wartha was an attack on Küstrin. Fermor was now resolved on Küstrin, but not entirely, because we will see him being deprived of the services of Rumyantsev by engaging him too far to the north, as if he could not completely give up thoughts of an offensive on Pomerania. Invaluable time had been wasted, and here is the man who never lost any time, the man with whom "one cannot jest," Frederick II in person, who struck like the lightning. The distress cry from his threatened fortresses, from his fields held for ransom by the bold incursions of the Cossacks, of his plundered and stripped peasants robbed of their last shirt, added wings to the feet of his marching troops.

On 13 August, Fermor directed a strong reconnaissance on Küstrin. There arose a sharp engagement in the Kurze-Vorstadt or "Little Suburb" of the city. The Prussian hussars were pursued through the city to the bridge over the branch of the Oder that separated the city from the Kurze-Vorstadt. The city's ramparts erupted with fire as 20 cannon shots were fired on the Cossacks. Küstrin is situated on a sort of island at the confluence of the Oder and the Wartha, an island enveloped by the two branches of the river, which was smallest on the side of the suburb and largest to the west of the city. The soil, softened by the water, formed a fortress surrounded by a belt of swamps. One could regard Küstrin as impregnable or at least very difficult to take. In 1806, however, it capitulated upon the appearance of a single French division, but this was purely due to the cowardice of its commander. The commander in 1758 was much more willing to fight. Attacked by the Russians from the east, he communicated freely by bridges to the west with Brandenburg. He also knew that Dohna was not far away, and that Frederick was rushing to his aid. He had a garrison of 2,000 men, many cannon on the old ramparts, and ammunition in abundance, while the Russians lacked it.

On 14 August, Fermor, stopped at Gross-Kamin, called together his council of war. It was decided that the following morning they would proceed with an attack on Küstrin. When Fermor made such a decision in the face of a strongly fortified city, in the presence of Dohna's 14,000 men, and with Frederick on the way, was this not an act of insanity when the army was weakened by the separation of Rumyantsev's corps? However, the council agreed with the order which it had already received from Fermor. Rumyantsev was to rejoin Riazanov, march with him on Kolberg, a port on the Baltic Sea, summon it, besiege it, bombard it, and take it before making a demonstration on Stettin. This was an error for which Fermor would pay dearly.

On 15 August, Fermor left Gross-Kamin and directed the attack on Küstrin. Before becoming master of Kurze-Vorstadt, it was necessary to remove a strong battery established on an eminence and two cemeteries where the Prussians had entrenched themselves. The Russians opened a sharp cannonade on these positions; then, in an impetuous charge, the Cossacks swept across the flat ground, threw themselves into the streets of Kurze-Vorstadt, drove back the Prussian hussars, and carried all these obstacles. Masters of the suburb, they tried to push out of it; but between the suburb and the bridge of the city, they found a ground marshy and slick, and swept by cannon and musketry fire from the ramparts. The grenadiers, running up to support them, were no more successful. The Prussians, after having evacuated the suburb, had taken refuge in the fortress, destroying the bridges behind them. The Russians, before reaching the ramparts, had to cover a piece of ground swept with Prussian fire and a branch of the Oder. Stoffeln audaciously sent a parliamentarian to summon the place. He was not received. The remainder of the day was occupied by a violent cannonade between the suburb and the city, which then continued all night. In the suburb conquered by the Russians, Viazemski, Herbel, and Demoline, very good engineers, were directed by Fermor, also an engineer; they worked on erecting three batteries connected by trenches and equipped with guns. In the morning of the 16th, 22 guns were positioned in them. Fermor also added some mortars to them. Once established they began bombarding the city with shells, bombs, and red-hot shot. At 5:00 p.m., Küstrin was in flames. So general and so violent was the fire that the arsenal, with its cannon foundry, and the piles of the bridges were burned. In the magazines 1,200,000 hectoliters of wheat, Frederick II's food reserve, were reduced to ashes. The Prussian artillerists who served the cannon on the ramparts were obliged to leave their posts because of the fire. However, the Russians, forced to save their ammunition, had fired only 85 shots. The fortress had fired 517 in response, but without causing any substantial damage to the Russians. Fermor, in his daily report, was most pleased with the results. "It will be enough to say that the noble volunteers attached to the army declared that in history one will not find an example of such an army, which on the same day that it arrived in front of such a redoubtable fortress, had it advanced directly before it, without approach works, under the cannon of the city, chased out the enemy, conquered the suburb, and bombarded the place, while losing only 11 dead and 29 wounded." The fire in the city was a single blaze; the works remained intact; the branch of the river still flowed before its walls. And Frederick II approached! Fermor had to bitterly regret the days lost spent idle in the camps on the Okra and the Netze. During the night of the 16th/17th, the Russians continued to strengthen themselves in the suburb and to bombard the fortress. The bombardment slackened over the next two days. Ammunition was running short and Russian soldiers were sent about to collect the expended cannon balls fired by the Prussians. The Küstrin Garrison, constantly reinforced and resupplied, took advantage of the artillery battle, which continued throughout the 19th and 20th. In response to the Russian fire, the Prussians fired 1,353 projectiles and made the situation of the grenadiers and Cossacks intolerable, destroyed the bridge that the Russians had thrown over the Oder at Schaumburg, and succeeded in destroying the bridges that connected it to the left bank of the river.

Fermor understood that he could neither make a breach with the ramparts, nor to force the passage of the Oder. At the same time, he recognized the error he had made by dispatching Rumyantsev, which could be repaired only by half measures. He learned that, on the 18th, Major Strick had surprised the bridge at Schwedt, 60 versts downstream from Küstrin, and threw back the Prussian corps on the left bank of the river. It was a strategic point of great value which fell into Russian hands. Fermor related this beautiful feat of arms in a most favorable report to the Tsarina, who then sent a letter of congratulations to Strick and granted to him a gratification equal to one years' pay. Fermor dispatched couriers to Rumyantsev, who continued to march on Stargard to try to join the Swedes. Fermor enjoined him not to go beyond Pyritz and to beheld himself ready to support Strick against a renewed attack by the Prussians or an attempt by the Stettin garrison. Rumyantsev, who already found himself in a very risky situation, was very happy to receive the order to march on Schwedt. Fermor might have acted more wisely if he had ordered him to return to Küstrin. However, at this time the Russian generalissimo was convinced that it was at Schwedt that Frederick would try to cross the Oder so as to fall on the right flank of the forces besieging Küstrin. This strategic point thus acquired in his eyes an extraordinary importance. He wished, at all costs, to prevent the King of Prussia from crossing the Oder. While he could prevent this from happening at Küstrin, he sent courier after courier to Rumyantsev directing him to hold Schwedt to the last man. He sent reinforcements to Strick, particularly Stoyanov's cavalry and Tchougouyiev's Cossacks. Between Schwedt and Küstrin he deployed the Don Cossacks and the Khomutov Dragoons. Unfortunately, on the day of the great test, these so valuable troops would be lost to him. It was the same for Krasnochtchokov's Don Cossacks, who, swimming across the Oder, had spread devastation far into Brandenburg, and, on 17 August, captured 1,500 cattle and 150 horses, and then on the 20th, took a further 2,000 cattle and another 250 horses, levied contributions, and audaciously camped upstream from Küstrin, on the same road along which Frederick would soon be advancing.

CHAPTER VIII

THE BATTLE OF ZORNDORF (25 AUGUST 1758)

Fermor knew well that the King of Prussia was moving. But what forces did he bring with him? The reports varied between 40,000, 30,000, 18,000, and 15,000 men. Which direction did he follow? The Russians were absolutely unaware of the details of Frederick's actions. Prince Sulkowski, one of Fermor's "confidants," assured him that Frederick marched on Posen, in order to throw himself on the rear of the Russian Army. One thing that was certain was that one could not count on either the Swedes or the Austrians. The first did nothing to link-up with Rumyantsev. The second marched quietly on Lusace, though Daun knew perfectly well that the common enemy had just left his camp at Landshut and rushed towards Brandenburg to engage the Russians. He had promised not to lose sight of him and, if he moved, to follow him step-by-step, close on his heels. When Frederick began his movement to the north, Daun did not stop his movement to the west. He did not seek to move before the Russians. Instead, he simply continued one of his march-maneuvers, where he demonstrated all his military science and concern about the elegance of his maneuvers. Frederick was quick to benefit from this.

Frederick, despite Lehwaldt's defeat at Gross Jägersdorf, persisted in his inaccurate understanding of the Russian Army. He continued to ignore the reforms that had fortified it, thinking always that he would have an action with the troops that had been earlier led by Marshal Münich.[10] They would not fail to, upon the approach of the enemy, form themselves in an oblong square, embarrassed by their baggage and unable to maneuver or even move, to face the musketry and canister of their enemies. This living and inert fortress would first be swept by violent artillery fire and then opened up by impetuous cavalry charges. The battle would be won by volleys of musketry and a liberal use of Prussian bayonets. At that moment Frederick left Silesia to move in front of the Russians, he once again sought to consult with the old Marshal Keith, who had commanded them at the time of Anna Ivanovna.

What are these Russian troops? — Sir, these are good troops who will defend themselves well, but are badly directed. — Good, good! You will learn that I have attacked these rascals and in that first attack I will put them to flight.

---

[10] Frederick II still employed this expression, even regarding Zorndorf, in his *Histoire de la guerre de Sept ans.*

– Sir, these rascals will not flee so easily, and I believe it my duty to tell Your Majesty this truth and this interest which I owe them. — Well, you will see that these are not the same Russians that you knew.

However, it was not really the same army, because the reforms of 1755 to 1757 had made it much more redoubtable than the armies commanded by Keith and Münich. Frederick would soon learn this, and upon his return from Zorndorf, one commented on "the silence that he maintained between himself and the Marshal about the battle, and everything that he could have said about the Russians."[11]

It was on 10 August, from his camp at Grüssau, that he informed his brother Henry of his resolution.[12]

I beg you to maintain in complete secrecy everything that this letter contains, as it is for your information alone. I will march against the Russians tomorrow. As the events of war can produce all kinds of accidents and I might easily be killed, I believe it my duty to bring you up to date on the steps I have taken, especially as you are, with unlimited authority, the tutor of our nephew: 1.) If I am killed, it is necessary that you have our armies immediately take the oath of allegiance to my nephew; 2.) It is necessary to continue all activity so that the enemy does not see any change in the command; 3.) Here is the plan that I actually have: to defeat the Russians outright, if it is possible; then to immediately redirect Dohna against the Swedes; and, for me, to return with my corps against the Austrians.

Evidently, Frederick, in his first encounter with the Russians, counted on a new edition of *Veni, vidi, vici.*[13]

Of the 50,000 men that he commanded in Silesia, he left 40,000 to protect his positions and observe the Austrians. He left with only 15,000 men: 14 battalions and 38 squadrons, among whom were the best of his cavalry. He marched as rapidly as possible. He ran, as he would say, "like a Basque." This did not prevent him, at night, from reading *De natura Deorum* by Cicero and the *Tusculanes*, to reason with Catte on philosophy and metaphysics, and to write poetry.

On 12 August he was at Liegnitz; on the 13th at Heinzendorf; on the 15th at Dalkau, on the 16th at Wartenberg; on the 17th at Plothow; on the 18th at

[11] Henri de Catt, *Mes Entretiens avec Fédéric le Grand, memoirs et journal*, Leipzig, 1885.
[12] *Politische Correspondenz*, Vol. XVII, p. 158.
[13] Translator: Julius Caesar, "I came, I saw, I conquered."

Krossen; and on the 19th at Ziebingen. On the 20th he entered Frankfurt, where he found Dohna. With the 18,000 men that Dohna had brought with him from Pomerania, and the 15,000 he brought with him from Silesia, he found himself able to deploy 33,000 men and 117 cannon, not including regimental guns. He passed this army in review and was struck by the contrast between the troops from East Prussia and from Pomerania, who were well rested, well fed, well-dressed, and those of his own who had suffered through so many campaigns, with uniforms in rags and their faces tanned by summer's sun and winter's frost. He did not conceal his confidence in his "devils from Silesia" and his "bearskin bonnets"[14] from Prussia. The defeat at Gross Jägersdorf was always at his heart.

As soon as he entered the lands that had been overrun by the Cossacks, he had unfortunate subjects to console and burnt-out peasants to assist. Everywhere he was greeted by the acclamations of the peasants, who saluted him as their liberator and father.

Frederick was in Wartenberg when he learned of the Russian attack on Küstrin. Immediately he wrote in Dohna: "No matter what happens, it is necessary that Küstrin holds, under penalty of death and of the greatest torments if somebody speaks of abandoning it!"[15] From Frankfurt he could hear their guns thundering against his city. Bolotov tells us, undoubtedly according to some German account, that he was seen, upright on the steps of the house where he was staying, throwing furious glances in the direction of Küstrin, and, with each detonation, dipping from his snuffbox, with a rag, and inhaling it up his nostrils. It was even worse when, the following day, he entered Küstrin, which was reduced in ashes, and he could study the extent of this disaster. His riders shouted on his passage: "Father! Be peaceful. We will saber these poor wretches and we will give no quarter. All of us sharpened our sabers."[16]

The letters in which he describes the excesses committed by the Russians in the villages, the burned thatched cottages, the massacred men, the raped women, makes one think of the bulletins where Napoleon denounced in Germany and Europe the atrocities of these "barbarians" that had been brought into Germany by the cruel policies of Austria. Did Frederick not mix a bit of politics into his philanthropic protests as did Napoleon? Did Frederick, if moved by the misfortunes of his subjects, forget how he had treated those of the Elector of Saxony? If he was sincerely pained upon seeing the process of war applied to his patrimony, were not his exclamations of grief calculated either for his own justification or to affect the opinion of the 18th century Europe?

---

[14] Translator: "Bearskin bonnets" is a reference to the headgear worn by grenadiers of this period. They were an "elite" unit. However, at this time the Prussian grenadiers wore a miter cap, not a bearskin.

[15] From Wartenburg, 18 August. *Poliatische Correspondenz*, Vol. VXII, p. 178.

[16] *Politische Correspondenz.*

"The Muscovites," he wrote in his *Relation,* "make a war with barbarians on the States of the King; every day they burn villages; they pillage in an inhuman way; they kill women, the children, and old men, and commit horrors that make nature quiver." — "These are horrors that a sensitive heart supports only with the cruelest bitterness," he would write to his brother Henry. He will repeat the same thing with his minister Finckenstein, by sending to him a "summary of the exactions, cruelties and horrors committed by the Russians." But he will add: "I believe that the best use we can make of it would be to have it printed in the gazettes, both French and German, to inform the public of it."

The Prussians sometimes showed themselves as "wild" as the Cossacks. Henrich von Catt has preserved for us an instructive anecdote:

> One had brought to His Majesty's headquarters a Kalmuk who had been taken prisoner. A general, who saw him, advanced and started to insult the poor devil, in terms which he did not understand. Seeing that the Kalmuk had an image which hung to him on this chest, the general attempted to touch it with his cane. The prisoner, who thought the general wanted to take his religious medal, hid it with his two hands. The general, furious, struck him blows on his hands with his cane such that they swelled and became black. As the Kalmuk continued to clutch his medallion and looked at the general who struck him in such a cruel way, struck him in the face and drew blood. Losing his temper at this spectacle; I said to him that if one accused these Kalmuks and Cossacks with cruelty, there were many other people whom one could accuse of even greater cruelty.

A sharp discussion followed between the two Germans; but on the observation that Catt made that the King would learn of this scene and that it would ruffle his principles of humanity, the general softened and requested that he never speak about this business.

Frederick, in order to engage them, had resolved to pass, not at Schwedt, which would have been too far away, nor at the Küstrin bridges, which would have brought him before the face of the Russian positions, but at an intermediate point, where Fermor did not expect him. This was Gustebiese-am-Oder. There he could seize the advantage of cutting Fermor off from Rumyantsev, to whom the former had reiterated his order to vigorously hold Schwedt. The King made his preparations in the greatest secrecy, and even misled his two adversaries by demonstrations downstream and upstream from Gustebiese. During the night of 22/23 August, he moved rapidly over bridges constructed by his advance guard, commanded by Manteuffel. The

King followed with the 1st Hussars. At 3:00 a.m., all the army had moved to the far bank. Frederick II initially stopped at Zellin; he pushed Malachowski on Klossow, following him and arriving there on the 23rd. His soldiers were enthusiastic with this first success: "Father," they shouted to him, "you lead us quickly to the enemy. We want to overcome him or die for Your Majesty."

From the 21st, patrols by the Don Cossacks informed Fermor they had seen large Prussian troop movements to the north, descending from the left bank of the Oder. Fermor did nothing but to enjoin Rumyantsev even more strongly to strongly hold Schwedt. Fermor did destroy his bridge at Schaumburg and concentrated his forces in his trenches under Küstrin's guns. But on the 22nd, Khomutov, one of the chiefs of his light troops, who had seen his cordon of cavalry broken and found himself obliged to withdraw in the direction of Schwedt, warned Fermor, by a picket which had to make a great detour, of the pending crossing of the Prussians at Gustebiese. Then the Generalissimo destroyed his batteries before Küstrin, reinforced his outposts to conceal his retreat from the Küstrin garrison, and moved off to the northeast. During the day of the 23rd, Prussian deserters and Russian fugitives, among whom was the Austrian Military Attaché, Saint-André, and finally new couriers from Khomoutov confirmed the first reports to Fermor.

The movement that Fermor executed had brought him so close to Frederick that it was not impossible for him to avoid a battle.

The battlefield, on which the two armies would collide, forms a sort of enclosed field, approximately 10 kilometers from north to south and 12-15 from west to east. It is delimited on the west by the course of the Oder, which was separated from it by the Drewitz Wood; in the south by the Wartha which winds among its marshes; on the north by the Meitzel, another affluent of the Oder; and on the east by the vast, brushy Zicherwald. Küstrin was in the southwest corner. In the northwest corner was the village of Kutzdorf. Along the Mietzel were scattered, from west to the east, the villages of Quartschen, Darrmietzel, and the Neudamm Mill. In the Zicherwald were those of Zicher, Bartzlow, and Wilkersdorf. In the center of this plain stood the village of Zorndorf. On the right bank of the Wartha ran the highway from Küstrin to Bromberg, which ran through the villages of Warnick, Tamsel, Klein-Kamin, and Gross-Kamin, before reaching Blumberg.

The situation of the Russian Army was extremely dangerous. In truth, on the northern side, the Mietzel still separated him from Frederick II; but this river offered only a very weak defense, being passable at each village that it watered. If the Russians moved back, they would be thrown into the marshes of the Wartha, or back on Küstrin, in the angle formed by this river and the Oder. Its destruction would then be certain. Its only line of retreat was by the Küstrin-Bromberg road, running along the right side in the Wartha marshes, leaving its left flank exposed to Prussian attacks. This angle, with Küstrin at its corner, formed the most frightening trap of the battlefield. It is true that the northwestern angle, towards Kutzdorf, was another cul-de-sac where the Prussians could be driven back if their attack on the face or the left flank of the Russian Army failed. They were the the two "pockets" of this game of billiards.

It was not without emotion that Fermor felt committed to such a play, against such an opponent, only had the protection of the Mietzel Brook, which would delay the Prussians for only a few hours. Any wihdrawal by Gross-Kamin was even more perilous than the resistance in front of Zorndorf.

Fortunately for Fermor, in this marshy or brushy plain, from where one could be driven back step-by-step towards the marshes to the south and inevitable destruction, there arose, north of Zorndorf, a line of low heights. They had their most abrupt face towards Mietzel, with their soft slopes towards Zorndorf, which was drawn up on a projection of ground. These positions, known as the Quartschen Heights, were flanked, in the west, by the Zabergrund Ravine; to the east, by that of Hofbruch. They were divided, in their middle, by a third ravine, the Galgengrund[17] Ravine, which formed two mountains. Further to the east was a ridge called Mount Lyssia. It was on these heights that Fermor positioned and anchored himself so as to avoid being swept away on the plain.

From Zabergrund to Hofbruch, which straddles the Galgengrund, ranges from the west to the east, facing Meitzel, Fermor deployed his army in two parallel lines. For each of these two lines, the western flank and the center were formed of his own regiments. The east wing, the Observation Corps, were placed under the orders of Brown.[18] At the fold of the Galgengrund the two lines broke at an obtuse angle with the peak pointing to the north. Thus, the main body of the Russian Army, three miles before Zorndorf, and a few hundred meters behind Quartschen, was about 10-11 kilometers from the "little suburb" of Küstrin.

To watch the passages of the Mietzel, the Russians had posted, before Zicher, directly across from the Neudamm Mill, some companies of Brown's grenadiers. At Quartschen there were posted a few companies of Fermor's grenadiers. The army's cavalry was posted on both wings. To the south, at Gross-Kamin, on the only line of retreat, the Russians had massed all their heavy baggage. It had formed into a *wagenburg*, surrounded by ditches and palisades, and guarded by a few regiments. The light baggage had remained with the army.

This force contained 30,000 infantry, 3,282 regular cavalry and about 3,000 irregular cavalry. It had 190 regimental guns and 50 field guns.

---

[17] Translator: An interesting note. "Galgengrund" translates "Gallows Ground." This was probably the local execution site.

[18] Because the battle was one of maneuvers and things changed, the author has chosen to describe the wings as the "east" and "west" wings, instead of the right and left flank.

When Frederick was informed of these dispositions, he decided not to attack the Russians frontally. As for turning them by their western wing, it would, in the event of success, simply drive them back on their line of retreat, and, in the event of failure, the Prussians would be pushed into the dangerous angle on the northwest of the battlefield. While turning their eastern wing, they would push the Russians into the Zicherwald, and there was a chance of pushing them into the Oder, the Wartha, or under the guns of Küstrin. However, Frederick II chose something more audacious than a simple turning movement of the eastern flank of the Russians. Instead he chose to move into Fermor's rear, cut him off from his heavy baggage at Gross-Kamin, occupy the village of Zorndorf which had initially been the location of the Russian headquarters, in order to strike them precisely up the soft slopes of the heights they occupied, towards the village.

In this bold offensive, Frederick gained one other advantage. This was to strike a great blow against the Russian's morale, by appearing successively on their front, their flank, and then their rear; to throw disorder into the maneuvers of this still novice army; to inspire terror in them by causing them to see that they had been turned, cut off, and enveloped, before they knew from what direction they would be attacked.

All the morning of 24 August, the King of Prussia rested his troops on the far side of the Mietzel. At 1:00 p.m., he sent Manteuffel's advance guard to the Neudamm Mill and deployed it in a circular double line, presenting a line of bayonets to the Russians at every point. At 2:00 p.m., the rest of the army, moving to the river, took up position between Darrmietzel and Neudamm.

At 5:00 p.m., only, the Russians were informed of this movement, and they maintained their positions.

The night passed in this manner. The Russian Army, expecting some surprise, some sudden crossing of the river, slept with arms in hand. At 3:00 a.m., on the 25th, Fermor slightly modified his positions. His two lines moved some 1,200 paces to the rear.

Frederick passed the evening of the 24th discussing with Catte the Ode in general, Malherbe, and the lyrical poet Racine. He amused himself by reading some stanzas of *Athalie* and J. B. Rousseau. He was up at 3:00 a.m., on the 25th. He had his infantry pass over the bridges that had been erected at the Neudamm Mill. His cavalry, which had made a great detour, crossed the river, a few kilometers upstream, at the Kersten ford, and moved into the Zicherwald. A few hours later the Russians were stupefied to see the King's infantry turning their positions, his squadrons passed by Batzlow, and then this infantry continued its march on Zorndorf. The surprise Frederick had prepared for Fermor was complete. Fermor was cut off from his heavy baggage and he no longer possessed his line of retreat.

Frederick did not congratulate himself on his success, even though his maneuvers were brilliant. He had his infantry do an about face, so that his second line became his first line and his right wing was now his left wing. He prescribed lengthening these two lines and gave them an absolute straightness, without any angle. The artillery, which had earlier lined the banks of the Mietzel, passed between the battalions and presented a new face on the side of Zorndorf. He had the lines send out all their "light baggage" and concentrated it at Quartschen, along with the army's treasury, his headquarters' secret files and the ambulances. At 9:00 a.m., all movements were finished.

At this time, it was Fermor's corps that formed the left wing. Fermor's first line consisted of the 1st Grenadiers, the 3rd Grenadiers, the Rostov, and Novogord Infantry Regiments, forming Lubomirski's Brigade; the Schüsselburg and Tchernigov Infantry Regiments, forming Ouvarov's Brigade; the Kexholm and Lagoda Infantry Regiments of Leontiev's brigade, and finally the Sousdal Infantry Regiment. His second line consisted of the Voronezh and Petersburg Infantry Regiments, of Panine's Brigade; a battalion of dismounted dragoons, the Riazan, Smolensk, and Mourmon Infantry Regiments, the 4th Grenadiers, and the Troitski and Kazan Infantry Regiments. Brown had in his first line two regiments of Manteuffel's brigade, the grenadiers of the Observation Corps, and the 4th and 5th Musketeers, a new formation. In the second line were the Nevsky Infantry, 2nd Grenadiers, and the 1st and 3rd Musketeers, also newly formed. The right wing, supported on the Zaubergrund, was flanked by Haugreven's cavalry, that is to say the Kargopol Horse Grenadiers, and the Archangel and Tobolsk Dragoon Regiments, a total of 9 squadrons or 1,260 sabers. The left wing, supported on Hofbruch, was held by the Empress, 3rd and Novotroitski Cuirassiers, under the orders of Demikov: a total of 12 squadrons and 1,680 men. The artillery deployed across the front of the army its 200 cannons, heavy guns grouped here and there by batteries.

In reality, the situation of the Russian Army was not good. It now had behind its back the deep Mietzel ravine and on its right flank the Oder. On that side it had no line of retreat. On its new front, it had nothing more than the gentle slopes descending to the south and the heights it occupied were commanded by the Zorndorf heights. It found itself, by its center, on the Galgengrund, divided into two armies that could barely communicate. Of these two armies, Fermor's was excellent, while that of Brown, though reinforced by some of Fermor's regiments, remained very mediocre. It was the most encumbered with artillery and the least able to serve itself well with them. The disadvantages of the annoying duality that already existed in the Russian forces were worsened by their separation by the deep Galgengrund Ravine. Finally, the two factions, Fermor as Brown, lacked space to fully maneuver and were excessively massed on the heights. When Frederick II had examined their position, he was extremely satisfied: "Not a bullet will be wasted there!"

he exclaimed.

The King of Prussia continued his turning movement by Wilkersdorf. He took up position behind the village of Zorndorf; but, as the Russian light cavalry had hastily set it afire, this fire greatly bothered them. The smoke concealed from them part of the battlefield and they would not take their ammunition caissons through the streets of the burning village.

To the south of Zorndorf, supporting his right on Wilkersdorf, Frederick formed an advance guard, followed by two parallel battle lines. In his formation, he put the lower quality regiments in the second line. The advance guard, under Manteuffel[19], contained eight battalions of grenadiers. The first line, with 20 battalions, consisted of: on his left, Kaunitz's infantry; on his right that of Dohna. The second line, containing 10 battalions, was commanded by Forcade. On the right of the army there were, under Schorlemer, 12 squadrons of hussars. On the left, under von Seydlitz, one of the greatest cavaliers of history, were 56 squadrons to which one should add 15 squadrons, a bit detached to the right, belonging to the Karabinier Regiment and the König Friederich and Kronprinz von Preussen Cuirassier Regiments.

At 9:00 a.m., the Prussian artillery, grouped into two large batteries, one of 20 guns and the other of 40, opened the most violent fire on the Russian right. The Russians responded. In this artillery duel, the advantage went to the Prussians. They occupied a dominating position, and the Russians were absolutely uncovered. Finally, the pieces on which Fermor founded his greatest hopes, the famous Shuvalov howitzers, had been grouped on the left wing, under Brown's command. In the dense masses of Russian infantry, the Prussian balls caused massive casualties. One shot killed 48 men. Russian batteries were dismounted, caissons exploded. A Prussian officer was later heard to say that in the history of warfare, one had never heard such a din.

The Russian infantry, for two hours, withstood hell's fire with a stoic patience: "With an intrepid and amazing firmness," according to Fermor's report. The foreign volunteers had to give the same homage to the Russian soldier.

Everyone, however, did not share this heroic endurance: there were some who ran away, and among them was Prince Charles of Saxony, who had been received in the Russian camp with royal honors and a salvo of 21 guns. He fled with such haste that, not being able to cross the village of Quartschen, as its streets were clogged with baggage, and the soldiers fired on him[20], he ran to Kutzdorf, and from there he reached Soldin.[21] It was at this time, or perhaps after Seydlitz's first charge, that Fermor appears to have disappeared,

---

[19] There was a General Heinrich von Manteuffel in the Prussian army and a General Manteuffel-Szoeggen in the Russian army.

[20] Second account of Saint-André.

[21] On the contrary, the French military attaché, Baron von Wittinghof, remained and during the battle he was wounded with a shot to the wrist.

without it being ever being known where he had gone. The Prince of Saxony was accused of having said to Saint-André: "I will go, if it is necessary, as far as Schwedt." What is certain, is that he issued no orders, leaving the brigade commanders and colonels to act at their discretion. Later it was said that he had been wounded; undoubtedly it was a very light wound, or a simple contusion.

On the Russian right, already cruelly tested, around 11:00 a.m., Frederick II launched Manteuffel's eight battalions. They were to push past the right and left of the village of Zorndorf. As soon as they did so a fusillade began, and the Russians responded. They also advanced their batteries. Frederick threw Kanitz forward to support Manteuffel, but Kanitz, following the ravine, moved too far to the right, and instead of cooperating with the attack against Fermor, he found himself in contact with Brown. Thus, two distinct battles began simultaneously.

Fermor's Russians immediately profited from this error. At noon, this right wing took the offensive. Haugrewen, with his 9 squadrons, fell on Manteuffel's flank and threw him back. Then the 1st Grenadiers, the brigades of Lumbomirski, Ouvarov, and Leontiev descended from the height and completed Manteuffel's rout. The Russians captured 26 cannons. *Removed space* Then they fell on Kanitz and dispersed seven of his battalions. Kanitz was grievously wounded. Fermor's Russians now discovered they had ventured too far, especially since Brown's troops, on the Lyssia Heights, had made no movement.

Now Seydlitz was close by, with his 56 squadrons. He had also recalled the 15 squadrons that had been detached to the right. During Fermor's attack, Frederick had already sent him orders to charge. In the last note he said that after the battle he would pay with his head for his disobedience. To this Seydlitz responded: "After the battle my head is at the disposition of the King." Finally, when he saw the Russian infantry and cavalry well engaged, and with his infallible eye, he judged the moment had come, he assembled under his hands all his squadrons (the Russians had only 9 squadrons and 25-26 battalions there), and he threw them beyond the Zabergrund. At the head of this mass galloped the 5 squadrons of cuirassiers, then the 18 squadrons of Ziethen and Malachowski's hussars. These were followed by the 3 squadrons of the Gardes du Corps under the intrepid Wakenitz, plus 5 squadrons of Gendarmes, under Colonel von Schwerin. They were then followed by 25 squadrons of dragoons. The hussars and cuirassiers fell on the squadrons from Haugrewen, the others on the Russian battery, which they captured, then on the Russian infantry. In this amazing charge, unparalleled in the history of warfare to that time, of which we will see parallel examples at Eylau, Friedland and Borodino, the Russian infantrymen, surprised by the disorder following their first offensive, folded and broke. The storm had fallen initially on the 1st and 3rd Grenadiers. They showed, in this disaster, a marvelous intrepidity and coolness: one saw the soldiers, under the shock of the Prussian riders, reform in small groups, leaning on one another, and fighting the Prussian sabers with Russian bayonets:

> The infantry, attacked in their front, in their rear, and on their flanks, was massacred without mercy, but it is not astonishing that all its bravery was of no use to it and our right wing was thrown into such confusion and disorder that there was no front, no lines, and the soldiers, violently scattered in small groups, struggled against the Prussian cavalry, and fought less for victory than to sell their lives dearly. The Prussians themselves relate that they had never before seen such a spectacle. They saw everywhere the Russians, in small groups and little heaps, after having exhausted their last cartridges, as firm as rocks, defending themselves to the last drop of their blood. They said that it was easier to kill them than to put them to flight. Many pierced here and there continued to stand up and fight until they could no longer stand up. Others, having lost an arm or leg, already laying in the dust, seeking to defend themselves and to kill the enemy with the hand that remained to them. None of them asked for mercy.[22]

Catt, the confidat of the King, notes in almost the same terms this desperate resistance: "The Russians were lying in files; they kissed their guns, when they were sabered, and did not leave them... Wounded and laying on the ground, they still fired. One did not give them quarter!"

A cry of admiration also escaped the Prussian officer already quoted: "With regard to Russian grenadiers one can say that no soldier is comparable to them."

The stubborn resistance of the 1st and 3rd Grenadiers gave time for the regiments of Lubromirski, Ouvarov, and Leontif to reform. This saved the Russian right wing from total destruction. However, these three brigade commanders were wounded; many guns were lost; all the units were confused. The higher command still gave no signs of life. As a result, Fermor's second line remained motionless while the first was crushed. At least the second line's firm capacity stopped the Prussian offensive on that side. Seydlitz, whose soldiers had been in the saddle since 3:00 a.m., brought his cavalry back, behind Zorndorf to let it catch its breath.

---

[22] Bolotof, Vol 1, p, 788. His account had of value only this eyewitness account. He commits the gravest errors. Suddenly after this event he related the scene of disorder and drunkenness on the left wing. Beyond that, most of the accounts of the eyewitnesses, including that of Catt and Frederick II (*Histoire de la guerre de Sept ans*), are worth little more than that of Bolotof.

As a result, Frederick had to renounce completely destroying the Russian right. He was very affected by this half-success. Upon seeing his right wing coming back, he was heard to say in a strong voice: "Dass sich Gott im Himmel erbarme!"[23] But, the eyewitness Catt says: "Prince Maurice von Anhalt-Dessau, well aware of the misfortune, and who envisaged a continuation of it, perhaps not too content with the King's comment, took his hat, threw it into the air and, with a decided air and a very loud voice, shouted: "The King lives! The battle is won!" Then prince Maurice and General Bülow, seeing the poor bearing of their infantry, said: "Comrades! What you see there are Russian prisoners that one brings back. Let us go! Long Live the King! March!"

Frederick II, although he had not been able to finish with the Russian right wing, had decided to direct all his effort on their left wing, against which Kanitz's attack had failed.

By this time, the Prussian army occupied a line almost perpendicular to that which it had occupied at the time of the initial attack.

Against Brown's 27 battalions, Frederick could only present Dohna's 13 or 14 battalions and his second line. Having little faith in this infantry, mostly formed of "bearskins" from East Prussia, and wishing to let his cavalry rest a little, Frederick advanced his artillery, established a large battery very close to Zicher, and sought to resume the terrible cannonade of the morning against the Russian left wing.

Brown resolved to take the offensive, which was a bold resolution in light of the quality of his infantry. However, on this side, his cavalry was superior in number to that of Frederick, and it contained Demicou's cuirassiers. His artillery, which contained the Shuvalov howitzers, was also excellent. His first action was to try to take the Prussian battery by Zicher, and a battalion of the Prinz von Preussen Regiment, which defended it, with his cavalry. The battery and the battalion were disengaged by Schorlemer's cavalry. Then Brown had Demicou charge, whose armored horsemen exchanged blows with the lines of Dohna and Forcade's infantry.

The Prussian infantry could not hold. It was decimated by the Russian howitzers, terrified by the advancing phalanxes of bayonets, and charged by Demicou. It was seized by terror; it broke and fled even before the Russian infantry reached it. Vaguemeister[24] Ilia Semenov, of the Kazan Cuirassiers, captured a Prussian flag. A new charge by Schorlemer only served to delay the rout.

Frederick now found himself in great personal danger. Around him, his pages were killed and one of his aides-de-camp was taken prisoner.[25]

---

[23] "God have pity on us in Heaven." Account by Heinrich von Catt.
[24] Translator: A "vaguemeister" was a sergeant major in Russian cavalry.
[25] Bolotof.

Vainly, for the third time[26], seizing a flag[27], he attempted to bring the Silesians back to the battle.

The battle, on this side, was lost for Frederick; but two incidents saved the situation for the King. First Brown's infantry suddenly fell into disorder. The second was a second great charge by Seydlitz. As for the first, we will leave Bolotov to tell the story:

> The soldiers threw themselves on the casks of brandy belonging to the sulters that appeared before their eyes. They broke them open and drank the liquor like brutes, becoming so drunk they were uncontrollable. Their officers and leaders vainly broke the casks and poured the liquor on the ground. The soldiers threw themselves on their stomachs and licked the ground. A great number drank themselves to death. A large number died from the inflammation produced by this alcohol in their guts. Many, in their delirium, threw themselves on their own officers, cutting their throats. Others, insensible and enraged, wandered here and there, listening to nobody....[28]

It was at this time that Seydlitz reappeared with his 60 squadrons; that is to say, 8,000 sabers. He threw his cavalry on the Russian left wing, which was already in disorder. His cavalry advanced in the following order: first the cuirassiers, then the dragoons, the Gendarmes, the Gardes du Corps, and finally the hussars. He drove back their cavalry; then he charged their infantry. He threw it into such disorder that he could climb the Lyssia Heights. Everything he encountered there he threw into the Galgengrund. The Observation Corps suffered a complete disaster. Brown received 10-12 wounds, at the moment he was about to surrender[29], and was left half dead on the battlefield. His soldiers gathered him up and carried him to the ambulance. Tchernychef had two horses killed under him and he too was wounded. All the brigadier generals were wounded or captured. It was there that the Prussians captured many cannons and flags.

What saved the debris of Brown's corps and stopped Seydlitz's pursuit was the Galgengrund Ravine and the firm countenance of Fermor's on the far side of this natural ditch. The Prussian horsemen could only turn the Lyssia by the north, running on Quartschen, where they engaged Fermor's veteran soldiers, after which the Russian baggage was pillaged and the generals in

---

[26] Catt, p. 307
[27] Schaefer.
[28] Bolotof, p. 789. This episode, which Bolotof reports occurring on the right wing, actually occurred on the left wing and it was the troops of Brown's Corps, or the Observation Corps.
[29] *Journal d'Elmpt*, commander of engineers of the Observation Corps, cited by Masslovski.

the aid stations, Soltykov, Tchernychef, Tysenhausen, and others were taken prisoner.

As for the Prussian infantry, whose attack at this time could have decided the victory, it was impossible for them to cross the Galgengrund or even attack Quartschen. It is here that one places the anecdote regarding Frederick II[30], which is an interesting illustration of the military customs of the period. If Frederick had sought to excuse his infantry from an accusation of cowardice, it appears that he accuses them of an equally grave offense. "We sought on several occasions to advance the troops; but they returned after a short period of time, without our being able to understand the reason. It was because the Russian military treasury and all the equipment of their generals was in the bottom of the ravine. The troops, instead of pushing on, as they could have, amused themselves with pillage, and returned loaded with booty." Fermor's reports admit to a loss of 30,000 rubles from the army's treasury. However, it was not only the love of pillage that stopped the Prussian infantry, it was also the salvos of musketry and artillery from Fermor's regiments.

At 7:00 p.m., Frederick attempted once again to renew the combat, by Zicher and Wilkersdorf, with the troops of his second line. Vainly Rauther, the successor to Kanitz, Dohna, and Forcade, attempted to push forward their infantry. However, it was impossible to put them in order. Everyone fell back, even the Brandenburgers, with whom the King defended the land of his birth, the East Prussians, and the Silesians.

It was only then that one felt in the Russian Army that they had a commander-in-chief. Fermor ordered his troops to form a front along the side of Zicher. He crossed the Galgengrundand swept the Lyssia; but to go down to Zicher, it was necessary to expose to himself to an attack by the Prussians who remained in Quartschen. Consequently, until 8:30 p.m., the battle was nothing more than an artillery duel. The Russian Army held its positions on the heights; but it gave up part of the ground that it had occupied that morning, and it was there that many of its cannon, left without support and useless, were gathered up by the Prussians. The Prussian army had to camp in a dispersed manner, between Zorndorf and Wilkersdorf, abandoning part of its positions and consequently some of its artillery; but, during the night, they managed to recover all their guns.

The evening after the battle, Frederick II embraced Seydlitz: "I owe you this victory," he told him. Then, using a drum as a writing desk, he wrote letters to the Queen, his sister the Margrave of Bayreuth, his brother Henry, and the Minister of State Finckenstein. He announced that he had "defeated" the Russians. Only "the obscurity of the night had prevented pursuing them." He received at that same time, that "Fermor was going to surrender;" even that "he has surrendered; but I am not sure." The next day he wrote down the details.

---

[30] *Histoire de la Guerre de Sept ans.*

He swore to Prince Henry that he had not "always found all the assistance possible in the infantry."[31] He was more sincere and more expressive in his confidences to Catt:

> It was terrible, this day, and I have seen the moment where everything was going to hell. Everything would have gone there, my friend, without my brave Seydlitz and without the courage of my right wing and above all that of the regiment of my dear brother and Forcade. I tell you: they have saved the state and myself. Also, my gratitude will live as much in the glory that they acquired in this day, as my indignation against these regiments of Prussia, on which I counted, will never end. These idiots fled like old whores and give me instances of cruel sadness. These bastards suffered a panic, and one could not recall them. It is so cruel to depend on this collection of rogues."

In Catt's eyes, the King was more of a victor than he was. Everywhere the losses were significant. The Russians admitted to 10,886 dead and 12,788 wounded. The total loss was later reduced to 18,000 men, plus 2,882 prisoners. They also lost 100 cannon and 30 flags. The Prussian losses were about 12,000 men, 26 cannon, and no doubt a few flags.[32] Both armies had fought from 9:00 a.m. to 8:30 p.m. Many officers and generals had been wounded. The Prussian army lost the brave Ziethen. The situations of the two armies were equally critical, but that of the Russians was somewhat better. Even though they were cut off from their wagon train and their line of retreat, they strongly occupied the heights, while their adversaries were spread across the plain. In addition, they expected Rumyantsev, with 10,000-12,000 men, to arrive at any minute, while Frederick could not hope for any reinforcements.

In sum, in the battle, the risks were offset. The Russian artillery had almost always maintained its superiority over that of the Prussians. However, the number of guns that they had lost showed how badly organized and served the Russian guns were. It was, above all, the guns abandoned that had been gathered up by the Prussians on the battlefield that hurt. The Prussian cavalry had shown itself incomparable. However, that of Haugrewen and Demicou had revealed they were markedly better than in 1757. The two infantries had suffered equal disasters, but that of the Russians had forced the admiration of the Prussians, while that of the Prussians had been struck by a strange cowardice. It was easier, the next day, to bring the latter back to the battle. To suppose that Frederick would have had the advantage during the day of the

---

[31] *Politische Correspondenz*, Vol. XVII, p. 194 and following.

[32] These figures are accepted by Schaefer and modern historians, but Frederick, in the *Histoire de la guerre de Sept ans*, reduces it to 1,200 men and 20 cannon.

25th, nothing indicates that a second battle, given the second day, would have ended to his advantage. In any case, Fermor had not surrendered and did not consider surrendering.

Frederick II singularly anticipated this when, the following day, he wrote to the King of England: "We have defeated them after a 10-hour battle; they now flee into Poland." He spoke more truthfully, when, the same day, he wrote to Finckenstein: "It is even more necessary to raise the price of this victory... The King will the next day engage in a second battle with the Russians, who appear to want to try their luck against the victors.[33] One has never seen a more obstinate enemy."

In the morning of the 26th, Fermor had made dispositions that looked more offensive than suggestive of a retreat. He had drawn back all his army on the right and on the left, concentrating almost all of it on Mount Lyssia, moving his baggage from Quartschen to Zorndorf, and, as there was no water on the heights, descending finally on Zorndorf. The Prussians had withdrawn a bit to the north, the infantry on Zicher and the cavalry on Wilkersdorf. It appeared as if the Prussians wished to give the Russians free passage to their wagon train and the road to Bromberg; in a word, to prepare for the Russians a golden bridge. However, the Russians did not appear to execute the movement Frederick II favored and appeared to desire. Some cavalry, and Efermof's Cossacks, who moved to rejoin the Russian Army, moved to brave the Prussian cavalry as far as Wilkersdorf. Meanwhile behind a mobile screen of this cavalry, Fermor proceeded to establish formidable batteries. He then resumed bombarding the Prussian positions and, 1,200 paces from the Prussians, appeared ready to accept a second battle, as the King had written to Finckenstein.

Throughout the day of the 26th Frederick held firm. A peasant, ruined by the burning of Zorndorf, who came to the King to request a little place for his son was told by the King: "My poor good man, how can I give you a place when I am not sure I can hold my own?" To explain his inaction Frederick wrote in his *Memoirs*: "If we had had sufficient ammunition, we would have attacked then; we were obliged to content ourselves with a cannonade, which was not as heavy as one might have desired, because it was necessary to husband our powder." Before Catt he devoted himself to reflections showing that the words of Field Marshal Keith restored his spirit and he reproached himself for having scorned his enemy. He was caught up saying: "good infantry, bad generals"; or: "good infantry to hold firm, yet still a beginner in its evolutions; that cannot be moved." And he added, with sorrow for his "Prussians": "They held firm." Withdrawn into his tent, he read Lucrece's poem *Nature des choses* [*On the nature of things*]; however, he read it only with sadness in his heart. It was his *Bible* on dark days. "You see me with my Lucrece," he said to Catt; "that

---

[33]At this time Frederick believed they had no more than 11,000 men.

proves to you that I am grief-filled." At that moment, the following words escaped from him: "Tomorrow morning, we could well decamp from here and to take leave of those whom I could not destroy." Obviously, there was no longer a question of throwing the Russians into the Wartha, or of pursuing them, or of receiving Fermor's surrender, or of assisting in his "escape" to Poland. Frederick was no longer Caesar with his *Veni, vidi, vici*: Instead, he was a philosophical, melancholy person. After pondering affairs, it was Frederick, not Fermor who decided to retreat.

Fermor, on the part of the battlefield that he reoccupied, had a *Te Deum* sung with the inevitable salvoes of artillery and musketry.[34] He dispatched to the Tsarina, by Baron Rosen, his report, on the "victory."[35] He credited Frederick with 69,000 men; but we know that the King had only 32,000 men. After discussing the various Prussian attacks, he adds: "The army of Your Imperial Majesty did not lose an inch of ground.... It opposed bravely the enemy's attacks which could not gain the least bit of ground. He had, nonetheless, the advantage of the wind, which covered us with smoke, without counting the number of his soldiers.... The King, finally, was constrained to abandon the battlefield. We spent the night in sight of the enemy, and we arrayed ourselves [for battle] anew in the morning." Fermor acknowledged that he did not dare to attack and now only used his guns. The account of an offensive movement by the Prussian cavalry follows; but "the extraordinary fire of our artillery obliged them to escape." Fermor stated that his loss had been considerable, but that he had "taken a large number of prisoners, captured guns and flags, unquestionable trophies of our victory." He took a poke at Prince Charles and Saint-André, who had fled "because they did not expect a happy outcome of the action." (We know that Prince Charles and Saint-André amply responded in kind by disparaging him to their respective courts.) Fermor then explained why he had not attacked during the day of the 26th. The manpower of his regiments was greatly diminished, and Brown's corps was in worse condition than ever. All in all, there was at least as much truth in the report of the Russian Generalissimo as in most of the reports by Frederick II, which Finckenstein spread to the winds of European publicity.

The only error of the first was, while he fired victory salvos, he sent a parliamentarian to Dohna to propose an armistice of two or three days to him to bury the dead. This provoked the natural response that the King was the victor, and he would do this. Since both armies occupied part of the battlefield, this duty in truth should have been shared.

---

[34] Moreover, "the two armies both sang at the same time the *Te Deum* to the sound of cannon and musketry." The second account of Saint-André to the Viennese Court. The Archives of the Department of Foreign Affairs of France. Correspondence, *Russie*, Vol. LVII.

[35] I reference the translation, which is attached to a dispatch of L'Hôpital, in Vol. LVII, of the Correspondence, *Russie*. Archives of the Department of Foreign Affairs of France.

If we believe Bolotov, inhumane acts were committed by the Prussians: "The peasants were so furious against the Russians that, the Prussians having assembled a few thousand of them to dig ditches and bury the dead, these threw pell-mell into the ditches, not only the dead, but also the wounded who lay defenseless and buried them alive. Vainly these unfortunates cried out, imploring mercy and bleeding, exhausted their last breath and efforts attempting to climb out of the piles of the dead. Others simply shoveled dirt on them until they had given their last sigh." However, Bolotov is inclined to pathos, and we know that he was not present to witness this. The King did not show himself very concerned about the well-being of his prisoners, including Lieutenant General Tchernychef. They were taken to Küstrin, where they were thrown into the casemates. Glum, they complained about the conditions. Frederick responded that if they had not wanted it so, then they should not have burned the city.

It was not Frederick's prisoners who had the greatest concerns. It was those who persisted in occupying the Quartschen Heights, where, at any moment, Rumyantsev could rejoin them and from where there came such annoying cannon fire.

Catt tells us that Frederick was exposed to Russian canister fire and that Colonel von Schwerin, who accompanied him on this reconnaissance, said to him: "Do you not see that they're trying to shoot you?" – "I do not see it." – "Well, by all the devils, if you do not see it, do you not at least hear the balls that whistle around us and plough up the ground a few paces from your horse?"– "Nonsense, Mr. von Schwerin!"–"Well, remain here if you wish. As for me, I'm going to the regiment that I have the honor of commanding and I will put myself at its head."

On 27 August, Frederick II again wrote to Finckenstein "that he might still have a battle here, in case that General Rumyantsev moves to join this army." Nonetheless, as Rumyantsev never arrived, it was up to Frederick to fight or not.

Frederick II had taken up position to the south-west of Zorndorf, approximately three kilometers from the suburbs of Küstrin. Perhaps he had the idea of affecting his retreat by the city's bridges if Fermor did not decide to retreat. But, on 27 August, Fermor, circumventing Zorndorf by the south, advanced deliberately on Gross-Kamin, where the Prussians had not even disturbed his wagenburg. He could have withdrawn to the north, since Frederick had fallen back to the southwest; and, if he had been in a mood "to flee," he would not have moved in the direction of the Prussians. He marched in two columns, and like the interval between them, his head and rear, were closed by an advance guard and a rearguard, the whole forming a great oblong square. In the center, Fermor had placed carriages full of casualties: the guns that had lost their limbers were drawn by hand by the infantry. This was a poor formation from which to push back a serious attack; because each of the two columns, separated from the other by all these impedimenta, could not have moved to the other's assistance. The temptation to attack it was all the more natural as after having passed almost within musket range of the position occupied by Frederick II, the great Russian square was going to present its right flank to him, then oppose him with a simple rearguard, and finally it would march, having the Wartha marshes on its right, where any attack would drive it. However, Frederick resisted temptation and watched the imposing movement of the Russian Army with crossed arms. Instead of pursuing it, he rather had it escorted off the battlefield. Those of his hussars who moved too close to Fermor's rearguard were received with cannon shots. When the Prussian infantry moved to support them, they found the Russians ready to cross bayonets.

This day Frederick could announce to Finckenstein "things here take a better turn." Rumyantsev had abandoned his station at Schwedt and was withdrawing on Landsberg, where he was going to join the great Russian army. On the 29th, Frederick II received news that the Austrian army (Laudon) was approaching, which decided him to prepare his own retirement. He gave himself the pleasure of announcing to the Margrave of Bayreuth that he had killed in this battle 30,000 Russians.[36] With Catt, he still allowed himself to rant against the enemy: "I have nothing today of my barbarians, but their sick and poor baggage. Weren't you informed of how they damaged this poor village? ... If Voltaire saw all this, as he would exclaim: 'Ah! Barbarians! Ah! Brigands! how inhuman you are! How can you hope to inherit the Kingdom of the skies?'" In addition, he said: "Shouldn't the princes who use such troops redden with shame? They are guilty and responsible in front of God for all the horrors that they commit." But finally, he did not launch out in pursuit of these "incendiaries" and was satisfied to gather up on their heels some bits of their "poor baggage."

While Fermor joined Rumyantsev's division in Landsberg, Frederick, as of 2 September, again took the road from Küstrin, then that to Silesia. The Zorndorf campaign was finished.

This is the moment to determine who was victorious at Zorndorf, because now all the direct consequences of the 25th are in front of our eyes. In general, the winner can be defined as follows: he who obtained by the battle the results that he proposed to obtain by engaging in the battle. However, Frederick II proposed to capture the Russian position and "to throw them into the Wartha," which he failed to do. Frederick had initially placed himself in the south, then east of the heights occupied by the Russians, to turn around them like a lion, *quaerens quem devoret* [seeking whom he may devour], he could not dislodge them. After having occupied Mount Lyssia, he saw himself

---

[36] *Politische Correspondenz*, Vol. XVII, p. 199, 30 August 1758.

thrown into the plain. Throughout the 26th, he suffered the provocations of their cavalry and the inconvenient fire from their batteries, without making an effort to drive them out. On the 27th, it was he who withdrew on Tamsel, leaving to the Russians their wagenburg and their line of retreat; and it was the Russians who almost arrived at Tamsel, then marching under the Prussians' beard, and forming a front between Tamsel and Gross-Kamin, as if to offer to them a battle for the third time. If they had persisted in occupying their initial positions, we would have seen it, but it was Frederick who resigned himself to decamping. When, subsequently, he only had in front of him their rearguard, with this double column encumbered with wagons loaded with wounded and guns drawn by hand, moving along the dangerous banks of the Wartha, he had not attempted an aggressive pursuit. Frederick restricted himself to escorting them as far as Blumberg and capturing some straggling wagons.

Undoubtedly Fermor failed in his campaign plan, which was to take Küstrin; but one can also state that Frederick failed in his to destroy the Russians. As a consequence, resulting from the battle that occurred in the following days, one can assign to the battle the disintegration of Brown's Observation Corps. Its destruction and the grave losses suffered by Fermor's corps had prevented the Generalissimo from attempting some great blow in an autumn campaign. However, Frederick's losses had a no less significant impact, as on 14 October, he encountered the Austrians at Hochkirch and he found himself lacking the "devils from Silesia," who had died at Zorndorf. One can consider his defeat as the epilogue of the butchery of 25 August.

The battle of Zorndorf, considered in itself and in its consequences, was, therefore, for the Prussians one of those where patriotism consoled them by calling it "undecided." The toast made a century and a half later by Kaiser Wilhelm II to the "Victors of Zorndorf" was revisionist.[37]

---

[37]Translator: The author makes the assumption that Frederick sought to destroy the Russian army and that was his only goal. Surely it would have been highly desirable to achieve it, but then again, the Russians were threatening the Prussian heartland before the battle of Zorndorf and after it they were back in Poland. Surrounded on all sides; the French to the west, the Swedes in the north, the Austrians to the south, and the Russians to the east, Frederick constantly shuttled across his country driving back one invading army after another. Every time he drove back one enemy he preserved his country, his army, and his throne. If destroying the Russians was desirable, keeping the Russians out of the Prussian heartland was critical and, in this Frederick, succeeded. Though the author seems to contend that Frederick lost this battle, I would argue that the Prussian strategic goal of the battle was achieved.

On the other hand, Fermor's objective was to take Küstrin and penetrate further into Prussia. In this he obviously failed.

Senior Officer of the Russian Guard Cuirassier Regiment

CHAPTER IX

THE RUSSIANS AFTER ZORNDORF

It is not in the 1758 campaign that Fermor showed himself a great captain. He did not dare to attack and destroy Dohna before he could be joined by Frederick II. He spread his forces on the right bank of the Oder, from Küstrin to Schwedt. It did not appear to him that this dispersion was too great, since it had not stopped pushing Rumyantsev further to the north, when he had himself turned back, it was the repeated orders of the Generalissimo that stopped him at Schwedt. Had Rumyantsev moved to Zorndorf he would have assured a complete and indisputable victory and the total destruction of Frederick II. When Fermor raised the siege of Küstrin and took position south of Zorndorf, he did nothing to seriously obstruct the passage of the Prussians over the Mietzel. As he had deprived himself, at the same time as he had dispatched Rumyantsev, of almost all of his light cavalry he could not detect Frederick II's approach and allowed himself to be surprised on the battlefield. He could not deploy his artillery. It was crowded on his left and his right. Two things, however, must be praised: first the choice of heights from which he could not be dislodged, and then for the rapid change of facing by which he could face the Prussians on the south side.

During the battle, almost from the beginning, the Generalissimo disappeared. At no time did a single hand control the Russian side of the battle. As a result the organized and bold attacks, initially with the right wing, then with the left wing, ended in a disaster for the infantry. This is the source of the immobility of the left wing while the right wing was engaged in bloody combat, and it produced the inertia of the second line on right while the first was crushed. It was only after the cruel tests of the day that the talents of the tactician suddenly appeared as Fermor was almost defeated. The uncertainty and timidity of the 25th were followed by prompt decisions, a firm attitude, and the bold offensives of the 26th, and finally the bold and imposing triumphal withdrawal of the Russians on the 27th.

For all these reasons, even though Frederick II had ranked him among the "bad generals," Fermor deserves a position in history between Apraxine, the victor of Gross Jägersdorf and Saltykov, the victor of Kunersdorf. An indecisive battle, defeat or victory, Zorndorf is one of those names that an army can inscribe in golden letters on the flags of its regiments.

The scenes of disorder, pillage, and drunkenness, which compromised the success can only be assigned to a few battalions of a corps that was born disorganized. However, during the battle the Russian infantryman showed the qualities of marvelous endurance, tenacity, courage, and by turns stoicism and impetuosity. The cavalry, not very numerous, showed itself enterprising and brave. The artillery, despite the vices of its organization, maintained its superiority over that of the Prussians and even over that of all the European armies of this period.

The army, for which Frederick II had had such contempt, now showed him that it was a force with which to be reckoned.

> The conceited King was seized with terror upon seeing the intrepidity, the steadfast solidity with which our infantry fought. The Prussians, in their accounts wrote that it was easier to kill our soldiers than to put them to flight; that the soldiers, sure their guns or on the brandy barrels, had to be killed, and that to run them through was not enough to cut them down. In a word, all the Prussians of this time started to think differently about our troops and ceased considering our soldiers as the pigs that they did before.

The Tsarina's government did not give this army the recognition it merited. In his report of the 26th, Fermor had made the following derogatory statement: "If the soldiers had always obeyed their officers and if they had not drunk more than a cup of brandy that one had ordered for them to encourage them, it would have been possible to gain as complete a victory as could have been desired." This was an illusion to the unfortunate incident on the left wing. The Conference wished to have a clarification of these enigmatic lines. What were the acts of indiscipline? What brandy was given out? Fermor had to provide additional information. He then even imputed on them undisciplined plundering of the military treasury. The result of this denunciation was a ruling by the Tsarina against the army in the harshest terms, not distinguishing between the various units, which was most unjust. The ruling of 13 September, addressed to "our beloved army, regular as well as irregular," after a rather short praise for the "bravery and intrepid courage that it had shown in the battle," continued in these terms:

> But, moreover, to Our great sorrow and ire, We learned that, even at the time where the victory was entirely gained on our side, and where the overcome enemy fled in the greatest disorder, some undisciplined soldiers, remaining unpunished, but worthy of capital punishment, yelled to stop the victory and to cause a retreat; then, that the number of these undisciplined increased and that while moving back they involved in their escape many of those who still held firmly; that they disobeyed the chiefs established by Us

under the terms of the authority that We have received from God; that they were devoted to an abominable drunkenness, at the moment when their duty, their oath, the love of the fatherland, obliged them to pour their blood. Large and legitimate is Our ire when We think only of this indiscipline; larger still it becomes when We think of all the pernicious continuation of this misconduct, on which We do not want more to hear. Today, undoubtedly, each soldier understands, with the remorse of his conscience, that if each one had done his duty and his station had not been deserted, the enemy, who otherwise was defeated, would have been completely destroyed; that there would be no more to fear of new attacks by him nor to overcome new resistance; that nothing would have remained but to collect, in all peace and safety, the fruits of the victory. It is with horror and fear that everyone is reduced to thinking that the great losses suffered by our army were not inflicted on it by the enemy, but because of this indiscipline, by fire that the runaways directed on those who remained at their station, and who with a steadfast firmness covered their shameful escape and ensured victory, and who deserved to be used forever as glorious an example of fidelity to their sovereign, to their fatherland, and not as a target for a fusillade that was disordered and worthy of punishment...

I am forced to shorten this strange piece of literature, baroque, diffuse and streaked, where the *conceitti* [concepts] alternate with the unction of an episcopal mandate. The scribe Dmitri Volkov could gaze at himself there and the generals in the anteroom could take great delight in watching. But one can imagine the bewilderment into which the Cossacks and grenadiers were plunged by the publication of this homily of interminable, inextricable, and bombastic sentences, filled with terms that were unintelligible to them. When one read it to these rough soldiers, they surely listened, stupefied, to the monotonous chant of the Chancellery which unceasingly droned on using phrases like "our maternal affliction," "the just and inevitable punishment of God," "divine blessing and divine assistance," and "the eternal crown which, in the Kingdom of Heaven, girds the face of those which showed a infrangible fidelity." I do not ask the reader, to compare Elisabeth's order of the day to bulletins of Napoleon to his Grande Armée. But during the epoch of Frederick II the style of the Russian Chancellery was such that nothing proves better Elisabeth's Russia still had much ground to cover before it could merit being called European. Though the Russian armies were able to engage those of Frederick II on an equal basis, Elisabeth's records and

Elisabeth herself were on the intellectual level and literary style were still Byzantine.

Fermor, who had culture, had to shrug his shoulders upon receiving the ruling. However, as he was a courtier, he directed that one "draw up exact copies; that a copy be given to each company; that each battalion and squadron commander, on the days fixed by the report, read it [to the soldiers], and that the soldiers better understand it, to comment on it themselves; because thus the will of the sovereign be achieved and those who had been guilty of excesses and indiscipline would feel the remorse of their consciences, and, recognizing and deploring their crime, be corrected." This idiotic prose was thus put at the order of the day of the army, and twice per week, was read, and interpreted, with accompanying notes to all the companies.

Masslovski was indignant that Fermor did not feel the affront that resulted from this for his soldiers; that he did not better defend their honor; that he, if courteous to the small, landed proprietors and the academics of Königsberg, was this discourteous to the heroes of Zorndorf. This was further aggravated by these heavy instructions of the unjust reproach which St. Petersburg dropped on them. Masslovski points out the "unsympathetic" side of Fermor's character. He quickly denounces Fermor as a German commanding a Russian army. He seems to have forgotten that Volkov, the probable author of this proclamation, the ministers and the generals who signed it, and the empress who had approved it, were also Germans!

That which most seriously scandalized the Conference was the disappearance of the army's treasury, given up, as we saw, in a ravine on the battlefield. It had contained some 30,000 rubles. We saw Frederick II denouncing his own soldiers for having stuffed their pockets. The Conference and Fermor accused the Russian soldiers of that deed. On an order apparently coming from St. Petersburg, the Generalissimo had them all searched, even those of Rumyantsev 's corps, which had not participated in the battle, and which had joined the army only at Landsberg. One has never seen a government humiliate the honor of its soldiers or the dignity of its citizens in this manner.

It seemed that when compared to some battered alcohol barrels and a few packages of paper money that disappeared, the marvelous resistance of the infantry of Lubomirski, Ouvarov, and Leontiev, the exploits of the Demicou and Haugrewen's horsemen, the glory acquired by the artillery, the bravery, and the devotion of so many officers, and so much blood spilled for the glory of the Russian army, were of no value.

After this had been so cruelly humiliated no one thought to compensate it. Fermor made a limited excuse for his absence or his escape at the most critical moment of the battle when he was unable to indicate the regiments or the men who had best deserved the praise of Russia. He recommended only those who had contributed with him (with Fermor when he had reappeared on the battlefield) to get the army into order and to reform the ranks. Generals Mordvinof, Fast, Iazykov, Demicou, Dietz, and General of Artillery Nottelfeld were praised. Only Prince Lubomirski intervened to request a decoration for Brandt, the colonel of the heroic 3rd Grenadiers. There was no question of a *donativum* [gift] for the regiments that had fought the best; all the army seemed wrapped in the demerit and the disgrace of the Observation Corps; one treated it like a vanquished army, and one which had been overcome by its bad behavior.

By this injustice or this meanness, the St. Petersburg Court accredited Frederick II's account of the battle, namely it was the Prussians who had been victorious at Zorndorf. The battlefield was at Fürstenfelde, as one said in the European chancelleries, though the town of Fürstenfelde is north of Mietzel, 7 kilometers from the battlefield.

As the military attaché Saint-André, states in his reports to his court, he believed himself obliged to describe the "battle of Fürstenfelde," as a Russian defeat though he only watched it from afar, probably from Fürstenfelde. It was the same for the ambassador from France, the Marquis de l'Hôpital. He confirms "the valor that the Russian troops showed," "the great resistance that they presented to the King of Prussia" and who "had to make him pay dearly for his victory;" but finally he gives the victory to Frederick II. Bernis, in his answer to l'Hôpital, expressed the hope that the Tsarina in will not be discouraged: "It is known that the fate of arms swings daily, all the powers engaged in the current war successively had triumphs and failures."

Elizabeth showed, in effect, the same firmness and the same ardor for the war. Doctor Poissonier finally assured himself of the state of her health and sent to Versailles reassuring letters. The Young Court did not disarm itself, but it was reduced to impotence.

It remained to be seen what profit Generalissimo Fermor would draw from the absence of Frederick II, as he was then quite occupied with Laudon. On 30 September, we find the Russian Army concentrated in Stargard. They had returned to the idea of an offensive in Pomerania, a completely secondary field of operations, where success would be limited to making a junction with the Swedes. The army remained in Stargard until 18 October. The Conference pressed Fermor to attack Dohna and to destroy him. Fermor claimed that he did not know where the Prussian general was and that he lacked cannonballs. Dohna himself was no better informed of the location of the Russians and Cossack raids prevented him from collecting any information. It was only on 27 September that he reappeared in Mietzel and occupied Neudamm; the 29th, he was in Soldin; 2 October, he went from Lippehne to Pyritz. During the morning of the 3rd he found himself facing entrenchments at Passkurga and began erecting his own entrenchments that he could finish owing to morning fog. When the fog cleared the two trench lines began firing on each other.

At 9:00 a.m., Dohna formed two attack columns and launched them against Rumyantsev's position. After a rather sharp combat, he was pushed back and pursued to Pyritz by Efremof, Krasnochtchokov and Souline's Cossacks.

During this time, a corps of 6,000 Russians, under General Palmenbach, arrived by sea from Pillau to Kolberg, beginning a siege of that fortress. Important as a seaport, cutting the communications between the Vistula and the Oder, it prevented the Russians from saying that they were masters of Prussian Pomerania. Kolberg, in 1807, would resist Napoleon's soldiers, under the command of Loison and Mortier, for 35 days.

In 1758, the place was already strong by its situation and its works. Palmenbach, despite the reinforcements brought by Stoffeln and the opening of the trenches, raised the siege during the night of 28/29 October. On 8 November, he rejoined Fermor at Tempelburg.

Fermor, despite the demands of Kaunitz who had constantly demanded the dispatch of 30,000 Russians into Silesia, considered the campaign as ended. He had reorganized his army and replaced some of his lieutenants wounded or taken at Zorndorf. The 1st Corps was now commanded by Frolov-Bagreev, the 2nd by Riazanov, the 3rd by Rumyantsev, and the Observation Corps, somewhat reconstituted by Golitzyn. Frolov-Bagreev had to march on Marienwerder, Riazanov on Kulm, Rumyantsev also on Marienwerder, and Golitzyn on Thorn. They decided to shift Russian operations to the lower Vistula. On 26 November, the Russians recrossed the Vistula. They then established themselves in winter quarters.

The Russians were spread around Elbing, Dirschau, Marienburg, Heiligenbeil, Braunsberg, Graudentz, Kulm, and Marienwerder and in East Prussia. The light cavalry was charged with covering the army, to scout, and to observe Posnania and Posen. Much too in front of their lines of outposts, the Russians had their magazines at Posen, Nakel, Friedland, Vronki, Oberjitsi, Rogojno, Khodjewo, etc. Their magazines, especially those at Nakel and Posen, were not sufficiently protected. In the winter one had to protect them from the incursions from the Prussian cavalry, under Wobersnow.

The Russians were very concerned for East Prussian. The Conference decided that, if they were obliged to evacuate this province, the army, in retiring, would leave nothing intact, everything would be burned or destroyed; that the men of military age would be taken away, in order that the King of Prussia could not take them into his army. Though well understood, this was nothing but a threat, an intimidation by the King of Prussia and his enterprising generals, because the order was given to distribute these decisions to the Prussian advance posts.

Fermor occupied himself with replacing the vacancies in his army that resulted from the Zorndorf campaign. He requested St. Petersburg send him 422 officers, 23,000 recruits, and 6,000 horses.

After promoting the noble non-commissioned officers of the Guard, to the young gentlemen who were unemployed, and the Corps of Cadets, only part of the necessary officers could be found. The recruits did not start reaching the army until the end of 1759. However, Fermor did receive 5,664 horses, including 3,484 pack animals.

Fermor preoccupied himself with reforming his artillery. He had lost 100 cannons at Zorndorf, but for the most part they were regimental guns. It was decided to rebuild the regimental guns to a total of 208 guns, and that of the field artillery to 260 guns, and to replace, above all, the missing guns with howitzers. He received 181 regimental guns and 105 field guns. The principal source of this failure to meet the desired goal was the number of specialized troops charged with serving and protecting these guns. It was decided to form three regiments of artillery, but for the next campaign, they only existed on paper.

In St. Petersburg, they were very dissatisfied with Fermor. He wanted to guarantee to the province of East Prussia wider privileges than those it had enjoyed under her kings; in addition, he was highly criticized by Saint-André and Prince Charles of Saxony. He was reproached for not having reached any of his goals that had been proposed to him for this campaign, neither in Silesia, nor in Pomerania, nor in Brandenburg. His finances were criticized. His enemies again began to find fault in that a German Lutheran commanded the army of the Orthodox Tsarina. He was replaced in spring of 1759 by an old stock Russian, Saltykov.[38]

Other changes had occurred in the world. The poor success of the campaign, the French defeats at Minden and Crefeld (defeats followed by success at Sandershausen and Lutternberg), the loss of Ohio, Acadia, and Chandernagor, the little results from the Austrian victory at Hochkirch, and the lack of Swedish co-operation, had thrown the germs of dissolution into to anti-Prussian coalition. The Russians were dissatisfied with the Austrians who had not helped them, the Austrians were dissatisfied with the French who were too often defeated. It was the Russians who endeavored to justify the efforts of the Versailles Court to that of Vienna. Vorontsov pointed out that after all the French defeats they were still committed to persist in the war. However, France's allies had begun to be suspicious of Cardinal de Berni, who they suspected of thinking of peace. On 13 December 1758, he fell from favor and was replaced by the Duke de Choiseul. The Duke hastened to give a new impulse to the war and diplomacy. On 30 December 1758, he signed, with Austria, the third Treaty of Versailles, which Russia signed on 7 March 1760.

Europe, united against Frederick II, was going to try a new and general effort.

---

[38]Translator: It is interesting to note that in 1812 Barclay de Tolly, of Scottish extraction, was criticized for his not being Russian, on top of his failure to stop Bonaparte's invading army. He was then replaced by Kutusov, who was seen as a "true" Russian.

CHAPTER X

THE BATTLE OF PALTZIG (OR KAI OR ZÜLLICHAU)
28 JULY 1759.

In the spring of 1759, Daun, the Austrian Generalissimo, expressed the best intentions to undertake an energetic offensive. This attitude, rather new in him, had initially an excellent moral effect on the French and Russians. It surely contributed to hastening Fermor's return to his army. After a rather long sojourn in St Petersburg, where he justified and defended himself, he also prepared his instructions for the 1759 campaign, reappearing at his general headquarters, on the Vistula, at Thorn, on 26 March.

His light cavalry, which stood before the river, covering the Russian winter quarters, now became more active and bolder. Colonel Orlov, with a pulk of Cossacks, had executed a raid as far as Neu-Stettin, in Prussian Pomerania, which was an enormous distance from the line of Russian outposts. Preceding his pulk with 200 Cossacks, it had charged a picket of Prussian hussars, then had run up against the squadron, and was then obliged to fall back on Orlov's main body. During his retreat he was obliged to cross through a village, but the peasants had closed the village gates to them. Then, with part of his forces, he charged the Prussians who pursued him. He ordered the rest of his force to break in the doors and saber the villagers, who were armed with clubs and pitchforks. In this manner the Cossacks could affect their retreat, but they had lost 14 killed and many prisoners. Among those was the bold colonel, whose horse had been cut down (1 April 1759).

This incident shined a light on the prodigious audacity of the Cossack scouts, but also on the hostility of the rural population in the Prussian provinces. Fermor thought he should address a proclamation to the inhabitants of Pomerania and Brandenburg: "If they permitted themselves in the future to arm themselves, in whatever fashion, against the troops of Her Imperial Majesty, to block their successes, in a word, to show themselves non-submissive, conforming to the laws of war and without mercy, they shall be put to the sword and fire. Those, who in contrast, submit and continue to attend in their homes to their habitual work, shall be assured of Imperial clemency and protection. The most rigorous discipline shall be maintained among [the Russian] troops." This proclamation was communicated to the diplomatic agents of Russia to the various imperial courts, in order that they would be in a position to "dissipate the slanderous rumors that might arise, spread by the enemy and to give them the means to refute them." The Conference enjoined them, in its turn, that "if some village permits itself a parallel insolence, all the inhabitants will be taken with their wives and children, sent to Königsberg, and then sent on to Riga and Revel."[39]

However, the marvelous offensive that Daun had promised did not occur. He did not leave his cantonments during the months of February and March, leaving Frederick to ransom the territories of Saxony and the neighboring states, laying a contribution of 300,000 florins on Erfurt, 25,000 on Fulda and Hirschfeld, and even threatening the Free City of Frankfurt, occupied by the French. Prince Henry launched an enterprise against the Austrian magazines in Bohemia. Prince Ferdinand von Braunschweig attacked the French at Bergen and defeated them on 13 April.

The impunity of the Prussians was all the more shocking as the Coalition joined together far more forces than those of Frederick II. There were 125,000 French, divided in two masses, under Contades and Soubise; 45,000 men from Austria or the Circles of the Empire in Franconia and by Cassel; 16,000 Swedes in the fortress at Stralsund and on Rugen Island; and 155,000 Austrians with Daun. The Coalition had, not including the Russian army, a total of 400,000 soldiers. Frederick II could oppose them with only 225,000: that is, 70,000 with Ferdinand von Braunschweig; 37,000, with Prince Henry, in Glogau and Breslau; and 48,000, under Frederick's direct command, between Landshut and Schweidnitz; 9,000, with Dohna, in Pomerania; and the remainder in the fortresses. Three years of constant war had decimated and exhausted the Prussian armies. They had lost their best elements and some of their bravest leaders. Frederick II was deprived of his income and his recruits in his possessions along the Rhine and in Westphalia, in East Prussia, and in parts of Pomerania.

Frederick hoped to hold all his enemies, to contain the Swedes and the Russians with Dohna; the French and the army of the Circles with Ferdinand; to worry Bohemia with Henry, to throw a reinforced Fouqué into Moravia, and with his 48,000 men, Frederick planned to occupy Daun's 155,000 men. At least these were the intentions that Daun provoked in him, because of Daun's timorous inaction, to whom he gave the name of the tactician Fabius Cunctator.

Which role was the Russian army going to play on this vast chessboard? This was the object of many discussions: in Vienna, between Kanitz and the ambassador of Russia; in St Petersburg, between Esterhazy and Chancellor Vorontsov, the Conference, and the General Tillier; at the Austrian general headquarters, between Daun and Springer, Russian military attaché. On 16 March, Tillier declared to the Conference that, since the Russians refused to detach 30,000 men in Silesia, his government renounced it; if they proposed to operate in Pomerania or Brandenburg, Daun would try to help them there by threatening the King of Prussia's rear, "but without any hope of success." The Conference assured that the Russian army would advance on the Oder, either

---

[39] Masslovski, Vol. II, p. 405 and following.

towards Frankfurt, or towards Lower-Silesia.

From this exchange of ideas was born the 3 April campaign plan. It was agreed that the Russian army would be raised to 100,000 men, "if not more": 10,000 would remain on the Lower Vistula and Russia would try to reinforce them with 20,000 recruits; the 90,000 others would affect a junction with the Austrians; this junction would take place around 6 July. Thus, the meeting of the two large Russian and Austrian armies was ordered, in theory. Even its date was fixed.

Another plan was ordered by the Conference and was signed in Peterhof, on 14 June, by Elisabeth. Fermor's army was to cross the Oder at Korolath, but he would not advance with more than 60 or 75 versts on the other bank. If the point at Korolath were not acceptable to Daun, one would choose Krossen. The junction completed, Fermor would not be subordinated to Daun, but he was "to listen to his councils" and "not to move away from what he could ask," understanding that the great capacities of the Austrian Generalissimo "were proven by experience." In the event of a victory over the enemy, of a victory that would not be decisive, Fermor would be careful; he would avoid "risking the integrity of his army for Austrian interests." He would not go further and would try to persuade Daun to be satisfied with taking Glogau, Liegnitz, Krossen, Frankfurt-am-Oder or Schweidnitz. Only in the case of a decisive victory would Fermor have the right "to give to the operations all possible support." If one could carry out the junction neither at Korolath nor at Krossen, Fermor was to seek another point upstream on the Oder, and if needs be, as far as Breslau, but after having destroyed the Frankfurt Canal, levying contributions on the cities, and making a raid on Berlin, in a word, was to seek to appropriate all the resources of Brandenburg. If Fermor were exposed to fight alone against the Prussians, he was to accept battle only if he had a "well-marked superiority of forces." If, on the contrary, Frederick II threw himself, with all his army, on Daun, and it would not take more than two marches to join him, Fermor was to advance and to complete his victory, or to attack the victorious Prussians. In the latter case, it was necessary that it was two days later at the latest (no doubt because a longer delay would have made it possible for the King to restore his army). The same if the Russians were defeated and that Daun was not with more than two marches away, Fermor was required to attack the Prussians. One sees that the Conference endeavored to anticipate everything, on all possible assumptions, and to the least detail. Lastly, what shows that the Conference did not have complete faith in its allies, is that it was strongly recommended to Fermor that he take care that "the Austrians did not make a separate peace" with the common enemy.

In April, Fermor was at Marienwerder, where his main body was to cross the Vistula. To the degree that his regiments arrived there, he passed them in review. Then when all the army was assembled, it moved in the direction of

Posen, where it was to concentrate.

The days of the supreme command were numbered for Fermor. He had not succeeded, during his stay in St. Petersburg, in dissipating all the biases against him. It was always the same complaints: he had granted to East Prussia such privileges as were superior to those of similar Russian provinces; he had enriched himself by the passage of the Russian armies and the movements of supplies, while all the charges for the war fell on the Russian lands; he had witnessed too much sympathy for the Germans; and finally, there were many irregularities in his accounting.

To replace him, the Court threw their eyes on a Generalissimo who, by race and religion, was a true Russian. It was Count Peter Semenovitch Saltykov.

He was probably about 60 years of age, because he was one of the 20 young men that Peter the Great had, in 1717, sent to France as students at the School of the Gardes-Marine. He had remained in Europe for 20 years. We find him in favor at the time of Anna Ivanova. He had family ties with the Empress. This favor can be one of the reasons of the type of lapse of memory into which he had fallen under the reign of Elisabeth. Though he had studied to be a sailor, he was relegated to the command of the Ukrainian *landmiliz*, in Kharkof. He had appeared at the head of either a fleet or an army; he owed his rank to his seniority in the grade of General-in-Chief. Why was he chosen to succeed Fermor, who, junior in rank had been initially chosen in preference to him? The Vienna Court would have praised his capacities then he was ignored in Russia. The German testimony was decisive in favor of the Russian general who they intended to replace the German. The taste of the court had nothing to do with this choice. It was Soltykov who asserted himself. Masslovski compared his situation with that of Kutusov who, in 1812, was *persona non grata*, but to whom Alexander I was obliged to entrust the post of commander-in-chief.

The great difference between Soltykov in 1759 and Kutusov in 1812 was that the former had no popularity in the army. He was almost unknown. His nomination was a surprise. Bolotov, who pushed paperwork in the bureau of the Governor General at Königsberg, gives a good idea of the impression of the young officers:

> All were astonished upon hearing of this new commander, because, previously assigned to the Ukrainian *Landmiliz*, almost nobody knew him. There had never been great discussion of his merits. Those who had had the opportunity to meet him could not answer the questions asked about him beyond that he was a good man, but an old man who was a bit simple (*prosten'koï*), without instruction or particular merits,

and who had not yet been characterized by any important act.

Bolotov and his comrades in the chancellery did not crowd into the streets when one announced Soltykov's arrival at Königsberg:

You cannot imagine the curiosity with which we awaited him, with what particular feelings we looked at him when he walked on foot in our city. He was a grey old man, small, unpresuming, dressed in the kaftan of the *landmiliz*, without any badge or any luxury. He walked in the street in the company of only two or three men. Accustomed as we were with ostentation and the magnificence of the Generalissimo, this was quite astonishing and strange to us. We could not understand how, with this so simple old man and, according to appearances, if unimportant, one was able to entrust him with the command of the great army that was ours, and how he could hope to oppose an adversary as the King of Prussia, who astonished Europe by his bravery, his heroism, his promptitude and his military engineering. He had on us the effect of a poor small hen (*kourotchka*). Nobody dared, I do not say "to hope," but only to imagine that he could do anything that was great, his exterior and behavior promised little. Our general would have liked, according to custom, to give a great feast in his honor. Yet he contented himself with the simplest hospitality and food. It was for this reason that his passage through our city was so little noticed and made little noise; and, though he remained with us for two days and he walked on foot through almost all of the streets, the major part of the city did not even know that he was in its walls. He left with no more brilliance than when he came. At least he was accompanied by our enthusiastic wishes that he would be more successful than Fermor; but our hearts were sad and one did not cherish the least hope.[40]

Soltykov had taken no action to provoke his elevation to this post; some lines of the correspondence of Shuvalov with Vorontsov even give one to think that he had to be requested and encouraged to accept it: "I hope," wrote Shuvalov, "that a word from Your Excellency for General Soltykov will be enough to make him content."[41]

The steps taken with regard to Fermor were couched in the terms that were most honorable for him. He was told, "Count Soltykov was senior to

[40] Bolotof, Vol. I, p. 872.
[41] *Archives of Vorontsof*, Vol VI, p. 292. Dated 16 July 1759.

him, so that it naturally belonged to him, the right to take command of the whole army." – "We are persuaded," one later said to the Empress, "that you will continue your service no less." He was therefore offered the command of the 1st Corps (Frolof-Bagreef, who command and then received another job). Fermor did himself great honor by accepting a lower situation in the army that he had earlier commanded. He gave his thanks in a manner we can find quite humble, but which was that of the country and the time, and which he employed with Elisabeth and the Grand Duchess Catherine:[42]

> Very gracious Sovereign, I am the humblest slave of Your Majesty; I fall to Your Imperial feet, and I take the boldness to attest that I will be always subjected to Your very high will, that not only will I continue with the greatest zeal my very humble service, but I will help Count Soltykov, by my actions and council, with all the intelligence which I have. I do not doubt that this general, as my superior, shall not return testimony from there and that I do not deserve his approval.

The court was very happy with these good dispositions: Soltykov was still unknown, and Fermor was always "the skillful Fermor." Chancellor Vorontsov, by a letter dated 14 July, acted quickly to inform Soltykov of the happy news:

> One can only hope for victory over the enemy and envisage all successes which will result from this, since the agreement between Your Excellency and Count Fermor begins so happily: it will not change with time, but on the contrary will be strengthened by a mutual trust and a cordial collaboration... The harmony between the chiefs, united with the well-known heroism and the intrepidity of your troops, gives us the best and the joyous hope that the present campaign will be, if not decisive, at least completely ruinous for the King of Prussia, with the greatest glory for both your names, of the army and the Russian nation. All of Europe awaits Her Imperial Majesty, our very gracious sovereign, with the achievement of a work worthy of an immortal glory: the re-establishment and strengthening of a peace that is as sure as it is glorious.

The new Generalissimo, supported by Fermor's "actions and council," directed by the wisdom of the Conference, could not fail to be victorious. Soltykov was victorious; but let us see, as of the beginning, him emancipate

---

[42] See *Papers of Catherine II*, College of the Historical Society of Russia, Vol. VII.

Prince Nikolay Soltykov, 1736 - 1816

himself from the supervision of the Conference, avoid resorting to the councils of his subordinate, to take in his hands the full direction of the army, and this unknown, this easy-going and simple old man, to appear suddenly, to the stupefaction of the young officers at Königsberg, to be like one born for command.

As for Fermor, he served loyally under Soltykov's orders. He could scorn the reproaches made against him for his German sympathies, which were first leveled at him he entered triumphantly into Memel, Tilsit, and Königsberg, that they had produced the indecisive victory at Zorndorf and at Kunersdorf when he was to complete the defeat of the King of Prussia. The future held another justification for him. While the government of Elisabeth, primarily Russian and national, had been so careful of his feelings, it was by Peter III, the servile imitator of Frederick II, that, on 1 April 1762, he was banished into retirement: "at his request," as related in the *oukaze* of the new emperor.[43] Perhaps, in this change of rulers, which was a total revolution, he was unhappy with the success the new ally, the friend of Berlin.

No general had shown as much confidence as Soltykov in the solid virtues of the Russian infantryman; none better appreciated the services of the irregular cavalry and knew better how to utilize it. While his predecessor had only thought to disembarrass himself of these irregular horsemen, Soltykov wanted, in contrast, to augment the number of Don Cossacks and to make a similar call in the Ukraine. No general had better understand the duties of a commander-in-chief. He did not spend a day when he was not out on a reconnaissance, without provoking, controlling and coordinating the reports

---

[43]Masslovski, Vol. II, p. 434.

of his scouts. In his marches, he was frequently with the advance guard; in the battle, he was in the center of the army. He had many of the traits of a great general. The *simple old man*, the *poor little chicken* was for Frederick II a more redoubtable adversary than the wise tactician Daun.

During the evening of 28 June 1759, Soltykov arrived at Posen and Fermor handed command over to him. The new Generalissimo found the headquarters established in this city, which Colonel Herbel had fortified, to the point of putting it in a state, if not to sustain a regular siege, at least to withstand a *coup de main*. The main body of the army was concentrated there. Krasnochtchokof's Cossacks, posted at Oborniki, on the Wartha, observed the movements of the Prussians. On 1 July, Soltykov passed the troops that he found at hand in review. They came to a total of 40,000 men. Colonel Botta, the Austrian military attaché (apparently replacing St. André), was pleased to state that it was in a good material state and the morale of the army was also good.

The first reform that Soltykov realized almost from the beginning was a reorganization of the light cavalry, looking to give a unity in its operations by placing it under the command of a single commander. That new commander was Count Tottleben: "You shall have," he wrote to Soltykov, on 1 July, "authority over all the hussars and Cossacks; you shall maintain them in good order and report directly to the Generalissimo."

The army, whose rear echelons were still on the Upper Netze and the Bromberg Canal, at Nakel and Usci, completed its concentration on Posen, while the Cossacks pushed their incursions to the frontiers of Pomerania and Brandenburg.

Conforming to the instructions given to Fermor and which had been maintained for Soltykov, it was decided that he would seek a junction with Daun. Therefore, the Austrian field marshal, who knew Frederick II as a man "of rapid action," need not care about moving along the Queiss to link up with Soltykov, or to expose himself to a flank attack. All his calculations, which were to avoid the first blow, required that the Russians receive that first blow. Therefore, he limited to himself to marches and maneuvers, but not moving himself far from his camp at Reichenberg (Bohemia).

Frederick II wanted, at all costs, to prevent the junction of the main Russian and Austrian armies. While, from his camp at Reichhennersdorf he watched Daun, at the same time he occupied himself with reinforcing Dohna. He sent him Wobersnow, one of his most enterprising cavalry generals and Hülsen with about 10,000 men, drawn from the corps of Prince Henry.

This army, initially pushed to Stargard, arrived, on 12 June, at Landsberg on the Wartha. It contained, then, 28 battalions and 52 squadrons, a total of 30,000 men. Then moving up the Wartha, it advanced on Neu-Schwerin; on the 27th it was at Birnbaum; on the 28th, it moved more to the south and established itself at Betsche (or Pszczeow). It appeared to wish to block to the Russian army the roads from the Upper Oder. Then it moved in the northeast. It pushed squadrons from Wobersnow on Murawana-Goslin. Dohna, on 21 June, appeared at Oborniki and fortified himself there. He spread the rumor that he was awaiting Frederick, at the head of 40,000 men. Now he was on the right flank of the Russians and on their rear if they took up position.

Soltykov was reasonable to believe that they sought to cut off his communications with East Prussia, or perhaps move into that province and liberate it.

Soltykov took the positions most plausible for such a theory. He stopped the convoys that moved from Thorn to Posen until the Russian army's rear had been assured. He directed Korff, Governor General of East Prussia, and Frolof-Bagreef, who commanded on the Netze, to assure the security of Königsberg; he moved the main body of his troops to the right bank of the Wartha, to cover Posen on that side. On the same right bank of the river, he directed Boulatsel, with the Tchuguiev and Don Cossacks, on Oborniki. He had them followed by the Eropkine's cavalry. Further to the right, on Rognojno, he directed 500 Cossacks and hussars, under Haudring, which were to support Mordvinov's advance guard. He then had the Lowecin Monastery occupied by Perfiliev's Cossacks. On the left bank of the Wartha, he threw Krasnochtchokof, who was to support Stoffeln. This famous Don leader was to push as far as Neu-Schwerin and from there to Landsberg, in order to cut Dohna's communications to Brandenburg.

Thus Dohna, who had initially threatened the Russian lines of retreat, now in his turn found his threatened. These perplexities manifested themselves by some movements, without apparent objective, from the left bank of the river to the right, and back, around Oborniki. Basically, he could be reproached for his inopportune slowness, for having lost this part of the campaign. He had allowed opportunity slip away where he could have fallen on the Russian divisions scattered from the Netze to the Wartha, from Nakel to Posen, and to have defeated them in detail. Now he found himself facing a Russian army, strongly concentrated and superior in number, and risked being cut off and surrounded before Frederick II could make any movement to assist him.

That same day (2 July) when Soltykov expedited the commander of the Don Cossacks on to Neu-Schwerin and Landsberg, he personally went to the right bank, leaving on the left only Lubomirski's division. He maintained communications with him by means of six pontoon bridges and had directed him to erect a seventh.

On 3 July, Wobersnow, who had attempted to establish himself at Murawana-Goslin, was chased out by the Russian cavalry and forced to withdraw on Oborniki. At this time all the Prussian army, like the main body of the Russian army, were on the right bank of the Wartha. On the 4th, Soltykov resolved to march, along that same bank, from Posen on Oborniki, and to give battle. When his forces marched out, they found the road free and the city abandoned. They were greeted only by a field ambulance, some caissons, and 43 soldiers and surgeons. The Prussian army had already returned to the left bank.

The following day, the Russian army moved there, in its turn, and occupied Jankowici. On the 8th, it fought, at Cerwitz, a brilliant light cavalry skirmish. It was noted that in this combat the Prussian hussars fought weakly and frequently withdrew to their supporting infantry, to regain their force and confidence, while the Cossacks limited themselves to maneuvering and to gaining ground, but never seeking the protection of bayonets. After this affair, Dohna, apparently intimidated, withdrew in the direction of Obra, and, on 12 July, took up a position at Mezeritz.

Soltykov conceived the plan to cut off his retreat, to engage him and, after having beaten him, throwing him on the Oder and then affecting his junction with Daun, the supreme goal of the ambition of the two courts, and which would throw against the King of Prussia a mass of 250,000 men. On 10 and 11 July, the Russian army followed the road laid out by Janowici, Pinne, and Zamorji. It marched in two columns containing all the infantry; between them marched the artillery park; at its head ran the light cavalry; in the rear of each infantry column formed the regular cavalry, the dragoons, the cuirassiers, and the horse grenadiers.

Soltykov marched at the head, with the advance guard, commanding the infantry. In the advance guard he was in constant contact with Tottleben, and it was there that this brilliant and ambiguous commander of the light cavalry succeeded in gaining his confidence. Soltykov showed himself more and more happy with the services provided by the irregular troops. The Cossacks, above all, did not cease to harass the Prussian rearguards, gathering prisoners everywhere, capturing posts and convoys. He informed the Conference of his desire to see the number of Don Cossacks raised to 8,000 men and to obtain 2,000 Ukrainian Cossacks for service on his lines of communications.

On 13 July, the Russian army was at Zamorji, about 40 versts from Mezeritz, which is situated on the other side of the Obra and which was occupied by Dohna. At this time, Soltykov sought to obtain a complete picture of his situation. It was difficult to attack Dohna since it was necessary to cross the Obra under his cannon. But one could turn him to the south and march on Züllichau, or even on Glogau.

In the first case, there was a chance of cutting Dohna off from Brandenburg. In the second, the desired junction with the Austrians would be realized. But the news that he had of the theater of war gave him much to consider. On one side, news came of the pending arrival of Frederick to support Dohna. On the other hand, they could see that Daun had made no movement to close on the Russians. The march on the Silesian Oder, when no hand was extended towards him, would expose Soltykov to seeing the King of Prussia suddenly appear on his flank, cut him off from Posen, and drive him into the swamps of the Obra.

Soltykov convoked a council of war. It decided that at all costs they should seek to affect the junction, directing that they pass the Obra close to Bentschen (Zbaczyn), approximately thirty versts upstream from Mezeritz; then turn to the south on Züllichau; from there they would try to cross the Oder either at Krossen, or at Korolath, according to circumstances. All the Russian generals were well aware of the danger of such an operation. It was a very "chivalrous" resolution according to Masslovski, that they took, and nothing testifies better to the sincerity of the Russians to seek a junction with Daun.

At this time Daun had moved his headquarters from Reichenberg to Marklissa, in one of the northern valleys of the Bohemian Mountains. He had moved no more than two or three marches. He had his lieutenants close to him as Laudon was in Lauban, de Ville was at Görlitz, Esterhazy was at Friedrichsdorf, Bukow was at Friedrichsburg, and Hadik was near Bautzen. All this was far from Soltykov.

The King of Prussia was much closer. From Landshut he had moved to Laken, where he arrived on 8 July. He then moved to Düringsvorwerk and Schmottseifen, a bit to the south of Löwenberg. He installed himself at Schmottseifen on 10 July and remained there until the 29th. With at Bautzen and Finck at Sagan, he watched all the movements of the Russians and Austrians, ready to throw himself on the point of the Oder where they looked as if they would make their junction. His confidant, Catte, tells us the monarch distracted himself in his ordinary manner, reading Tacitus, Sallust, Cornelius Nepos, and devoured the *Pucelle*.

It is in Schmottseifen that he learned the piteous results from Dohna's offensive. He had however promised himself much of it, and, still on 1 July, he seemed persuaded that Dohna would completely remove the Russian threat, attack them in detail and in *flagrant délit* in the process of formation, initially destroying the delayed units at Nakel and on the Netze, then giving him a "good report on the others," disseminated in Posnania. "This oracle is surer than that of Calchas," he affirmed to Catt, and "in a few days I will be able to assure you of good news." However, he learned now that Dohna, "by his pitiful operations and, to be plain, his ignorance of the trade of a general, despite all his vain presumptions, did not only fail under the most favorable circumstances to beat the Russian army in detail, but, by his miserable conduct, acted such that the beautiful and nimble army under his orders was obliged to withdraw shamefully in front of the enemy, who pursued it."

Thus, once more the Russians were going to enter Brandenburg. Frederick had done everything to draw them away from the main theater of war. His minister to Constantinople had neglected nothing to provoke a diversion against the Tsarina on that side. On 9 January 1759, he expressed to Baron Motte-Fouqué the hope that the Turks were already moving and that in the spring they would not remain idly by the side with their arms crossed. "If the nation that does not wear a hat turns against the Barbarians, their hordes will invade." The Turks not having acted, he had opposed the Russians with Dohna and a "beautiful and nimble army," which he had reinforced several times. As for him, he had exhausted his manpower resources and officers, so he was obliged to hold himself on the defensive. And when the Russians came to attack him on his home ground in Brandenburg, he grew angry against these frightening pests as well as against the unlucky Dohna.

Dohna, since his retreat behind the Obra, had little idea what the Russians were planning. Fearing that they had not turned south to link up with Daun, he decided to move up this river in the direction of the Oder. On 17 July, he broke camp at Mezeritz and, by forced marches, moved on Schwiebus, where he arrived on the 21st. However, that same day, 17 July, Soltykov had crossed the Obra at Bomst (in Polish: *Babie most*, "Bridge of the Good Woman.") and on the 20th, he entered Brandenburg. There resulted from this double operation that Dohna, pursing his road to the south, without knowing it, passed almost within musket range of Tottleben's cavalry. Then at Züllichau, he fell on the Zoritch Hussars, which he chased from this city. It was there that he took up position to attempt to block the road to the invaders.

It was also there that he received a note from the King, a very dry note, which read: "You are too sick to continue in command. You would do well to go to Berlin, where you can recover your health. Adieu."[44]

This note arrived at the same time as Lieutenant General von Wedell. In addition to the command, the King had given him the most extensive powers. "I have made him dictator during the duration of this commission." he wrote to Prince Henry. Thus, it required a dictator, as in ancient Rome at the moment of supreme dangers, such as the Gaulish tumult and the Barbarian invasions. Frederick II did not conceal from Wedell the difficulties in his mission. "He must do what the dictators did in the time of the Romans."[45] - "You understand," he wrote Henry, "that an empty hand does not redress itself in 24 hours. There are still heads that turn. Great God, men are such a sad species! The crisis is great, but there is nothing to lose."[46]

Not only was Dohna's army in the riskiest situation, but it was exhausted and demoralized. Without having suffered the enemy's fire, it was notably decreased by desertion, which was the plague of these troops, recruited partly from defectors, forcibly enlisted foreigners, and even prisoners of war.

---

[44] *Politische Correspondenz*, Vol. XVIII, 2nd Part, p. 425, 20 July 1759.
[45] *Was ein Dictator bei der Roemer Zeiten vorstellte. Ibid.* Letter to Dohna.
[46] *Ibid.* p. 425, 20 July.

A French officer wrote on 15 July:

> Desertion is very great in Prussia. One estimates that
> Dohna has lost 3,000 deserters since his stay in Poland. The
> deserters vanish. The Mecklenburgers taken by force return
> home; the Poles remain in their territory, and barely 200 were
> returned to the Prussian Army. In this number there are some
> Frenchmen who were taken prisoner at Bergen.[47] Forty saved
> themselves, but twelve were recaptured and taken to Stettin.[48]

The "dictator" Wedell first had to rebuild the morale of the army, to take actions against the indiscipline of the soldiers and the "cowardice" of the officers. Here are a few lines of the *Instruction* given him by Frederick II:

> ... Maintain a rigorous discipline. Prohibit
> the officers, on pain of being cashiered, from making
> discouraging lamentations and remarks. To also despise
> those who, under any circumstance, exaggerate the enemy's
> forces. Any officer who acts in a cowardly manner will be
> taken before a war council.

After these precepts of moral dictatorship, came the tactical precepts:

> Initially contain the enemy by taking a strong
> position. Then attack him according to my manner. To hold
> in respect his light cavalry with our hussars, dragoons, etc.
> If, that which God does not want, the army is beaten, take
> up a position on the point where he wishes to invade, either
> behind Frankfurt or Krossen, or under the fortress of Glogau.

Wedell, who arrived in the camp the day before the battle, barely had time to receive a report on the situation. This brisk change of command, in the presence of the enemy, would surely influence the conduct of operations in an unfavorable way. It would have been better to leave Dohna in command; but, in summary, he had taken the best course by marching to the south. He had the chance to escape Tottleben's cavalry. Finally, the position that he assumed at Züllichau was well-chosen. It allowed him to present a redoubtable front to the Russian army. Wedell could not have done better.

Soltykov resolved to turn the Prussian position by the north; that is to say, the Prussian left. From his arrival in the presence of the Prussians he had not ceased his personal direction of reconnaissances. As a result, he had a

---

[47] Bergen was a battle lost, on 13 April 1759, by Ferdinand von Braunschweig to the Duke de Broglie.

[48] Archives of French Foreign Affairs. *Russian Correspondence*, Vol. LX., piece 65.

very good understanding of the Prussian's situation. He also understood that his communications to both Posen and to the Austrians were compromised. In addition, he had to hasten, because Wedell would certainly receive reinforcements, be it Prince Henry or Frederick himself.

The position at Züllichau, which dominated the plain, was surrounded, except the north, by natural defenses, such as a swamp and brush-filled woods. On the north side was Eichberg. The Prussians, to guarantee for themselves this side, had to occupy this height. They had moved there the bulk of their forces, such that they were strong at Eichberg and weak at Züllichau. Eichberg was evidently the key to the battle.

On 22 July, Soltykov's headquarters was established in the village of Goltzen. The Generalissimo had under his command three corps: 1st with Fermor, 2nd with Villebois, and the 3rd, formerly the Observation Corps, with Golitzyn. He had moved to Bukow, on his right and far forward, Tottleben's light cavalry; at Langenmeile, on the left and forward, were Zortich's hussars. He deployed 28,000 infantry, 5,000 regular cavalry, 7,500 irregulars, and 140 cannon. That was a total of about 40,000 men.[49]

To oppose the Russians Wedell had only 18,000 infantry and 9,380 horsemen: a total of 27,380 men.

Both men thought the other far stronger than he was. Wedell thought Soltykov had 90,000 men and Soltykov thought Wedell had 60,000 men.

During the day of the 22nd, Soltykov made a last reconnaissance. At 3:00 p.m., he returned to his camp at Goltzen and issued orders for a night march that would allow him to turn the Prussian right wing.

The march of the Russian columns was completed under the protection of Tottleben's advance guard. The Russians moved out at 4:00 p.m. and moved to spend the night at Bukow. They left this position on the 23rd, at 3:00 a.m., reaching the stream that watered Schönborn and Nickern, and moved on Paltzig. The turning movement was completed with great precision and such secrecy that the Prussians, in the morning, discovered the Russian columns behind their left wing. Soltykov had shown that the "Barbarians" had profited from the lessons of Frederick II. His maneuver was like that which Frederick had executed at Zorndorf.

Wedell learned of this movement at 5:00 a.m., on the 23rd, when he placed himself with a strong reconnaissance and moved on Langenmeile. He counted on finding Zoritch's hussars, but he found nothing, and he quickly determined that the Goltzen camp was evacuated. Seized with great concerns, he rapidly returned to Eichberg where he arrived at 7:00 a.m., and immediately prepared his forces for battle. At that time the Russians appeared at Nickern and opened artillery fire, followed by an offensive, on the Prussian positions.

[49]Not taking part in the battle was the Troitski Infantry Regiment, which remained at Posen; nor Mordvinof's advance guard, which did not arrive until the evening, nor Fast's brigade, which a false maneuver had forced to move from Bukow to Goltzen.

Soltykov, seized by a concern similar to that of Wedell, decided to send back to Goltzen a part of Tottleben's cavalry and Fast's brigade. Therefore Fast did not re-appear during the day, but Tottleben did succeed in returning in the last stages of the battle.

Wedel, until 11:00 a.m., contented himself with observing Soltykov's march, then he had the Russians charged by part of Malachowski's cavalry. Malachowski was driven back. The Russians continued from Nickern on Paltzig. They arrived there shortly after noon and arranged themselves forward; that is to say, on the east of the village, turning their backs on Krossen, facing Züllichau and Eichberg, separated from the Prussians by the stream running from Schönborn to Nickern. Their infantry, as usual, formed two elongated lines. On the left, the two lines were formed by Golitzyn's regiments, the center with those of Villebois, and the right by those of Fermor.

On the face of the first line the Russians established, dominating the bank of the stream, five batteries of heavy field artillery. A sixth battery, on the right, stood on a mound between the two lines and a seventh, on the extreme right, formed a true redoubt. Fermor also had it covered by four elite regiments: on the left by the Siberia Infantry and the 1st Grenadiers; on the right by Vyborg and the 2nd Moscow, placed at a right angle to the former and closing the interval between the two lines.

The cavalry was deployed as follows: On the extreme left, the Don Cossacks watched the crossings of the stream between Schönborn and Nickern. Then came the New Siberian Hussars. Behind them, moving against the village of Paltzig, and under the orders of Eropkine, came Galatzin's infantry; the Novotroiski, the 3rd and Kiev Cuirassiers; and the Riazan and Kargopol Horse Grenadiers. Between the two lines of infantry, resembling a reserve, Demicou commanded the Kazan Cuirassiers and a squadron of the Nijni-Novgorod Dragoons. It was on the right that the masses of cavalry stood. In the first rank were the Imperial Highness, Petersburg, and Narva Cuirassiers; in the second Georgia, Hungary, and Slavo-Serbian Hussars; and in the third line the Don and Tchuguiev Cossacks. All this cavalry, with the infantry of the Vyborg and 2nd Moscow Infantry Regiments were placed under the orders of Panine.

This right wing of the Russian army, by its composition in artillery (commanded by Borozdin), in infantry, in cavalry, and by its dominating position on the valley, was very strong and almost unassailable. The center was also covered by the stream and the Eckmühl Pond. The left wing, in contrast, was formed of less solid troops, and was exposed to seeing itself turned by the Prussians, if they succeeded in crossing the bridges at Schönborn and Nickern. In the case the Russian army was taken in the flank and its rear threatened, it could be thrown from the heights and into the stream, the swamp, and the brush, cut off from its lines of retreat on both Krossen and Goltzen, having no other alternative than to perish or cut a path to safety with its bayonets.

The Prussians, abandoning their position at Eichberg and Züllichau, had taken up a position on the east bank of the river, which dominated the western bank occupied by the Prussians. Their double line of infantry had its right near Nickern, its left on the Heidenmühl Pond, and the village of Glocksen. In their rear, the village of Kai and on their front, the Eckmühl Mill, with its pond and stream. Five batteries of field artillery crowned the stream bank. For over an hour, they maintained a violent cannonade on the Russian batteries and lines.

Wedell prepared his attack on two points. He left to the rear and as a reserve Wobersnow's cavalry. He massed his infantry into two columns. The right column, under Kanitz, was to cross the river at Nickern and assail the Russian left. His left column, divided between himself and Manteuffel, was to attack Saltykof's formidable right.

Saltykov, in order to be less concerned about his left wing, directed the Cossacks to destroy the Nickern bridge and to burn the village. He then moved all his attention to his right wing.

Against this wing, Wedell, with four infantry regiments and three squadrons, led the flank attack. Manteuffel was, with the bulk of the column, to attack it frontally. There was no unity in this attack, because while Wedell was delayed in his turning movement, Manteuffel grew impatient and launched his attack prematurely. He launched his attack with much energy; but,under the fire of the two heavy Russian batteries, under the musketry of the 1st Grenadiers, the Siberia, Perm, and Ouglitch Infantry Regiments, his troops were driven back. Manteuffel even fell grievously wounded. Wedell hastened to reinforce him with Hülsen's five battalions, but Soltykov, on the same point, brought up from his left wing the 1st and 5th Musketeers. A second effort by the Prussian infantry, under Hülsen, suffered a second check. The Prussians broke under the fire of the Russian musketry and artillery, never crossing bayonets with the Russians. Colonel of Engineers Mouravief, an eyewitness, tells us: "The Russian regiments showed themselves unshakable, in that, in the most perfect order, they directed a well-nourished fire and as the artillery and musketry fire reached its height the enemy precipitated his retreat; to the extent that when their [the Russian] dead and wounded fell from the first line, they filled the holes with troops from the reserve."[50]

Wedell's flank attack had no more success than the frontal attack did. There the Prussians had also not crossed bayonets with the Russians. The terrible fire of the heavy Russian batteries put to flight their four regiments of infantry. Their rout across the woods and swamp was so complete that only much later did they rally and return to the Prussian army. The other regiments that followed them, to take their place, were charged in the flank by Tchuguiev's Cossacks. They were driven back with blows of the lances and

---

[50] In Masslovski.

lost their regimental cannon.

Wedell had produced this partial disaster by badly coordinating his attacks and attacking the much more powerful Russian right wing in little packets. Now the Prussians waited for the outcome of Kanitz's attack, and above all, the arrival of Wobersnow's cavalry, which alone could save the debris of the Prussian left wing.

Kanitz had been stopped by the burning village of Nickern and the destruction of the bridge. This is what permitted Saltykov to reinforce his left wing with the 1st and 5th Musketeers.

As for Wobersnow, he did not arrive on the battlefield, strewn with the soldiers of Manteuffel, Hülsen, and Wedell, until 5 a.m. All the chiefs being wounded on this side, he took command. He reduced Kanitz's attack to a simple diversion and resumed with the left wing the attack which had already failed three times. He resolved to initially attack the Russian infantry with his cavalry. The marshy and brushy ground offered great difficulties to the charges of his squadrons. The Prussian cavalry charged the Russian infantry with such élan that it broke a hole in the line between the Perm and Siberia Infantry Regiments. He then found himself faced by a large Russian battery between the two lines that crushed his ranks with its projectiles. Thus, caught between the two lines of Fermor's infantry, caught between the fire of the two large batteries, he had still to undergo on his two flanks a double charge by the Russian cavalry: on his left flank he was charged by Demicou with the Kazan Cuirassiers and the Nijni-Novgorod Dragoons; on his right flank he was charged by Eropkin with the Kiev, Novo-Troïtski, and the Imperial Highness Cuirassiers. These riders did not even take time to fire their carbines. It was with blows of the saber that they attacked the Prussian squadrons. The fray was so hot that Demicou, a worthy rival on this day of the "great cavalier" Seydlitz, fell pierced with blows. His soldiers avenged him. The Siberia Regiment, by them released, opened a fire by ranks on the Prussian squadrons. At the same time Panine came up with fresh squadrons and battalions. He completed the rout of the Prussian cavalry, driving them into the small valley. Then Panine charged the Prussian lines with infantry. Wobersnow made vain efforts to disengage them. He fell dead. All the Prussian left wing was now destroyed: they fled in disorder on Züllichau, towards the Tschicherzig bridge, into the Oder marshes. Kanitz, abandoned to himself, had to follow the rout. The Russian regular cavalry pursued the Prussians to Glocksen and Heidenmühle. It could go no further because it was as exhausted as the Russian infantry. It was 8:00 p.m., and the troops had marched or fought since 3:00 a.m. It was Tottleben, returning from his reconnaissance on Goltzen, who was charged, with his hussars and Cossacks, to continue the pursuit. He gathered up much abandoned equipment and many prisoners. However, he had will stop at the Oder. The remains of the Prussian army passed this river at Tschicherzig, and then continued to on Zawade, Kühnau, and Grunberg.

Such was the battle of 23 July, which the Prussians call the Battle of Züllichau or Kai, and which the Russians call the battle of Paltzig. The Russian infantry had shown its usual tenacity, the artillery had maintained its usual superiority over that of the Prussians, and finally, for the first time, the Russian cavalry had constantly held the advantage over the Prussian cavalry. As for Saltykov, the success of his turning movement by the north, the happy choice of his position, the foresight that he had to fortify his right wing, his dispatch of reinforcements from the left wing, revealed him to be a general worthy of comparison to Frederick himself.

The disaster suffered by the Prussian army was as complete as a disaster could be. Frederick II, who worried less about minimizing the losses in the battles where he did not command in person, readily admitted those suffered at Paltzig. That day Wedell lost 4,000 to 5,000 men. The Russians did not suffer an equal loss, as the terrain was to their advantage.[51]

Saltykov, in his report, states that he buried 4,220 Prussian bodies and took 1,200 prisoners. This is very close to the truth. Masslovski evaluates the Prussian losses at 4,269 dead, 1,394 wounded, and 1,495 unaccounted, of which 1,406 deserted and there were 600 prisoners. Wedell's army was thus weakened by 7,000 or 8,000 men. The figures given by Schaefer, who indicates 8,000 dead or wounded, shows that the Russian historian who came after him, had not exaggerated the Prussian losses.

Russian losses are estimated at 900 dead and 3,904 wounded.

On both sides the losses among superior officers were substantial. On the Russian side Demicou was killed, while Generals Borozdin and Elchaninov and four colonels were wounded. The Prussians lost Wobersnow and Generals Manteuffel and Galentz were wounded.

As trophies of his victory, Soltykov had four infantry flags, three cavalry standards, 14 cannon, and 4,000 muskets.

Saltykov, who could fear an offensive return of the Prussians, had quickly rectified the position of his regiments, sent to the third line the Siberia, Narva, and Ouglitch Regiments, which had suffered greatly, and replaced them in the first line with the 1st and 5th Musketeers. Then he had three victory salvos fired and presided over evening prayers on the battlefield covered by the dead and dying. On the 24th, he gave his report to the Tsarina to Lieutenant of the Guards Saltykov.

In his report, which happily contrasts with some of the statements by Fermor, he gives a brilliant witness to the bravery of his army:

> The enemy returned five consecutive times to the charge with
> fresh troops and always in greater numbers. All these times,
> the troops of Your Imperial Majesty behaved with as much

---

[51] Frederick II, *Histoire de la guerre de Sept ans.*

valor as the first line alone, without the help of the second, without losing an inch of ground and without being shaken; not only did they receive the five attacks, but they even gained a complete victory, drove the enemy off of the battlefield, put them to rout, made them flee and captured many of their cannon, standards, flags and other trophies... There was no one, from the generals to the last soldier, who did not do all his duty as one promises to be faithful subjects and people of honor...[52]

Saltykov had shown to Daun the *Cunctator* how one knows to acquit oneself, at all prices, of a given word, and how, for the success of the common cause, one must face "the first blow" of a redoubtable enemy. After his victory, as before the battle, he seemed to have no other concern than to maintain or establish communications with this ally, who concealed himself. He stretched out to move closer to the points from where he could affect a junction with the Austrians. On the 25th, he decided to occupy Krossen on the Oder, with Volkonski's brigade. However, at that time Wedell marched from Grünberg on this same city. On the 28th, his advance guard, formed with Malachowski's hussars, arrived there before the Russians. He was immediately chased from the city by Volkonski, who carried the city and the Prussian magazines located there.

This general sent, by the bridge over the Oder, Perfiliev and his Cossacks. They pursued Malachowski on the other bank of the river, capturing two cannon and forcing Wedell to change his itinerary.

Finally, on the 26th, Saltykov, who had spent three days at Paltzig, occupied with burying the dead, caring for the wounded, and singing a *Te Deum*, broke camp. On the 28th, he was personally in Krossen. He sent Tottleben's cavalry and Golitzyn's corps, to the other bank of the Oder River to sweep the land and prepare for the junction with the Austrians. In the direction of Frankfurt, he sent Villebois, with 5 regiments of infantry, 2 of horse grenadiers, some hussars, some Cossacks, and some artillery. Villebois arrived, on 31 July, in sight of Frankfurt. Frankfurt, on the left bank of the Oder, was a city of 1,300 houses, which was greatly enriched by commerce. It was not in a state of defense. Frederick II had carried away all the cannon to reinforce Küstrin and had left there only a battalion under the command of Major Arnim. Villebois, upon arriving there, found the bridge broken. He desired to spare the city and immediately sent a parliamentarian to Major Arnim. Arnim consented to enter into discussions, but he demanded the free exit of the garrison with all its arms and baggage. Villebois refused these

---

[52] Translation of this document in Vol. LX in the Correspondence with Russia. Archives of the Department of Foreign Affairs of France. — Soltykov expresses himself in the same terms in a letter to Vorontsof (Imperial Society of Russia, Vol. X., pp. 489-490).

conditions and opened fire on the city. Barely had he fired a few cannon shots than the secretary of the magistrate arrived, announcing that the garrison had departed, and the inhabitants were surrendering. Villebois demanded that before everything the bridge over the Oder be rebuilt; if not, the bombardment would resume. The bridge was immediately re-established and Villebois sent over Zortich's hussars and Bülau's horse grenadiers, with orders to pursue the garrison, which was retreating on Küstrin. Loukovkin's Cossacks had already swum across the river at Lebus. They were the first to fall on Arnim's little column and, without pushing the attack home, they held him s until Zortich and Bülau arrived. Then, this Prussian troop, which contained 645 men, surrendered.

Villebois entered Frankfurt escorted by the Vyborg Infantry Regiment. He was received by the inhabitants with the accustomed honors, but he still immediately imposed on the city a contribution of 200,000 *thalers*, demanded a large quantity of food, and had the city's smiths produce the cuirasses that his heavy horsemen had lacked since 1757.

The following day, on the far bank of the Oder, the Austrian corps of Laudon appeared. He had attempted to anticipate the Russians by the occupation of Frankfurt and then he attempted to take from them their conquest. He demanded that Villebois at least hand over part of the contribution and requisitions, but Villebois refused, sending it to Saltykov.

Saltykov made his triumphant entrance into Frankfurt, on 3 August, saluted by the ringing of bells and salvos of Russian artillery. He was greeted and addressed by the magistrate who presented him with the keys to the city. They were immediately sent to the Tsarina.

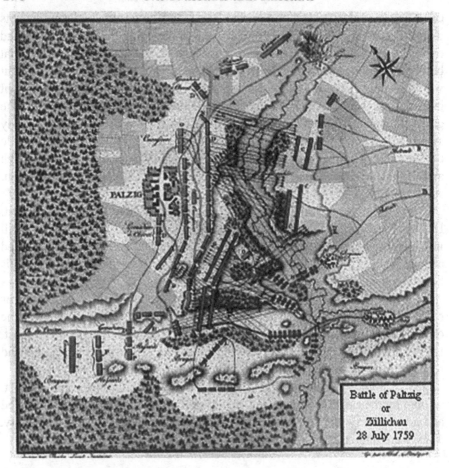

Battle of Paltzig
or
Züllichau
28 July 1759

CHAPTER XI

THE BATTLE OF KUNERSDORF (12 August 1759)

The news of the victory of Paltzig had spread enthusiasm in the Austrian districts. Laudon, who had advanced from Lauban on Rothenburg, had learned of it on 25 July. On the 26th, Daun arrived at his camp at Marklissa. Saltykov, by means of an Austrian courier that the riders of Volkonski had encountered on their raid beyond the Oder, requested Laudon to advance at the same time as he on Frankfurt; the purpose of this operation would have been to draw to the other side Prince Henry, who had arrived from Saxony, and to prevent him from making a junction with the King of Prussia: "It is all the more necessary," added Saltykov, "as I am no more than 15 miles from Berlin."

Then only Daun considered it "possible" to obey the requests of his Russian allies. He reinforced Laudon with 12 battalions of infantry, 12 companies of grenadiers, and 3 regiments of dragoons; which raised his forces from 18,000 to 20,000 men. He also directed Hadik to march in the same direction, to worry Prince Henry and, if the opportunity arose, "to beat him without fault." Daun maintained himself in Marklissa, only moving his left wing to Lauban on the Queisse. He was determined to leave his positions only when the King of Prussia had decamped from the positions, he occupied in Schmotlseifen and Löwenburg. He swore at this time that he would take the offensive at once and "march on his heels." One had only to let him do it: what he would do, was "a secret." At the bottom, he was less interested in helping his allies than to see the King move a bit away from him.

Even the movements which he ordered were carried out with an extreme slowness. On 27 July, Laudon was still in Rothenburg. It was only on 1 August, as we saw, that the heads of his columns appeared in the vicinity of Frankfurt, on the left bank of the Oder.

Saltykov wrote to his court that he was extremely embarrassed to act, as long as he would not have penetrated the great "secrecy" of Field Marshal Daun. With his refined good sense, he guessed all there was in this great secrecy was inertia, hesitation, and perhaps timidity. The King of Prussia was not mistaken on what his Austrian adversary would do. He constantly joked about the "blessed toque." He acknowledged frankly: "It is not the Austrians who will embarrass me."[53] It was the Russians. He impatiently awaited and feared news of "what would occur at Züllichau." It was only on 24 July, at 3:00 p.m. We leave it to the words of Heinrich von Catt, an eyewitness:

---

[53] *Politische Correspondenz*, Vol. XVIII, 2nd Part, p. 440, to Prince Henry, 23 July 1749.

The King spoke with me... He asked me how much philosophy could help in violent positions... I answered him... then I saw at a distance his aide-de-camp Bonin advancing in great strides. When he was in range, I realized that his hat was pierced in one of its wings: "Lord, here is your aide-de-camp; his hat has been struck by a musket ball, and there has surely been a battle." With these words, the King became very red: "Where is he, where is he? — He will enter." His Majesty opens the door himself: - "Enter! Well, what is it? What has Wedell done? — Lord, he gave battle to the Russians, and it lost it. His aide-de-camp Wobersnow is killed. — Lost!" To this the King said. "And how devil did he do that? Speak to me true, but quite true, you hear!" When Bonin had completed his report, the King began again: "What silliness are you telling me here? Is it possible to act in such an amazing and such an inept way? Go! Tell Herr von Wedell that I will soon join him. You shall not stop. Hurry, and do not say a word of this to those that you may see while leaving at home...

When the aide-de-camp had left, the King devoted himself to all the sorrow which he felt of the loss of a battle: "Am I not unhappy? Is this a similar position to mine? I am alone to defend myself. And the means of holding? ... Is it not possible to post oneself across an uncrossable brook, to force the troops to march on a narrow bridge and to thus expose them to a cannonade? All those b[astards] lose their heads. You are not great a soldier, but surely you would not have made all these stupid mistakes... But this Wedell, this Wedell, will force me to make a similar push there! This army does not have, as of the beginning, done anything good. A f... disagreement which reigned between the generals of this army, and in particular between Dohna and Wobersnow, both very spoiled, and officers and soldiers, and the devil and his grandmother...And this gentleman, the most amiss and most inept in the world, loses me a battle! I will pass by again on all that, to see what there is to do. Good evening! You will sleep surely better than me."

As a result of events Frederick II had everything to repair at once: Ferdinand von Braunschweig's defeat at Bergen and that of Wedell at Paltzig. Where to find the resources to repair all this? Where would he find the men, the officers, and the generals to fill the ranks? After each battle lost, after each battle won, he found himself more alone.

However, from 24 to 29 July Frederick remained in Schmottseifen. He encouraged his lieutenants, speaking with Prince Henry of the battle of the 23rd as an action "that had not absolutely turned to our advantage;" he assured Prince von Württemberg that he would be set right "with all honors;" affirming to Ferdinand von Braunschweig that they had only lost 1,400 men, while the Russians suffered "14,000 dead and wounded." At the same time, he borrowed soldiers from the other army corps. Finally, on the 28th he said to Catte: "I leave tomorrow. Thus, the wind of fortune is against me. I do not know what fate will decide against me. If you should not see me anymore, think sometimes of a being who was the toy of fate, and which wished you well." And, thinking of the remote Tsarina who hated him so much, parodying a verse from *Athalie*, he added:

Deign to do, deign to do, my God, on Kaunitz and on her....

On 30 July, with 10,000 of his best troops and the incomparable Seydlitz, he was at Sagan. He made his junction with Prince Henry, who brought with him 14 battalions and 25 squadrons, and with Prince von Württemberg, who had 6 battalions and 15 squadrons. He joined all of those troops and sent his brother back to take command of the army he had left at Schmottsiefen.

The Austrian Hadik had let flee the opportunity to attack Prince Henry and "to beat him without fault," as Daun had prescribed to him. Daun then enjoined to him to worry the King in his rear and to place him "between two fires." But the King marched too quickly. On the 31st he was in Christianstadt; 1 August at Sommersfeld; 2nd in Merzdorf. It was there that he gave himself the pleasure of capturing all of Hadik's baggage, to capture the Würzburg Regiment, to seize 600 caissons of food. It is there that he learned of the entry of the Russians into Frankfurt. He wrote to Prince Henry: "As soon as we have some force, we will march on these people, and we will fight *pro aris et focis*." On the 3rd, he was in Beeskow: "I have just arrived," he wrote in Finckenstein, "after long and terrible marches... There were six nights where I did not close my eyes." On the 4th, he was in Müllrose, where it completed his junction with Wedell's army. He had also drawn to him the 10,000 men that Finck had close to Torgau. However, he well realized of gravity of the situation: "I wish," he sent in the same correspondence, "to give you a little good news from what I have just received (victory of Ferdinand von Braunschweig at Minden, on 1 August), but my "bearmen" are not Frenchmen, and Saltykov's artillery is a hundred times better than that of Contades."[54]

While Frederick ran in the direction of Frankfurt, what did Daun do, when he had sworn to "march on his heels?" The action of the convoys

[54] *Politisches Correspondenz*, Vol. XVIII, 2nd Party, p. 471

captured from Hadik had intimidated him. He did not even attempt to attack Sagan where Prince Henry remained with the rest of Frederick's troops. He directed Hadik to rejoin Laudon. By this he proposed to Saltykov a new plan of cooperation that one might find strange.

Laudon had begun by asking for a corps of 30,000 Russians, which would receive 500,000 *thalers* of the million *thaler* contribution that he would impose on Frankfurt. On 4 August, after Saltykov had passed in review the Austrian contingent, its leaders saluting him with their drawn swords, drums rolling and trumpets blaring, and their Imperial standards dipped. However, in a visit with Laudon, Laudon informed him of the thoughts of his chief and revealed the great "secret" that Saltykov had not been able to penetrate. This consisted of a retrograde march of the Russians on Krossen, from where they would attempt to join Daun in Silesia. The Russian Generalissimo objected to the difficulty of retracing his steps with all his wagons and wounded. His artillery material was already fatigued by its long marches. Many of the gun carriages had suffered as a result of the terrible cannonade of the 23rd. He had lost many horses in the battle. He lacked projectiles and was awaiting them from his rear. An epidemic raged in his cattle herd carrying off 80 cows a day. Laudon then proposed that he leave his wagon train and 10,000 Russians at Frankfurt and as forage was lacking in Silesia, the Cossacks should be left on the right bank of the Oder. Saltykov asked how long he would have to remain in Silesia. "All winter," responded Laudon. Then the Generalissimo, though consenting to retreat on Krossen, refused to engage himself so far or so long. If the Austrians thought only of their Silesia, Saltykov was well obliged to think that his army would perish in this dispersion into three parts, from the province of East Prussia, where such a long exposure would leave him at the mercy of the enterprises of the Prussians. Later, the Conference was to justify him on all these points. In his turn, he asked the Austrian generals to cross to the right bank of the Oder. He had already constructed a bridge for their use at Tschetschnow.

The presence of the King of Prussia at Merzdorf was already known and did not permit the Allies to wait with impunity on the left bank. For the same reason, and for others given above, it was necessary to postpone the projected attack on Berlin. At the very most one could direct on Berlin Rumyantsev's corps, with the mission to collect, there or on the road, contributions, food, and horses. Thus, for the second time, the day after a battle Rumyantsev saw himself on the point of being sent off. Due to the imminent approach of Frederick this was abandoned.

Although Laudon was united with Saltykov, it was the light Russian cavalry that alone assured the security of the army. Tottleben was charged with the organization of a line of advance posts and reconnaissances. The Croatians were not employed for this. The Cossacks and the hussars of this general continued to distinguish themselves. Colonel Turovinov led a raid as far as the suburbs of Küstrin, capturing prisoners and burning military magazines. Other detachments infested the road from Frankfurt to Berlin. On 7 August, Lieutenant Wenzel, with the hussars, crossed the Oder near Lebus, moving as far as Müncheburg, captured Fürstenwald, and after having thrown alarm into a Prussian corps, withdrew on Tschetschnow. He reported that the entire region along the Spree, between Rauen and Pilgram, was already occupied by the Prussians, and that the Prussians had gathered boats from everywhere. Saltykov directed his light cavalry to redouble their attention.

Until that point one thought that Frederick II was moving only to cover Berlin. Now one began to think that he would attempt a crossing of the Oder. On the 9th, cannon were heard on the far side of Waldow. This was the King firing salvos of joy to announce the victory of Minden. This was the day earlier designated, in a council of war held between Saltykov, Fermor, and Laudon, for their march on Krossen. On the 10th, they learned that Frederick was preparing to cross the Oder at Lebus, between Frankfurt and Küstrin. They had no preparations to block the passage, since the retreat on Krossen had been decided on, in principle. Frederick crossed, without difficulty on the 11th.

This event completely changed the situation. One could no longer think of retreating. The least perilous step was to accept battle.

The Russian army consisted of four corps: 1st Fermor, 2nd Villebois, 3rd Rumyantsev, and 4th Golitzyn or the Observation Corps.

It contained 33 regiments or 68 infantry battalions, 5 cuirassier regiments, 5 horse grenadier regiments, 1 dragoon regiment, 3 hussar regiments, plus the Tchuguiev Cossacks: a total of 45,000 men and 200 cannon.

As Hadik had written that he would not move beyond Kottbus, and in effect he had withdrawn on Daun, the Austrian army contained only the corps commanded by Laudon. It contained six infantry regiments, some grenadier companies, and 33 squadrons of regular German and Croatian cavalry. It contained a total of 18,523 men, including 7,000 infantry, 6,000 cavalry, 5,000-6,000 Croats, and 48 cannon. Against these 60,000 men, Frederick could deploy 48,000 men, or 53 battalions and 93 squadrons, with 114 heavy cannons, which, in large part, he had drawn from Küstrin. This army had two distinct elements: Wedell's army, formerly Dohna's army, where most of the regiments had suffered heavily at Gross-Jägersdorf, Zorndorf, and Paltzig; and the troops coming from Silesia and Saxony, the 10,000 men that Frederick had brought from Löwenberg, with those that he had taken from Prince Henry and Finck's Corps, which he had called to him. These two distinct elements, one of the East Prussian Army and the other of the Armies of Silesia and Saxony were in approximately equal numbers.

One notes, in the numerical inferiority in its total number that the King retained his numerical superiority in cavalry: 93 squadrons against 71. If he had fewer cannon, they were of heavier caliber than those of the Austrians and Russians.

The description of the battlefield of Kunersdorf offers many things in common with that of Zorndorf.

During the morning of 12 August 1759, like that of 25 August 1758, the Russians still had their left wing near the Oder and near a Prussian city. However, here they occupied Frankfurt, while Küstrin, in 1758, had resisted them. And Frankfurt was much closer to them, because it was in its suburbs and near them that the battle would occur. One found ravines, in this line of heights, like those that had been so useful at Zorndorf. There were parallel lines of heights oriented from the west to east, but they were much larger here. In going from the west to the east they diminished: the Judenberg ("Jewish Hill", which contained a Jewish cemetery), the Grand Spitzberg Plateau, and Mühlberg (Mill Hill). The first was separated from the second by the Laudongrund (Laudon Ravine). The second was separated from the third by the Kuhgrund (Cow Ravine).

These three heights, thus cut by two ravines, formed a crest about 6,000 paces long, and 200 paces wide from the Judenberg, and no more than 1,200 to the Mühlberg. The Judenberg was the highest, dominating the Grand Spitzberg, and the Grand Spitzberg dominated the Mühlberg. The Spitzberg Plateau formed a culminating point on its west part with another bulge: the Sieben-Ruthen-Berg (Seven Poles Hill). This plateau was, of the three heights described mentioned above, that which presents the greatest extent of level ground, being 2,500 paces by 1,400 paces, but it was very uneven and rough.

At the foot of the Mühlberg was another ravine, the Beckergrund, which bypasses and communicates with a great depression of ground occupied by a series of ponds: Dorfsee, Blankesee, and Faulesee [Village Lake, White Lake, and Rotten Lake]. In these extensions of the Kuhgrund [ravine] there ran two streets, the village of Kunersdorf, enveloping on its two extremities, the Dorfsee. On the opposite back of the heights the ground was the same; because on the other extremity of the Kuhgrund, there was the marshy Els-Busch [Service Tree Wood]. This swamp was drained by a stream that flowed on the north flank of the hills and moves almost to Mühlberg. This is the Hühnerfluss [Chicken River], which was very muddy, and which could only be crossed at a few fords or at the points where the roads crossed it.

Of the heights close to these, it is necessary to mention two of them: small Spitzberg, an hillock isolated in the east, which dominates Kunersdorf, and the hill that supports the village of Trettin: today it is called Finck-Berg; as the small Sptizberg is called Seydlitz-Berg, Judenberg is called Laudons-Berg to, to a small hill, the Pech-Stauge, north of Mühlberg, is called Kleist-Berg.

These names recall to the villagers the exploits or misfortunes of Generals Finck, Seydlitz, Laudon and the death of the soldier-poet Kleist.

To the northeast is the village of Bishofssee with its two lakes. To the south is the brushy wood called the Kunersdorfwald [Wood].

Frankfurt is so close that its suburbs on the left bank and its small fort, the Rothvorwerk, almost touches the Judenberg. From Frankfurt there runs, to the northeast, a road that passes through the villages of Trettin, Leissow, Gohlitz, Frauendorf Ötscher, and Göritz. This last village almost touches the Oder, which from Lebus swings towards the northeast. The highway from Frankfurt to Göritz is the capital line of the battlefield. Another important highway is that which runs from Frankfurt, passes by Judenberg by the south, and continues to the southeast, moving on Krossen.

Thus, Saltykov's army had clung, in this brushy and marshy plain, on a line of heights. If it were to climb down and move towards the west or the south, it would be thrown into the marshes of Oder. But these were also dangerous angles for the Prussians, some pockets: because Frederick, according to the positions that he would occupy, would have on his rear either the Oder or the Wartha.

During the morning of 12 August, the Russian army was arrayed on the three heights. Its western wing, with Fermor and Villebois, occupied the Judenberg; its center, with Rumyantsev, was on the plateau of the Grand Spitzberg; its eastern wing, with Golitzyn, was on the Mühlberg. As to the Austrian troops, they had not yet taken up position on the heights and were massed near the Rothvorwerk.

As the army faced to the north, the western wing was then the left wing and the eastern wing was the right. Saltykov awaited an attack from the north and covered his front with engineering works which somewhat sharpened the profile of the hills and he had deployed his heavy batteries on that front. In this situation, there were two lines of retreat: one by the highway from Frankfurt to Krossen; the other by the four bridges over the Oder. A first disadvantage of this situation, similar to that which had already been seen at Zorndorf, was that the Russian army was divided into three parts separated by two deep ravines, and that these factions could barely move from one height to the other to provide mutual support. Another disadvantage was that the Observation Corps, reduced to five weak regiments, still suffering from its original problems, occupied the lowest hill of all three, the least well defended against an attack, the most exposed to the fire from of the Little Spitzberg and the Trettin Hill, which would be occupied by the Prussians.

Saltykov had moved the Russian and Austrian heavy baggage to the far bank of the Oder at Tschetschnow. There it formed a wagenburg, to which an infantry regiment was assigned as its guard. To communicate with it, Saltykov had constructed a fifth bridge. That was covered, on the right bank by a bridgehead or a redoubt that was guarded by the Austrian Warasdiner,

Liccaner[55], and Leopold Passy Infantry Regiments.

In the city of Frankfurt, Saltykov had only left five officers and 260 men, entitling it the "Lifeguard" for the inhabitants.

The regular and irregular Russian cavalry found itself massed between the redoubt of the Tschetschnow bridge and the Judenberg, or at the foot of the north slope of the plateau on the Grand Spitzberg and in the Els-Busch. The Austrian Regiments, Kalnoki, Nadasty, and the Russian Serbia Hussars camped beyond the Rothvorwerk, against the Frankfurt suburbs.

And finally, the advance posts occupied the course of the Hünerfloss and the Beckergrund.

Frederick II crossed the Oder at Lebus over five bridges. From there, as he did not expect to attack the Russians frontally, but to turn them by their eastern flank, he moved to the east making a large detour. This march was very difficult, because his horses had to pass through forests and through swamps, and they were pulling the heavy guns taken from Küstrin. At 2:00 p.m., on 11 August, the bulk of his forces took up positions on the heights between Tretten and the Bishofssee. He established his batteries on the hills and pushed his advance guard on the Hünerfluss.

Saltykov had already understood Frederick's movement would take him to the village of Kunersdorf, i.e. in the rear of the allied army, such as it was then laid out. He ordered a general about-face. Consequently, there occurred the same phenomenon as at Zorndorf: the western wing of the Russians, the left wing, was going to become the right wing, and the eastern wing was to become the left wing.

Saltykov put all the time that Frederick II employed in marching, the afternoon of the 11th and part of the following night, in transforming his position. It was now on the southern face of the heights he that he covered with works and the groups of heavy cannon. Judenberg was now covered with three large batteries, one of which could direct its fire on the bridges of Frankfurt and Tschetschnov; another, aimed to the south, could sweep the southernmost side of the hills. On the culminating point of Spitzberg was an enormous battery, flanked on the right by the second, covering the plain to the south, which could fire on the passages between the three Kunersdorf ponds. On Mühlberg there were two more, also projecting, plus a star shaped redoubt, to cover the course of the Hühnerfluss. All these batteries were connected to each other by trenches that formed a curtain, and through which one could draw infantry and their regimental guns. At the foot of the hills, he had dug wolf holes which would break the élan of the squadrons. The three hills formed a citadel with a continuous enclosure, whose large batteries were the bastions. Saltykov had

---

[55] Translator: The Prussian General Staff work, *Der Siebenjährige Krieg (1756-1763)*, Berlin, Mittler, 1901-1914, does not indicate that the Warasdiner or Liccaner Infantry Regiments (Croatian Grenz formations) were present. I suspect that the author has confused the Loudon and Bethlen Freikorps as being Croatians (i.e. light troops).

little concern for Judenberg, which the enemy could not attack without having the river at their backs, nor for the northern face the heights, whose work remained and which the Els-Busch marshes seemed to make inaccessible.

It was necessary to have the Austrian infantry regiments climb the Judenberg and have Villebois's corps move onto the Grand Spitzberg Plateau.

On the Judenberg, the first slopes on the side of the Oder were occupied by the Vyborg, Narva, and Archangel Infantry Regiments, which could move to the defense of the bridges if they were threatened. The southern front and its three batteries were guarded by the 1st Grenadiers, Voronehz, Perm and Azov, which also formed the first line. The north front was formed by Nizovski, 2nd Moscow, the Austrian Bethlen Freikorps, and the Baden-Baden, Los Rios, Ahrenberg, and Waldeck Regiments.

In the fold of the Laudongrund were the companies of Austrian grenadiers.

Between the Judenberg and the Tschetschnow bridge were the Croatian cavalry, Warasdiner, Liccainer, Leopold, Serbian Hussars, Slavo-Serbian Hussars, the Imperial Highness, 3rd and 4th Cuirassiers.

The Grand Spitzberg Plateau was occupied by 17 Russian regiments. The southern front was defended by Kazan, Nevski, 4th and 3rd Grenadiers, who occupied a screen that linked the large battery on Judenberg to the large Spitzberg battery; by the Vologda, Pskov, Apcheron, and Rostov Infantry Regiments, which were charged with covering that battery. The northern front was covered with, from Laudongrund to Kuhgrund, the Siberia, Viatka, Ouglitch, Kiev, Petersburg, Novgorod, Nijni-Novgorod, Bielozersk, and 2nd Grenadiers. At the foot of the front and in the Els-Busch were the Tchuguiev Cossacks, the horse grenadiers, the dragoons, all the rest of the cuirassiers, and the Austrian cavalry.

Saltykov stood on the plateau, with Villebois, who commanded the regiments closest to Laudongrund and Rumyantsev, who commanded the group closest to the Kuhgrund.

Finally, the Mühlberg was occupied by Golitzyn's five regiments, the 1st, 3rd, 4th, and 5th Musketeers, and the Grenadier Regiment that crowned the most exposed point of the hill and guarded the two batteries.

Throughout the afternoon of the 11th, Frederick II had thought that Saltykov, threatened by the position that he had assumed between Trettin and Bischofssee, would profit from the night to decamp by the Frankfurt bridges or by the Krossen highway. The night flowed by without anything happening. He now had to make dispositions for battle on the following day.

Frederick's attack was to begin with a double attack, one directed by Finck and Schorlemer on the side of Trettin and the other by the King, in person, on the side of Bischofssee. At 2:30 a.m., Frederick began his movement, moving between the lakes of that village and crossing the Hünerfluss.

Saltykov did not react. He thought it a simple reconnaissance. At daybreak, Laudon set fire to the village of Kunersdorf in order to make the passage between the lakes more difficult.

At 9:00 a.m., two Prussian batteries opened fire from the Trettin heights. Others occupied Little Spitzberg and the slopes neighboring the Kunersdorf lakes. The Mühlberg was then "embraced and surrounded by the Prussian batteries rather like a polygon in the form of a chair."

At 10:00 a.m., the cannonade became furious. At the same time the Prussian infantry and cavalry began deploying.

The King deployed his infantry in four lines: first was an advance guard, 8 battalions, under Generalmajors Lindstädt and Jung-Schenckendorf; then the first line, 22 battalions under the King, with Generalleutnants Wedel on the left and Hülsen on the right; then the second line, 15 battalions, with Kanitz on the right and Itzenplitz on the left; and finally, a reserve, 8 battalions, under Finck and three generalmajors.

His cavalry was formed into four divisions commanded by Prince von Württemberg, Seydlitz, Platen, and Schorlemer.

One sees in the *Ordre de bataille* [*Order of battle*] prepared by the Prussian General Staff (1860), that the King, distrusting Wedell's troops, which had so often been defeated by the Russians, had dispersed them throughout all his divisions and had amalgamated them with elements drawn from his own army or that of Finck, Prince Henry, and Prince von Württemberg.

Saltykov, attentively following all the movements of the Prussians, and who retained to himself the opportunity "to conform his dispositions to those taken by the enemy," understood that Mühlberg would be furiously assaulted and that the Russians could not hold it. As a result, he occupied himself with reinforcing the regiments on the Grand Spitzberg. He drew there the Laudon and Baden-Baden Regiments, and the Austrian grenadiers, then the Kolowrat and Wittenberg Hussars. He moved closer to the Kuhgrund and Laudongrund Ravines his cavalry regiments. He had the Austrian Liechtenstein and Löwenstein Hussars move up the Judenberg and had them posted between the two lines of Russian infantry.

At 11:00 a.m., the Prussian advance guard, descending from the heights it occupied, assaulted Mühlberg, led by Generalmajor Jung-Schenckendorf and protected by the fire of 60 cannon. When it descended into the bottom of the Beckergrund the Russian batteries had to cease firing because they could no longer see them. Golitzyn's infantry, already intimidated by the silence of its artillery, suddenly found itself attacked frontally and on both flanks. The grenadier regiment was, in an instant, thrown into the swamp to the north. The four regiments of musketeers, making conversions to the right and left, attempted to face the Prussians. Frederick II, who moved up with his first line to support his advance guard, brought his artillery with him, put it into battery, and opened canister fire on the Russians, who, in their turn, were driven into the Els-Busch.

This was a great success that Frederick had achieved. Of the three heights occupied by the Allies, that of the east, the Mühlberg, was in his power. It offered him the best position to bombard and assault the Spitzberg. He had knocked out 15 Russian battalions and captured 42 cannons.[56] By this first success Frederick threw a material and moral disorder into the Russian army, so "new to maneuvers," and obliged it to make a total conversion, finding itself pushed into a smaller place and piled up on the Spitzberg Plateau, giving the Prussian artillery a compact mass where every projectile struck home. "There was not a point," Saltykov says in his report, "where the enemy artillery did not cause ravages, and such that many caissons exploded, and many gun carriages were damaged."

No doubt Frederick thought himself victorious. He sent couriers to Berlin and to his army in Silesia. He returned to Prince Henry a courier who had brought him news of the victory at Minden, directing him to announce, in return, his own victory.

However, the most difficult task remained to be tackled. The Prussians had to cross the Kuhgrund ravine, some 50-60 feet wide and 10-15 deep, under the fire of the Spitzberg battery and under the fire of the Russian and Austrian regiments that stood on it.

In effect, Saltykov, always "conforming his dispositions to those of the enemy," executed a new conversion of his regiments, such that they now faced the Kuhgrund.

The Grand Spitzberg Plateau was so narrow, at least on this part of the battlefield, that one could only deploy two regiments across the new front. The Russians and Austrians, therefore, formed a series of echelons. In the first line were Rostov and the 2nd Grenadiers; in the second the Laudon Grenadiers, commanded by Campitelli; in the third Bielozersk and Nijni-Novgorod; in the fourth the Novgorod and Petersburg; in the fifth, the Laudon and Baden-Baden Regiments; in the six Archangel and the Tobolsk Dragoons; and then came Vologda, Piskov, and the 3rd and 4th Grenadiers, which continued to cover the great battery.

Bruce commanded these echelons. He attempted to pass the Kuhgrund and recapture the Mühlberg. He was checked, but he had delayed Frederick's offensive. If the King had been able to follow-up on his first success and captured the large battery, the Russian army would have been lost, but it was the fire of this battery, which swept the village of Kunersdorf and the passages between its ponds, that pevented the cavalry of Seydlitz from deploying in front of the Weissee and Fauler See and strike the right flank of the Russian positions.

---

[56] Not 180, as claimed by Bolotof.

Frederick had remarked that the Els-Busch swamp was less uncrossable that it was supposed, since the fugitives from the Mühlberg and the horse grenadiers had succeeded in crossing it. The Prussians began cannonading these fugitives who had begun rallying on Golitzyn. Then, taken by a new panic, they carried away the horse grenadiers in their new rout, fleeing to the Rothvorwerk. The Prussians could not attack the Grand Spitzberg Plateau on its northern front.

The King then prepared a triple attack: 1.) on its right by the Els-Busch; 2.) frontally by the Kuhgrund; and 3.) on its left by Seydlitz's cavalry.

On the right, the attack was affected by a column of infantry and cavalry. The infantry column ran up, close to the level of the Laudongrund and the Judenberg, against the Siberia, Nizovski, and Azov Infantry Regiments, supported by the Ouglitch and Kiev Regiments, which were by Brigadiers Berg and Derfelden. Borozdine reinforced these regiments with part of his Shuvalov howitzers. From Judenberg the Austrian artillery bombarded the Prussian column. The Prussians, struck by canister on the front and flank suffered tremendous casualties and were thrown back on the Els-Busch.

The cavalry of Prince von Württemberg, who flanked it on the left, charged, and if one believes Frederick II, at the wrong time[57] and uniquely because Prince von Württemberg was "impatient at the inaction of the cavalry." He climbed the north face of the plateau, at about the same level as the great battery on Spitzberg. He was initially successful. His cuirassiers climbed the slope and fell on the flank of the Novgorod Regiment, and as the Russian infantry were almost completely occupied with the Prussian infantry, the Prussian cavalry penetrated well into the plateau. Laudon and Rumyantsev only had time to call the Kolowrath, Tobolsk, and Archangel Dragoons to help him. In an impetuous charge they drove back the Prussian cuirassiers, who were exhausted by their great effort, and threw them back to the Els-Busch.

In the center, Frederick II directed the frontal attack. His advance guard, his first line, and Finck's reserve climbed the slopes opposite the Kuhgrund, drove back the Russians before them, moving within 800 paces, then to within 150 paces of the Russian battery. But them there arrived from the Judenberg the Azov Regiment, and the 2nd Moscow and the 1st Grenadiers, led by Brigadier Berg. On the other side, the Russian artillery did not remain inactive. General Borozdine, with the Shuvalov howitzers, covered the closely massed Prussian infantry with shells. The Russians defended themselves with their usual calm. The attack stalled and gained no ground. Here the genius and the finesse of Frederick's tactics did not serve him. It was a brutal face to face slugfest with sabers and bayonets and each foot of ground conquered was covered with the dead and dying.

---

[57]*Histoire de la guerre de Sept ans* and *Politische Correspondenz*.

Bolotov tells us:

> God himself had inspired our generals; in the place of the
> beaten first line, they hastily formed a new line, taking
> a regiment from the right, a regiment from the left, thus
> building a short and not very deep dam, but multiplied, it
> resisted the enemy one after the other, more regiments
> moving to the butchery, because the enemy, growing of
> number every minute, made new progress every moment,
> conducting himself with an indescribable bravery on these
> thin lines, destroying them one after the other. However, our
> men did not cross arms with them, but each line, putting a
> knee to the ground, discharged its muskets, until there was
> nobody alive, nobody intact in their line. Every step delayed
> the Prussians and gave our generals time to study the situation
> and determine the means of saving the army.

However, the Knobloch Regiment, from the first Prussian line,
succeeded in occupying the burning village of Kunersdorf and established
itself within the walled cemetery. From there, in climbing the ravines, the
Russians climbed to the Spitzberg Plateau and assailed the Allies in their right
flank.

This was, for the Allies, the most critical moment of the battle. If one
is to believe Bolotov, the Generalissimo should have been totally demoralized:

> The old man who commanded us found himself in despair
> that he forgot everything, threw himself off of his horse,
> kneeled on the ground, and raised his hands to Heaven, in
> the presence of everyone, supplicating, tears in his eyes,
> the All Powerful to come to his aid in such an extremity of
> misfortune and to save his men from certain destruction. In
> this prayer, which the virtuous old man raised to Heaven
> in the purity of his heart and soul, it appeared that Heaven
> heard him, for a few minutes later, there occurred something
> that could not have been anticipated.[58]

It was 3:00 p.m. Frederick II had conquered more than half the ground
that the Russo-Austrians had occupied in the morning. However, all the
Prussian infantry, including the reserve, had been engaged. It was exhausted
and further operations were necessary to drive the Russians from the Spitzberg
and Judenberg. Finck recommended that they stop and hold the positions

---

[58] Bolotof, Vol. I, p, 918.

they had conquered. He represented that that the Russian material and morale had been cruelly damaged; that they only awaited nightfall to withdraw; that this would achieve the result sought by the King, without costing him more soldiers. Retzow relates that "all the generals spoke in manner, except for one which sought to flatter [the King]. Though he does not name him, Bolotov does. "And you, Wedell," said the King, "what do you think?" Wedel, who was more the courtesan than a general, wished to flatter the King and gave him advice that conformed to his desires. Then the King, without thinking long about it, cried out: "Well, forward!"

Whatever the truth may be, it is certain that Frederick II, who saw in his heart an incomplete success and saw the same from Zorndorf, had decided to finish, once and for all, with the Russians, and sought, by an irremediable defeat or a total destruction, "to get rid of them" for all the campaign. He did not want a half-victory.

He now laid new demands on his infantry. Without taking the large Russian battery, it was turned by the right. Its defenders, disconcerted, began to abandon it. "One sees now to what victories are due!" Frederick would later say.[59] According to his account, Laudon ran off, but should have re-occupied or reinforced the battery, and had it fire canister from its heavy guns on his Prussians.

The attack on the left alone could determine the new operation. It was that which Seydlitz's cavalry would direct on the southern flank of the Spitzberg Plateau. The intrepid warrior hesitated to undertake it. He had first to move his squadrons through the intervals between the Kundersdorf ponds and to form up under the Russian guns on the Spitzberg and Judenberg, in an area where several firs converged. Then he had to charge not against cavalry or infantry in the open, but up steep slopes crowned with entrenchments, and before which were sprinkled wolfs holes. His military eye did not serve him as well as it had at Zorndorf, where one could see all the action as if it was "on the palm of the hand." He did not know where the King was in his attack on the plateau. He thus hesitated; but as he received from Frederick II courier after courier, as he would not answer "with his head" of the happy outcome from a new disobedience, he resolved to give the signal.

He debouched through the intervals between the ponds, put his squadrons in line under a terrible fire, and charged the entrenchments that were defended by the Pskov, 3rd and 4th Grenadiers, Nevski, and Kazan Regiments. Naturally he suffered great losses. His horsemen were decimated, hungry, and exhausted by 14 hours spent on horseback. The principal nerve of the Prussian Army, its magnificent cavalry, was not broken. The weak Allied cavalry took heart at Seydlitz's attack. Initially two squadrons of Austrian hussars and two of the Imperial Highness Cuirassiers charged them as they retreated. The rest

---

[59] *Histoire de la guerre de Sept ans.*

of the Allied cavalry then came up. In the first line were the Lichtenstein, Löwenstein, and Württemberg Hussars, with the Imperial Highness, Kiev, Novotroitski, and Kazan Cuirassiers. In the second line were the Archangel, Tobolsk, and Riazan Dragoons. In reserve, Tottleben had the 4th Cuirassiers and his Cossacks. The charge was led by Laudon in person. Seydlitz's cavalry was pushed beyond the ponds. Then the victorious squadrons arrayed themselves on the edge of the Frankfurt Wood, their front facing towards the Great Spitzberg. After this brilliant charge, they took almost no further action in the battle.

Saltykov's courage returned. From the Judenberg, where there remained only three regiments of Austrian infantry and three hussar regiments, he endlessly called for reinforcements to be sent to the Spitzberg Plateau. He sent all of Fermor's corps there, which was still fresh. The great battery on Spitzberg, once abandoned was now reoccupied. Under this irresistible pressure, the Prussians, who had no intact troops remaining, were forced to withdraw to the Kuhgrund. The crest of the ravine was again lined with artillery and Shuvalov howitzers. Projectiles rained on the Mühlberg where the troops thrown back from the Spitzberg mixed with the last troops Frederick had brought up. Frederick claimed that these soldiers now feared captivity and deportation to Siberia. A panic arose, and the Prussians began to tumble down the slopes. The Russians crossed the Kuhgrund and closed on the Mühlberg with their bayonets lowered. In an instant the hill was swept clean; Kunersdorf and its cemetery was recaptured.

Frederick II exhausted himself attempting to stop the rout. His clothing was torn. Two horses were killed under him. A musket ball struck the golden case that he carried in his pocket. He constantly drove back to the battle anything that looked like a formed body of troops, but his infantry refused to rally and dispersed immediately afterwards.

He did not have a single intact battalion left. Only Seydlitz's cavalry and some squadrons of the Guard cavalry remained operational. The King wished, at any price, to recover the victory that was escaping him. Seydlitz again moved past the Kunersdorf ponds, charged the entrenchments, and was struck down by a canister shot in the chest. Then everyone fled. Prince von Württemberg, turning around to call his dragoons to a new charge, found he was all alone. He was wounded. Puttkammer was killed at the head of his hussars. Finck and Hülsen were wounded.

Free from fear that still this cavalry inspired in them, the Russian battalions started down from the heights. The regular cavalry, Cossacks, and the Croats spread themselves across the plain at a gallop.

Frederick vainly attempted to dispute the passages of the Hühnerfluss with the von Leswitz Regiment, the Pioneer Regiment, and two squadrons of the Guard Cuirassiers. However, the Tchuguiev Cossacks, with their long lances, did not hesitate to charge the iron clad men, drove them back, captured their standard, and took their commander, Biedersee, captive. The fugitives of the Prussian army pushed through the narrow passages between the Bischofssee lakes. The Pioneer Regiment was captured. The King was almost alone; one already heard the hurrahs of the Cossacks as they rushed at him. Finally, Lieutenant Pritwitz succeeded in surrounding him with an escort of 40 von Ziethen hussars and covered his escape exchanging saber blows with the enemy riders.

Laudon pursued the debris of Seydlitz's cavalry on to Celowo; Tottleben galloped on Bischofssee and Trettin; the horse grenadiers, who had still done nothing, followed the hussars, the Cossacks, and the Croats. They gathered up wagons, caissons, cannons. Everyone who tried to resist was captured, sabered, or thrown into the swamp. At Bischofssee, Tottleben threw an entire squadron into the swamp. However, he stopped there, and the horse grenadiers did not move beyond Trettin. If the pursuit had been more energetic, or the Russian squadrons less fatigued, perhaps less occupied with pillage, not a Prussian battalion would have escaped.

During the day, a Prussian corps, under Wunsch, following the other bank of the Oder, had entered Frankfurt and had captured the 260 men that Saltykov had left there as a "lifeguard." Brandt, occupied with preserving the wagonberg, did nothing to prevent this, which the Russian army did not notice, and which had no influence on the operations, but would have had very serious results, if the victory had not been decided in favor of the Allies. Wunsch quickly evacuated Frankfurt and retired on Lebus.

The following day, Saltykov had a *Te Deum* sung and victory salvoes followed. It was not like Zorndorf. There were no more Prussian cannons to answer him with their salvos. He sent his first report to the Tsarina, which was carried to her by another Saltykov (Nicolas Ivanovitch), who would later become governor of the Grand Dukes Alexander and Constantine, and who would die a prince and a field marshal.

The Generalissimo wondered in his report, "if there had been in history a more complete and more glorious victory, where the zeal and the talent of her generals and officers, the heroism, bravery, discipline, and fraternal harmony of her soldiers, merited being cited as an example to the centuries to come."

He praised the artillery, which "had maintained the glory it had conquered on other occasions." Finally, he gave a delicate homage to his Austrian allies. "The corps of Imperial Roman troops, instead of envy and discord which has so often manifested itself between the troops of other nations, appears to have made its junction with the troops of Your Imperial Majesty so that the soldiers of the two armies could show their respective courage to the other and to give to the world a special example of concord and harmony between allies." Saltykov wrote also to Vorontsov: "What a blow for the King of Prussia, who came to exterminate us! And we trounced him!"

The Russians counted 2,614 dead and 10,863 wounded; the Austrians lost 1,399 dead or wounded. The Prussian loss was enormous: 7,627 dead, 4,542 wounded, and 7,000 prisoners. More considerable was the number of fugitives that never returned to the Prussian flag. All their generals were killed or wounded, or at least bruised; 540 officers were no longer in the ranks. They had abandoned to the Russians 26 infantry standards, 2 cavalry standards, and 172 cannon, among which were the pieces that Frederick had taken with such effort from Küstrin.

Among the Prussian officers who fell at Kunersdorf, was one who was mourned in all of Europe's newspapers: it was Ewald von Kleist, major of the Hausen Regiment, the poet who wrote *Printemps*, the author of so many other energetic and gracious pieces. Kleist, aged 44, found a glorious and cruel death. Frederick had drawn this regiment from the army of Prince Henry. With Finck's infantry he attacked the Russian positions. He already had a dozen contusions and two fingers on his right hand were cut. His saber in hand, he charged an Austrian battalion and received a ball in his left hand. Taking his saber from his mutilated right hand, he continued to fight. A canister shot then broke his right arm and knocked him from his horse. Two of his soldiers carried him to the ambulance, where a surgeon began the necessary amputations. The surgeon was killed by a ball. Some Cossacks came up, robbed him, took his hat, his wig, and his shirt. They would have killed him if he had not spoken to them in Polish. Taking him for a Pole, they contented themselves with throwing him naked into the swamp. During the night he was saved by some Russian hussars, who dried him off, gave him an old coat and a hat; they warmed him at a campfire, giving him some bread and water. One of them offered him an 8 groschen piece, and he refused it. The Cossacks returned, taking from him everything the hussars had given him. The next morning a Russian officer named Stackelberg, a cavalry captain, found him and had him taken to Frankfurt. Professor Nicolai received him in his house and cared for him. A number of Russian officers came to visit him and offer their services. However, the care arrived too late and, on 24 August, 12 days after the battle, Kleist died of his wounds. Professor Nicolai handled the funeral. The Russian commander of Frankfurt, Chettnov, rendered him military honors. The body was carried by a dozen grenadiers and the funeral procession was followed by the principal officers of the garrison.

The evening of the battle of Kunersdorf Frederick's despair was terrible. From the field of carnage, he wrote to Finckenstein: "My misfortune is very sharp… Out of an army of 48,000 men, I have no more than 3,000. Now I am writing, everyone has fled, and I am no longer the master of my men… It is a cruel reverse. I will not survive it. The results of the action will be worse than the battle itself. I have no more resources, and, not to lie, I believe I am lost. I will not survive the loss of my fatherland. Good-bye forever!"

These three last words cause one to believe that Frederick was momentarily considering suicide. And, in effect, all hope seemed lost. How could he anticipate that Saltykov and Laudon would not aggressively pursue the few thousand men that remained to him; that Prince Henry, weakened by the troops Frederick had taken from him, could hold against Daun; what would be the fate of Berlin and the Kingdom of Prussia? Becoming a prisoner of the Cossacks or the Croats was the only opportunity that seemed to await the King; escaping from Saltykov, he could only fall into Daun's hands. Total destruction seemed only days away.

He spent the night of the 12th/ 13th in Ötscher, to the northeast of Lebus. Then he crossed the bridges over the Oder, and, on the 14th, he was at Reitwin, on the left bank. He was sick with fatigue, emotion, chagrin, his contusion, where his coat was pierced by a ball, and stitched back up with white thread, bothered him immensely; and he turned command over to Finck. The number of men around him rose from 3,000 to 10,000 men. The weakening of Frederick's constitution was substantial. He could not stand. Profoundly discouraged, he had Finckenstein ask England that it intervene and negotiate a peace. The saddest reflections weighed down his soul; around him his companions in glory disappeared one after another. The great Schwerin had fallen at Prague, Keith and Brandeburg at Hochkirch; Wobersnow at Paltzig; Puttkammer at Kunnersdorf; Seydlitz, Prince von Württemberg, Hülsen, Itzenplitz, and Knobloch were in the hands of the surgeons. It was quite worse than when he wrote: "My generals pass to Acheron[60] at a full gallop, and soon nobody will remain." The "cruel war," that turned so bitterly against him as the three women[61] continued, had destroyed all his elites: "Ah! If I had ten of my 1757 battalions! … But what remains to us is comparable only to the worse."[62]

Later, Frederick made this comment: "If the Russians had known how to benefit from their success, if they had pursued these discouraged troops, it would have been the end of Prussians… Finally it would have depended only on our enemies to finish the war; they had only to give us the *coup de grâce*."[63] The evening of Kunersdorf, he already saw the enemy on the way on his capital: "In Berlin," he wrote in Finckenstein, "one will do well to think of his safety."[64] The following day he prescribed that this minister be transported with the government to Magdeburg and to "quietly" engage the rich and easy

[60]Translator: The Acheron is also known as the Hades River, or the path to the world of the dead. The phrase might be less romantically translated as, "My generals drop like flies."
[61] Translator: A reference to the three ladies of the period: Empress Elisabeth, Maria-Theresa, and Madame Pompedour, but it could also be to the three Fates who, in Greek mythology, determined one's fate.
[62] *Politische Correspondenz*, to Finckenstein, 16 August.
[63]*Histoire de la guerre de Sept ans*
[64] *Politische Correspondenz*, to Finckenstein, 12 August 1759.

people to withdraw themselves in Hamburg with their effects and capital, because the enemy can be in Berlin in two or three days."[65]

In this battle of Kunersdorf, Saltykov did not show himself as a mediocre general. In accounting for what he owed to the councils of Laudon, it is necessary to recognize that he had resolutely accepted battle, chosen the most advantageous positions, added to their strength with well-conceived works, made the most exact reconnaissances possible, and assured his retreat as he prepared his defense. He had known "to conform his dispositions to those of his adversary," broken with the routine great square of Münich, made convenient modifications as Frederick's movement developed, shifted forces from his western wing to the help his eastern wing, benefitted from all his resources, and showed coolness and tenacity at the most critical time. One could reproach him only for not having tried, at the beginning, to dispute the passage of Oder and, at the end, for not having supplemented the defeat of the Prussians by a more energetic pursuit.

The faults of the great Prussian captain appear much more serious. It is obvious that he had not taken time to make a detailed reconnaissance of the ground. In the strong positions where he met the Russians, it was perhaps imprudent to fight a battle, especially as if he had held himself on the defensive, he would have obliged the Allies to come down from their heights, either to attack him on his, or to withdraw. It seems that he recognized his boldness was an error later. Catt says to us that one day, seeking to comfort the King, he said to him: "But, lord, doesn't one need bold blows in war?" And Frederick answered him: "Yes, they are needed, but one does not have, my dear, to undertake them on the idea of the weakness or the lack of wisdom on the part of the enemy." Was the point of attack, on Mühlberg, well-chosen? Masslovski sometimes asks what the great Suvorov would have done if in the place of Saltykov. One can't but wonder what Napoleon would have done in the place of Frederick II. The position of the Austro-Russians at Austerlitz reflects, in certain aspects, their position at Kunersdorf; there was a height at Austerlitz that seemed almost as inaccessible, and which was the key to the battle. Napoleon did not use his forces against the others; it is the Pratzen Plateau that he wanted, and he took it. It is true that this was after having induced his adversaries to weaken themselves in the hope of benefitting from his apparent weaknesses. Napoleon, at the beginning of Kunersdorf, might have attacked Mühlberg initially; but he would not have crossed the Kuhgrund; he might well have quickly transformed the attack into a simple diversion, calculated to attract to this side the troops on the Spitzberg and the Judenberg; and it is apparently the Judenberg, as strong as it was, that he would have attacked in depth, before his infantry was decimated and demoralized in a secondary enterprise.

---

[65] *Ibid.*, 13 August.

To the contrary, Frederick II piled up on this point all his regiments and even his reserves. He was then obliged to assault the Spitzberg, which was difficult and strongly occupied, with Seydlitz's cavalry. He had the boldness to charge his squadrons at the entrenchments and batteries. He threw away this splendid cavalry and had no more when it was a question of supporting the Prussian retreat, which consequently changed into a rout.

For this act, later and in secrecy, he made bitter reproaches to himself. But initially he did not acknowledge this and preferred to throw the fault on the cavalry. On the 16th, writing to Prince Henry, he was satisfied to say: "Prince von Württemberg and Seydlitz were wounded, the cavalry had disappeared from the battlefield." It appears that he went further in his injustice, because on the 24th we find him almost in a polemic with Prince von Württemberg: "In reply to your letter of the 22nd, I must unfortunately say that the cavalry did not distinguish itself at all in this battle, as it charged badly; as a result it was put in such confusion that, when it became necessary at the end, one could draw no service from it." He persisted, and in a bad mood, in a reply dated the 28th: "I do not understand what there can be shocking for Your Highness in the letter that I wrote to you earlier. It is a constant that the cavalry withdrew one hour before the end of the battle and that it was no longer present when I had the greatest need of it... It is not astonishing besides that one was not prodigal with rewards after a lost battle." It is not very probable, however, that Seydlitz, if a little hasty in his first charge, allowed Prince von Württemberg and Puttkammer to charge on the second occasion without a direct order from the King. When they directed the attack in which the two first were wounded and the third killed, we see that the battle was already lost: actually, it is thanks to their devotion that the offensive of the Russian infantry was delayed and that the remains of the Prussian army could affect their withdrawal.

If one compares the faults made at Paltzig by Wedell, for which Frederick so harshly reproached him, perhaps one will find that Frederick committed all the same errors at Kunersdorf. He delivered a battle without pressing reasons, attacked very strong positions, persisting in this attack as the chances of success decreased, and used his cavalry against an entrenched height that was armed with batteries.

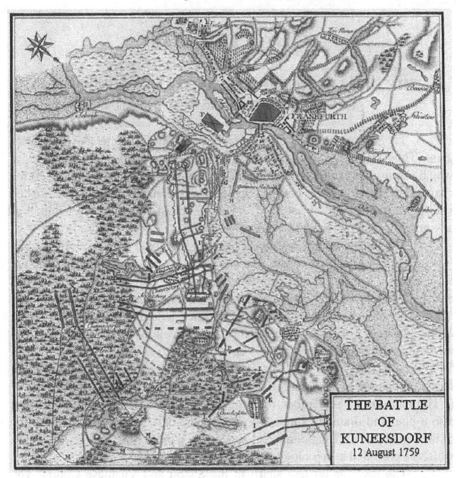

THE BATTLE
OF
KUNERSDORF
12 August 1759

CHAPTER XII

THE DAY AFTER THE BATTLE OF KUNERSDORF –
THE END OF THE 1759 CAMPAIGN

The effect produced in Europe by the battle of Kunersdorf was very great. The Tsarina was delighted. She had a *Te Deum* sung in her palace, to which she invited the French Ambassador. He gave his congratulations to the chancellor. He wrote to his court: "Our reciprocal compliments always finished with these expressions: Very good; a Russian must be a good Frenchman as any good Frenchman must be a good Russian.[66]

The ambassador noted that Elisabeth "received with modesty and an infinite religion this great event, that she regards a proof of divine protection for the good cause." She rewarded the happy Generalissimo with field-marshal's baton; a silver medal was struck in his honor with this inscription: "To the conqueror of the Prussians." The other generals were also the object of the Tsarina's generosity. Lieutenant Colonel Volkov, who had brought her the captured flags was promoted to colonel and given a gift of 2,000 rubles. "The Prussian flags and standards were brought to the palace by a detachment of the Leibgarde, to the sound of drums, and were placed in the throne room." (L'Hôpital.) On 17 September, the Empress' birthday, Brigadier Soumarokov, also a poet and dramatic author, director of the new Russian troupe and one of the founders of the national theater, directed a piece (*The Refuge of Virtue*), which he preceded by a prolog in honor of the great victory: *The New Laurels.*[67]

The joy was no less sharp in the Saxon and Viennese Courts. The King of Poland decorated Saltykov with the Grand Cordon of the White Eagle. Maria-Theresa sent a ring and a snuffbox to him encrusted with diamonds, plus 5,000 ducats. She made gifts of silver and jewels to Fermor, Rumyantsev, Panin, and Stoffeln. The Court of Versailles transmitted its congratulations to Petersburg. We know however that it always had the fear that the Russians might be too victorious. But French opinion was moved favorably by the bravery of the Russian troops. The poet Teissern composed a piece of poetry in Saltykov's honor, which was transmitted to Elisabeth by the French Embassy.

Finckenstein had written to the Prussia Ambassador and to the King of England: "Only a miracle can save us. Speak to Pitt, not as a minister, but as a friend. Explain to him the pressing danger that faces the most faithful ally that England has ever had. Perhaps he can make a peace."[68] The English

[66] A. Rambaud, *Instructions*, Vol. II, p. 94.
[67] Pierre Corvin, *Histoire du theater russe.*
[68] Vorontzof's Archives, Vol. VI, p. 370.

ministers did not show themselves shaken by this terrible failure: they assured the Prussian Minister Münchhausen that, as long as Frederick would be healthy and safe, they would not lose courage; but the moment was not favorable to speak about peace.

No author at the time of the writing of this work had any doubt that the day after the battle, in the disarray in which the Prussian Monarchy found itself, it would have sufficed for 20,000 or 25,000 Austro-Russians to occupy Berlin and, suddenly, bring an end to the war. The day after Kunersdorf, Hadik had moved to rejoin Laudon with his army corps. However, they were not going to Berlin. Suddenly, Daun, Laudon, and Hadik resumed their obsessing role towards Saltykov, seeking only to prevent him from gathering the fruits of his victory and to draw him into Silesia. Their pretensions and egotism shined constantly. It is believed that they attempted to persuade Saltykov to give the Prussian artillery and prisoners to them. The Field Marshal refused. He charged the Benckendorf brigade with the task of escorting the captured materials and prisoners to Posen, along with the Russian casualties.

As a result of this detachment and the losses sustained on the 12th, Saltykov had barely 20,000 men, but Laudon and Hadik had 15,000 men and they would give him 12,000 of them. The numerical preponderance, in the army, now passed to the Austrians. Saltykov could do nothing without them; and Hadik refused to march on Berlin. The reasons that he gave for his refusal appear futile. He feared that they would lack food; he judged the season too advanced, even though they were at the end of August. Finally, he feared that Frederick, profiting from his absence, would throw himself on Saxony.

Daun, who had advanced as far as Pribus, and had pushed Bukow to Lauban, Ahrenberg to Marklisa, Markner to Görlitz, and Harsch to Trautenau, did not put all his troops in motion because of the weak corps that Prince Henry had at Schmottseifen and Löwenberg. He was not to attack him, but only to observe him. He imagined that this prince would throw himself between the Imperial and Russian masses. This is what limited Austrian operations when Frederick II, still on the 24th, expected to see Daun making his junction with the Russians before Frankfurt and to give the *coup de grâce* to Prussia. In quick succession, Daun sent to Saltykov Prince von Lobkowitz, then Lascy, then the Russian attaché Springer, all with messages and propositions of the same order: one could not undertake new enterprises; it was necessary to think of going into winter quarters; he asked the Russian army to cover his operations in Saxony or in Silesia.

What would have happened if Saltykov could have moved on Berlin, without taking council of anyone other than himself, leaving his allies to their erudite "march-operations" and their sterile war of sieges? He could not, initially, because of the instructions given him to listen to the experienced councils of Daun, to not "move away" from what he asked of him. Even his two Prussian victories had not emancipated him from the supervision of the Conference. Suvorov, who appears otherwise as energetic and determined to us would later undergo the same obstacles and directions coming from St. Petersburg, which obliged to get along with his allies, suffering the egoistic and suspicious supervision of the Austrians: even after Gassano, Trebbia, and Novi; after the destruction of three republican armies, Suvorov could not attack French territory; it was necessary for him to follow the call of the Austrians into the maze of the Swiss mountains and to lose his victorious army there.

For purely military reasons, Saltykov could not act alone against Berlin. He required 25,000 to 30,000 men. He had close to that number, but many of his regiments, above all, those in the Observation Corps, were disorganized, lacking good cadres and good officers. If he complained, the day after Paltzig, of having worn out and broken gun carriages, artillery equipment that was damaged, insufficient horses to pull his guns and cartage, an insufficient supply of projectiles, his condition was even worse after the battle of 12 August!

He remained at Kunersdorf for four days after the action. On the 16th, he saw that the heat and the stench of the carnage made remaining intolerable and potentially dangerous. He moved to Lossow on the Oder, crossed the river, and then moved south to join the Austrians. On the 22nd, when at Guben, he met with Daun. It occurred in a small room and without witnesses. Little is known of what happened. It is certain that Daun rejected all movement on Berlin, asking that Saltykov remain beyond the Oder to cover the Austrians while they besieged Dresden, then proposed that together they invade Silesia.

Saltykov categorically refused this latter proposal. The security of East Prussia was too important for him. The Marquis de Montalembert, French military attaché, in a letter to de Choiseul, gives the following summary of a conversation he had with Daun:

> The Marshal has informed me that he had obtained from Count Saltykov, in his interview, that he would remain beyond the Oder, that he had offered to furnish his army with bread and forage which would be necessary, and that after the capture of Dresden, they would march together on Silesia, or the Russians would take up winter quarters if the siege of Neisse, which he had in sight, could succeed. He had greatly recommended to me that I maintain Count Soltykov in these sentiments.[69]

Frederick II, on his side, thought to summarize the famous interview thus:

---

[69] Montalembery, *Correspondance*, 2 Vol. In-18, London, 1777.

On that which Marshal Daun pressed Saltykov to push his operations with vigor, he responded to him: "I have done enough, sir, this year; I have won two battles, which cost Russia 27,000 men. I am waiting to put myself in action again, when you have won two victories in your turn. It is not just that the troops of my sovereign act all alone.[70]

Frederick II is not far from the truth here; because here is what Montalembert reports to us from his interviews of Saltykov and the sentiments that reigned in his general headquarters:

> From the camp at Lieberrose, in Lusace, 31 August 1759.[71]
>
> … I found, upon arriving, the Russian generals overpowered with the weight of this war. Count Saltykov repeated to me, — that which I saw that he had said to everyone, — that the Russian army had done enough; that if the Marshal Daun had not in mind totally sacrificing him, he would have no difficulty following the King of Prussia, and that it was up to him, with fresh troops, to complete the work so well started; that, for him, he was ready to support him and fight once again if the Marshal found himself in a position where his assistance was necessary; that while awaiting this, he had resolved to rest his army….' That finally he had decided to conserve the remainder of his brave men, who had fought so well at Paltzig and at Frankfurt [Kunersdorf].
> I unsuccessfully represented that in not following the King of Prussia further, he would allow the Austrians to gather up the fruits of his victory. He responded to me that he was not jealous and wished them with all his heart the greatest success; that he had done enough.
> I realized in St. Petersburg, but even more distinctly in this army, that all who are Russians are intimately persuaded that the Viennese Court cares little about sparing them, and that it is its intention to make them support all the weight of the war. They are very attractive since their victories and speaking of the Austrians in unsuitable terms. For the Swedes, they regard them with contempt; they do not wish to suffer speaking about them and Count Saltykov has told me that he would be most angry to have them in his army.

---

[70] Frederick II, *Histoire de la guerre de Sept ans.*
[71] French Foreign Affairs, *Russian Correspondence*, Vol. LX, the piece that follows piece 74.

"They are brave otherwise," he told me, "but it is no longer their time."[72]

Saltykov, later, when the Austrians had pushed the end of his patience, expressed himself in even sharper terms in his correspondence with Vorontsov:

It is not my business only to mix myself in political matters. But you point out the past...The battle of Zorndorf is instructive enough for the help which we then received from the Austrians. Closer to us still, is the battle before Frankfurt [Kunersdorf]. The King of Prussia spent 36 hours crossing the Oder; Daun was not with more than 9 miles from there: I sent courier after courier to him. Hadik was within 7 miles; I asked Daun: "Where is Hadik? He can still hasten towards us." Laudon says to me: "I do not know." The King crossed the Oder: I send a courier to Hadik. The King starts to draw up his batteries: I send another courier. The battle starts: my courier, who was a colonel, had the time to return before the end of the battle and to be wounded in a charge by his regiment. Therefore, the Austrians were not so far away; they could have arrived in time if they had wanted to. The battle is declared undecided, new courier. The battle is won, yet another courier. The King crosses the Oder in total disorder; Hadik was near; why did he not attack and take all his forces? Of Laudon's regiments there were, in all, two and they took part in the action; seven did not move from their places. We had only three regiments which were not under fire, because they were occupied with the convoy, artillery, with the casualties, with the patients. Our muskets were broken, our ammunition consumed or spoiled; in three days we could barely bury our dead, bandage the casualties, and repair our artillery. Not one part of our army was still in a condition to fight. As for them, the Austrians were all healthy, and safe, and paid. I do not recriminate, but who does not recriminate against me, under the pretext that I did not destroy the King? It is necessary to have been there to know how easy it would have been to destroy His Majesty. He was close to Fürstenwalde, and at most he had 12,000 men and 20 guns. I sent to Daun Major General Caramelli: "Let us attack!" He answered me: "I am not far from you; we will see; wait; hold the King in place, that is all that I ask of you." I did it to please him; I remained before Frankfurt,

---

[72] Translator: This is probably a reference to the soldiers of Charles XII and his army.

in Lossow, Hohenwalde, and Lieberose. Hadik was in front of him. Each day our hussars and Cossacks skirmished with them; thus, we took Gordt. Who thus was ahead? Who acted? We only received fodder at the point of the sword; we took it with our hands. The King held himself in the woods, in the marshes, incompetent to stir up... Daun did not cease saying to me: "Wait, I will attack Prince Henry, hold the King in respect." After that he sent me: "Impossible. I will not attack the King." This is what I awaited. I wanted to take the offensive, without him asking me. Suddenly I learn that Daun left for Saxony!...I do not blame the conduct of Count Daun. [It is] possible that he acts according to his orders. They undoubtedly consist of taking others' chestnuts from the fire and preserving his world... I would like to, however, know what they wanted. Who will attack the King? Why didn't they attack him themselves with such a large army, almost on their premises, having their backs against their Bohemia and their Moravia, with fortresses and stores everywhere, and in the event of misfortune an assured retreat? I only feel guilty for having advanced too far; because finally, if I had lost the battle before Frankfurt, it was all our army that would have been lost, being so far, I do not say from our borders, but even from Poland and the Vistula.

The fortress of Dresden resisted Daun. Saltykov was impatient. On 26 August, by means of the Austrian General Caramelli, he spoke again of a common operation against Berlin, declaring that if the Allies refused to assist him, he would withdraw on Guben. However, as he had received the order from St. Petersburg to cover the siege operations at Dresden, he moved on the 30th, to Lieberose. He took up position with Hadik on the right flank, with Laudon as a rearguard, in a fashion contained and observed by the Austrians, with his heavy baggage at Guben. He remained there, until 16 September, in the most complete inaction.

How much this inaction weighed on him; how much it irritated him against the demanding and generally inactive allies, as one sees in the letter that he addressed, on 13 September, to Chancellor Vorontsov:[73]

The end of the war, peace, or whatever denouement you could have desired would have been in our hands. The King of Prussia had been so well beaten and ruined that there remained to him no more than 30,000 men and about

---

[73] *Soc. Imp. d'histoire de Russie*, Vol. IX. P. 49 (in Russian).

20 cannon and how much he was terrified, as you know. His family had fled to Magdeburg, while Berlin waited to receive a visit from the Russians or the Austrians. Daun had allowed everything to escape, always in vain projects, in correspondence, in dispositions, in scattering his forces. And what was the result? He had let everything escape from his hands, received shame, and finally everything was lost. Could he find a better occasion than that which we had given him, when we had given him the King of Prussia beaten and ruined? He did not know what to do. In maintaining myself here two weeks while I sit with my arms crossed, we suffer shortages. I do not wish to irritate my sovereign, but I am forced to leave this place. If I persist in remaining here, our horses will perish; is it necessary to wait until we are afoot, carrying our own food? We lack that already. I am not able to trust the promises of our allies, so I am obliged to nourish myself. If they continue to delude us, I will withdraw myself to our magazines. It is really painful to lose these honest soldiers unnecessarily. Such an army could not easily be rebuilt. God give it health! I add the wish to receive some recruits to renew my veteran soldiers a bit. From our allies one can expect no good. They wish that we do everything and remain themselves without a scratch. During the entire campaign they have not seen the enemy.

In France as well, they were discontented with Daun. Choiseul expressed this to Ambassador Stahremberg in the presence of Ambassador Michel Bestujev, while giving praise for the behavior displayed by the Russians at Kunersdorf. He limited himself to reproaching the Petersburg Cabinet for managing too much in East Prussia, for not supporting its finances by imposing extraordinary contributions on the land, as Frederick II had never failed to do in Saxony and Mecklenburg. Vorontsov responded to him, as follows, by Michael Bestujev:

It is to not know the true state of the resources of East Prussia to imagine that one can raise contributions there similar to those raised in Saxony and Mecklenburg. We know, by experience, that the inhabitants of Prussia are not in a state to pay such contributions, be it by poverty, be it from the lack of specie, because the King of Prussia had taken care to withdraw this from the country. Moreover, it is not advisable to follow the bad example of the King of Prussia.[74]

---

[74] Solovief, Vol. XXIV, p. 280.

When Dresden fell, on 45 September, Daun once again refused to march on Berlin. He retired on Bautzen. Saltykov, furious at his inaction, was, however, forced to obey the letter of his instructions. He moved into Silesia, on the side of Glogau. He could do nothing here, but a simple demonstration, as he did not have an artillery park. He sent Rumyantsev to Daun to request one, as well as money because of his lack of food. On the 22nd, Daun promised cannon, but refused money, engaging his allies to live off the land by means of requisitions. He was prodigious with sweet words, excusing for not acting against Frederick II, always claiming the peril that Prince Henry presented to him.

The cannon did not come and soon the result was six weeks lost in "vain projects", which gave time for Frederick II to rebuild his fortunes and allow his offensive movement into Silesia against the Russians.

From 14-17 August we find Frederick II at Lebus, on the left bank, stuck to some extent on the Oder, not daring to make any movement, constantly expecting to see the Russians cross the river to Frankfurt, to move south against him, to reject them into the plains of Brandenburg, and to chase them to Pomerania.

However, Frederick's morale rose because he began to publish lies. He claimed to have destroyed 24,000 Russians and 9,000 Austrians. The sentiment of a supreme duty put him on his foot and his correspondence was studded with words, which at their depth, expressed a state of soul that was exalted and heroic. "If the Russians really want Berlin," he wrote on 16 August to Finckenstein, "we will fight them, rather to die under the walls of our fatherland, in the hope of overcoming them." "Our situation is dreadful," he wrote to Ferdinand von Braunschweig, "but the enemy leaves me time. Perhaps by his faults I will be able to save myself.... To count on our exploits, is to hang on a reed. So, if one wants to negotiate peace, I fear that it is not too late.... For me I will die fighting to defend you."

On the 18th, be it that he found himself sufficiently strong to maintain himself in the plain, be it that he had withdrawn before Saltykov's movement on Lossow, we find him at Fürstenwald. On the 19th, he wrote to Ferdinand von Braunschweig: "I am on the enemy's road. I fear that tomorrow or the next day at least we will have a battle. The officers and I are resolved to die or be victorious. I pray to Heaven that the common soldier thinks the same!... My compliments to Seydlitz, to all the honest men who have fought well and my malediction to all the faint hearted cowards who find themselves with you without wounds." At Finckenstein, he announced, on the 20th, that he would soon have 33,000 men in his camp: "This will be enough if my best officers were there and if the bastards will do their duty. So as to disguise nothing, I tell you that I fear my own troops more than the enemy."

Little by little, with marvelous activity, he assembled some forces, drew from his fortress's new artillery, rebuilt a park of 60 cannon, rallied fugitives and lightly wounded men, called four battalions from Pomerania, and drew from Ferdinand von Braunschweig, despite the Prince's protests, "stubborn as the devil,"[75] a corps of infantry and cavalry. He animated this heterogeneous army with his genius and his patriotism, giving birth again to its appetite for combat and the hope for victory, although "our brave men perish in war and I have only cowards to command;"[76] although he "had no more men among his troops; that the j.....f.....possesses almost all of them."[77]

He held to the field, always redoubtable; he complained against fortune, which, "is like young girls, and only takes for lovers those who, etc…"[78] He is piqued to have to fight "the reappearing hydra of envy." He wondered where he would find the troops to oppose so many adversaries. He was astonished that "his head did not turn a hundred times."[79]

Yet, this marvelous head did not turn. The campaign of 1759 furnished new proofs that the great captain was not the same who had never lost a battle, but the one who, in the grip of reverses, did not despair of anything and knew how to conceal from the victorious enemy the fruits of victory.

The 13 days passed at the Fürstenwald camp had not been lost. To the extent that they moved away from that fatal day of the 12th, the Allies let more and more time flow and lost the results of their triumph, while the resources to repair the defeat accumulated in Frederick's hands. The fortunes of one side declined, while those of the other rose.

On 30 August, Frederick II was at Borne and communicated to Finckenstein his joyous surprise at seeing the Austrians turning towards Lusace. "While I thought they would march on Berlin, they took the opposite path." On 1 September, he was at Waldow; the divorce between the Russians and Austrians appeared consummated. It was with a cry of triumph that he addressed to Prince Henry. "I announce to you the miracle of the House of Brandenburg."

The miracle was, as the English would say, that they alone could save themselves, and this miracle was accomplished. Marshal Daun, on one side, and the Conference on the other, had managed to break the rise of the Russian eagles already turned towards Berlin; the victorious army, subjected to a disastrous charm, bound by invisible bonds, fascinated, enchanted, bewitched, as if the aiguillettes had been tied to it, remained motionless in its camp at Lieberose.

---

[75] *Politische Correspondenz*, to Finckenstein, 26 August.
[76] *Ibid.*, to Finkenstein, 5 September.
[77] *Ibid.*, to Henry of Prussia, 5 September.
[78] *Ibid.*, to Ferdinand von Braunschweig, 5 September.
[79] *Ibid.*, to Ferdinand von Braunschweig, 12 September.

However, all the consequences of Kunersdorf had not yet vanished. The battle of 12 August constantly weighed on Frederick. If he could neither punish Daun for his bragging, nor save Dresden, forced to capitulate, nor drive back "these infamous Swedes," who profited from his misfortune to invade Pomerania[80] anew, it is that he also was tied by the presence of the Russian army.

This army did not march on Berlin but remained in Brandenburg. Frederick could attempt nothing so long as he was "embarrassed" with the Russians. Then only, he wrote, "we can move." He calculated what was lacking with their army, in food and in fodder. He then waited until the Russians were driven out by famine.[81] He was condemned to the role of its observer: he was as a result, its escort, at its disposal, almost at its service.

Finally, on the 16th, Soltykov, left in inaction, exasperated against his allies, moved from Lieberose on Guben. Like the Russian army, Frederick II moved from Waldow on Kottbus. He marched by Amtitz on Christianstadt. Frederick then moved on Forste, where he arrived on the 19th. He guessed that "certainly the Russians went to Glogau" and he wrote to Finckenstein: "I run like a beautiful devil to prevent them." He mocked the "ridiculous maneuvers" of Daun in his campaign, which was "worthy of minor houses." He amused himself at the expense of Laudon, always stuck to Saltykov, "trailing the Russians as far as Silesia" and "becoming the archconductor of the bear of the Holy Roman Empire." On the 30th, he arrived at Sorau and wrote to La Motte-Fouqué:

> The Russians want to besiege Glogau. I march with wings
> to prevent them. But I am so weak; I have only 24,000 men,
> men who are twice beaten, you hear me…. I will not suffer
> that they besiege Glogau; I will rather fight, arrive what
> may. Here is the fashion that the valiant knights had and my
> own way of thinking.

One sees that he refused the idea of giving battle. It should have occurred that day. However, on one side, Saltykov knew the terrible situation of his material and the defiance of his allies; on the other hand, the King of Prussia reported on the "bad state of his beggars." Frederick II allowed the Austro-Prussians to cross the Bober, on 21 September, at Langmeersdorf. He crossed the river himself and moved on Sagan. In taking position on that point, he cut all direct communication between Saltykov's army and that of Daun.

On the 23rd, the Austro-Russians were at Freistadt. A council of war was held, which decided to march on Beuthen. On receiving a message

---

[80] *Politische Correspondenz*, to Finckenstein, 7 September.
[81] *Ibid.*, to Prince Henry, 8 September.

from Daun which asked the Russians to return to Saxony, Saltykov was too discontented with Daun to not refuse this request. Then Laudon and the other Austrian generals declaring to him that they would withdraw on Christianstadt and rejoin their Generalissimo. Saltykov responded to them that they were free to do so, but that he renounced from that point on all operations in Silesia and that he would retire immediately on his magazines on the Lower Vistula. They remained. On the 24th, they marched on Beuthen, the Russian army in battle order, covered by Stoffeln and Tottleben's cavalry, Laudon marched towards Saltykov. In Beuthen, on the 25th, they had to organize the passage of the Oder; but then Stoffeln's scouts saw the Prussian advance guards, and behind them strong columns of infantry. For being able to cross to Beuthen, it was necessary to fight a battle with Frederick II. Saltykov preferred detouring towards the north. Frederick, wrote to Prince Henry from his camp at Baunau: "This morning, at 6 a.m., the enemy generals wanted to reconnoiter our position. It is obvious that these gentlemen still consider us formidable; because they had barely turned back than their army withdrew and encamped close to Neusalz."

Nonetheless, this was "certainly a critical day." One can be surprised that Frederick did not take the offensive; because the Russians, with their back to the Oder and its swamps would have received battle in perilous conditions, not dissimilar to those of the battle of Friedland in 1807.

Three days passed thus. Saltykov hesitated to cross, between the points of Korolath, Neusalz, and Költsen. He decided for the latter, and the operation was executed without difficulty, on the 28th, although Tottleben had announced that they would be attacked. On the 29th, he had the light baggage cross the bridges. It is possible that this operation, masked by a screen of light cavalry, had escaped Frederick, because on the 28th, he again wrote to La Motte-Fouqué: "The barbarians are still opposite me. I prepare for them a good tower. If I succeed, they will quickly discover it. I swear to you that I am most impatient to be delivered of them, not for me, but for the country that they burn and kill." What was this good tower that he prepared for the barbarians? We do not know. It was only during the morning of the 30th that the King, no doubt better informed, attacked Tottleben's cavalry, which remained on the left bank to guard the bridgeheads. Tottleben drove back his attackers and then crossed. "Then," states Saltykov's report, "after this happy passage, in sight of all the enemy army, and of an army that was commanded by the King in person, the bridges were destroyed."

On 1 October, the Russians continued their march on Glogau. They took up a position at Gross-Ostein and Kuttlau. They would remain there until the 22nd. Saltykov saw that he could neither capture Glogau by surprise, nor, lacking the equipment, take it with a formal siege.

On 2 October, Frederick made his entrance into Glogau. Then he successively encamped, during the rest of the month of October, in the surrounding villages: Zerbau, Köben, and Sophienthal. He felt his exasperation grow against his enemy: "You do not believe what infamies these infamous Russians have committed and continue to commit. You believe that you hear of it in the history of Blue Beard. Never were there a people more barbarous, more absurd, or more ferocious."[82]

The *absurdity* especially consisted in remaining before Glogau when they had so many things to do in Bohemia, in Saxony, and in Pomerania. As of the first day, he hoped, he watched for the departure of the Russians; their heavy luggage had already been dispatched to Poland; surely, they were going to follow it. We will see that Soltykov had the bad taste to immobilize Frederick before Glogau for five whole weeks: until November 5th!

The two armies, each as strongly entrenched as the other, observed each other. October 5th, the Prussians having tried to establish a battery opposite Schofsen, there followed, from one bank of the Oder to the other, a cannonade that lasted two days. There were all-in-all 15 or 16 killed or wounded men and 8 or 10 horses. After that noting occurred to trouble the boring glumness of the camps.

The King continued to maintain, from this corner of the earth, his vast correspondence, speaking of what was happening in Canada or Indonesia, hoping that the loss of their colonies would finally provoke the French to make peace, expediting orders to his government in Berlin, to his armies in Saxony, Westphalia, and Pomerania, and even fired salvoes of victory, on 1 November, to cause the Russians to believe that Prince Henry had defeated Daun. At Köben, he recalled that in this location the famous Schulenburg had executed, before Charles XII, an admirable retreat, and he conceived, "the idea to write on the military talents and character of this prince."[83]

The leisures of Saltykov were less varied, less literary. He did not tease the Muses, but he asked himself anxiously why Daun, while he held Frederick in check, had not come to his rescue. He knew that the Austrian marshal continued to do nothing, being afraid of Prince Henry and Frederick, who could "suddenly turn on him." He knew that Kaunitz, Esterhazy, and Saint-André continued to feel sorry for the Russian army, accusing Saltykov of remaining inactive before Glogau and of refusing to return Laudon with a reinforcement of 20,000 or 30,000 Russians.

He spoke bitterly of this in his letters and his reports.[84] All in all, one asked the impossible of him, for nonsense, or even of the crimes of lèse-patrie [hurting the homeland]. Could he make an attack to Glogau, in the presence of an army commanded by the King of Prussia? Could he begin a regular siege, when he had no siege train? To detach 20,000 Russians, when he barely had

---

[82] *Politische Correspondenz*, Vol. XVIII, 2nd Part, to Prince Henry, 2 October.

[83] Catt, pp. 255-256.

[84] See his correspondence with Vorontsof, *Soc. Imp. d'histoire de Russie*, Vol. IX, p. 493 and following.

40,000? Should he sacrifice the interests of Russia to the great projects of a tactician who let all opportunities escape him?

On 22 October, he broke camp and moved on Herrenstadt. He summoned its commander, Kleist, and upon his refusal, he bombarded the city. On the 24th, he was at Tribus; on the 26th at Punitz. Then Laudon proposed to him a return to the offensive on Glogau assuring him that the King had already left for Saxony. Saltykov consented. On 1 November he arrived at Dolsk and camped at Shrimm. However, Frederick II had remained at his post, not wishing to be duped by a false departure. Nothing occurred. Laudon once again asked for the reinforcement of 30,000 Russians. Saltykov opposed him with a quiet refusal. The Conference, less concerned than Saltykov about the national interests, had enjoined him to send 20,000 men. Saltykov authorized this, in theory, but surrounded his assent with such conditions that it was Laudon who refused.

And with this nothing opposed the retreat of the Russian army to its winter quarters on the Lower Vistula. With it the 1759 campaign was ended.

On 5 November, Frederick II, finally delivered from the Russians broke camp and moved to the west. On the 14th, from his camp at Krögis in Misnie he wrote to Finckenstein: "The Russians, disgusted at last, by the Austrians... will undoubtedly make a separate peace."

He was right on the first point; but he was mistaken on the second. The Russian Court recriminated against the inaction of Daun; it answered Esterhazy about the proposals made in August by Laudon to Saltykov which "would have wearied the patience of the most phlegmatic"; it allotted to "abusive bias" the criticisms directed against the field-marshal. It returned, in discussions with L'Hôpital, on the project of a direct and more intimate alliance with France; this was "to only be opposed to the aggrandizement of the House of Austria"; but it had no better success in these insinuations. Despite everything, the Russians did not discourage themselves: on the contrary, wrote the French Ambassador, "the two battles they had won increase their hopes."

Saltykov, in the 1759 campaign, had won two brilliant victories; he had taken from the King of Prussia his fortune. Then, when he had to move into Silesia, he had shown that he got along no better with Daun Cunctator in a defensive war; he had passed the Oder in sight of a Prussian army, established so strongly its camp under Glogau that the King of Prussia did not dare to attack him, forcing the first captain of the century to just watch, and for three months had alone occupied the principal Prussian army. He had obliged the King to weaken his other army corps and 15 days after its departure from Silesia, Finck was encircled at Maxen by the Austrians and, on November 20th, obliged him to surrender with 12,000 men, 540 officers, 71 guns, and 120 flags or standards. "I thus brought to Saxony the misfortune that persecutes me!" Frederick exclaimed. He realized that it was Kunersdorf that continued to weigh on him and that the disaster of 20 November was only one result of the defeat of 12 August.

General Masslovski gives to Saltykov this testimony: he did not let himself be misled by the Austrians, agreeing neither to expose his army in an attack on Glogau nor to let it be dismembered to please Daun or Laudon; he knew to resist unjust criticisms and the unreasonable injunctions of its own government: "Count Saltykov, being on location, saw clearly what was offered; without being moved by abusive reproaches which came at him from the Conference, he knew to maintain his dignity at the appropriate level; he prevented the disastrous consequences which could result for Russia from the breaking up of its army or operations in Silesia following Laudon."

Finally, Masslovski notes that Saltykov was not responsible for the little results that one collected from his brilliant victories. "Those results," he wrote, "come from the great errors of Russian diplomacy, which had submitted to a complete dependence on Kaunitz." If the Seven Years War was not finished by a decided and general offensive, immediately after Kunersdorf, the fault falls on Daun, and on Kaunitz, who had obliged Daun to be more concerned about covering Bohemia and to endeavor to involve Saltykov in Silesia, which ruined everything.

The Prussians and Russians
Rulers of Russia

Empress Elizabeth ruled from 1741 – 1762

Emperor Peter III ruled from Jan 1762
to July 1762

Empress Cathrine II ruled from 1762 - 1796

CHAPTER XIII

THE 1760 CAMPAIGN IN SILESIA

The war started to weigh heavily on certain powers: not only on the King of Prussia, who saw all his resources successively destroyed; but also Austria and Russia, though they did not want to agree to recognize this, keen as they were, one with the recovery of Silesia, the other with the conservation of East Prussia; but especially with France, which only gained in Germany successes mixed with reverses, and which, of all the European powers, had lost all its colonies. The effort to establish a separate peace between France and England had failed: England not having made sufficient gains in India and North America, and Pitt saw it as a point of honor not to separate his cause from that of the King of Prussia.

France had seen itself exhausted in Europe and ruined outside of Europe for Austria's cause. As for Russia, not only had Louis XV declined all propositions or all insinuations for a more intimate and direct alliance with it; but it retained all its biases with regard to this power. One saw this in the *Instructions* given, on 16 March 1760, to de Breteuil, who had been sent to St. Petersburg as the Plenipotentiary Minister and assistant to L'Hôpital, and also as the agent of *Correspondence secrete,* and as *surveillant de l'ambassadeur en titre* [observer in the title of the ambassador]:

A healthy policy would not allow the St Petersburg Court to benefit from the advantages of its actual position to increase his power and to extend the boundaries of its empire. A country almost as wide as the combined states of the greatest princes of Europe and which, needing only a small number of men for its safety, can send beyond its borders formidable armies; a country whose trade extends to China, and who is within reach of obtaining from Asia, easily and in little time, the products that the other nations can draw only by long routes and dangerous voyages; a country whose troops are battle hardened, and whose government is absolute and almost despotic, must with reason appear frightening to its neighbors, and successively to the people who would be joined to it by means of its new conquests...

The enlightened courts felt, when the Muscovite armies passed for the first time into Germany, how interesting it was for all the sovereigns to take care with attention on the views and the steps of a nation whose power has already started to become frightening...Who knows if the Empress-Queen and her successors will not one day repent having taken recourse to such auxiliaries?

The violence that Russia exerted in Poland in 1733 and 1734; its campaign against the town of Danzig, that it besieged against all the laws of justice and propriety, which it then severely punished for having sought to defend its freedom and its rights; an ambassador of France[85] and three French battalions were held in an humiliating and long captivity against the content of a formal capitulation[86], but artfully interpreted; another ambassador of the King treated with the greatest indecency;[87] the lengths to which Russia demanded the imperial title from the sovereigns who did not have the kindness yet to grant it to him; the little fidelity it demonstrated in the execution of its last treaty with the Turks[88]...the authority which it claimed to exert over the interior government of Sweden; the way in which it has acted towards the Poles for three years; the views that it has already announced when establishing the boundaries between the Russian Empire and Poland; and finally the system and the conduct of Russia, the form of its administration and its military state, must cause all the princes who have in their hearts public safety and repose[89] to fear the enlarging of this power.

This reason would be sufficient to cause the King to wish that the Empress of Russia desist in her claims on Ducal Prussia, nevertheless, His Majesty would not have a more powerful and closer reason to divert Russia from a project that could only multiply the calamities of war and the embarrassments of peace.

---

[85] M. de Monti.
[86] As a result of the affair of the Count de Plélo, de Monti, French Ambassador to King Stanislas, was held prisoner. A. Rambaud, *Instructions,* Vol. 1, p. 275 and following.
[87] The La Chétardie Affair. See footnote above, p. 4. Translator: In 1742 the French agents de la Chétardie and Lestocq arranged a complicated intrigue to slander both Natalia Fyodorovna and Natalia Lopukhina, two ladies of the Russian Court, thereby securing the downfall of the Austrophilic Chancellor Aleksey Bestuzhev.
[88] The Treaty of Belgrade, 21 September 1739.
[89] This long enumeration of the complaints can be found almost in the same manner in the *Instructions* given successively to the French ambassadors and agents in the first years of the reign of Louis XVI.

Such were the distrusts and the jealousies of Louis XV about the constantly increasing power of Russia, which when Choiseul, in his *Instructions* of July 1759 to l'Hôpital, proposed a means of restoring peace by an armed mediation by Russia between Austria and Prussia, the King vigorously disapproved of his Foreign Minister's action. "One must regard as happy for the interests of the King," wrote Louis XV to de Breteuil, "that the Marquis de l'Hôpital.... let the occasion escape that had been so highly recommended to him to seize."

Before this cooling of the French Court, Russia had outlined a rapprochement with the Court of Vienna. Unbeknownst to the Versailles Cabinet, they had signed the Treaty and the Convention of St. Petersburg, of 21 March 1760.[90] In the *separate* and *secret* articles of the convention, one clearly stipulated that the two imperial courts would try to take their compensation at the expense of King of Prussia, one by the re-conquest of Silesia and the County of Glatz, and the other by the final acquisition of East Prussia.

In the explanatory memorandum the precedes the campaign plan signed by Elisabeth, on 11 May 1760, the resolution to continue the war emerged with an extreme energy:[91] "Necessity will sooner or later oblige us to begin the war when the King of Prussia does not begin it, because this sovereign, who otherwise was dependent on all his neighbors,[92] claimed to reduce all the courts to dependence on him; he coveted all that belonged to everyone else; nothing could appease him; and at the beginning of the current war he showed that he would not allow the Court of Vienna to make the least movements even on its own territories."

Elisabeth said to Esterhazy, the Austrian ambassador: "I do not take decisions easily, but once I have done so I never change my mind. I will continue the war with my allies, even if I must sell half of my dresses and my diamonds."[93]

Since Elisabeth was determined to continue the war, it was necessary to be put in state to make it. Three years of hard campaigns, sometimes at more than 1,000 kilometers from the borders of the Empire, numerous engagements and four great battles had singularly tested the Russian army. To repair its losses it had only received, in 1759, 8,000 or 9,000 recruits. After Kunersdorf, Saltykov had required 30,000 replacements. On 29 September, there appeared an *oukaze* concerning recruitment; but the men that it raised could not reach the army quickly enough. The interior depots and the garrison regiments had been exhausted. The commander of forces of the Ukraine, in 1760, General Burturline, declared that to protect the vast country and its long border facing

---

[90] F. de Martens, *Traités et conventions de la Russia*, Vol. I, Austria, p. 269 and following, St. Petersburg, 1874.

[91] Solovief, p. 308.

[92] Frederick was a vassal to the King of Poland for his possession of East Prussia.

[93] Solovief, Vol. XXIV, p. 304.

the Tartars and Turks, he had only 3,651 dragoons and 7,000 men of the landmiliz.

Again, there emerged the idea of demanding recruits from East Prussia. General-Governor Korff once again defended his administration. By calculations that were more or less exact, he proved that the province could provide no more than 500-600 recruits. It was, therefore, a most mediocre resource in point of view of numbers; and was it not risky to enroll Prussians to fight the King of Prussia? The military obligation was therefore transformed, for the new subjects of the Tsarina into a light tax and numerous corvées to handle cartage and transportation.

Other measures taken had as their objective the reorganization of the army. It was resolved to disestablish the Observation Corps, the "badly born child" of Shuvalov, which had done so poorly at Kunersdorf. Using the best soldiers, it was decided to create the special artillery regiments that had been long projected to be formed and which the army still lacked, as in many other European armies. Conforming to the Feldzeugmeister's initial plan, they formed three artillery regiments with very high manpower. Two were artillery fusilier regiments and one was a cannoneer regiment. Further such regiments were later created, and at the end of 1760, the army had 14,000 artillery soldiers, while at the battle of Zonrdorf it had had only 1,576. The rest of the men of the Observation Corps were incorporated into the infantry regiments of the operational army.

These regiments, by this expedient or others, were reconstituted on the basis of two battalions at full strength and a third battalion of each regiment that was to remain in the cantonments on the Vistula where they would serve as a depot cadre and train new recruits.

The regiments of the horse grenadiers and dragoons were equipped in the manner of the Austrian dragoons. The Russians even asked the Viennese Court for samples of their uniforms.

The cavalry was reinforced by 10 squadrons of dragoons, drawn from the Pskov and Veliki-Louki Regiments, and with four squadrons of cuirassiers drawn from the Guard, called from St. Petersburg.

As Saltykov had expressed the desire to see the number of Don Cossacks serving in his army raised to 6,000 men, a new call was made to the Don camps; but only 5,000 men were raised. Saltykov had asked for 2,000 Cossacks from Little Russia, not for the same services of the Don, but to work on the lines of communications, in the army's rear areas. This was done by the creation of Ukrainian "field pulks" under the orders of Tchesnokov.

There were unfavorable rumors in the Russian Army relating to Shuvalov's new artillery. General of Artillery Gliebov and Colonel Tutschen were charged with going to the quarters on the Vistula, and in the presence of the Field Marshal, of all the generals, the officers, and a certain number of soldiers by company, and to proceed with artillery experiments with the plan of establishing the superiority of the new guns over the old ones. Saltykov wrote:

> I had to worry about the annoying results that may have come from the soldiers who were invited to assist with these experiments, instead of maintaining them in the practices of quiet obedience with what is ordered to them.

He asked that simple soldiers not be included in the assistance. However, the Court persisted in its views, responding to Saltykov:

> We have judged this measure indispensable; the experiments will convince the soldiers of the enormous superiority of the new artillery over the old: so well demonstrated shall be this superiority, it would not comprise the advantage which it is desirable to draw from it, to dissipate the doubt which is, on this subject, rooted in the army, to destroy it even among the privates, if one did not clearly show to them this superiority once and for all, if their chiefs cannot explain it to them and convince them. Consequently, we invite you to give the order to the officers of any rank to benefit from all opportunities to inform and persuade the privates, to inculcate into them the greatest confidence in this new artillery, to convince them that it has for them the greatest advantages, that its action is much more energetic and effective that of the enemy artillery. We thus enjoin, under the most severe pain [punishment], to carry out our orders for this purpose.

The experiments occurred at Marienwerder, from 8-11 January 1760. One report, signed by all the generals, was subsequently sent to St. Petersburg. Here is its conclusion:

> Assuredly the new artillery presents a great superiority to the old, which the tests demonstrated between the 3pdr cannon and the 12pdr howitzer, as well as between the other weapons of this size. However, the experience of the preceding campaigns shows that the weapons of both systems, in their respective roles are useful and advantageous. As a result, both systems can be used with success; it is also necessary to take into consideration the long experience in the older pieces held by their servants as well as the soldiers. We, the undersigned see, therefore, it to be advantageous to maintain

the old system of cannons and mortars as well as the new pieces.[94]

The field artillery was, therefore, grouped into brigades of 30 guns. The brigades were then subdivided into very unequal batteries, because some, those of the first line, could contain as many as 24 guns; while others, those of the second line, had only 18 guns; and those of the third line, only 5. The first line contained 68 guns; that is to say, three quarters of the total, both cannon, howitzers, and *edinorogs*. The Russian artillery contained 11 different calibers. The larger cannon opened fire at 750 toises[95]; the smaller and the regimental guns at 400 toises. At 250 toises, the first began firing canister, while the second fired canister at only 70 toises. The guns were, otherwise, well-guarded and well-served, as a result of these newly formed regiments. One also saw some progress in the Russian artillery since the beginning of the war.

For the train and cartage, as the army lacked horses, it was directed that there would be brought 7,000 oxen from the Ukraine.

There was always a shortage of officers. It was attempted to obtain some by negotiating with the Prussians for the exchange of prisoners. A conference between the Russians and Germans opened at Bütow, between the lines of advance posts of the two armies. It was inaugurated on 10 July and ended on 12 October. On one side or the other, one brought forward prisoners by detachments. The exchanges were made based on equality, in light of the rank of the prisoner, his state of health, and the severity of any wounds. If the quantity brought by one side was greater than that of the other, the surplus was not put at liberty until a ransom had been paid. The Bütow Conference produced, for the evaluation of ransoms, a most curious tariff. A commanding general was estimated to be the equal of 3,000 soldiers, or 15,000 florins; a brigadier general was worth 200 men or 1,000 florins; a colonel 130 men or 650 florins; a lieutenant colonel 60 men or 300 florins; and a captain was worth 16 men or 80 florins. A simple soldier was worth only 5 florins. For volunteers, of all ranks, the exchange was reduced to money: 1,500 florins for a gentleman and 50 for a volunteer soldier.

It was also agreed that in the future, the soldiers not liberated would not be obliged to serve in the ranks of the opposing army. The enemy would pay the salary they earned before their captivity. It would be accounted for by the two governments. Deserters would not be included in the exchange under the titles of prisoners; but one would not be forced to hand them over. The present cartel or exchange regulation was made valid for six years.

Among the Russian prisoners, who recovered their liberty because of this convention, were Generals Tchernychev and Ivan Saltykov. The first resumed service in the army, but the second retired because of age and returned

---

[94] Solovief, Vol. XXIV, p. 304-305.
[95] Translator: A "toise" is approximately a meter.

to Russia.

Now there remains to be laid out the campaign plan for the year 1760. To this end, Generalissimo Saltykov, on 19 February, handed command of the army over to Fermor on an interim basis and went to St. Petersburg in order to enter into deliberations with the Conference.

One can summarize the plan he proposed as follows: to conquer Pomerania as far as the Oder and to establish himself solidly there so as to take up winter quarters there; to prepare for this conquest, he proposed capturing Danzig, to utilize the resources of this city in food, horses, men, and money to establish it as a principal supply depot and a place d'armes for the army; to then besiege Kolberg with an army corps and to cover the siege with all his forces; and then not to cross the Oder until the Austrians had achieved some major success in their campaign. Saltykov was of the opinion that it was pointless to risk a major battle, because the previous victories had not produced political results in proportion to the sacrifices made.

This was a modest plan, but very wise. If it had been executed from the beginning of the war, the Russians, masters of East Prussia, Danzig, and Pomerania, would have obtained a preponderant position in Germany, had an easy supply situation, and could have passed the winters in the theater of the major operations.

The Conference set aside this plan. Instead, the Empress signed the plan of 11 May (30 April). The Russian army, raised to 70,000 men, would make its junction with that of the two Austrian armies destined to operate in Silesia with the Russians; the junction point would be, based on circumstances, Frankfurt-am-Oder or Glogau; the other Austrian army, that of Saxony, would cover the operations in Silesia and would threaten Frederick II, if he tried to oppose the main operation, by moving into his rear and cutting his communications.

This plan was obviously developed under the pressure from the Austrian Cabinet, its ambassador and its military attaché in St Petersburg. The Russian army, for the unique interest of Austria, was condemned to a sterile war of sieges in Silesia. It was Kaunitz who would determine how it would be employed. This plan swarmed with inconsistencies and impossibilities. Saltykov was prohibited to engage Frederick in battle before the junction with the Austrians; but what if this junction could not be obtained that at the cost of a battle?

Moreover, the Tsarina, who had signed these instructions, agreed with Saltykov that he should avoid great battles:

> The experience of previous years teaches us that it is all
> the easier to prevent them as they were bloodier and more
> desperate. Then King of Prussia had an idea about Our
> armies that was quite different from that which he must have

today. It appeared impossible to him that they could hold in
front of the Prussians. At the beginning of the war, he did
not doubt that Lehwaldt's army was sufficient to ruin all Our
forces...The battle of Zorndorf, about which he never speaks
except with bitterness, gave him a very different idea about
Our army. He ended up concluding that he could attack it
as he pleased, that it has many means of doing much evil to
him, but that it is difficult for him to gain a complete victory
over it, so great is the bravery of Our soldiers, even when
beaten!....After Paltzig he could be comforted by thinking
that it was not a general battle; but that which he fought with
us before Frankfurt was enough to show him, as well as the
whole world, that Our army is not beaten even when one
obtained over it all the advantages. Which other army than
the Russian army would not have been disordered and put to
flight, after it had been attacked in the flank, that a notable
part of it had been beaten, and much artillery lost, while
the major part of our forces was reduced to immobility?....
King of Prussia thus had to convince himself that there is
no profit to attack Our army, more especially as it has never
attacked his, and that there is no need for him to anticipate
us. As soon as autumn comes, our army is to withdraw on
the Vistula, whatever victory it has gained. Thus, what good
is it to risk a battle against it? Believe that the audacity of
the King especially arose from that fact that he did not fear
being attacked; from there comes this obstinacy and even
this insolence at being approached Our army, as soon as one
of his corps appeared in danger of being attacked by it.

It was not a great praise of Russian tactics by the Tsarina. One could,
indeed, reproach her army for having made a war of position rather than
an offensive war, as it never sought battle, but was always subjected to it;
to have made itself formidable when in immediate contact but not when it
was at a distance; to have thus left to the King of Prussia the choice between
accepting and refusing battle and, up to a certain point, the supreme direction
of operations. However, this tactic, which the Tsarina seems to criticize, is that
in which it chose to engage. The result is this unforeseen conclusion: "Today
less than ever, we have not chosen one of these battles, which it will have been
impossible to avoid."

This indirectly recommends the system of temporization of Daun,
and to reduce the role of the Russians to the subordinated role of a purely
auxiliary force. This is the inspiration and serves as the Austrian seal on this

entire document.

It was determined, in advance, that the projected campaign in Silesia would only be a war of marches, of maneuvers, and of positions.

Against the 125,000 soldiers of France or the Holy Roman Empire, which were divided into two armies, Frederick presented a force of 70,000 men under Ferdinand von Braunschweig; facing the 10,000 Swedes, the 180,000 Austrians, and the 70,000 Russians he could present only 120,000 men divided between himself, his brother Henry, and La Motte-Fouqué. He had a total of 190,000 men to face 385,000.

The disasters of the preceding campaign, the exhaustion of his army, his finances, of his provinces, made him resigned to a purely defensive system, thwarting the marches and countermarches of his enemies by a series of similar operations. In this calculation he realized that Daun would do little to oppose him. The Russians worried him more. However, he had come to the conclusions analogous to those that the Tsarina had imposed on Saltykov with her instructions.

In a letter to La Motte-Fouqué, dated 17 February, a letter that was intercepted and translated for the Tsarina, he wrote:

> I have an army in Saxony and another in Silesia. My Army of Silesia initially will have to cover Glogau or Breslau, to benefit from the least faults of the Russians to deliver to them, if it is possible, some terrible blow, before their main army begins its operations, occupies sites that are difficult of access and abandons the plains: because the Russians have as a rule not to attack; to move by woods and not on the plains; it is when they go onto a plain that one can find an occasion to beat them. The important thing with them is to act so that they can take fortified towns and establish themselves there: consequently, it is advisable to watch, above all, Glogau and Kolberg.

Thus, Frederick II laid out his campaign plan as if he had guessed that which was being developed in St. Petersburg. But did he guess it? Masslovski is persuaded that he had direct knowledge, and, so to say, it was given to him. But by whom? By some officer around Saltykov, or perhaps by some "observer" installed in Danzig?

While Frederick and the St. Petersburg Cabinet considered their campaign plans, Tottleben, far away, to the west of the Lower Vistula, with 4,000-5,000 light cavalry, covered the cantonments of the Russian army. He observed what was occurring in Pomerania and noted that the province was almost stripped of troops. Stettin had a weak garrison. Stargard had a weak corps of cavalry and infantry. At Damm there was an infantry regiment. He was directed to move into Prussian Pomerania, to levy requisitions on the population, to block recruitment, and to stop the movement of food convoys to Frederick II.

The light cavalry advance guards of the Russians threatened all the country, all along the line that runs from Kolberg to Glogau. On 30 January 1760, raids of an incredible audacity started. Loukovkin, with 3 pulks of Cossacks, moved against Militsch (Silesia), attacked the Prussian hussars he found there and took 30 of them prisoner, and, in February, he traversed Fraustadt, Lissa (Leszno), and Hemistadt. Another detachment of 100 hussars or Cossacks moved against Landsberg, drove out the militia located there, levied a contribution of 2,622 *thalers* and brought back 41 horses. Podgoritchani, with the Moldavia Hussars, occupied Stolpe, and Köslin, and, moving almost within sight of Kolberg, ransomed the surrounding fields. The Russian outposts were now pushed to Stolpe and Neu-Stettin in Pomerania, Arnswalde, and Landsberg in Brandenburg, and to Fraustadt and Lissa in Silesia. Tottleben established his general headquarter with Bromberg.

On 22 February, Captain Dekowatz pushed as far as Schwedt, on the Oder, held the city to ransom, took Prince von Württemberg and his family captive, but was satisfied with *wechsels* signed by the inhabitants and *revers* signed by the princely family: that is to say, IOU's instead of cash.

In his withdrawal, the bold partisan was attacked near Königsberg, in Brandenburg, and was obliged to cut his way out, saber in hand. He left in the hands of the Prussian hussars 18 men, 53 horses and, moreover, the bag which contained the *wechsel* and the *revers*. Another of his detachments, which brought back the captive Swedish Major Schwartz, was, close to Pyritz, dispersed or taken. Two of his Cossacks were drafted into the Prussian Army. This mishap of Dekowatz did not prevent Loukovkine from crossing the Oder, to ransom the left bank.

However, the region began to defend itself and assistance began coming. On 10 March, there was a fight at Arnswald. The Russians lost 52 men there.

A strong column of Prussian infantry and cavalry, under Generalmajor Stutterheim and Major Podewils, appeared at Neu-Stettin and fortified themselves there.

Tottleben saw himself obliged to advance all his cavalry to support his lost children. He brought back his line of outposts to Rummelburg and Preussisch-Friedland, but he advanced his general headquarters from Bromberg to Konitz, designating this city as the rendezvous point for his dispersed detachments. Podewils again drove back the Russians from Rummelsburg and Stolpe; one could believe that he was going to press this attack further, but abruptly he concealed himself and moved on Kolberg, where he reinforced its garrison. Tottleben moved on this fortress and took up position in the vicinity.

He realized his position would soon become perilous. In his mind and in his reports, he exaggerated the enemy's forces.

Fermor, *Generalissimo par interim*, started to worry about these bold acts. He wondered about the utility of these light cavalry raids. All in all, Tottleben had not been able to prevent Prussian recruitment operations in Pomerania; and, being given not very precise information his reports, beyond his adventurous boasts, the information that he transmitted to the headquarters was subject to great caution. To support this cavalry that had ventured so far, Fermor found himself obliged to bring his regiments out of their winter quarters. He was annoyed by this and tried to hold Tottleben under control. He complained that Tottleben lacked respect, sending his reports on unsigned scraps of paper, proud of having personal instructions from Saltykov and corresponding directly with him, over Fermor's head. Tottleben answered his chief in an impertinent manner. He asked to be relieved and replaced by "another general, who know better than he how to lead the troops to the satisfaction of His Excellency," — moreover, he added, "I am sick, I do not speak Russian, and the written business takes such proportions that I no longer have enough time to complete it… Each courier from the general headquarters brings me another reprimand; in all my very long service I have never received similar reproaches from any general." A few days later he offered to give to Zoritch the command of the hussars and Krasnochtchokov that of the Cossacks. In the end Fermor lost patience. He replaced Tottleben with Eropkine and submitted his report with the Conference. The new chief of the light troops had, on 7 May, sharp skirmishes with the Prussians at Dramburg and Falkenburg and threw them back on Tempelburg. However, the Conference did not support Fermor and Fermor had to return Tottleben to his command. This squabbling did not bode anything good, and it was time that Saltykov returned to take over direction of the army.

Around 20 May, the army received from Petersburg the order to concentrate on the Lower Vistula and to prepare to march. Only on 11 June did Generalissimo Saltykov arrive at Marienwerder. The year was already well-advanced, and the Russians had lost much time. This delay was, however, the fault of the Conference, which had retained the Field Marshal at St. Petersburg, constantly asking him about the campaign plans that they had laid out and to adapt them to all of their differences.

The army was divided into an advance guard, under the Count Zachary Tchernychev, and three corps: the 1st Corps under Fermor, the 2nd Corps under Brown, and the 3rd Corps under Rumyantsev; in addition, Volkonski had command of the cuirassiers, Olitz commanded the horse grenadiers and the dragoons, and Gliebov commanded the field artillery. Tottleben retained command of the light troops. Not including those, the total of the Russian forces came to 74 infantry battalions and 44 squadrons. In total there were

65,000 men in the first line and 15,000 to guard the base of operations on the Lower Vistula.

On 29 June, Tottleben moved on Köslin. Prussian General Beckendorf brought his troops out of the city and prepared them for battle. Tottleben charged them so aggressively that they barely had time to seek shelter under the city's cannon, losing nearly 300 men. Then the city was cannonaded and Beckendorf was obliged to sign a capitulation. He was given honorable conditions, "in consideration of the courage of the garrison and in compassion for the city." He could withdraw freely with all the equipment of his small army, including his cannon, caissons, wagons, and horses, with provisions for one day. It was agreed that the two parties would retain their prisoners of war, so Beckendorf could take with him his Russian prisoners.

After this exploit, Tottleben proposed marching on Kolberg; but he received orders to march on Driesen and Filehne, to occupy that side of the Netze. This would put him on the Nakel and the upper part of this river.

It then pursued its march on the Wartha. On 13 June, Tchernychev's advance guard reached Posen, and successively the other corps arrived and began concentrating there. In the interval, the Conference had sent the order to take as their objective, on the Oder, no longer Krossen, but Breslau.

To prepare for his junction with the Russians, at this point, Daun directed Laudon to occupy Landshut initially, then to begin a siege of Glatz.

Frederick II, from his camp at Meissen, did not cease sending instructions to La Motte-Fouqué, who guarded Landshut. He recalled to him that he was to act to prevent this junction and to destroy, in detail, the Russian corps that was so imprudently advancing.[96]

Fouqué, intimidated by Laudon's offensive, retired to the northeast, announcing to the King his intention to cover Breslau. A new injunction came from the King — to return to Landshut. Fouqué returned there on 19 June. However, on the 23rd, he was attacked by Laudon and so completely defeated that all his corps surrendered, while Fouqué was taken prisoner. This was for Frederick II another disaster like Maxen. He now had almost no troops in Silesia and the province appeared to be open to the Allies. All that he could do was to stop and immobilize Daun by a series of maneuvers.

What saved the province was the time that Laudon lost after his victory. During all the month he remained immobile between Liegnitz and Parchwitz before deciding to begin a siege of Breslau. In the second place, the slowness of the Russian march; the magazines that Suvorov organized at Kallies and Schrimm were not complete; the instructions from the Conference carried instructions that one was not to risk crossing the Oder before being assured

---

[96] On the 18th, he announced to them that it was very probable, at the end of the month, that the Turks would enter the field, which would have obliged the Austrians to send 60,000 men towards Buda and would permit the Prussians to invade Moravia. *Politische Correspondenz*, Vol. XIX, p. 353.

of the junction with the Austrians. Now Laudon gave no sign of life, and one knew that Prince Henry was at Züllichau, Forcade was at Königswalde, Goltz was at Mezeritz, and Werner was at Dresden. The Russian advance posts and their reconnaissances were almost in contact with those of the Prussians.

While one was in Poland, one marched as if in peace time. The advance guard and the three corps advanced in columns. They did not trample the ground where there was wheat. Saltykov took care to maintain a severe discipline, an exact service with frequent rounds. He had to fight certain habits which had arisen in Tottleben's forces, during their stay in Pomerania, who were now under the surveillance of Tchernychev, commander of the advance guard corps. In an order of the day, which Tottleben was obliged to publish, dated 17 August, one found the following findings: "Many [men] maintain and transport women with them. In the next 24 hours, they will have to be returned to the pulks. If any are fond after this period, they will be delivered to Cossacks and the chiefs of police will be taken before the Generalissimo. The guilty officers will be stripped of their rank and broken to the ranks; the privates will be punished with the knout. We also learn that some Cossack colonels are in friendly relations with the enemy, walk with them, and mutually give each other their word: "that is to say, after having exchanged safe conduct, they dine and drink with each other. Those troops which should have been lightly equipped are becoming encumbered with baggage so as to transport their booty. Saltykov had to end all these abuses. War was too serious for this behavior to be tolerated.

As they approached Prussian territory, at the stop over at Bolewo, the army now formed only a single column and began observing all the precautions of war as it marched. On 4 July, it was at Militsch, in the swamps of the Upper Bartsch. Tchernychev occupied, on his right Sulau. On the 7th, it was at Wilkensdorf. There it had to stop to await news of the Austrians. Daun had said that, forced to block the passages from Upper Silesia into Bohemia, he could not leave his camp at Reichenbach. Now Saltykov, from 30 June, wrote to the Conference: "Not receiving any assistance from the Austrians, the army might find itself exposed to the greatest danger." In order to besiege Breslau he required siege artillery. He asked for it from the Austrians. On 14 July, Springer informed him that Laudon was occupied with the siege of Glatz; that Daun had moved from Reichenbach on Bunzlau to prevent the junction of Frederick II and Prince Henry; that the latter, with 39,000 or 30,000 men was marching on Glogau.

A month passed in waiting. Tottleben and Tchernychev were constantly in movement to observe what happened on the Middle Oder, to assure that the Russian communications with Posen were not threatened.

Finally, Glatz succumbed, on 26 July. Was Laudon's corps now available? The Austrian general asked Saltykov to leave Tchernychev at

Wilkensdorf to watch Breslau and to move, himself, by Wohlau, on Lebus, one of the crossings of the Oder. Saltykov responded that he wished to hold his forces united and march with everyone on Breslau, because that was the rendezvous indicated in his instructions. Laudon consented and informed him that he would march on the city, Breslau having only a weak garrison and could only be relieved by Prince Henry. That same day, by a new courier, he indicated an offensive movement by Prince Henry. He again requested assistance from the Russians, declaring that if they did not advance on Breslau, he would be forced to withdraw.

Saltykov, disturbed on the side of Prince Henry, took the measures to observe his march, in moving along the road that he would have to follow a few squadrons of light cavalry. He then directed himself on Breslau. The Weide, a tributary of the Oder, which flowed to the north of this city, was crossed at Hundsfeld, on 6 August, and the Cossacks came within cannon shot of the city. Thus, he had done entirely and fully everything that Laudon had requested.

However, as usual, the Austrians were far away, and the Prussians were near. Prince Henry marched resolutely by the left bank of Oder to relieve the fortress. Laudon had let him pass and did nothing to disturb him. Perfiliev and Popov's Cossacks, followed by all Tottleben's corps, galloped on Leubus immediately, crossed its bridge, then spread out on the left bank of the river. They found nothing but the Prince's rearguard, of which they killed 104 men and made 100 prisoners. Gaining a march on the Russian army, Frederick II's brother made, on 6 August, his entry into Breslau. Then, at noon, Saltykov's scouts arrived before the fortress, encountering the Prince's hussars, and were forced to fall back on Hundsfeld.

Saltykov then fortified himself in this city, having the Weide on his front, raising batteries on the left bank of the river, enforcing his scouts with Tchougouiev's Cossacks, and began to dispute the left bank until the columns of his army arrived.

He understood that the surprise attack that had been attempted on Glogau and its weak garrison had failed. He could not explain to himself how Laudon, who had declared he was pressing his march on Leubus and Breslau, could have not found himself on the same road as the Prince, and how the Prince had been allowed to pass him. Everything became clear for him when his scouts announced to him that the points that should have been occupied by the Austrians had been evacuated. Not only had Laudon not accelerated his march on Breslau, but he had withdrawn to the south.

On the faith of the arrangements made in advance, the Russians had arrived before the fortress, but they were now there without his allies, and it was on them that Prince Henry would direct all his efforts.

Saltykov modified his positions by continuing to occupy, on the right bank of the Wiede, Weigeldorf at the same time as he occupied Hundsfeld. Bruce, who commanded the detachments left on the left bank, was attacked by the Prussians on the next day, 7 August. He was thrown back to the other bank and barely stopped the Prussians from crossing. Saltykov managed to disengage from the Prussians by the actions of the Kexholm Regiment, and in turn he attacked. The Russian artillery rolled up and threw back the Prussians from the far bank of the river. Bruce, now reinforced by six regiments, succeeded in recrossing to the left bank. Prince Henry was unable to drive this attack home and did not renew it. He accepted his brother's recommendations. The Prussian armies were, in this year, condemned to execute a defensive war.

The next day, 9 August, the Russians finally received news of Laudon. He had withdrawn to Striegau! He requested now that the point of junction be at Leubus, far upstream from Breslau, and that Saltykov construct bridges there. Once again, the Russian field marshal responded to his call. It was, however, a series of very dangerous operations that were asked of him. It was necessary first, behind the Weide, to execute a flank march in the presence of the Prussians, then to expose his rearguard to attack. Since he received the message from Laudon, he began to march his heavy baggage behind his positions from Weizeldorf and Hundsfeld, under the protection of Tottleben's cavalry. Then the army formed itself in column, with three cuirassier and three infantry regiments leading: then the main body, then the rearguard of one cuirassier and three infantry regiments.

Prince Henry did nothing to seriously disturb this operation. Instead of crossing the Weide and falling on the flank of the Russian column, he contented himself with having its rearguard pursued by a little cavalry.

Saltykov arrived at Auras. There his scouts informed him that the King of Prussia had arrived at Bunzlau; that Daun had withdrawn on Goldberg: that Laudon marched to rejoin his chief: that Frederick II continued his march on the Oder; and that he appeared disposed to cross the river at Steinau, which was downstream from Auras. If such were his dispositions, his goal was, no doubt, to cut the road to the Russians on the left bank, and to place them between his army and that of Prince Henry, allowing him to wipe them out.

Saltykov, seeing himself surrounded by his enemies and without news of his allies, ordered an evacuation of Auras and withdrew on Kunzendorf. Once there he received a dispatch from Laudon informing him that, in concert with Daun, he was moving on Liegnitz to block the road to the Oder to Frederick. The Russians now only had to hold firm. Saltykov convened a council of war. It was decided that they would await the outcome of events at Kunzendorf. If Daun allowed the King to push on the Oder and to cross it, they would then propose to Laudon that they affect their junction on the right bank, because it was impossible for the Russians to face, at the same time, two

Prussian armies. If the King did not cross the Oder, the Russians would send Tchernychev to the left bank, to join Laudon there and to assail, under Breslau, Prince Henry. To hold himself ready for all eventualities, the heavy baggage was sent to Militsch. Finally, the bridge at Leubus was destroyed, so that it was unavailable to the King, and another was constructed at Auras for the eventual crossing of the Russian army.

On 11 August, the Russians returned to Auras and threw two bridges over the river. The next day a new message came from Laudon. The King was about to hook around Leignitz on Goldberg. The Austrian generals were going to give battle. They requested that Tchernychev's corps be sent to them. Tchernychev received the order from Saltykov to cross the river and to await new instructions. Then two days passed without news. It was then learned that Daun had refused to attack the King, on the pretext that a traitor had betrayed his maneuver to Frederick. The King then took the offensive, defeating Laudon at Paffendorf, on 16 August, killing or taking 3,000 Austrians, though he claimed 8,000. Then Laudon informed the Russians that the King had only pursued him at musket range and that he then retired. In what direction? According to news brought by the Cossacks, Saltykov understood that Frederick had resumed his march on the Oder. Leaving the Austrians behind, it was against the Russians that he appeared to be marching. Saltykov, as a result, drew Tchernychev back to the right bank and directed him to lift the bridges at Auras.

Thus Daun, by pedantry or pusillanimity, had caused Laudon to be defeated. If he conducted himself thus against his own lieutenant, how could one expect him to act against his allies? However, Saltykov, faithful to his instructions, persisted in working towards the promised junction with Laudon. On 15 August, he had the bridges at Auras rebuilt, but the same day news arrived that caused him to decide on a retreat.

Frederick camped on the left bank of the river. Everything caused one to believe that he would force a crossing at Leubus. A letter he wrote to his brother was intercepted. It informed him that Laudon had been completely defeated; that he had suffered enormous losses, and that he had been mortally wounded. It also said that Frederick was preparing an attack on the Russians. These were great exaggerations, but not exceeding those that Frederick frequently allowed himself. Saltykov was inclined to believe that the King had written this letter with the intention that it should be intercepted.[97]

The situation of the Russians had become too dangerous between the two Prussian armies which, by Breslau or by Leubus, could make their junction on either bank of the Oder. Laudon had returned to Striegau. He no longer talked of a rendezvous, limiting himself to asking that Tchernychev's corps be sent to him. A Russian council of war refused to send it. They felt it would be to expose this corps to certain destruction. On the 17th, they began

---

[97] This letter is not found in *Politische Correspondenz*.

retreating by Peterwitz and Tzerkwitz, in the direction of Militsch.

Thus, all the efforts at a junction of the Austrians and Russians ended in a double retreat. Saltykov had, however, done everything humanly possible to execute his instructions. Three times the Austrians had led him under the Prussian cannons and three times they had failed to reach the rendezvous. In sum, if they had attempted to make the junction, it would have been easy for them, considering the magazines they had, the resources of the land, their knowledge of the area, to move before the Russians beyond the Oder, who had moved much farther from their base of operations. They had only been timid and undone in their operations. To the contrary, one must praise the calmness with which Saltykov dared to maneuver, to maintain himself, erecting or removing bridges over the Oder, having the army of Prince Henry on his left flank and the King on his front, ready "to attack rapidly."

What followed was hardly of less interest. Daun sent Laudon messengers to inquire what the Russians intended to do. Saltykov answered: "If prince Henry follows the Russians he will be attacked." With Prince Henry occupied by the Russians, Daun's hands were free to act against the King. What Daun proposed, on 6 September, was that Saltykov march on Steinau and Köben; that he erect bridges there; that he draw Prince Henry and the King there; during this time Daun would move on Schweidnitz. This request essentially requested that the Russians fight, alone, the two Prussian armies. At the same time Laudon required that they move before Glogau, promising to join them to besiege the fortress in concert with them. Thus, the two Austrian generals were not even in agreement on what they were requesting of the Russians. The military and diplomatic imbroglio was at a peak.

On 24 August, the Russians retired on Trachenberg. On the 25th they were at Herrnstadt, where they recrossed the Bartsch.

They remained there, immobile, until 12 September Saltykov had fallen sick at Tzerkwitz. He had recovered, then he had several relapses; several times he handed command over to Fermor, then took it up again; but from 12 September to 30 October, he had to give it up completely. He remained with the army but did not mix in its affairs. This illness of Saltykov's undoubtedly contributed to the failure of the Silesian campaign.

CHAPTER XIV

THE CAPTURE OF BERLIN (OCTOBER 1760)

Thus, from 4 July to 12 September, for ten weeks, the most precious weeks of the military year, the Russians had only made marches and countermarches. A large Austrian army of 180,000 men, with a wonderful Russian army of 70,000 could only witness the maneuvers of two little Prussian armies, to the provocative demonstrations of Frederick II, who disguised his firm resolution thus to hold to the defensive. The Russians, undoubtedly not by their fault, had neither been able to fight a battle, nor capture a fortress; as for the Austrians, they were reduced to two combats and the capture of Glatz.

Dissatisfaction was great in St Petersburg and in the Russian army. De Breteuil was correct to write to Louis XV that Russia had made "the most pitiful of all the campaigns." Bolotov represents to us the impression of the young officers: "Both Generalissimos were ashamed of what they had done." Shame fell especially on the Conference which, against Saltykov's recommendations, had insisted that the Russians invade Silesia.

It now returned to the plan that Saltykov had proposed as of the beginning and that it had rejected. We saw that this plan consisted primarily of a campaign in Pomerania, with the capture of Kolberg as its objective, and an attempt on Berlin. The siege Kolberg should be carried out by corps detached from the principal army and by the dispatch, by sea, of a new corp. The attack on Berlin would be entrusted to a light unit, supported at some distance by the principal army. All that one would now request from the Austrians, would that they occupy Frederick II and Prince Henry in Silesia: Daun would retain the former by a demonstration on Schweidnitz, and Laudon would worry the latter by besieging Glogau.

On 14 September, Fermor informed the Conference of the actions that Saltykov had already taken before passing command to him. The first was to occupy Korolath with the main body of the army. Tottleben had been sent to the left bank of the Oder so as to maintain communication with Loudon. Meanwhile the Russians were preparing a secret expedition on Berlin. The conference made its objections. It wanted Glogau taken at all costs. Fermor held strong. He had himself examined Glogau and was convinced that without heavy artillery nothing could be attempted against the city. It was then that the Conference returned to Saltykov's plan.

On 18 September, the main body of the Russian army was concentrated on the Oder, between Korolath and Beuthen. They remained there the time necessary to prepare for the two expeditions on Kolberg and Berlin. On 21

September, it was decided by a council of war that, on the first of these two cities, they would send Olitz's corps to join that being sent under Admiral Michukov. Against the second, they would send Tchernychev's corps, preceded by Tottleben's cavalry. The main body of the army would then descend the Oder by the two banks as far as Krossen, to the confluence of the Obra, and then act "according to circumstances." The heavy baggage was returned to Posen and Thorn, along with the sick and wounded.

On 22 September, Olitz left Korolath to move into Pomerania.

The Russians now occupied themselves with organizing Tottleben's expedition. Tottleben states, in his memoirs, that success depended on three conditions: 1.) rapidity over numerical forces; 2.) measures well calculated to cover the cavalry column; and other measures to cut all the roads by which the enemy, no matter from where, to permit him from sending reinforcements to Berlin. He asked that his 7,000 to 8,000 Cossacks and hussars be reinforced by two regiments of dragoons, 2,000 horse grenadiers, and a detachment of horse artillery. It was to consist of nothing but cavalry so as to allow it to move as rapidly as possible, thereby assuring the surprise of the city. His intention was to move by Guben, Beeskow, Storkow, and Wusterhausen. Tchernychev, who was to follow with the advanced guard, consisting of the three arms, was to move by Krossen on Frankfurt. From this latter city he was to send down the road to Berlin an infantry brigade.

The only modification that was brought to the plan was that the itinerary assigned to Tchernychev now passed through Beuthen, Freistadt, Christianstadt, Sommerfeld, and Guben. From Guben it followed the same path as Tottleben, to be ready to support it with all his forces.

Behind him moved Fermor with the 1st and 2nd Corps; Rumyantsev, with the 3rd Corps, was to move from Krossen on Frankfurt to solidly occupy the Middle Oder.

Thus, all the Russian army would be echeloned from Korolath in the direction of the Prussian capital. Thus, three successive irruptions, more and more irresistible, would be directed at the heart of Prussia: Tottleben, Tchernychev, and the main army.

This was not the first time that Berlin had been threatened. On 16 October 1757, Austrian General Hadik, with 14,000 men, had forced his way into the Köpenik suburb, tearing to pieces two Prussian battalions, obliging General von Rochow to evacuate the city and take with him the Queen and the ministers to Spandau, imposed on the mayor a contribution of 600,000 *thalers*, who only had time to gather 185,000 *thalers*, because at daybreak, on the 17th, he judged it prudent to evacuate with the money, six flags (taken no doubt from the arsenal), and 426 prisoners. In 1758, before the battle of Zorndorf, the capture of Berlin was one of the goals assigned to Fermor. In 1759, after Paltzig and Kunersdorf, we saw that Frederick II expected his capital to become the prey of the Russians.

In the instructions sent to Tottleben, he was directed to impose a very large contribution on Berlin. If there was no money, he was to take *wechsel*, the payment of which would be guaranteed by the taking of hostages, among whom were to be two members of the *Rathaus* and several of the notable merchants. He was to destroy all the royal establishments, the arsenal, foundry, magazines of weapons, food, and ammunition, powder mills, and uniform cloth manufacturers. This was to be nothing more than "just reprisals for the services exercised by the King of Prussia in the Electorate of Saxony and notably Leipzig."

Tottleben's corps was definitely organized with the Moldavia, Croatia, and Serbia Hussars, under Colonels Podgoritchani, Tsvietinovitch, and Tekeli, a total of 1,000 horsemen; five pulks of Don Cossacks, under Turovierov, the two pulks of Popov Cossacks, and the two pulks of Lukovkine Cossacks, a total of 1,400 Cossacks; the Petersburg and Riazan Horse Grenadier Regiments, 1,200 men under Brigadier Meltchugov; four battalions of grenadiers (infantry), under Brigadier Bachmann, assisted by Colonel Masslov, Lieutenant Colonels Prozorovski and Burmann, and Major Patkul. These five battalions, drawn from the Kiev and 2nd Moscow Grenadiers, came to a total of 1,800 men. Lieutenant Colonel Gliebov commanded the artillery, which consisted of two Shuvalov howitzers and 13 other howitzers of various calibers. The total strength of this force was 5,400 men.

The corps supporting Tchernychev consisted of seven infantry regiments, totaling 12,000 men: 4th Grenadiers, 2nd Moscow, Kiev, Viatka, Petersburg, Nevski, and Vyborsk, all of which were covered with glory in the preceding campaigns.

On 16 September, the corps of Tottleben and Tchernychev left, without drums or trumpets. They followed pretty closely the designated itinerary but moved with an unequal speed.

In route, to better conceal the objective of this operation, they sent incursions, not along the same road to Berlin, but to the right and left. Colonel Tchorba captured a Prussian detachment at Fürstenwalde; Rjevski fell on Frankfurt, where a *wechsel* was taken, but no other payment was demanded.

Tottleben marched very quickly, moving the infantry on carts. On 2 October, he arrived almost within view of Berlin, at Wusterhausen. There he learned that the garrison of Berlin, commanded by General Rochow, consisted only of three battalions of infantry and two squadrons of hussars. However, to secure the city, Hülsen arrived from Torgau and Prince von Württemberg was coming from the north.

Tottleben was no less resolved to attempt a surprise attack. He informed Tchernychev that he wanted him to cover this attack, in order that "his back would be free."

At this time Berlin proper was on two islands in the Spree, and the suburbs extended on the two sides of the river.

One of these two islands was ancient Berlin, the Verolin of the Vendes Slavs, the heart of which was a fisher's village; the other island was called Köllin, from the Slav word "Kolin" (the hill) and was probably another fisher village. In the middle of the huts and nets, in 1452, Frederick Iron Teeth, Margrave of Brandenburg, had founded a city, and this feudal castle gave birth to the city.

The Island of Köllin was now joined to Berlin by a bridge called the "Royal Bridge." Together they formed three quarters: Köllin, Neu-Köllin, and Friedrichswerder; the two latter having been constructed under the Great Elector. It is there that the Royal Castle, the Cathedral, and the Arsenal were found.

On the left bank of the Spree, from north to south, there extended the suburbs of Dorotheenstadt, Friedrichstadt, Köpelnik, and Köllin. The second was constructed under Frederick I, and the three others under the Grand Elector. In Dorotheenstadt, up against the Spree, was the Opera and the Palace of Prince Henry. From there ran the large avenue, *Unter den Linden*, which led to the Brandenburg Gate, beyond which was the Tiergarten.

On the right bank, from north to south, was the suburb of Spandau, then called *Spandauerviertel*; that of the Royal Gates, otherwise called Oranienburg and Rosenthal; that of Stralau or *Stralauerviertel*. The second dated from the father of Frederick II, the two others from the great Elector.

The two islands forming the city proper were surrounded by a bastioned wall, where the branches of the Spree served as ditches. A vast wall, constructed of dirt, was on the right bank and one of masonry was on the left bank, enveloped the suburbs. In the same order as listed above, the wall was pierced by the following gates on the left bank: Brandenburg, Potsdam, Halle, Kottbus; on the right bank Ostvorstadt, Hamburg, Rosenthal, Schönhausen, Alt-Landsberg, and Frankfurt. Only the Kottbus Gate was protected by a flèche, a low-profile work which was armed with one 3pdr cannon.

Berlin, from the military point of view, was essentially an open city. From the architectural view, it offered only a collection of mediocre buildings and vulgar masonry suburban homes. There were no triumphant arches or victory columns, or heroic statues or museums enriched with the spoils of Greece. Frederick I had given it a château, an arsenal, the Academy of Sciences, and the Academy of Beaux-Arts. Frederick-Wilhelm I had constructed squares called today Parisplatz, Belle-Allianceplatz, Döhofplatz, constructed the Zimmerstrasse and the Kochstrasse, and raised many of the palaces on Wilhelmstrasse. Berlin was, above all, a city of soldiers, courtesans, and functionaries. However, because of Frederick I and a bit by Frederick II, it had become little by little the intellectual center of Germany.

PLAN OF BERLIN

The industry of Berlin, as its commerce, it was greatly favored by its situation in the middle of a network of lakes and rivers, and because it was still in its infancy, few men had made great fortunes there. Berlin was poor like the Prussians and its King. As to its population, it had fallen to 6,000 inhabitants at the end of the 30 Years War. It had risen to 50,000 under its first king, to 90,000 under the second king; Frederick II found it with 145,000 souls. When the Russians invaded, however, it had fallen to about 120,000 inhabitants.

General Rochow nearly lost his head when he heard the Russians were coming. His three battalions, with a strength of about 1,200 men, could not compensate for their low numbers with quality. They were formed of Saxon prisoners, Swedes, French, and Russians. He thought about evacuating the city. However, in the city there were several retired and wounded generals, the former including Lehwaldt, and the latter Seydlitz and Knobloch. They shamed him for his weakness and convinced him to attempt to resist. He hastily constructed some flèches before the city's gates, on the model of that before the

Kottbus Gate. He brought forward some cannon, manned by retired soldiers. He had murder holes cut in the walls. He sent an officer and 30 men to occupy the Köpenik Château, in order to dispute a crossing over the Spree. He sent couriers in every direction requesting help, to Hülsen, who garrisoned Torgau, on the Saxon frontier; to Prince von Württemberg, who was at Templin, on the point of attacking the Swedes. These generals responded to his appeals. The day that Tottleben entered Wusterhausen, Hülsen was no more than seven miles away and Prince von Württemberg was six miles away.

These dispositions by the military authorities had thrown panic into the city. Among the bourgeois, many fled to Magdeburg or Hamburg, carrying with them their money and most valuable effects. One minute they reassured themselves that one had taken as Tottleben's advance guard Prussian forces being sent to defend the city. Then began the great role of Gotzkowski, "the patriot merchant", who left us a set of curious memoirs on this event.[98] He engaged the citizens to subscribe to offer refreshments to the liberating troops. They bought bread, beer, *branntwein*[99], and cattle. This appears to be the limit of the citizenry for the defense of the city. Gotzkowski's house, who surely had had previous relations with Tottleben, became a place of asylum for all those alarmed for their lives or their possessions. The Jews took their gold there.

Tottleben[100] spent the night of 2/3 October at Wusterhausen. During the morning of the 3rd, he directed the Croatian Hussars on Potsdam, with the mission of destroying the weapons magazines that were there. He then marched on Berlin, having as his advance guard the Tourovierov Cossacks.

At 11:00 a.m., he occupied the heights in front of the Kottbus and Halle Gates. He sent Lieutenant Tchernychev to summon Rochow. The parliamentarian returned with a refusal. Tottleben now prepared to bombard the city and assault the suburbs' gates.

At 2:00 p.m., Lieutenant Colonel Gliehov opened fire. As the Russians only had small caliber howitzers, they could not set large fires in the city. The Prussians quickly extinguished the fires. As for the wall surrounding the city, their bombs had no effect on its masonry. They then began to fire heated shot on the city and a fire started that lasted until morning.

Rochow, on his side, opened fire, from the flèche before the Kottbus Gate. The afternoon passed without the Russians being able to establish artillery superiority.

At 9:00 p.m., Tottleben resolved to assault the two gates simultaneously. Prince Prozorovski was to assault the Halle Gate with 300 grenadiers and 2 cannons. Major Patkul, with equal forces, was to attack the Kottbus Gate. Each of the two columns had 200 grenadiers [infantry] and 2 squadrons of horse

---

[98] *Geschichte eines patriotischen Kaufmann*, 1768.
[99] Translator: Schnapps.
[100] Tottleben's account on the capture of Berlin was published in the *Vorontsof Archive*, Vol. VI, p. 458 and following, Moscow 1872.

grenadiers in reserve.

At midnight the signal was given, even though the artillery preparations were very insufficient, particularly at the Halle Gate. Prince Prozorovski captured it, however, but could not maintain himself at the gate, evacuating it at dawn. Patkul was checked immediately before the Kottbus Gate.

The bombardment resumed and lasted until morning. They had already fired 655 projectiles, including 567 bombs and howitzer shells.

It was learned, during the day, that the advance guard of Prince von Württemberg, with seven squadrons, had entered Berlin and that his infantry was coming by forced marches. This would bring the garrison a reinforcement of 5,000 men.

Tottleben retired on the village of Köpenik, calling to him Bachmann's infantry. The evening of 4 August, there remained before the Kottbus and Halle Gates only the Tsvietinovitch and Tourovierov Cossacks. During the morning of 5 August, they were frequently attacked by Prince von Württemberg and forced, in their turn, to withdraw on Köpenik.

In their failed surprise attack, the Russians lost 92 men hors de combat and they lost eight howitzers, whose carriages were broken.

The responsibility for this failure fell on Tottleben. With so little infantry at hand, why did he still divide it to attempt two simultaneous attacks. He attempted to justify himself in reports that exaggerated his losses, while raising the number of projectiles fired on the city to 6,500. He accused Tchernychev of not having supported him; now, he knew perfectly well that this general could not arrive at Köpenik until the 5th. Yet, he had never asked of him anything more than "covering his back." Obviously, he had launched his attack solely to grab all the honor for himself. Later he would claim that if he did not launch his men more aggressively, it was that he feared, once they penetrated such a large city, he could not rally them and get them in hand. Otherwise, all of Tottleben's reports on the siege are a web of contradictions and lies. While waiting, to borrow the words of the Marquis de Montalembert, the French attaché to the Russian army, Tottleben "broke his nose on the walls of Berlin."

On 3 October, Tchernychev occupied Fürstenwalde and, taking a better account of the difficulties of the enterprise, sent to the headquarters for reinforcements in the form of Haugrewen's cavalry, announcing that he heard a strong cannonade in the direction of Berlin. On the 4th, he received from Tottleben a request for reinforcements in men, cannon, and projectiles. That night he was sent two infantry regiments. During the evening of the 5th, he arrived at Köpenik, affecting his junction with Tottleben and took command from him. His authority was precarious and always contested, because of Tottleben's difficult personality. At the same time, he received a dispatch from Fermor. Panine's division advanced by forced marches to join him.

Tchernychev spent the day of the 6th awaiting Panine, a new dispatch from Fermor directed him to risk nothing before Panine's arrival. If, by chance, he had already made an attack, which had been checked, he was to dig himself in in a strong position. Otherwise, Fermor announced to Tchernychev the pending arrival of an Austrian corps and the Saxons, under the orders of Lascy. As a result, Tchernychev limited himself to reconnoitering the right bank of the Spree. He took up positions at Biesdorf and made no move to engage Prince von Württemberg before the arrival of the announced reinforcements.

On his side, Prince von Württemberg wrote Hülsen to expedite his march, by Potsdam, on Berlin. He took up position on the Lichtenberg heights, thus covering the Frankfurt and Alt-Landsberg Gates. Soon, on the other bank, Cossack scouts appeared, indicating Hülsen's approach. In the lead were military bakers under the escort of two battalions and a few squadrons, under the command of Cordier; then the advance guard, properly said, under Kleist's orders, containing five battalions and 12 squadrons.

On 7 October, Tchernychev received a dispatch from Panine, who, after a march of 30 versts, had reached Fürstenwalde. That same evening, he was before Berlin. Tchernychev was resolved to attack Prince von Württemberg, and if the attack was successful, to then attack the eastern suburbs. He reserved to Tottleben the execution of a diversion on the left bank.

Tottleben, to regain his independence, profited from the Spree being between him and his superior, Tchernychev. That same day, without awaiting the imminent arrival of Lacy, he resumed his attack against the western suburbs. He again distributed his squadrons and battalions before the Kottbus and Halle Gates, but he found that the heights that dominated them were occupied by Prince von Württemberg. After a three-hour cannonade, he obliged the prince to withdraw behind the curtain wall.

At this time Hülsen's bakers, under the escort of Cordier's infantry and cavalry squadron, Tottleben resolved to launch his assault. Leaving part of his troops to observe the gates, he threw the rest of his cavalry and about 1,000 grenadiers against Cordier. In his rush, he outstripped his infantry, charged with only the cavalry, and was repulsed. He prepared to renew his attack as Kleist's advance guard appeared. At the same time, he was informed that Lascy's corps was arriving. Tottleben did not wish to await the Austrian reinforcement and hastily attacked Kleist. There followed a very confused and indecisive battle, not far from Tempelhof. Tottleben lost four cannons, but his Cossacks recaptured them, but the general found himself unable to support them. It was then that the Austrian squadrons arrived, and the fate of the day was decided as Kleist withdrew, while Cordier and his bakers profited from the disorder to slip into Berlin.

Tottleben was furious at Lascy's arrival. He had not succeeded in making himself independent of Tchernychev to fall under Lacy's authority.

Because he commanded 14,000 men, he naturally would take command over the chief of the hussars and Cossacks. This intruder had come to snatch from him the glory of surprising and reducing Berlin. Discontented, he resumed his positions before the Kottbus and Halle Gates, turning a deaf ear to Lacy's first requests. As a result of this Hülsen's entire corps was able to enter the city that evening.

During this time, Tchernychev had acted on the right bank of the Spree. From Biesdorf he had marched on the Lichtenberg heights, his right covered by the Moldavia Hussars. These hussars charged some Prussian cuirassiers and supported by Haugrewen's cavalry; they drove the Prussians back. Then Tchernychev carried the heights, occupied them, and placed a battery of six guns which then bombarded Zedmar's infantry. At the third cannon shot the caissons began exploding among the Prussian troops. Threatened by the victorious Russian cavalry, they did not await the bayonets of the Russian infantry and retired into the eastern suburbs. Panine arrived during the evening with five squadrons of cuirassiers and six companies of grenadiers. He announced that the main body of his troops could not arrive before the morning of the 9th.

During the morning of the 8th, because of the operations of the day before, Tchernychev occupied, on the right bank, positions at Weissensee, Lichtenberg, and Friedrichsfelde, with the Moldavia Hussars and the Krasnochtchokof Cossacks in the woods and swamp along the Spree. On the left bank, Tottleben remained before the Kottbus and Halle Gates. The 14,000 Austrians camped around Lichtenfelde.

Tchernychev proposed attacking Prince von Württemberg and the eastern suburbs that day. However, the arrival of Kleist's corps has raised the Prussian forces to 14,000 men, there being 16 battalions and 20 squadrons on the right bank, under the Prince's orders, and 10 battalions and 21 squadrons on the left bank, with Hülsen. The Allies opposed them with 15,500 Russians on the right bank, and 4,400 Russians and 14,000 Austrians and Saxons on the left bank. The Prussians, masters of Berlin, could move their forces across the Spree with ease and oppose either, but only one of the two Allied forces had an equal force. The Allies were further weakened by the jealousies between the Russians and the Austrians, as well as the rivalries in the command between Lacy and Tottleben, and Tottleben and Tchernychev.

Tchernychev was profoundly discouraged. He called a council of war, but it was attended only by Panine, Baron von Elm, quartermaster of the army, and the Marquis de Montalembert, the French military attaché, who had accompanied Tchernychev in his march on Berlin. We owe to this officer the report of what occurred in this council of war. Tchernychev was disturbed by the reinforcements that the Prussians had received, the possibility of seeing himself attacked the next day by all their forces, the difficulties of communicating with the Russians and Austrians on the left bank, so "he proposed to retire that evening on Köpenik, to gain the time to organize a plan with Lacy; otherwise, he would leave seeking bread, as he had only enough for one day; and finished by asking my advice. Here is what the Marquis recommended to him:

> I said to him that to remain longer in his position before Berlin appeared me to have many disadvantages since the arrival of Generals von Hülsen and Kleist; but to withdraw to Köpenik appeared to me to be worse, in addition to the shame of such an operation, since it would expose the Count de Lacy to seeing all our enemy's forces coming out to engage him, who would oblige him to withdraw so as to avoid an unequal battle, and that they ran a great risk of failing in this operation; that I believed finally that one should not hesitate to attack at daybreak, by sending a courier to advise Count de Lacy of this resolution... The opinion of the two assistants was rather for a withdrawal than for a battle, without however deciding anything. This obliged to me to return at the charge several times. Finally, I persuaded Count Tchernychev to decide for the attack, and he immediately wrote of his resolution to Lacy...[101]

Tchernychev prepared for an assault the next day. Initially he organized the troops on the right bank into four columns: the 1st under Palmenbach, the 2nd under Lebel, the 3rd under Prince Dolgorukov, and the 4th under Nummers. At the head of each column, organized like those that Field Marshal Münich had used in his assault on the works at Danzig, were to march companies of grenadiers. The first one was to take the heights neighboring the curtain wall, then they were to move into the eastern suburbs. The cavalry would cover the columns against an attack by Prussian cavalry. The field artillery would maintain a heavy fire on all the Prussian positions. The regimental guns would follow the regiments. The heavy baggage and the non-combatants would move into the Friedrichsfelde Wood; the wagons and chariots were to remain with their horses attached in case of a retreat. The signal to attack was to be given, at 7:00 a.m., by three cannons firing heated shot. The column commanders were "directed to execute the attack with all the perfection possible and that each one was to bring to it what related to him, to the main effort while thinking and acting well....to thus deserve the majestic favor of the Empress...to maintain this honor and this glory which the arms of sovereign Russian had conquered by such long campaigns." The morale of the chiefs and the soldiers

---

[101] Montalembert, *Correspondance.*

was excellent; was excited to the highest degree: "One could not describe," said Tchernychev in his report, "the impatience and the heat with which the troops awaited this attack; hope shone on the face of everyone." The soldiers approached the sacraments with religious enthusiasm and drew from the bags their white blouses for the attack, in order to be able "to look death in the face, in the Russian manner."

The opposite process occurred in the Prussian council of war. During the day of the 8th, Prince von Württemberg had resolved to fight Tchernychev. However, during the night his colleges had convinced him the Allies were too numerically superior, that it was impossible to receive reinforcements, and that the prospect of making the city the scene of the horrors of war and capture by assault was to be avoided. It was decided that the troops brought by Kleist, Hülsen, and Prince von Württemberg should retire under cover of night, on Spandau and Charlottenburg. They gave Rochow the task of negotiating a military capitulation, but only for his weak garrison and the municipality encumbered by the care of its population and their goods.

On his side, Tottleben, who, still posted before the Halle and Kottbus Gates, interposed himself as a screen between the city and the Austrian army, had not renounced taking his revenge on Lacy. This Austrian general sought to rip from him the honor of capturing the place by himself. Tottleben profited from his advance position to negotiate a capitulation to the exclusion of Lacy, as well as of Tchernychev. No doubt he already had contacts inside the city, possibly his friend the rich merchant Gotzkowski. In truth, the presence of Hülsen and Prince von Württemberg appeared to take from him all hope of succeeding. He was still unaware of the decision taken by the Prussian council of war. How could he imagine that Hülsen and the Prince, who had come from so far, the one from Saxony or the other from Pomerania, would have done so only to declare that they could not defend Berlin?

During the same night of 8/9 October, he sent a new summons to Rochow. It was premature, because Rochow was obliged to hold firm until the relieving troops had affected their retreat. Also, a herald, around 1:00 a.m., came again with the commander's refusal. Tottleben, who did not understand this refusal, directed that a few cannon shots be fired on the city. At 3:00 a.m., Major Weger and Squadron Commander Wagenheim presented themselves at the Kottbus Gate, bearing Rochow's proposals for a capitulation. It was at this moment that the relief troops were making their exit from the city. One could ask how Tottleben, who was charged with the service of the scouts, had seen nothing, and heard nothing of this troop movement.

At the same time the bourgeois, warned by Rochow, had gathered at the Rathaus. The council of war had given the municipal council the choice to capitulate to the Austrians or to the Russians. It was the merchant Gotzkowski, who contributed the most to inclining the population in favor of the Russians, speaking with pride of his good relations with Tottleben. He had long resided in the city and counted many friends among its population. In addition, Berlin had served as the asylum for many Russian wounded and prisoners, generals, officers, and soldiers. They had been humanely treated and had been received into Gotzkowski's house as well as those of many other notables. One could count on them serving as protectors for their compatriots.

At 4:00 a.m., the military capitulation was signed by Rochow. He surrendered himself and his forces as prisoners of war and turned over all his equipment. The Austrian, Saxon, Swedish, French and Russian prisoners were liberated. The Prussians, who for the most part, laid down their arms were put on parole or left at their liberty with a caution. Of the 1,200-man garrison, only 700 were sent to Russia.

At 5:00 a.m., the civilians capitulated. Tottleben initially demanded 4,000,000 *thalers*: "40 tons of gold" according to Gotzkowski. This was reduced to 2,000,000, then 1,500,000, and finally 500,000 in coin and 1,000,000 in *wechsels*, guaranteed by hostages. In exchange for these concessions, the bourgeois handed over 200,000 in *douceur-geld*[102]*;* that is to say a bonus for the soldiers of the Expeditionary Corps. The magistrate executed it, persuaded by Gotzkowski, who promised to use his influence with the generals and the Russian Government to obtain a new reduction in this contribution, in demonstrating to them the extreme poverty of the citizens of Berlin. Tottleben otherwise guaranteed the inhabitants the security of their persons and property, the maintenance of their privileges, liberty of commerce, and mail, the exemption from military lodging, and a promise that the irregular troops would not be cantoned in the suburbs.

It was through General Bachmann that Tottleben, in the greatest secrecy, had handled the negotiations. This was a triumph of his skill and spirit of intrigue. No hint of this had been given to Tchernychev's camp or to Lascy's camp when, at 5:00 a.m., General Bachmann had the Kottbus, Halle, Potsdam, and Brandenburg Gates occupied by his grenadiers.

The Austrians on the left bank were the first to notice that something new was afoot. When they saw Russian sentries at the gates of the western suburbs, they became furious. At the Halle Gate they forced a Russian post. Then Lacy sent a complaint to Tchernychev demanding that he be given control of the Potsdam and Magdeburg Gates; that the Austrians receive part of the contribution, and their soldiers receive a share of the 200,000 *thalers douceur-geld*. His anger went further, as we will see. He affected to hold the capitulation as not having occurred, sent his troops into the city, and lodged his soldiers in the homes of the inhabitants.

---

[102] Translator: This word is a mixture of French and German – *douceur* being French for *sweetness* or *softness; geld* being German for *gold* or *money*. This is apparently something between a tip and a bribe.

Tchernychev received, at the same time, the messenger sent to him by Tottleben, who had passed through Berlin, and Lacy's complaints. His troops were already under arms, formed in assault columns, awaiting the three cannon shots, the signal for the attack. At 5:00 a.m., the corps leaders had sent their aides-de-camp to Tchernychev to receive any last instructions. The army breathed impatiently; the attack was to be launched at 7:00 a.m. Suddenly the word spread through the astonished troops: Berlin had capitulated!

One of Tchernychev's first actions was that which Tottleben had neglected: the pursuit of the Prussian army. He ordered General Panine, with the Moldavia Hussars and the Krasnochtchokof Cossacks to head down the road to Spandau. The main body of the Prussians was already long gone. Panine only found a few abandoned wagons and Kleist's rearguard.

Kleist had 10 squadrons of Prussian cuirassiers, one regiment of infantry, the Busch Freikorps battalion, and some companies of light infantry — a total of 3,000 men. The Cossacks and hussars bravely charged the cuirassiers, threw them back, but had to stop before the infantry concealed in an ambush in a defile on the road. The Serbian Hussars arrived, after finally being dispatched by Tottleben, then the cuirassiers, and horse grenadiers. The Prussians were driven from their positions. The Busch Freikorps was surrounded and forced to surrender. The rest of the Prussians were vainly chased to Spandau. The Russians lost 45 dead and 21 wounded, while the Prussians lost 2,000 dead or wounded, plus 1,000 prisoners and a quantity of horses. Kleist's rearguard was completely destroyed. If Tottleben had earlier advised his superior, all of Hülsen's corps would have suffered the same fate.

The true trophy of the campaign was Berlin in the hands of the Allies; Berlin, the capital of the Margraves of Brandenburg and the first three Kings of Prussia. However, the joy, in the Coalition Army, was mixed with other sentiments. Tottleben's conduct appeared ambiguous. The Austrians were upset at his success, which they felt was at their expense. The Saxons were indignant that the capitulation was so advantageous for Berlin, complaining they were deprived of the chance for reprisals for what Frederick had done in their lands. Even the Russian generals and officers felt that Tottleben had been too soft on the Berliners. The capture of Berlin did not have the impact of a victory. No *Te Deum* was sung and there was no solemn entry. Tchernychev was satisfied to examine the eastern posts, having Lascy at his side. He did not go into the city. He affected to leave Tottleben to dispose of his conquest as he wished. Lacy complained that Tottleben was master of the city and that the Austrians were there only in the capacity of spectators and like his slaves. Tottleben had distributed the 200,000 *thalers* of the *douceur-geld*; 75,000 went to the Expeditionary Corps, 25,000 to Panine, and 50,000 to Tchernychev's troops, with the same going to Lacy's troops. The Austrians and Saxons were not content. Fights erupted in the city between them and Tottleben's troops.

This produced a relaxation of discipline and soldiers of every arm and nation entered the city, irrespective of the capitulation and their instructions. Bolotov tells us the following:

> The soldiers, dissatisfied with their food and drink, extorted money and clothing from the inhabitants, taking all that they could carry or drag away. Berlin filled with Cossacks, Croats and hussars who, in broad daylight, broke into houses, raped, beat, and wounded the inhabitants. People were stopped in the streets and stripped head to foot. 282 houses were plundered and stripped. The Austrians, as the Berliners themselves say, went far beyond the excesses of our soldiers. They wanted to hear nothing of conditions, nor of capitulation; they were given up to their national hatred and their love of plundering. Also, Tottleben was obliged on several occasions to send into the city many Russian soldiers and to fire on the plunderers. The plunderers went like madmen into the royal stables, which, under the capitulation, were to be guarded by the Russian soldiers. They took the horses; the King's coaches were stripped and broken. Even the hospitals, the old people's homes, the churches, were not saved, but everywhere was plundered and devastated. The fever of plundering became so sharp that the Saxons themselves, the best and the most disciplined of all the Germans, became barbarians at this time and ceased to resemble themselves.
>
> They then went to their quarters in Charlottenburg, a city within one mile from Berlin and famous for its royal pleasure palace. With cruelty and ferocity, they fell on the palace and destroyed everything on which their eyes fell. The rarest pieces of furniture were torn and broken; glass and porcelain were broken, invaluable carpets were torn, tables slashed with sabers; parquet floors, panels, and doors, split with blows of axes; an infinity of objects were removed and stolen. What caused the greatest sorrow to the King of Prussia, was the destruction of the splendid cabinet of rarities which he had gathered, which was composed only of antiquities, gathered with great effort and great expense. The petty thieves did not save it: they broke and mutilated the statues.
>
> The inhabitants of Charlottenburg had hoped to spare themselves by a contribution of 15,000 *thalers*, but

they were fooled. All the houses were emptied; all that the pillagers could not carry off was broken, ruined, destroyed; men were beaten and wounded with saber blows; women and young girls were outraged; some of the beaten and wounded were so cruelly injured that they died under the eyes of their torturers.

The same plague and the same misfortune struck many other towns around Berlin, but most of the pillaging was done by the Imperials, not our Russians; because they effectively observed, there as in the city, an exact discipline.

Berlin suffered less than its surroundings. Tottleben succeeded in establishing there a bit of discipline, by reinforcing the Prussian posts. Only the establishments of the crown were pillaged, but not destroyed from roof to foundation as prescribed by Saltykov and Fermor's instructions. In the Arsenal, the Russians and Austrians came to blows. The latter wished to take everything. Tottleben only granted them 12 Prussian cannons, in addition to the Austrian and Saxon guns that were there as trophies. The Russians found 143 cannon and 18,000 muskets there. Lacy wished to blow up the Arsenal. Tottleben opposed him, anticipating the disaster that would result for the city. He had already taken the care to drown the powder and ruin the mills that served to make it. The royal mills producing military cloth were stripped and the cloth sold at minimal prices. The Mint and the cannon foundry were destroyed. In the royal chests they found 60,000 to 100,000 *thalers*. "One saw the infamous individuals show the enemy the army's depots; one also saw, and in greater number, dedicated citizens make every effort to save what belonged to the King."

It was visible that Tottleben protected the Berliners. He was subject to the influence of Gotzkowski. When Bachmann, the morning of the capitulation, at 5 a.m., entered the city, it had met, at the Kottbus Gate, the Magistrate's delegation. A curious dialogue, which was preserved for us by the patriotic merchant, occurred between them:

Turning to the bourgeois, Bachmann asked who they were. On their answer that they were the delegates from the city and the corps of merchants, he asked to them whether Gotzkowski was not there. I said to him: "It is me; what do you wish?" Then he began again: "I am charged, gracious Sir, to greet you on the part of the former Brigadier Siwers, now general; he recommended to me and requested you to render you all possible honors; I am called Bachmann and I am named, for the duration of our stay, commander of the city; if I can be useful to you in some way, just ask."

As soon as Gotzkowski could take this interview elsewhere, he asked that Brink, the aide-de-camp to Tottleben, be lodged in his house. This gave him every facility to obtain audiences with Tottleben. Bachmann then set about preventing excesses, maintaining discipline, and protecting the people and their property. He punished a Russian officer who had stolen 100 *thalers*: the culprit remained tied, for 48 hours, to the mouth of a cannon. Gotzkowski saved the people's shotguns, which the Russians wanted declared as weapons of war: one delivered only a few hundreds of them at worst. He prevented two imprudent journalists from being beaten with rods; their writings were simply burned by the hand of the torturer. He persuaded Tottleben to only impose a contribution on the Jews. He even succeeded in preserving from destruction the depot and manufactures of gold and silver, ensuring that their product was not thrown into the royal chests, but only devoted to the maintenance of the Potsdam orphanage. For the guarantee of the million in *wechsel*, instead of taking two counselors and several notable merchants as hostages, Gotzkowski arranged that they be satisfied with a junior clerk, two cashiers, and two Jews named Itzig and Ephraim. The patriotic merchant was night and day in the streets, Bolotov tells us, or in Tottleben's anteroom. He had enough influence over him to make him violate most of his instructions. Did Tottleben receive for his softness a large sum from the King of Prussia? Later on, we will see that it is extremely probable.

Gotzkowski limited himself to saying, in his memoirs, that Tottleben conducted himself more as a friend than an enemy. When he saw the Russian army about to leave, he expressed his joy at seeing his house finally delivered: "During all the period when the enemy was in the city, I had to feed and water all those who presented themselves; which was at my cost, without speaking of the numerous gifts that I was obliged to distribute to obtain what I requested, but all this is in my ledgers of profit and loss. One can be certain that in a parallel case one obtains nothing with nothing."

Another man who greatly contributed to diminishing the rigors of the occupation was Verlst, the Dutch Envoy. He shamed the Russian and Austrian authorities for the disorders of the first day and stopping the pillage. Later Frederick II thanked him[103] and gave him the title of "count."

We now return to Fermor and the Russian main army.

On 28 September, he had crossed the Oder and marched by Wartenberg, Grünberg, etc., on Berlin. It was while enroute that he dispatched Haugrewen's cavalry to reinforce Tchernychev. On the 29th, Rumyantsev had left Korolath and marched on Züllichau. Upon his arrival at Guben, Fermor had detached on Berlin, as we have noted, Panine's division with Eropkine's dragoons. On 8

---

103   *Politische Correspondenz*, Vol. XX, p. 25; of 22 October 1760.

October, he had affected his junction, with Rumyantsev, at Frankfurt. On the 10th, he handed command back to Soltykov.

Saltykov, seeing the expeditionary corps so far out on a limb, troubled by the new march of Frederick II on the Spree with 70,000 men, fearing that his forces might be cut in two and destroyed in detail, directed Tchernychev and his lieutenants to retreat to Frankfurt. During the night of 11/12 October, Panine's corps left Berlin; the next day, Tchernychev and Lacy left; the evening of the 12th, it was Tottleben, who covered the retreat. Bachman left last. This is what Bolotov says on the subject:

> Upon the departure of our soldiers with Brigadier Bachman, who had been for some time Commander of Berlin, the inhabitants offered him, through the Magistrate, a present of 10,000 *thalers* in recognition of his wonderful and magnanimous conduct; but his response was no less generous; he refused the present saying that he was sufficiently compensated by the honor of having been Commander of Berlin for a few days.

During the course of the evacuation, Saltykov was in a trance. He then had only 20,000 men in Frankfurt. Finally, from the 13th to the 14th, the army found itself reunited with the trophies it had collected in Berlin.

The capture of the Prussian capital had produced great excitement in Europe. Voltaire wrote to Count Alexander Shuvalov: "Your troops in Berlin, made a more wonderful effect than all the operas of Metastasio."[104] The Allied Courts and the ambassadors did not fail to present their congratulations, though little sincere, to Elisabeth. The Austrians told her that they hoped, for the honor of Russian arms, that they would maintain themselves in Berlin. There they had, in Brandenburg, magnificent winter quarters. The compliments continued even though Berlin had been evacuated.

Irrespectively, the Russians were proud of this bold campaign. One of the paintings inthe Winter Palace, among the other battles of the Seven Years War, represents the entrance of the Russians into Berlin; and one can see at Our Lady of Kazan, the keys to Berlin. The Marquis de L'Hôpital, in a dispatch of 5 November, observed that "the coup de main on Berlin gave to this court a tone of audacity, if not to say insolence." The chances of making peace appeared to it, for the same reasons, to be farther away. Vorontsov was inclined to make peace, but the young favorite Shuvalov and the Conference moved the Tsarina in the other direction.

Frederick II had suffered great losses in Berlin: his grand central depot, its arsenal, its foundry, and its magazines which had cost him much pain and

[104]Voltaire, Oeuvres, *Correspondance général,* 25 October 1760.

money. He was both humiliated and irritated that he had not realized earlier that the Allies might enter his capital. "It is not without reason," Catt tells us, "that he groaned at his incredulity."

That same witness, Catt, gives us the impression that this misfortune was greatly felt by the King's entourage. "Berlin only offered a sad vestige of what it had been previously." There were praises for Tottleben: "Generals Tchernychev and Lacy were fortunately attached to the commander of the Cossacks. Praise also came for the Dutch envoy; the King said to him, with tears in his eyes: "The Royal Family, myself, and the Prussians, owe prayers to this worthy minister;" And finally, praise for the merchant Gotzkowski, "who at the peril of his life or being carried off as a prisoner, did all that was humanly possible to prevent excesses." Justice was also given to the Russians: "They saved the city from the horrors with which the Austrians threatened it; they held an admirable order," except that they had soiled the chambers of the King and Queen at Charlottenburg. They had mutilated the statues: "The Goths, those barbarians, committed the same excesses in Rome." They looked for even more against the Saxons, and justified in advance, by their violence in Berlin, those which they proposed to later make in Saxony and Poland.

The Russian Court was proud of their success in Berlin. When it undertook to justify itself, to the British envoy, for the accusations of barbarism which Frederick II directed at the Russian army, there was a certain irony in the "note to be read to Mr. Keith, Envoy Extraordinaire to His Britannic Majesty," an assignment to point out the misdeeds of the accuser, to juxtapose them against the so moderate and so humane actions of the Court of St. Petersburg, the whole joined with the pleasure of triumphing at the same time over King of Prussia and his ally, England:

> Saxony was deprived of a large number of its inhabitants, enrolled by force as recruits or taken away for other ends in the States of Brandenburg. In exchange, one had not carried off a single [East-] Prussian man and, in addition, one has furnished from the treasury of Her Imperial Majesty to the inhabitants of this province money to replace the animals that have died, in order that they may continue, without interruption, their tilling. The King of Prussia has forced prisoners, by blows, by hunger, and by other very rough treatment, to enter into his service, in violation of their first oath. Her Imperial Majesty has, by contrast, put at liberty the men enrolled by force when they have fallen into her hands and returned them to their legitimate masters.
> The capture of Berlin which, according to appearances, has newly turned the King of Prussia sour, should nevertheless be

used only to give relief to the arms of Her Imperial Majesty, which being a monument to her generosity and softness, as well as a reason for the King of Prussia to imitate the nobility of the soul of Her Imperial Majesty, far from thinking of revenge. Certainly, all this residence cannot refuse to testify, though it had deserved a punishment compared to the resistance which one had vainly undertaken there; it was however spared so much so that one did not even allow the soldiers to take up quarters in private houses, except for the Lifeguards that were placed at the specific request of the inhabitants. Leipzig, in exchange, was never put in a state of defense against the Prussians; but this city never tasted such a soft fate.

It is true that, in Berlin, the Arsenal, foundries, and weapons manufactories were destroyed, but it was principally for this purpose that the expedition was launched.

In taking a contribution from this city, one followed the normal practices; and, in truth, it does not compare to the vast sums that the Prussians took from Saxony and alone from the city of Leipzig.

Until now the Almighty constantly blessed the arms of Her Imperial Majesty, and, though she entrusts fully in the subsequent assistance of Divine kindness, however up to now Her Imperial Majesty did not allow that her victorious arms were to be used to ruin the enemy cities that her troops had seized. But in case that the King of Prussia, far from conforming to Her Imperial Majesty's manner of behavior, he wants to misuse the temporary success of his arms to push his revenge, especially as he persists in forcing his non-military subjects to take up arms, in these cases results of such conduct can become disastrous beyond what one can provide and will undoubtedly rather contribute to pushing away the desired return of peace that to advance it.

And as the envoy on every occasion acted with a praiseworthy zeal for the re-establishment of peace, one hopes that he would succeed, as much with his court as with that of the King of Prussia in order to prevent the war, already so disastrous for both, become even more cruel.[105]

Frederick II moved to take his revenge on the Austrians in the bloody battle of Torgau, fought on 3 November of the same year.

---

[105] This unedited document is found in the Archives of French Foreign Affairs, in a document attached to a dispatch from L'Hôpital (*Correspondence*, Russia, Vol. LXV, 11 December 1760.)

The other expedition attempted by the Russians, that on Kolberg, had less brilliant results. Olitz, moving from Korolatah, on 12 August, with six regiments of infantry, the Archangel Dragoons, the Georgia Hussars, 1,000 Don Cossacks, and 12 cannons, with a total of 12,000 men, had to stop at Driesen to wait there for new orders. During this time, Admiral Mikouchov brought into the roadstead of Kolberg 5,000 men on a flotilla of transports escorted by 17 warships. The fortress was defended by Colonel Heiden. Against these 17,000 Russians he had two battalions of *landmiliz* and 800 men of the Puttkammer Garrison Regiment. The Admiral, who had begun, on 27 August, to bombard the fortress and landing troops and material, was interrupted for nine days by a terrible storm. On 6 September, the bombardment resumed. The trench was opened. Suddenly, General Werner, leaving from Glogau, on 8 August, with three battalions, who had rallied two others in Stettin with eight squadrons, appeared on 18 August, before the walls of Kolberg. He maneuvered audaciously and succeeded in entering the fortress. The Russians, discouraged, raised the siege, re-embarked, and abandoned 22 cannons. The conference showed such anger at this check that it brought the Russian commanders before courts martial. However, they were acquitted on 21 November.

After the concentration of the Russian army at Frankfurt, on 13 and 14 October, Saltykov had it recross to the right bank of the Oder. He waited there to be attacked by Frederick II, furious at the devastation of his capital. However, we have seen that the King of Prussia had already turned against Daun. After having vainly waited at Zielenzig, where he occupied an advantageous position, Saltykov decided on the 17th, to order a retreat on the Wartha, then onto the Vistula. This movement provoked complaints from the King of Poland and Daun. They insisted that he send at least Tchernychev's corps to the Austrian Army in Saxony. This request was not accepted by the Conference. The Russian army had suffered greatly in the campaign. It lacked forage, as usual. They had such a lack of horses that they were obliged to burn 55 forges and 54 pontoons to turn their horses over to the artillery. On 26 October, they went into cantonments on the other bank of the Wartha. On the 30th, Saltykov, sick again, handed command over to Fermor. Already his successor was designated: it was Count Alexander Borissovitch Burturline. He was much in favor with the Tsarina; he had no military qualifications to justify this charge, beyond his title as being the most senior of the generals-in-chief. They did not wish to name Fermor; Rumyantsev was judged to still be too young, leaving no other choice. Burturline had been a member of the Conference and commander of the Ukrainian forces. In addition, there is no doubt that Elisabeth designated him; it had to be the Conference.

On 14 October, he had informed Fermor that his intention was to take up winter quarters in Silesia or in Pomerania. When he arrived at the army, he could assure himself that this was impossible. He directed, therefore, that the retreat continued to the Lower Vistula, where the army would canton as it had in the previous campaigns.

It was not only the Russian army that was fatigued by the campaign. The war weighed heavily on everyone, but above all on the King of France. In India, Pondicherry had succumbed on 10 January. In America, the debris of the French forces capitulated with Vaudreuil in Montreal. In Germany, the French had only one victory, that of the Duke de Castries at Clostercamp (6 October). This winter, the French moved to take up winter quarters in Westphalia, on the Werra and the Fulda. It was a weak compensation for the disasters they had suffered. On 18 December, Louis XV sent to the Marquis de L'Hôpital a "Declaration to the Allied Courts." Louis XV gave it to be understand that he considered the goal that coalition had proposed to reach in this war had been achieved: "The Prussian power was weakened to the point that one could hope that one would have no further reason to fear the ambitious spirit who counted too daringly on his forces." As for the compensations that Austria, the Elector of Saxony and the Crown of Sweden had hoped to tear away from him, Louis XV invited his allies to reflect on the chances of obtaining them: "He did not envisage the possibility that the coming campaign would place, by its events, the alliance in a different position than that in which it was at that time." Lastly, going quickly to the main question, the King spoke of the miseries and the exhaustion of his people. He could not "conceal from his faithful allied only he was obliged to decrease his military assistance," and that if the war lasted longer, he could not "answer that it would be possible for him to completely fulfill all his engagements."

The defection of France was close, at least for the affairs of Germany. Choiseul intended to devote his last resources to maritime defense.

CHAPTER XV

THE 1761 CAMPAIGN.

The 1761 campaign was about to begin. Since France had made its statement of 18 December, one could no longer hope in St Petersburg for a very active continuation of hostilities in Germany, or even a final success; that is to say, a continuation of Russian domination in East Prussia.

Elisabeth had already ceded to the requests of Louis XV in rejecting Saltykov's projects on Danzig, also making concessions for the Province of [East] Prussia. In the fall of 1760, she had said to the King of France that this would be no obstacle for the negotiation of a peace. The *Instructions*, dated 31 January 1761, which Baron de Breteuil received from Paris, showed at why Louis XV, always for the same reasons, discouraged the ambitions of Russia:

> Baron de Breteuil will represent to the Empress of Russia, if she will give him the time, all the reasons of justice and humanity which must urge this princess to adopt the salutary project to stop the effusion of so much blood from the belligerent nations and to prevent, if it is possible, the chances for a new campaign...One cannot reasonably any more hope to obtain peace by a war, which experience has too much taught us that the dangers are more certain than successes...Such a great princess, after having given the most authentic marks of her fidelity to her engagements, should not currently seek any other glory than to procure public repose and happiness.

The first result of this state of spirits among the Allies was the *very secret* rescript addressed by the Tsarina, on 2 February, from Generalissimo Burturline: "Now are changed or can change the circumstances which led us to make all our efforts to maintain East Prussia in a good state. Other circumstances occurred, demanding that one occupies oneself before providing our army with all the things necessary and to produce fear in the King of Prussia." Consequently, Burturline was to make the province heavily feel the cost of the state of war. He was to replace all the Russian wagon drivers, laborers, and service people, with peasants conscripted in Prussia, with their carriages and beasts of burden. They were to be released only upon the end of the war.

Another result was a conference held in Paris, on 25 March 1761, between the representatives of the Courts of Austria, Russia, Sweden, and Saxony-Poland. It occurred in the home of the Duke de Choiseul. It issued a declaration from the five courts, dated the 26th, addressed to the Kings of England and Prussia. They were offered to designate a city, Augsburg or any other, where they would send plenipotentiaries to negotiate a peace. Parallel negotiations would be held in London and Paris. They would offer, at the same time, a suspension of arms "in all the parts of the world where the fire of war is burning." On 8 April, Pitt responded that the war could only be ended overseas after the conclusion of a definitive peace. He therefore reserved to himself the ability to complete the conquest of the remaining French colonies. The Congress of Augsburg as well as the conferences in Paris and London were equally blocked. Maria-Theresa wanted Silesia; as for Frederick, rather than renounce this province, he was resolved to continue the war. "Should I in charge of six kitchen boys, I will support the indivisibility of my possessions."[106]

The war was renewed everywhere, but principally outside of Europe. Elisabeth attempted to profit from the deception suffered by Louis XV to propose a new, direct and formal alliance with Russia. The insinuations of Ambassador Dmitri Golitzyn to the Court of Versailles and, those of Chancellor Vorontsov made to Baron de Breteuil, were equally checked by the position taken by the King of France. Choiseul had accepted this alliance with joy. Louis XV obstinately rejected it. He locked de Breteuil in the most rigorous instructions. When one spoke to him of a treaty of alliance, he was to shy away from it and speak only of a treaty of commerce. England took good account of the repugnancies of Louis XV. Sensing that it had nothing to fear from a Franco-Russian alliance, it redoubled its demands and bitterness towards an isolated France. It is this which produced all the checks to the efforts at negotiation and the furious resumption of the naval and colonial war.

Choiseul, who Louis XV prevented from extending a hand to Russia, turned to Spain. He succeeded in conquering its hesitations and brought it, by the Treaty of Paris of 15 August 1761, into the *Pacte de famille*, into which also came the Bourbons of Italy. This alliance only offered a new object for English greed. After having completed the ruin of the French colonies, it could now attack those of Spain. The naval war continued for the French and her allies, with new disasters.

On the Continent, the pessimistic expectations of Louis XV were realized. Frederick II, reduced to the defensive by the exhaustion of his resources, appeared to have found a means of imposing this same attitude on his enemies. He had no more than 190,000 men against 385,000. He succeeded in not giving a single great battle and not allowing the Russians or the Austrians any great conquest. The 1760 campaign ceased to be "the most pitiful of campaigns;" it left that honor to the 1761 campaign.

On the Austrian side there was but one success of any importance, the capture of Schweidnitz. On the French side, there was the defeat at Willighausen

---

[106] De Meissen to Councilor Kniphausen (charged with his affairs in London) 12 April 1761. – Vol. XX, p. 330.

(15 July). The Russian balance was summarized in a new campaign of marches and maneuvers in Silesia and the capture of Kolberg.

We know already Generalissimo Burturline. The praise given him by the Empress to the Conference, at the outcome of the 1760 campaign, is very characteristic. The following note was signed by all the members of the Conference.

> It is necessary to give to his good services this justice to all the provisions that he took to that point are founded on the noblest zeal as well as on the most careful wisdom. His labor and his solicitude extended to all the parts of the service without exception. Usually, the army, in its withdrawal to its winter quarters, completed the exhaustion and loss of its horses; quite to the contrary, thanks to the efforts of the field-marshal, the army was reconstituted on this march. He could exchange bad horses for good ones. In a word, if the zeal of the generals who are subordinate to him correspond to his zeal, we are permitted to hope for their good performance and glory in the next campaign.

From this certificate it appears that Burturline was a good administrator; that he could spare the men and the horses. However, one knows nothing of his strategic talents. On this point, we will see that history has the right to be mute like the Conference.

According to Bolotov, the Generalissimo would have affected by a serious defect. Perhaps this officer, for whom, undoubtedly, there was an echo of scandal that ran in the Army, but this was an exaggeration; however, for the bottom, his testimony agrees with that of Frederick II. He assures that, in the most critical moments, Burturline was devoted to frequent and almost uninterrupted orgies:

> There have reached us accounts, sometimes comic and sometimes humiliating to a very great degree. In these orgies, the general uttered insults without number; he spent whole nights accompanied by grenadiers, obliged them to drink, sing songs, and to shout; those that pleased him the most, he appointed officers and even majors; then, when he had slept, he made them come and requested them to surrender these ranks and to remain such as they were before…

However, in his dispatch of 26 January 1761, the Marquis de L'Hôpital gave to the Russian army reorganized by Burturline, the most favorable evaluation: "It is in a very good state. It continually receives new recruits. It lacks no more than 1,000 horses in the cavalry."

The 1761 campaign began, as usual, with movements of the Russian light cavalry. "There are 8,000 Russians who have re-entered Pomerania," wrote Frederick II. "Acknowledge that I am in charge of the work of Penelope. God! That I was there!" On 29 January, the Russians had a skirmish with the Prussians, at Schlawe, on the road from Stolpe to Kolberg. They there had the advantage and took many prisoners. Tottleben benefitted from this to go before Kolberg and occupy with his lines of outposts Treptow, Greifenberg, Plathe, Regenswalde, Neu-Stettin, Czarnikow, and Oborniki; that is to say, the major Prussian part of Pomerania and Posnania. On 17 February, Tottleben announced that he held Kolberg in a state of blockade. With the reinforcements that Beketov had brought him, he had 14,000 men.

At the end of February, he entered negotiations with the Prussian leaders, Prince von Braunschweig-Bevern and General Werner. He had concluded with them a four-day truce for the exchange of prisoners. Then other truces followed. Tottleben was not disavowed. He initially received the approbation of the Generalissimo, then that of the Conference. The latter also authorized Tottleben to extend this truce to 27 May. Masslovski was shocked, because, from then on, the general of the light troops could be seen as an ambiguous and even suspect personage.

Meanwhile the plan for the 1761 campaign was being negotiated between the St. Petersburg and Vienna Courts. Daun wished to act in Saxony. He designated Laudon to act in Silesia. He desired that he be reinforced by Tchernychev's corps; as for Burturline's army, he did not have any employment for it. He declared "Send it anywhere." On its side, the Conference sent to the Russian Generalissimo very incoherent instructions. He was to enter Silesia and to set up his headquarters at Kosel; or to act against Küstrin, that a simple bombardment was to reduce. Masslovski says to us: "From the strategic point of view, one could not imagine a plan of a more unfortunate campaign. The Generalissimo had no specific objective; the abundant essay of the Conference on the advantages and the disadvantages of the various lines of operations could only muddle and confuse a novice commander such as Burturline."

The first general to act was Ferdinand von Braunschweig. He drove back the Duke de Broglie on Hanau; but de Broglie, having received reinforcements, resumed his position at Kassel. Then Soubise made his junction with Broglie on the Ruhr. The first operations of Ferdinand von Braunschweig had as their results the slight untying of Frederick II's hands. On 14 May, he made his junction at Schweidnitz with Goltz's corps. By this, he placed himself on the line by which the Russians and Austrians might possibly reunite.

Burturline, tied by the truces that Tottleben had made, which would last until 27 May, had made no movement. However, on 14 May, he received, at his headquarters in Marienwerder, the order to enter Silesia and make his junction with Laudon, who was from then on the autonomous commander of the Austrian army in Silesia, while Daun commanded that in Saxony.

The Russian army, on that date, was distributed as follows: 1st Corps (Fermor), 9 infantry and 6 cuirassier regiments; 2nd Corps (Prince Golitzyn), 8 infantry regiments, Narva Horse Grenadiers, and Tver Dragoons; 3rd Corps (Prince Dolgorukov), 8 infantry regiments, Nijni-Novgorod Dragoons; Tchernychev's Corps, 7 infantry regiments, the Petersburg, Riga, and Riazan Horse Grenadiers; Tottleben's Corps, the Kiev and Mourom Infantry Regiments, Kargopol Horse Grenadiers, Serbia, Hungary, Slavo-Serb, New Serbia and Moldavia Hussars, the Yellow Hussars, and eight pulks of Cossacks; the Artillery Corps (General Gliebov), the bombardier Regiment, the 1st Cannoneer Regiment, the Grenadier Regiment, the Fusilier-Musketeer Regiment, and 5,000 train soldiers. General Vassili Suvorov, charged with the administration, had under his orders 45 battalions and the Macedonia Hussars. [107] We will later see the composition of Rumyantsev's corps, destined to execute the siege of Kolberg.

The negotiations that Burturline had undertaken with Lautingshausen, the Swedish Generalissimo, to assure coordination with his 10,000 men, produced no practical result.

In the councils of war held on 17 and 19 June, Burturline had decided that he would give Rumyantsev all liberty to act in Pomerania and against Kolberg, and that the principal army would march on Breslau to unite with Laudon. Word had been given to the Austrian General Caramelli. Tottleben's cavalry, recalled from Pomerania, was to scout and cover the march of the army.

On 3 July, the Russian advance guard occupied Rawitz, Zduni, and Krotoschin. On 13 August, Burturline crossed the Oder at Leubus; on the 25th it was at Jauer; on the 27th, at Striegau, where the Russian advance posts joined those of Laudon.

At Striegau, Burturline rested from 27 August to 9 September. Then he began a withdrawal and recrossed the Oder at Leubus.

The Austrians complained loudly; the Conference asked explanations of its Generalissimo; he did not know how to respond to the recriminations, and to the questions of Austria: "Why have the Russians obliged the Court of Vienna to take command away from Daun and give it to Laudon? Why have

---

[107] Translator:The French word used was "intendance," which, at the time this work was published, included 1.) services of pay, military subsistence, clothing, camp equipment, cavalry (horse) equipment, travel and transportation, military bedding and the approval of all disbursements connected with these services; 2.) the approval of the outlays made by the troop units and establishments, the verification of issues in cash and material made from military chests or from magazines of these units or establishments, 3.) the approval and verification of the disbursements of the recruiting service, and finally the administration of such personnel as are not attached to troop units and of all detached persons who draw pay, salary, or gratifications.

they forced the Austrians to make such great expenses, create magazines for their army, etc.?...."

The truth is that Buturline was afraid. Frederick II had moved into Silesia, assigning his brother Henry to handle the war in Saxony. On 4 May, he had crossed the Elbe at Hirschstein; on the 10th he was at Löwenberg, without having encountered the Russians; on the 13th, he was before Schweidnitz. Until 7 July he had his headquarters at Kunzendorf, with his army in position from Schweidnitz to Freiburg. He had detached Goltz, with 12,000 men, on Glogau to observe the Russians. Glotz was established in a fortified camp, before Glogau and on the right bank of the Oder. Glotz had succumbed to a fever and was replaced by Ziethen. Frederick II had also moved Bülow's cavalry corps to Nimptsch, in order to maintain communications with the fortress of Neisse. From Schweidnitz to the Oder, Frederick II had 70,000 men, not having to depend on either a Conference and a Hof-Kreigsrath, nor any other council or other commander than himself, terrifying his adversaries by his speed of passing from resolution to action, ready to fall, at his choice, on the Austrians or Russians. However, it made a difference between them. As he said in his *Memoirs*, "he took the resolution to fight against the Austrians, if a favorable opportunity presented itself, but to hold himself scrupulously on the defensive with regard to the Russians, by the reason, that if he won a victory over the Austrians, the Russians would retire by themselves, and that if he won the same victory over the Russians, it would in no way slow Laudon from continuing the operations of his campaign."

The Russians, who had done so much to join Laudon, from whom the Generalissimo had received, on 13 August, a visit by the Austrian general, not seeing himself realize any of his projected plans, had not received any reinforcements from his allies. The King of Prussia maneuvered with a shocking dexterity and audacity. From his headquarters in Kunzendorf he moved, on 8 July, on Pulzen, where he formed a camp; on the 23rd, on Giesmannsdorf, near Neisse; on the 27th, on Nimptsch, then onto Münsterberg. He was not constrained by prudence and very embarrassed to send out scouts. On 1 August, he complained "I can see nothing, because of the horrible multitude of vermin Cossacks."[108] He, thanks to skillful operations, had broken the communications between the Russians and Austrians and forced the former to recross the Oder.

On 17 August, the King of Prussia had once again divided his forces, occupying Wahlstatt himself, with 40,000 men, facing Laudon with 30,000 under Margrave Charles von Preussen. At the Russian headquarters, one found that Frederick had taken a risk, placing himself, as it were, between two fires. It was resolved to attack him in his position. Leaving a sufficient force to guard their camp, the Russians marched, in one night, on Jauer. They arrived there during the morning of the 19th, without having encountered any Prussians.

---

[108] Schäfer.

Their scouts indicated the Prussian presence at Jarischau. As Laudon had promised to closely observe Frederick and to fall on his rear if the Russians engaged him, the Russians moved on Jarischau, where they did not find the Prussians; then onto Hochkirch, when it was learned that the Prussians had withdrawn on Schweidnitz. As to Laudon, fearing that he might be turned by Frederick II, he had retired on Freiburg. Thus, the Russians found themselves hanging in the air in unknown territory, finding nothing before them, neither friend nor foe. The King of Prussia, with 70,000 men in hand, maneuvered at will between the two armies, each of them almost equal to his own, since Laudon had 75,000 men and Burturline had 50,000.[109] Less excusable were the Austrians, since they were the stronger.

The Russians were angry at being left in a war without glory. Burturline repeated in his report the words of Saltykov: "The Austrians only seek to have their chestnuts drawn from the fire by someone else." Perhaps it is appropriate to cite the commentary by Frederick II, although a bit suspect: "So as not to expose himself, Mr. Laudon never left the foot of the mountains, and had the audacity to expose, on every occasion, the allies of the House of Austria to the most hazardous enterprises."

However, on 24 August, Burturline occupied Jauer; on the 25th he could rally part of the Austrian army near Hohenfriedberg. Laudon moved to join him there in person, and as the Russian Generalissimo was his senior, he placed himself under his authority. All they had to do at this point was march, united and in mass, against Frederick II.

Frederick was near Buntzelwitz, to the southwest of Schweidnitz, on the right bank of the Striegau River, a formidable position. The Striegau River protected his camp from the north and west. The Schweidenwasser River was on his east. He had covered all his front with fortified villages, entrenchments, redoubts, batteries, palisades, chevaux de frise, and an abatis of trees.[110] He could also draw reinforcements of men and material from Schweidnitz.

The Austrian army took up position on the southern front, behind the village of Kunzendorf. Burturline's army was before the western front, to the south of Striegau, on the two banks of the Striegau River. Tchernychev's corps, an Austrian corps, and Berg's Russian corps observed the northern front. Only the eastern front remained open, because to do so would require the encirclement of Schweidnitz Fortress and Burturline, even when united with Laudon, did not have the forces necessary for this.

Otherwise, one could not blockade such an extended camp as that occupied by the Prussians, separated from the enemy by the two rivers and a swamp, which obliged them to maintain a respectful distance, and to extend

[109] It is notable that Frederick II estimated Bourtourline at 30,000 men, that is: 13,000 infantry, in 23 battalions, 7,000 regular cavalry, and 10,000 Cossacks. *Politische Correspondenz*, 23 April 1761, Vol. XX, p. 608.
[110] See the detailed description of this camp by Frederick II, *Histoire de la guerre de Sept ans*.

their lines indefinitely, which would weaken them. One could not attack it. All the advantage was with Frederick II. With the Allies so widely separated, he could fall on one of the blockading armies and beat it long before the other army could come to the first's defense. It was still Frederick who commanded the situation, determined the movements of his adversary, and was the leader of his maneuvers.

Laudon had initially decided to attack on 27 August. Then, on the 29th, Burturline called a council of war in which Laudon assisted and where he showed himself very pressing. He said that one could, in these two locations, finish the war with a single blow. The Russian generals appeared shaken. As the Chevalier Ménger French military attaché, would write on 30 August, only "when Laudon appeared, everyone celebrated him and agreed with his opinion, even before he proposed it; but every day he held his own councils which revoked that evening what was done in the morning." The account of Frederick II seems to confirm this testimony: according to him, both Generalissimos would have ceased to agree that the attack would take place on 1 September: "Buturline, who held long meetings where the wine was not spared, had authorized, in a moment of cheerfulness and glass in hand, that which Laudon had proposed to him. The provisions of the three attacks had been put in writing; one had sent them to the principal officers of the army who had commands, and Laudon returned to his headquarters satisfied with the Russians. Buturline slept on it, and having consulted his prudence in the morning, countermanded the orders that had been given, because he feared, with some reason, that the Austrians would not sacrifice their army, and that if the enterprise did not succeed, the Russians would only gain blame and shame."

Masslovski's observations produce today in the debate over this affair yet another turn. According to him and the *Journal des opérations* (verbal account of 4 September), it was the Russians who had resolved to attack. Laudon, on the contrary, had arrived on 2 September, at Burturline's headquarters and had made objections to the attack. It is said that "no doubt it had been agreed in a common accord that they would attack the enemy and that one would bombard Küstrin… but that he found many difficulties and few advantages there; that he did not believe that the two armies could remain united, because of the lack of forage." He asked that one attach to the Austrians 10 regiments of Russian infantry, one of cuirassiers, and one of hussars under the command of Tchernychev; that the rest of the Russians operate on its side and to its account. In exchange for this assistance, he offered Burturline 30 squadrons of Austrian cavalry, under the orders of General Beck, on the condition that they would not be taken beyond the Oder.

One can barely understand the utility of such exchanges and of this bargaining for battalions and squadrons. On the other hand, the reasons given to Laudon by Russian chroniclers in the *Journal des opérations* do not hold together. The lack of forage would have been a reason to hasten the attack, at all risks, since it was the best result that could have been expected from the junction of the two armies.[111]

Whatever may be the reasons for these two contradictory accounts, the two Allied armies remained immobile until 10 September, contenting themselves with firing a few projectiles that could not even reach the Prussian trenches, soon renouncing even this as the Prussian artillery occupied all the dominating positions. On 10 September, Burturline, having granted Laudon the reinforcement he requested, - it is not known that he had accepted Laudon's offer of 30 cavalry squadrons - ordered his army to break camp and retire in the direction of Jauer. On his side, Laudon, "who thought himself exposed if he remained in the plain after the Russian departure,"[112] withdrew towards the mountains and his old position at Kunzendorf.

The King of Prussia remained, alone, on the bloodless battlefield, but ordered Platen to disturb the Russians by threatening their magazines in Posnania. Platen destroyed those in Kublin, where he took 5,000 wagons and 7 cannon.

Frederick II surely would have desired to maintain his position in Bunzelwitz longer: "If the food supplies had permitted the army of the King to maintain itself there, the campaign would have run out in Silesia without the formidable preparations of the enemy producing remarkable events; but the Schweidnitz magazine, which had provided food to the army during most of this campaign, was empty." It contained food for only one month. On 26 September the King had all his works in his camp blown up, leaving 5 battalions, the convalescents and 100 dragoons in Schweidnitz, under the orders of Zastrow. On the 28th, he occupied a camp at Siegroth and, on the 29th, at Nossen, close to Münsterberg.

The main Russian army, having lost the 18,000 men left with Tchernychev, recrossed the Oder and moved on Posnania.

Burturline's retreat had been a relief for Frederick. None of the belligerent armies gave him any concerns and could do him any damage other than the Russians. His hatred towards them is visible in his letters to Voltaire. Frederick reproached Voltaire for having written the *Histoire de la Russie sous Pierre le* Grand [*History of Russia under Peter the Great*]: "Tell me,

---

[111] Translator: This issue of forage for horse dependent armies was absolutely known and understood by all generals of the period. It was known that a large force would soon exhaust the forage in an area and that a large body could not long hold together. Napoleon, recognizing this, marched his forces in multiple columns and only brought them together for the express purpose of battle, most likely because of this and related logistical issues. The author is correct, there is absolutely no reason to bring the armies together unless it was for the purpose of quickly engaging in a battle.

[112] Frederick II.

I beg you, who recommended that you write the history of the wolves and bears of Siberia? I will not read the history of these barbarians. I wish I was unaware that they inhabited our hemisphere." However, to that time he not been permitted to be unaware or even to forget their existence.

It was at this time that the most important action of this "pitiful" campaign occurred. If Laudon lacked the decisiveness to attack frontally, if in 1761 he still exaggerated the "cunctatrice" prudence of Daun, he had the kind of stubbornness of a fly; after a failure, it moved away very little and at once resumed to the same point. Never was Frederick II completely free of him for a long time. At the time Frederick moved on Münsterberg to attract Laudon in that direction, the Austrian general made a hook, reappeared suddenly under Schweidnitz and, during the night of 30 September/1 October, captured it by surprise. The fortress did not have time to fire 12 cannon shots, and the Austrians would have suffered few losses if a powder magazine had not exploded. Frederick II gave great importance, in this event, to the actions of Major Roca, who was a prisoner in the fortress along with 500 Austrian soldiers of Italian ethnicity. It was he who, having gained the confidence of Zastrow, provided Laudon with the indications which ensured the success of the attack. Resistance seems to have been more serious than Frederick says it was: the Austrians suffered, in the fight, the loss of 63 officers and 1,394 soldiers, of which 400 only were victims of the explosion. The Russians lost only 5 officers and 92 men. It is true that their allies had made little use of them. Of the 18,000 Russians available only 800 grenadiers participated in the attack. They were placed at the head of the columns. In the plundering that followed, according to the testimony of the historian Sukhotin, only the Russian soldiers showed discipline; only they remained under arms on the ramparts, while their allies were ransacking the houses and magazines.

Overall, it appears that Laudon was pleased at the departure of the main Russian army: since both had abandoned the attack on Frederick's camp, both Generalissimos had shame to share; Laudon, who proposed no major enterprises, would not have known how to employ 50,000 Russians; he did not care to be, even in very nominal way, under Burturline's orders; and if there were some glory or some spoils to be taken, as in Schweidnitz, he preferred not to share it.

Nothing remained for Burturline, if he wished not to lose all the campaign, to press by Rumyantsev the siege of Kolberg and to support him from a distance.

The siege of Kolberg was the fourth of this war.

The corps under Rumyantsev consisted of the 3rd Grenadier, Novgorod, Bielozersk, and Voroneje Regiments. The latter contained three battalions and there were a few Cossack squadrons. He was to march quickly, and without baggage. He was joined, en route, by the 15 battalions of Neviedomski's brigade, the Archangel and Tobolsk Dragoons, the Georgia Hussars, and the Slobodes Cossacks. It appeared that he could count on the support of Tottleben's corps in Pomerania. Finally, he was to be reinforced before Kolberg with 12 battalions under the command of General Durnovo, which the fleet had brought there from Revel and Kronstadt.

The expedition was to be secret. It was not enough that Frederick II be preoccupied as of its beginning. Rumyantsev, forming his troops in two columns under Generals Eltchaninov and Bibikov, reached Tuchel, on 30 May; Konitz, on 1 June; the 5th, he was at Steinfurt, where he was reinforced by a section of engineers and the Eropkine Dragoons; the 9th, he was at Rummelsburg, where he was directed to await reinforcements. On the 23rd, he reached Köslin. He then had about 8,000 men; but the halts quickly revealed the secret.

Rumyantsev, during his stop, on 9 June, to Rummelsburg, had written to Burturline, informing him of the inadequacy of his tiny corps for such an enterprise. The nine infantry battalions that had been given to him did not have the authorized strength; the men assigned to them had been chosen from the least solid and lead well equipped; many of the officers were lame or maimed and barely recovered from their wounds. They had been given to him because they had just come out of the hospital. He had no regimental canons and almost no other field artillery. Burturline agreed with this but invited Rumyantsev to reassure himself. Once before Kolberg, he would have 20,000 men and 60 cannon, including the regimental guns.

The fortifications of Kolberg had barely been increased since the first attacks. We find there the same commander, Colonel Heide, who had already withstood the first sieges of Kolberg. It had a garrison of four battalions. But first of all, Frederick II had sent Prince Frederick-Eugene von Württemberg to help him. The Prince had been wounded while leading the charges at Kunersdorf. He was only 30 years old. He was the younger brother of the reigning Duke of Württemberg; he was to be Duke in his turn (1795-1797); he was to be the father of the first King of Württemberg (Frederick, 1797-1816), and his daughter became an empress of Russia; he was the grandfather of two tsars (Alexander and Nicolas), of a viceroy of Poland (Constantine); he was the grandfather of the Queen of Westphalia, Catherine, and the great-grandfather of Prince Napoleon and Princess Mathilde.

Frederick-Eugene had brought with him 16 battalions and 20 squadrons, a total of 12,000 men. His cavalry was excellent, and the grenadiers formed the elite of the infantry. The Corbière and Wunsch Freikorps were full of ardor; however, in the rest he had too many recruits, deserters, and even prisoners of war. As the Kolberg Fortress was not particularly large, the Prince had established, to the southeast of the city, a fortified camp. He supported his right on the Persante River, his left on the fortified village of Ballenwinckel.

It extended over a length of 1,500 to 2,000 paces. On its front, there were raised 11 boulevards or redoubts, placed at a distance of a musket shot between them. Other works lined the Persante River and filled Ballenwinckel. It was, in reality, a double siege that the Russians had to make that of the city and that of the camp.

In addition, since 5 June, the corps of General Werner occupied Körlin. The Prussians had, in total along the banks of the Persante, 26 battalions and 45 squadrons, facing the 8-9 battalions and 10 squadrons that Rumyantsev commanded.

With Tottleben's corps, Rumyantsev should have had about 11,000 or 12,000 men, but the commander of the light troops did not care to place himself under Rumyantsev's orders. He held himself at a distance, alleging that the rivers or Prussian detachments prevented his coming. When Rumyantsev reached Köslin, Tottleben retired on Schwiefelbein. However, he wished to send to Rumyantsev the infantry brigade of Beketov, containing the Mourom, Kiev, and Viatka Infantry Regiments.

Skirmishes multiplied. Already on 19 June, General Werner, wishing to observe Rumyantsev's march, took a detachment of cavalry in the direction of Köslin. At Fachmüne, he threw himself against the Don Cossacks. A brilliant action resulted under the eyes of Rumyantsev. The Cossacks drove back the Prussians with such success, that Rumyantsev, in his report to the Tsarina, declared "that he could not have believed it if he had not been present and if he could not attest to it on his word of honor." He also wrote to Buturline of the excellent discipline observed all the way by his small army: "The inhabitants, as well, in this city of Köslin as in the others and in the villages, even along the extreme lines of my outposts, continue to live peacefully in their houses, but they are exhausted and reduced to misery."

Now Rumyantsev occupied the right bank of the Persante, from Belgard to its mouth. To begin his siege operations, he awaited only the arrival of the fleet, which was to bring 6,500 men and the siege park.

On 28 June an incident occurred which produced great distress in the Russian army: this day, Tottleben and his son were arrested, in Bemstein, and sent as state criminals to St Petersburg. "The Tottleben Affair" is one of the strangest episodes of the Russo-Prussian War. To explain it, it is necessary for us to reconsider a bit of past history.

Tottleben was a German from Thuringia, who, formerly, had been extremely in favor at the Court of Augustus III. After having sought his fortune by various means, in 1757 he had entered Russian service. During the first campaigns, he initially appeared only as a mercenary, a bold leader of partisans, with a passion for boldness, not very scrupulous when it came to discipline and plundering, unleashing his Cossacks and hussars, making and letting them take spoils, a kind of "Father of Petty Thieving," adored by his light, vigilant, untiring troops, always surprising the enemy while never being surprised; impatient of any authority higher than his own, in creating high relations over the heads of his chiefs; not very concerned regarding the exactitude of his scouting reports, and a braggart. The capture of Berlin had brought him into the light. He had shown himself to have little skill, but being tenacious in attacks, but of an undeniable superiority in intrigues, mixing secret negotiations with the attacks made in the open, simultaneously fooling the Austrian General Lascy and his own commander, Chernihiv, negotiating, in a word, the capitulation of Berlin as being his affair. He had entered this capital as a preferred guest and almost like a friend. It had softened, in favor of the defeated, the rigor of his instructions, directly saving even royal establishments. The Austrians were jealous of him, and even the Russians. They did not forgive him for having snatched the glory of an attack from them, having reduced their share of the spoils and and making treaty with excessive regards the residence of the King who had shown so little concern for the capital of Saxony. In Petersburg one was astonished by the inaccuracies and contradictions of his report, which Tottleben had addressed directly to the Generalissimo, refusing to pass it by Tchernychev; in Vienna, the Austrians were indignant at his charges against the Austrian chiefs. This was the first "Tottleben Affair." He received from the Conference, in the name of the Empress, a rebuke on five issues: 1° the irregular manner of his reports that constituted a most serious fault against discipline; 2° the audacity with which he took all the honor of the enterprise for himself and his task force, accusing the main army of having obstructed, instead of supporting him; 3° his charges against his superior, Tchernychev; 4° his recriminations against the Austrian army which tended to ignore the services rendered by it and to make Europe believe that there was disagreement between the allied armies and a coldness between the courts; 5° his "perfidious attacks that lacked any sincerity" against the role of the Russian artillery. This accusation was signed by all the members of the Conference, Prince Nikita Trubetskoi, Chancellor Vorontsov, Alexander Shuvalov, Ivan Nepluiev, Iacob Chakovskoi.[113] Tottleben had refused to issue the retraction, as required of him, of the charges he made in his report against the generals and the troops of Austria, and even against Tchernychev. He had complained greatly, threatening even "to give further particulars, to uncover many people and to make known to Her Imperial Majesty the reasons that prevent the success and the glory of her arms."[114]

All the superior officers had had cause to complain about him. Misusing the confidence that he had inspired in 1759 in Saltykov, he had benefitted from it not to obey Fermor in the Pomeranian campaign of 1760: Fermor had been constrained by his insolence to withdraw command of the light troops from

---

[113] *Vorontsof Archives*, Vol. VI. – Masslovski, Vol. III, Supporting Document No. 69.

[114] Letter of Chevalier Ménager, French Military Attaché to the Russian Army, to the Duke de Choiseul, 10 January 1761 (Archives of French Foreign Affairs, Correspondence, Russia).

him, then forced, by the Conference, to return it to him. Tchernychev had complained about him as well when in Silesia, during the 1761 campaign, as before Berlin. It was in Tottleben's corps where one saw Russian officers going into Prussian cantonments, after an exchange of words, and going to drink with the Prussian officers. Field Marshal Buturline, at the time when he took command, had initially given a warm welcome to the Thuringian adventurer; then he had seen himself constrained to let him run free, to let him act in his own way, for his partisan war, the results of which appeared to him to be very low, and for his intrigues, which already inspired suspicions in him. When Tottleben was accused so sharply by the Conference about his report from Berlin and that he went to Burturline's general headquarters to offer his resignation, pleading the state of his health and his desire to pass the remainder of his days "in loneliness and rest," the Field Marshal requested the Conference not to not pursue the Tottleben affair; but the arguments with which he supported his request are most strange:

> I fear that, by receiving this reprimand and this testimony of
> the ire of Your Imperial Majesty, and especially the request
> for explanations to Tchernychev, Tottleben, with his ebullient
> and unwise character, resigns from command in the season
> when he would be most useful for us; I even fear that with his
> force of troops he could make some demarche which would
> be infinitely harmful for me and which he uses, to the profit
> of the enemy, of the secret orders that I gave to him with my
> observations, more especially as those contain [my] plan of
> operations against the Prussians, the disposition of his corps,
> with all imaginable detail.

It is impossible to say more clearly that Tottleben was capable of everything, even compromising his corps in some disastrous perfidiously premeditated adventure, even to give over to Frederick II the most secret papers of the staff. He was, however, such a man that, for these same reasons, one maintained in charge of an important command: much more, one sacrificed Tchernychev to him, who had to give up obtaining explanations, which, "in his zeal for the service of Her Imperial Majesty," was satisfied with the resentment that Tchernychev expressed for offenses that he had received.

Tottleben no longer had anything to constrain him. Immediately after, we see him acquiring in Pomerania in Prussian territory and perhaps with Prussian money, the domain of Lüpow, for which he paid 96,000 *thalers*. All while continuing to make war against Frederick II, he prepared to become his subject: from a general in the Russian service, he became a member of the Pomeranian landed gentry.

Russian Cuirassier

Tottleben was such an ambiguous character that when, on 22 June 1760, postal carriages were plundered on the road from Stolpe to Danzig, and that someone had removed 17,169 *thalers* from them, voices arose in the army claiming this armed robbery was at the connivance or with the complicity of Tottleben. One said that the attack had been conducted by his subordinate Brigadier Stoianov, of the Serbian Hussars. An investigation followed and did not provide any proof. It was those who had denounced Tottleben who were punished. Some, including Vaguemestre Matveev, were beaten before the regiment, while others passed through a gauntlet of soldiers armed with rods.

In the winter campaign that preceded the 1761 campaign, it was noted that Tottleben had some strange consideration for the Prussian territories of Brandenburg and Pomerania and that, while making much noise and making lots of movement, he never attacked in depth and took nothing seriously. It was he who had the idea of the armistices and who pursued the negotiations, qualified by Masslovski as criminal, but which, however, Burturline and the Conference weakly approved.

At the time of the operations on Kolberg, he did nothing to support Rumyantsev: as soon as this one approached the fortress, Tottleben moved away and fell back on Greifenberg. Tottleben continued to operate in an autonomous manner. It required reiterated orders from the Generalissimo to surrender to Rumyantsev a brigade of infantry.

To assure complete liberty in his intrigues, he had finished by terrorizing his officers to such a point that when the order came to arrest Tottleben, Colonel Bülau refused to put his hands on him.

Lieutenant Colonel Asch, one of the officers that Tottleben had personally chosen to serve under his orders, suspected, from January 1761, that his chief, by the most diverse means, almost without taking any precautions, was sending to the Prussians information on the division of troops, their strength, and operations. Asch, to have a clean heart, worked to gain Tottleben's confidence. He watched his frequent conferences with Prussian officers; his relations with the merchant Gotzkowski; the correspondence that he passed by Stolpe; the exchanges of encrypted notes, and his persistence to avoid any effective operations, despite the most formal and frequently reiterated orders from the supreme authority. He carefully avoided making a premature denunciation, instructed, by previous experience, of the dangers that he was running. It was only on 27 June that he succeeded in completing his dossier. The following day he secretly convened the superior corps officers, gave them a look at his proof, and had arrested the Silesian Jew Issac Sabatky or Sabatka, one of Tottleben's most active agents, with suspect papers in hand; or, more exactly, in one of his boots.

These documents are conserved in the Moscow Archives or the Depot of War, reproduced by Masslovski in his supporting documentation, which permitted him to accuse Tottleben of treason, a treason that the historian Soloviev had only suspected.

The Jew Sabatky also made some revelations. He swore that he had been frequently employed to carry concealed letters to Frederick II's camp or to the camp of Prince Henry, and back. Sabatky had a brother in Breslau, with whom Tottleben had deposited money. The two of them had carried letters from Tottleben to the Prussian commander of Glogau, without an address on the envelope. The commander, in receiving these letters, had said: "It is perfect;" then he sent the two Jews to Prince Henry, who had sent them back to Tottleben with some letters. Only Tottleben had said to Sabatky that the Prince simply asked him to spare his lands in Pomerania. The packet that was seized in Sabatky's boot had been given to him by Tottleben with the mission to give it to either the commander of Breslau or to Prince Henry or to the King of Prussia. Sabatky affirmed to having never been charged verbally by Tottleben with asking for an interview with Frederick II. Tottleben had only expressed the wish to have, before his death, an interview with the King of Prussia.

The results of the interrogations of Tottleben and Sabatky, with the pieces published by Masslovski could indicate but one thing: that Tottleben undertook suspicious correspondence with Frederick II, Prince Henry, the Prussian commandant of Glogau, the merchant Gotzkowski, and other people. We have not, to the present, any specimen of this correspondence; it was unfortunate that the rest of the documents found in Sabatky's boot were not reproduced. There are, without a doubt, great holes in the dossier, such as that which Masslovski had in his hands. Perhaps also Colonel Asch could seize nothing more. It is this which explains the refusal made by Colonel Bülau to arrest Tottleben. This also explains the actions taken later, pursuant to the affair.

Before Masslovski had gone over Tottleben's trial, we already have the very precise testimony, so scornful, so withering, of Frederick II:

> There is not an impregnable town into which one cannot send a mule loaded with gold; there is not an army where one cannot find a cowardly and corrupt soul. In this crisis of affairs, it was important to have news from a good source, and with so many enemies, it was necessary to be at least informed of some part of their plans. That had caused eyes to fall on Tottleben, as a man capable of entering parallel propositions and proper to provide the best news. One did not fool oneself in the judgment of his character. He did all that one could ask of him and even more. However, because of this spirit of lightness and imprudence in which he had engaged in this unworthy trade, he betrayed himself by his little measured conduct; and he was arrested precisely at the beginning of the campaign, when his services had become most essential and most useful.

However, this testimony of Frederick appeared to other historians subject to caution. It is only by the recent publication of Volumes XIX and XX of *Politische Correspondenz*, that is to say after the appearance of Masslovski's work, that the Tottleben Incident has been exposed to a full, dazzling light, which is overpowering for the defendant. We see Frederick II, in his *Memoirs*, had not exaggerated anything; that his most intimate and most secret letters, even those addressed to his beloved brother, are in agreement with the writings intended by him for the posterity. Prince Henry, in a letter from Landsberg, 26 June 1760, said to the King of Prussia: "The Jew Sabatky came to inform me that a Russian officer wants to be used as a spy, if you want to give him a note signed by you, saying that he will be a lieutenant-colonel and will receive a pension with peace." And the King sent a blank sheet of paper bearing his signature. Perhaps it is not this Tottleben who is in question here; but here is what becomes indisputably clear. From Leipzig, in February 1761, the King wrote to the Governor of Stettin, the Duke of Braunschweig-Bevern: "I strongly approve of the Tottleben Affair by money and the Jew; but one must be careful, that the fellow (*Kerl*) does not mislead us. If he wants money, good (*wenn auf Geld ankommt, gut*). Tell me how much he wants (*Mir sagen wie viel will*)."[115] Later, to Prince Henry: "I will say to you that the Jew carried out the commission very thoroughly; that my intention was to give Tottleben an amount of money in order to spare, firstly, our country from his excursions, not to treat it so cruelly, nor to devastate it so cruelly, and in the second place, to secretly inform us of the true plan of operation of the Russians, their intentions to open their campaign and to begin their first operations and the movements which they will want to execute elsewhere. According to my idea (sic), it is not necessary thus that he is dismissed, since then he would not be useful to us and that the Russians will always find another subject, such as him, to command the troops with his skill. If Tottleben accepts the aforesaid conditions, then I want to give him my promise that after peace is made, he will be able to remain quietly on his lands in my country, and to have them without being disturbed by anything - Here is what you will want to inform the Jew mentioned above."

The market was held. In May, the King announced to his brother that "the Jew Sabatky arrived yesterday: I was informed, by the channel by which you know him, that the operations of the Russians, during the coming campaign will be the same ones as those of the year past; that is they will attempt to join a corps of 35,000 Russians to Laudon, that they will detach another towards Kolberg, and that, according to all appearances, the main body of their army will move towards the borders of Silesia... that all these operations could begin only when the green grass is in the fields...."[116] In June, the King wrote: "I intend to know, by a person who is known to you, the plan that the Austrians have negotiated with the Russians for this campaign." In a margin of a report from Goltz, the King wrote in pencil: "Wait until I

[115] *Politische Correspondenz*, Vol. XX. P. 223, Frederick to the Governor of Stettin.
[116] *Ibid*, Vol. XX, p. 317. From Meissen, 8 April 1761.

have received a letter from Tottleben."[117] Tottleben also informed the King about the diplomatic facts, for example the Austrian negotiations, and issues relating to the war. This is also "a pure result of chance," says Frederick, who had in his hands "the project that Laudon sent to the Aulic Council of War in Vienna, to have it approved."[118] Still on 4 June, he awaited "the letters of this person whom I do not have need to name to you, to know what was positively resolved between the two generals (Russian and Austrian) and to know what to do."[119] - "I still await every day for news from Tottleben."[120]

There are 20 references of this type in Frederick's correspondence. It appears that he made no decisions without having received a courier from Tottleben. He evolved and maneuvered with certainty. There were some of his generals who were in on this secret; for example, the General of Cavalry Ziethen.[121] He finishes with the letter from Frederick II, of 6 July 1761, where he says to his brother: "Here is Tottleben who was arrested. His indiscretion has betrayed him. You can imagine this occurs at the wrong time."[122]

Transported to Petersburg with his son, Tottleben was interrogated anew. The inquisition lasted until 1763. A new sentence of death followed, but almost immediately Catherine II commuted it to banishment, an insignificant punishment for a man who was not a Russian subject and who had lands in Pomerania. In addition, in 1769 Catherine II completely pardoned Tottleben and took him into her service. The conqueror of Berlin died in 1773, in Warsaw, with the rank of lieutenant general.

In June 1761, suddenly after the arrest of Tottleben, Berg was designated as his successor in command of the light troops. Masslovski considered him as infinitely superior in this difficult role; that his service was far superior. He showed less indiscipline and less imagination, but was braver and more active, and Rumyantsev found in him a precious collaborator.

On 12 July, Admiral Polianski, leaving from the Russian Baltic ports, arrived in the Danzig Roadstead; but from Danzig to the port of Rügenwalde, driven by contrary winds, he took 12 days to complete a passage which normally took 16 hours. At Rügenwalde, on 21 August, he landed the troops and heavy material that he had transported, which was then to move to Kolberg overland. He, personally, arrived there on the 24th, in sight of this place, with another 20 ships of every type, to cooperate with the siege operations. The equipment that he delivered to Rumyantsev consisted of 150 cannon and a large quantity of ammunition. Among the troops he had two companies of engineers and 23 engineering officers. It was General Demoline who was to

---

[117]*Ibid,* Vol. XX, p. 432.
[118] *Ibid,* Vol. XX, p. 441.
[119] *Ibid,* Vol. XX, p. 443. From Kunzendorf.
[120] *Ibid,* Vol. XX, p. 446.
[121] *Ibid,* Vol. XX, p. 503.
[122] *Ibid,* Vol. XX, p. 513.

direct the operations.

During the day of the 24th, Admiral Polianski began operations. He sent three armed gunboats to study the shore defenses of the fortress. They were received with cannon shots. The next day he advanced the *Varakhil*, a ship of 34 guns. As the fire of the city redoubled, he supported the *Varakhil* with his bomb ketches and the ships-of-the-line *Archange-Raphael, Astrakhan,* and *Archangel-Michael.* During the evening he received a reinforcement in the form of a Swedish squadron, under Admiral Ipsilander, with six ships-of-the-line and three frigates. However, the cannons of the fleet could only act against the city of Kolberg, not on the Prussian camp, which was masked by the city, and therefore the projectiles swept the road from the city to the Port of Münde. It was, as a result, the ground forces that had to capture the camp. Polianski reinforced the army with 2,000 sailors.

Russian operations began by clearing the Prussians from the Kolberg Wood and closely pressing the Prussians in their camp.

On 2 September, Neviedomski's brigade, which had remained in Rummelsburg to assure communications, joined the siege army. It had been hoped that the small Swedish army would support the operations. The French military attaché, Caulaincourt, was attached to it. However, the Swedes were haughty, offering advice, recommending Caulaincourt and their own officers as indispensable to the Russians to manage the siege to a good result, proposing nothing more than the support of 2,000 or 3,000 men, and then at a great distance. Rumyantsev feared that, for such a mediocre agreement, they would demand all the honor for the success. Therefore, he limited himself to asking them to operate on the Prussian lines of communication. In sum, they provided no service.

On 4 September, Rumyantsev occupied the siege positions with his troops. On the right was Neviedomski's brigade, with the Ouglitch Regiment, a force of volunteers, and 2,000 sailors. In the center was Rumyantsev and Eropkine with the main body and on the left, on the right bank of the Persante, was Bibikov's column. From the 6th to the 12th, he directed a continuous fire on the Prussian camp and city. It was turning cold and to keep warm the besiegers were obliged to dig holes in the ground and build hovels.

On 12 September, the Russian scouts indicated a cavalry movement on the road from Kolberg to Treptow. This was the advance guard of General Werner, who, with 2,000 hussars and dragoons, 300 infantry, and 6 cannon, had come out of the besieged camp, which the day before had occupied Treptow and the neighboring villages. He estimated, no doubt, that he could gain more advantages operating on the Russian rear than he could by sitting in the camp, already filled with the troops of Prince von Württemberg, while the Russians bombarded it. Rumyantsev immediately directed Bibikov, who formed his left, to advance on the Prussians. Bibikov left command of the infantry and his works to General Durnovo, taking his dragoons, Cossacks, and two battalions of grenadiers. The Cossacks enveloped Treptow on all sides. Profiting from the panic that their sudden appearance produced, Bibikov formed his two battalions in an assault column, advanced into the city, and fortified himself there. Then with the dragoons and Cossacks, he attacked the neighboring villages, driving out the Prussians, and pursuing them to Greifenberg. The Russians took General Werner, 8 officers, and 524 men prisoner. Their trophies included 6 cannons, 20 supply wagons, and 200 horses. In addition, the Prussians lost 600 dead and wounded. The Russians lost only 5 officers and 100 men. The prisoners were taken aboard the fleet. Admiral Polianski insisted that General Werner not be released on parole, because he said, "not a single Russian officer had obtained his liberty on parole, and asked Count Tchernychev and General Saltykov how they were treated during their captivity."

Colonel Massow brought in the debris of this Prussian corps and from Greifenberg retired on Naugard. Once there he received a reinforcement of 400 hussars. The Swedes could have destroyed this force since they were masters of the region as far as Wollin and Kammin. However, they gave no sign of life.

Bibikov fortified Treptow and left a small garrison there in order to observe the arrivals of reinforcements and materials that the garrison of Stettin might send to Kolberg. Later he evacuated Treptow.

The desperate effort made by Werner to come out of the city showed the situation of the besieged, already lacking food and placed between the crossfires of the Allied fleet and Rumyantsev's batteries.

However, the situation of the Allies was not easy either. Kolberg and Prince von Württemberg's camp formed a vast fortress; on the fronts of the camp there were batteries that crossed their fire on the approaches, deep ditches, palisades, redoubts, wolf holes, and fougasses[123] prepared to blow up any attacker. On the 13th, there was a fight with Lieutenant Colonel de Corbière, who was thrown back on the Prussian entrenchments.

In a council of war held on 14 September, Prince Dolgorukov, a staff officer, proposed continuing the preparation with an incessant artillery bombardment, then an assault on the Prussian camp by four columns. His opinion was supported by Generals Neviedomski, Brandt, Durnovo, and Eltchaninov. In opposition, Dewitz and Kochkin argued that no assault be launched, but that one maintains a strict blockade. Such a fortress, so well-defended with men, could only be reduced by famine.

Rumyantsev decided for an attack. He ordered the preparations for a double assault to be launched on the 18th, at 4:30 a.m. Neviedomski was to attack the redoubt called the Verhackschanze, near the Bodenhangen Wood. Schultz was to attack the Grünenschanze. The assault occurred. Neviedomski

---

[123] Translator: A "fougas" is a primitive type of land mine that was set off using a burning fuse and intended to detonate under the feet of an advancing enemy column.

captured Verhackschanze, taking 15 cannon and 200 men; as for Schultz, his column took the wrong road and could not attack in time. The attack was resumed, on the 19th, at 2:30 a.m. Neviedomski, wounded, was replaced by Durnovo, who would attack the Sternschanze, a star redoubt which fired on the shore. Popov was to attack the Grünenschanze. Durnovo was no more fortunate than Schultz the previous night. Popov initially succeeded and took 200 prisoners, but not supported in time and pressed by the troops of Prince von Württemberg moving against the work, and despite the eventually support of two regiments sent by Rumyantsev, he had to evacuate the Grünenschanze at daybreak, after suffering nearly 3,000 casualties. Prince Dolgorukov was mortally wounded. Rumyantsev had to console himself by writing in his report "that the grenadiers and soldiers had fought like lions."

It became apparent that Rumyantsev did not have sufficient forces to take such a place d'armes, where the enemy constantly multiplied the works. He was also unable to establish an effective blockade and assure the security of his communications.

On the 19th, he received grave news. Platen had arrived with 10,000 or 12,000 Prussians.

We have seen that the King of Prussia, as soon as the Prussians and Austrians had lifted the siege of his camp at Kunzelwitz, had detached Platen on Breslau, where he would cross the Oder, fall on Burturline's magazines in Posnania, and profiting from the disorder thrown into his communications would march to the north to relieve Kolberg and affect his junction with Prince von Württemberg. It was only at Landsberg on the Wartha that the Russian detachments, scattered to the north of the watercourse, attempted to block his passage. Berg detached, on Landsberg, Lieutenant Colonel Suvorov, who encountered Platen in the city, killing 2 officers and 26 men, but was unable to destroy the bridge. Soon all of Platen's forces arrived, driving Suvorov back. Suvorov disputed the Prussian advance step-by-step, until he was in his turn reinforced, and, with Popov's Cossacks, and the Zoritch Hussars, threw himself on the Prussian advance posts, dispersing three squadrons, killing 100, and capturing 50, including an artillery officer, who was an aide-de-camp to Platen, throwing the Prussian advance forces back on the main body. However, in the end, Suvorov was obliged to withdraw.

Thus, as in the previous year with Berlin, Kolberg became the hasty rendezvous point, the goal of a steeple chase, which brought troops, Prussian and Russian, from all corners of Germany.

In the Russian camp, under Kolberg, they were unaware of the true destination of Platen. Was it to trouble the siege? Or was it to move against the magazines on the Lower Vistula? In the council of war on 20 September, several generals urged the breaking of the siege and marching on the Wartha and the Netze, to engage Platen. Rumyantsev decided that they would remain before Kolberg; that a new assault would be attempted, this time on the Bollenwinckel, and that one would ask the Generalissimo to stop Platen's movements. He sent couriers to request reinforcements from Burturline. However, Burturline was occupied with his projects on Breslau and limited himself to saying that Rumyantsev did not have "to be disturbed." He was to refer to the Empress about it:

> I am in the greatest embarrassment... I do not know anything of the principal army... According to what I read in the newspapers, I suppose that the King of Prussia, seeing the Imperial Army divided into two armies, threw Platen on our communications, in the hope that, not wanting to let myself be taken between two fires, I would be forced to raise the siege. Even without fighting a battle, Platen can establish himself in the entrenchments here and thus paralyze the siege army. I fear, in addition, that Platen will seize Posnania and our magazines in that country; that he may even have in mind those on the Vistula. God will that he does not have this idea, [which would be] most dangerous in the present circumstances!

On 23 September, Rumyantsev received news of Prince Dolgorukov's 3rd Corps. He asked him to enjoin Berg, Tottleben's successor, to move into Platen's rear. In effect, they moved seven squadrons of dragoons on Naugard, Daer, and Lebes. Platen broke through this cavalry cordon, cutting anew the communications of the various Russian armies. On the 28th, he was at Schiefelbein and Regenwalde. Now he acted only to know if he crossed by Belgard or Körlin, that is to say, by the right bank where he arrived by the left bank of the Persante.

On the 29th, he was at Körlin, dispersing a post of 200 Cossacks or infantry commanded by Major Wettlitz, and who, after "a defense in the manner of the Russians," was killed or captured. However, it was by Körlin that Prince Dolgorukov's division was to arrive. Rumyantsev expedited a courier to this prince to invite him to attack Platen. Rumyantsev moved before him, declaring the enemy lost if he allowed himself to be taken between two fires. Platen succeeded in avoiding an encounter with Rumyantsev, making a hook on Spie, occupying the Selnow Heights, and, from there, made his junction with Prince von Württemberg.

The situation of the siege forces became very grave. The arrival of Dolgorukov's division had brought their forces to 20,000 men, but the Prussians now had 17,500 men. In a council of war, held on 3 October, most of the Russian generals, including the brave Eropkine, urged the siege be lifted;

that they retire on Belgard, and that they take up a strong position there to await the arrival of reinforcements. Rumyantsev assured that the main Russian army would soon arrive but feared that it would not arrive in time. On the other hand, Admiral Polianski informed Rumyantsev that he was out of provisions and that he would retire on 11 October. Rumyantsev asked him to remain for one more week. This week passed and Polianski set sail for Revel.

That the siege was not broken three times, was due solely to the tenacity and energy of Rumyantsev. It was for him a point of honor to succeed. The Austrians had taken Schweidnitz, and it would be a great embarrassment if the Russians could not take Kolberg.

Burturline's slowness was inexplicable. The Conference was desperate. It had informed Rumyantsev that, if the junction between Platen and Prince von Württemberg was affected, he was fully authorized to raise the siege.

Finally, on 3 October, Berg, with the light troops, arrived at Soldin and pushed before him as far as Stargard Colonel Chetnov. On the 11th, he arrived at Stargard. That same day, the Russian main army camped near Arnswald, and Fermor left for Kolberg with his division. The communications of the camps before Kolberg were threatened in their turn. Several of their convoys were taken and the escorts dispersed or captured. On 15 October, Berg occupied Naugard and learned of a Prussian detachment moving from Treptow to Weissenstein. He enveloped it in the latter village and, the next day, after preparing his attack with a cannonade, and as the Prussians sought to escape into the woods, he charged them with his horse grenadiers, dragoons, and hussars. As the other Prussians moved from Greifenberg to the rescue, Suvorov (the future field marshal and Prince of Italy) threw himself on them with his hussars and Cossacks. One officer and 40 soldiers were taken prisoner. The rest were pursued until nightfall and dispersed into the woods. On the 19th, the Russians attacked Lautlow, near Treptow, the detachment of Lieutenant Colonel de Corbière. Platen, who had moved to Treptow, assisted in the retreat of the Prussian forces. Corbière was captured, along with 40 officers and 1,000 men. The Russian light troops learned them that they had had an action with Platen's main forces, which had, the day before, left the Selnow heights and moved on Treptow. All this movement of enemy and friendly troops had occurred because Platen had learned of the arrival of a large convoy of food and ammunition coming from Stettin, which he wished to protect and allow to enter the fortress. However, Platen already had Fermor pursuing him. He barely had time to decamp from Treptow. Prince von Württemberg had already sent a corps, under General Knobloch. Terrible idea! The latter arrived on the 20th. Rumyantsev moved there in person. Knobloch was encircled. Unable to be assisted by Platen or the Prince, on the 25th he was obliged to capitulate with 61 officers and 1,635 soldiers. Fifteen flags and 9 cannon were the trophies of that action.

Fermor, continuing his pursuit, found Platen in a strong position at Gollnowo. He had to content himself with bombarding the Prussians. The bold Prussian commander only wanted to decamp. He remained there only long enough to move out the convoy while the Russian howitzers destroyed a few caissons. He left with the last wagon during the night of the 22nd, about 3:00 a.m., hotly pursued by Suvorov. He finally reached Damm, where he rested his troops.

By this brilliant action, the Russians had re-established their communications, covering their siege operations by pushing away or destroying the Prussians.

On 5 November, Burturline arrived at Tempelberg. However, judging that Rumyantsev now had sufficient forces to reduce Kolberg, he turned towards the east. On the 21st, he was at Dirschau and, on the 26th, he made his solemn entrance into Marienwerder, the center of the Russian army's winter quarters.

At this point the Russian army was divided into four parts: Rumyantsev and Berg were before Kolberg; Volkonski's corps was on the Wartha, that of Tchernychev was in Silesia with the Austrians, and finally, the main body was in its winter quarters on the Lower Vistula.

With the reinforcements that had successively flowed to him, Rumyantsev now had 35,000 men, while Platen was reduced to 4,200 and the camp at Kolberg could not be reinforced or relieved.

There was only one hope for relief that remained for Kolberg. Frederick II had ordered, on 2 November, Generalmajor von Schenckendorf to march from Silesia into Brandenburg. He brought a bit under 5,000 men with him. On the 9th, he was at Bernstein and joined Platen. On the 10th, he reached Arnswalde; on the 14th, he was at Naugard. He found Berg on the road and could go no further.

The siege continued. On 14 November, the Prussians, under cover of a fog, evacuated their entrenchments. Prince von Württemberg abandoned the garrison, with a few reinforcements, to its fate. In the greatest silence, without being noticed by the Cossack patrols, he moved to Treptow, then empty of Russian troops, during the morning of the 15th. On the 16th, he continued on Greifenberg and Plathe, where he joined Platen.

It was only in the morning of the 15th, that the Russians found the Prussian camp abandoned. They immediately occupied it. Delighted to be rid of the Prince, of having "drawn him from his nest," and to no longer have to deal with anything but the body of the fortress, they moved their siege lines closer and closer to the city. An assault, launched during the night of 15/16 November, resulted in the capture of Wolfsberg. The next day the Russians occupied the mouth of the Persante. At this point a regular siege could be begun, which was directed by Colonel Herbel. All the subsequent actions could now be envisaged, as well as the inevitable outcome. On 3 December, a practicable breach was made in the fortress wall. On the 14th, a powder magazine exploded. On the 15th, the last ration of bread was distributed to the garrison. On the 16th, Commandant Heide, an energetic and brave officer, who had seen the Russians raise their siege of his fortress, signed a capitulation. All the garrison became prisoners – 88 officers, 2,815 men and 20 flags. The Russians found 28 other flags in the Arsenal, as well as 140 siege guns, and a notable quantity of weapons, artillery projectiles, and ammunition, fell into Russian hands. Rumyantsev granted the garrison the honors of war, i.e., the garrison marched out to the sound of drums, before laying down its arms before the Mühlen Gate. The garrison remained prisoner with its sick and wounded. The officers, on their parole, were sent to East Prussia.

One last battle occurred on 20 December, at Klempin, between Berg's and Württemberg's cavalry. After this action, Prince von Württemberg was ordered into his Mecklenburg winter quarters by the King.

Prussian Pomerania was now conquered as far as the gates of Stettin. The fortress of Kolberg, where Colonel Herbel had been named commander, assured for the coming campaign, a decided preponderance to the Russians.

On 7 January, Burturline handed command over to Fermor and left for Petersburg. He was unaware that upon his arrival he would not find the Tsarina Elisabeth and that the cannon shots under Kolberg would be the last fired on the Prussians during the Seven Years War.

CHAPTER XVI

THE END OF THE WAR.

On 5 January 1762 the Tsarina Elisabeth died. She had always had a weakness for Louis XV since there had been a question, from the time of Peter the Great and Catherine I to make her the Queen of France. It was especially thanks to her, with her personal will, that the two courts could have been joined again in their relations. She had initially accommodated the secret agents of diplomacy, then to the brilliance of the representatives of French official diplomacy. She had lent herself with kindness to the "small commerce;" that is, with the exchange of secret letters, which Louis XV had proposed to her. Her dearest wish had always been to establish a more intimate and more direct alliance with France, which would have freed it from heavy Austrian dependency. On every occasion she had expressed the sincerest joy at French successes, and an honest resentment at French reverses. Even at the time when she had resigned herself to facilitate the peace so much desired by Louis XV, "to make a question" of East Prussia, she insisted that the Versailles Court did not treat with England before it had restored to France her lost colonies. Inside, her reign was marked by the expansion of French civilization in Russian society; the French language became in vogue, as did French literature, arts, and customs. Because of Peter the Great Russia had long been a student of the Germans, but now she entered the school of France. Its Academy of Science became populated by French scientists and counted among its corresponding members Voltaire, the author of the *Histoire de la Russie sous Pierre le grand* [*History of Russia under Peter the Great*], written on notes that Ivan Shuvalov had provided him; French artists were already numerous in the Academy of the Art schools. There was a French theater in St Petersburg, directed by Sérigny, and at the Russian theater, that Soumarokof directed, where one played translation of Corneille, Racine, and Molière. This was the moment when the most distinguished Russians came to complete their education in Paris, like the poet Trediakovski and Cyrille Razumovski, the future president of the Academy of Science; where the Russian ambassador Kantemir corresponded with and was the friend of Montesquieu and our principal writers; where one saw Vorontsov, in the uniform of light horseman, stand the guard in the galleries of Versailles; where the aristocracy started to adopt French as a second mother tongue.[124] The reign of Elisabeth was the preface to the century of Catherine II, which was the French period of Russian

---

[124] Translator: The use of French in Russia became so universal that the infantry drill regulation published in St. Petersburg, in 1799, was in French.

history. One thus sees that the alliance with France rested on the depth of incipient sympathies for France.

As for Elizabeth's successor, he was only a prince who was weak of body and spirit, without education or culture, a badly raised child deprived of intelligence and heart that Catherine III depicts for us in her memoirs. He was something terrible in the eyes of the Russians, a pure German. He cared only for his title of Duke of Holstein and disdained his title of Emperor of Russia. He knew nothing of the Russians and openly despised them and took pleasure in deriding their religion and their customs. During all the war with Frederick he was aggrieved by the victories of the Russian army and always rejoiced at its reverses. His sympathies for the Prussians bordered on treason; as a result, he was excluded from the deliberations of the Conference because it was feared he would give their secrets to the Prussians, and certain comments from Frederick II appear to confirm this.

Peter had conceived a fanatical admiration of the King-Captain, imposing on his Holstein Guard the uniforms and maneuvers of the Prussian Army, threatening the Russian Army with the same transformation. He sincerely saw himself as a student of the great man, but the one thing he could not copy was his genius and courage.

The Allied courts knew too well what to expect from the Grand Duke. The correspondence of L'Hôpital abounds with accounts of his character. In a dispatch of 22 May 1759, the year of Kunersdorf, this ambassador recounts to us the Future Peter III saying to the young Schwerin, "that he would find it glorious and an honor to make a campaign under the orders of the King of Prussia and, if he was the master, he [Schwerin?] would not be a prisoner here." L'Hôpital attempts to attach no importance to this comment which comes "from a badly stamped brain." However, the Allied courts were disturbed by these dispositions, and the Tsarina was alarmed. It was held for certain that she had the intention of removing her nephew from the succession and designating as her successor, his son, the Grand Duke Paul, the future Paul I.[125]

When Versailles learned that the Tsarina Elisabeth was dead and that the Emperor Peter III had succeeded her, they addressed to the Baron de Breteuil a set of curious instructions dated 31 January 1762.[126] They saw three alternatives: "the first, that the new Emperor would follow the old system; the second, that he would adopt a totally opposite one by linking himself with our enemies; the third, which he might take was something in between." Baron de Breteuil was to neglect nothing that "Russia might remain attached to the great alliance; that it would not recall its armies; that it would not make any separate peace. — Otherwise, they added, they would maintain the same vigor in their operations was a subordinate issue of much less importance."

---

[125] Translator: Paul I was a equally a Prussophile as his father and as mentally unstable.
[126] A. Rambaud, *Instructions*, Vol. II, p. 183 and following.

Of the three options that were anticipated by Versailles, the most disastrous was what was realized.

Peter III acted suddenly, not as Emperor of Russia, but as the Duke of Holstein, as a German impassioned for the Greatest of Germans.

Frederick II, who had Keith, the British Ambassador, deliver his felicitations to the new Tsar, could not hope that he would find Peter III so completely imbued with the old dispositions of the Grand Duke's heir: He found in Peter "A basis on which one could hope that the negotiations in St Petersburg could take a good turn? The Versailles and Vienna Courts had guaranteed the Kingdom of East Prussia to the late Empress; the Russians were in peaceful possession of it; would the young prince, who had ascended the throne give up this province of his own free will, a province that was guaranteed to him by his allies? Won't the interest and the glory of such an acquisition at the beginning of a reign cause him to hold it? For whom, for what, for which reason would he surrender it?"

The very night of Elisabeth's death, couriers left the Winter Palace headed to the headquarters of the various Russian armies, carrying orders to not take one more step into Prussian territory and to abstain from all acts of hostility. There then appeared in the camp of Frederick II, under Breslau, Gudovitch, the favorite and clown of Peter III. The words that he transmitted were such that Frederick II saluted him as the "peak of the arch bearing the olive branch." Immediately the King of Prussia enjoined his troops from disturbing the lands of the Princes of Anhalt, the parents of the new Tsar; that they put at liberty all Russian prisoners, and expedite the dispatch of Goltz, who was a confident of the Tsar. He then sent in his footsteps Count von Schwerin, who, taken prisoner at Zorndorf, had during his internment at Petersburg, placed himself in the good graces of the heir to the throne, and who the Tsar had manifested a desire to see again. On his side, Peter III placed at liberty the Prussian prisoners, while expressing the wish to retain Generals Werner and Harte.

In the Russian Court, where there was a return of all the Germans who had been proscribed or punished under Elisabeth's reign. They hoped to see the return of the wonderful days of Anna Ivanovna and Anna Leopoldovna. Once again one saw the Mengdens, the Lilienfelds, and many others, including the old Field Marshal Münich, now 80 years old; the old surgeon Lestocq, who was 78 years old; the old Duke Biren, who was 80 years old, surrounded by all the other Birens. All these Germans basked in the Imperial favor with Prince George von Holstein and Feld Marshal Holstein-Betski. The ambassadors of France, Austria, Sweden, and Saxony-Poland were now as if in disgrace, while Keith, the English Ambassador, the Prussian envoys, and above all Goltz, a young man of 28 years, received invitations to all the parades and, above all, all of Peter III's drinking parties, where among the pitchers of beer and alcohol, in the smoke of the pipes, the traditions of the *Tabacks-Collegium* of the King-Sergeant Frederick Wilhelm were reborn.

The instructions that Frederick II had given to Goltz can be summarized as follows: If the Tsar desires to retain East Prussia until a peace is signed, agree to it; if he wishes to keep permanent possession of it, seek some compensation; if he asks for a guarantee for his Duchy of Holstein, ask him for the same for Silesia; if he proposes to make, as Duke of Holstein, war on the King of Denmark, preserve Prussia's neutrality, and above all offer our good offices and mediation.

Never was a negotiation an easier task. Peter III abandoned everything, even on the points that Prussia was resigned not to ask of him. What was even better was that he offered an alliance. He acted not only to withdraw the Russian armies from Prussian territory, but even to place them at the disposition of the King of Prussia.

Frederick responded to these generosities with praise that was not without some irony:

> It was that Peter III had the excellent heart, and the most noble and elevated sentiments that one does not ordinarily find in sovereigns. Lending himself to all the desires of the King, he went even beyond what one could expect…He hastened peace negotiations and asked in return only the friendship and the alliance of the King. Such a noble and generous process, also not very common, not only must be transmitted to posterity, but should be engraved in gold letters in the cabinets of all the Kings.[127]

Goltz initially had a most curious audience with the Tsar. Peter III showed him a portrait of Frederick II which he wore on his finger in a ring. He pointed out what he had suffered for the King when he, the Grand Duke Heir, had been excluded; from the Conference; the King had to only to say a word in his ear and he would march to his aid with all his army. Goltz was more than a favorite. He was like the Prime Minister for the Tsar; he disgraced or gave credit to those he saw fit. Peter III surrounded himself by portraits of Frederick, and out of respect for him, refused to allow Russian currency to be struck with his effigy crowned with laurels, saying modestly that he did not have the right to resemble Frederick II thus. On the subject of the treaty, he declared that the King had only to write it himself. Frederick sent a project which was adopted without modification. When Vorontsov, directed to negotiate it, had tried to raise some objections, Goltz went over his head and spoke directly with the Tsar. The following day he turned over to Vorontsov the treaty with

---

[127] Frederick II, *Histoire de la guerre de Sept ans.*

this note: "I have the honor to transmit hereafter to Your Excellency the project of peace treaty which I yesterday morning had the happiness to read with His Imperial Majesty and which was approved by him in all its parts." This was the treaty of 5 May (24 April) 1762: the tsar gave up all the conquests for which so much Russian blood had flowed in four great battles. Much more, on 19 June, a treaty of alliance was signed. The two sovereigns reciprocally promised to provide a corps of 12,000 infantrymen and 8,000 cavalry. The King of Prussia guaranteed Holstein to the Tsar and authorized him to put forward its old claims against Denmark; in the policy to be followed in Courland and Poland, they were in complete agreement.

Bérenger, the French Chargé d'affaires, relates a scene which occurred in one of the banquets given by the Tsar for the conclusion of the peace. "In a drunken tone he said to Goltz, 'Let us drink to the health of the King, our Master.' He [Frederick] did me the honor of giving me a regiment in his service. I hope that he will not give me my leave. You can assure him that, if he orders it, I will make war against hell with all my empire.'"[128]

Thus, not only did Peter III buy peace with Prussia for the price of East Prussia, but he subordinated his politics to Prussia's in Courland, which Elisabeth regarded as already being a Russian province; but he did give his people the consolation of peace. To the contrary, he assumed the burden of two heavy wars, absolutely strangers or at least of no concern to the interests of the Empire. One was a war against Denmark for the personal affair of Holstein and the other against Austria to assure Silesia to Frederick II.

It was the corps placed under the orders of Rumyantsev, the corps that had captured Kolberg, that was to conduct the war against Denmark. It was Tchernychev's corps, to that point an auxiliary force serving with the Austrians, that would turn against Austria in Silesia.

From 21 March, Tchernychev, on the first orders, was to separate himself from Laudon, and cross the Oder at Auras and had withdrawn into Poland. In May, he received new orders. He was then to recross the Oder and make a junction with the Prussian army.

We will now examine what happened in the Russian army of East Prussia and that of Pomerania.

Peter III, from 15 December, had replaced, in the government of East Prussia, Vassili Suvorov, with General Peter Panine, who was to surrender command of the 2nd Corps. As successor to Burturline, as Generalissimo, he gave it to Saltykov, the victor of Paltzig and Kunersdorf. We have seen that Fermor, the victor of Gross-Jägersdorf and Zorndorf, had fallen, at this time, into a sort of disgrace. Finally, in the camp before Kolberg, Rumyantsev received the order to immediately return to St. Petersburg.

---

[128] *La Cour de la Russia il y a cent ans*, p. 382.

The Russian armies had learned with a dumb pang the news of Peter's ascension to the throne. Out of instinct, the soldiers felt than the new emperor was not sympathetic to their successes against Prussia; that he would not approve of their glory; that the fruit of so much spilled blood was going to be lost for Russia. They knew that in St Petersburg all the military traditions of the nation were being overthrown; that there would be imposed on all units the drill regulations, the operations, and the equipment of the Prussians.

Rumyantsev's recall, which was part of the handing over of command to Volkonski, appeared to be a new indication of the goodwill of the master. Perhaps Peter III suspected, at the beginning, the sentiments of the young and ebullient General. A single interview sufficed to dissipate the Imperial biases. He had revealed himself as not only one of the most capable of the army's leaders, but a man so in love with war for war's sake, and who presented a second plan focused on interior and external politics.

A month later Rumyantsev reappeared before Kolberg, charged with the command of the army that was to operate against Denmark. He prepared for the war with Denmark with an ardor equal to that he had displayed against Prussia. The corps which, under his orders, had forced Kolberg to capitulate, would be raised to 50,000 men and reinforced with a contingent of 6,000 Prussians. On 1 June, he received orders to occupy, with an advance guard of 10,000 men, in Mecklenburg, the fortresses of Rostock, Güstrow, and Waren, and to establish magazines there, and to establish communications with the Baltic Fleet, commanded by Admiral Spiridof.

Denmark, so directly threatened, prepared, as it had on other occasions, without allowing itself to be intimidated by the inequality of forces, an energetic defense. King Frederick V had given the portfolio of war and command of his army to one of the most distinguished of France's generals, the future reforming Minister of Louis XVI, Count de Saint-Germain. The Count, who had been a Danish field marshal since 1761[129], had raised the forces of his new sovereign to about 70,000 men. However, only 30,000 could be put in line and the greater part were poorly trained, equipped, and armed. Saint-Germain, however, took the offensive, and moved before the Russians in Mecklenburg.

Rumyantsev, who had raised no objections to the new political ideas of the Tsar, however, was disturbed by the strategic dispositions imposed on him by St. Petersburg. Forced to extend his army across Pomerania and Mecklenburg, from Kolberg to Rostock, and soon to Lübeck, he feared that he could be surprised and destroyed in detail.

In a minute, things appeared to take a disastrous turn. Saint-Germain, after an otherwise insignificant cannonade, had succeeded in throwing from Lübeck the Russian advance guard. Then he deployed his army between

[129] For the details of this episode in the life of Saint-Germain, see the curious work by Mention, *Le Comte de Saint-Germain et ses réformes*. Paris: Clavel, 1834.

Wismar and Lake Schwerin, and projected to move against the magazines in Warin, while the Danish fleet, cruising along the coasts of Pomerania, commanded the inaction of the Russian fleet under Spiridof and disrupted the resupply of the Russian army. The worst part was that Peter III had manifested the intention of going to the Russian headquarters and personally directing operations. The chances of a Russian defeat had singnificantly increased.

In the first half of July 1762, the Russian army from Kolberg, now called the "Army of Mecklenburg", consisted of the following corps: Olitz's corps, which was still on the march from the Vistula to Pomerania; the corps of Plemiannikov and Tysenhausen, then around Kolberg and Treptow; Haugrewen's cavalry, Treptow's at Netzburg and Artensteinitz; the reserve, under Volkonski, more or less in the same region. Finally, the "flying corps" of General Brandt was in front of the army and pushing its advance posts beyond Anklam. Rumyantsev's artillery had a total of 102 cannons.

During this period, Tchernychev had left Thorn to operate in Silesia and make his junction with Frederick II. He brought with him a reinforcement of 20,000 men. However, this took 20,000 Russians from Laudon, and placed them on Frederick's side, which constituted a 40,000-man advantage to Frederick. Add to this that Maria-Theresa had seen herself obliged, for economic reasons, to disband 20,000 Austrian soldiers. The difference between the two sides, over the previous year, was now 60,000 men in Frederick's favor. "If the King," he remarked, "had won three battles, they could not have given him a greater advantage." It was, with the most wonderful hopes that the new Silesian campaign was about to begin. In awaiting the arrival of Tchernychev, Frederick had his cavalry harass that of the Imperials, who subsequently underwent a series of checks.

Tchernychev was proceeded, by a few marches, by an advance guard of 2,000 Cossacks. Frederick II distributed them between the two corps of Lossow and Reitzenstein. On 30 June, the main body of the Russian army crossed the Oder and marched on Lissa. Frederick II quickly used this reinforcement by throwing the Cossacks into Bohemia. He tells us this himself:

> They spread throughout all this kingdom, sowing terror. As of the second day of their entry, one their troops arrived before the gates of Prague. The terror that their presence inspired was so great that de Serbelloni was on the point of leaving Saxony with his army, to oppose, in person, the disorders which they produced. It is true that their actions were cruel: they ransacked, plundered, and burned the places which they found along their path. This irruption would not have been unfruitful if one had been able to prolong it.

Frederick II added that these undisciplined bands, once they were loaded with booty, left for Poland to sell or safely store away their booty. As a result, eight days later Bohemia was evacuated. Frederick now found himself in the strange role of the "archdirector of the bears in the Holy Roman Empire," something for which he had so reproached Laudon.

Frederick did not have time to relish this irony. He planned to attack the army of Daun by his right and, as his first operation, flush out the Austrian forces which occupied Burkersdorf and Leutmansdorf. The roles were already distributed, and he had assigned to Tchernychev the positions that he was to occupy. Suddenly, in the afternoon, Tchernychev appeared before the King of Prussia and, tears in his eyes, announced to him that Peter III had been deposed; that his wife had taken the throne under the name of Catherine II, and that he had received orders from the Senate to have his troops take an oath to the new Empress and "to leave the Prussian army without delay and withdraw into Poland."

"The loss of Peter III," added Frederick, "was a sad blow for the King, who esteemed his admirable character and who animated him with a heart filled with gratitude." Frederick did not oppose Tchernychev's departure. "The only kindness that he asked of him was to defer his departure for three days. To this the General assented. These three days were precious. It was necessary to put them to profit by striking some decisive blow. The presence of the Russians imposed on the Austrians, and they were still unaware of the revolution that was about to occur." Frederick II profited, to this end, from the circumstances to capture the positions that he coveted. He threw Wied's corps on those of Leutmansdorf; the corps of Knobloch and Möllendorf on those of Burkersdorf, while the Russian army, weapons in hands, appeared to cover his wings and serve as a reserve corp. In the joy of this success, Frederick II embraced Tchernychev and, despite the penury of his treasury, he gave him a sword of honor, estimated at a value of 27,000 *thalers*. Three days passed (19-22 July), and the Russians left the Prussians and headed for Poland, "without the Imperials having the least news of their departure."

The revolution that was accomplished in St. Petersburg, on 9 July 1762, which cost Peter III the throne, and which would eventually cost him his life, had been anticipated by Frederick II. The excessive manifestations of Peter's Prussophilia; his indiscrete expression of his being the servant of the King of Prussia; the discontent that he had provoked by his contempt for the Orthodox Religion and the national practices; the feverish haste by which he pushed reforms; the hostility raised in the army and especially in the Guard regiments by the new military regulations; the disappointment felt by the aristocracy following a detrimental peace from which sprang two new heavy wars, in which the interests of Russia were completely sacrificed to that of the Duke of Holstein, over the attitude of the Empress, who on several occasions, was humiliated in public; offended by the passion of the Tsar for Elisabeth Vorontsov; that Catherine was threatened to be thrown in a convent and seeing her son disinherited had not escaped the clear-sighted eye of the King.

More than once, Frederick II had attempted to convince Peter III to renounce his unpopular war with Denmark. More than once he had him advised by Goltz and Schwerin of the dangers that threatened him, begging him to "not neglect the essential precautions for his personal security." Peter III did not wish to hear this; he had pushed the army, the clergy, and the Tsarina too far. He had put them in the position of choosing between losing their legitimate rights or conquering the Empire by a coup de force. He was surprised by the promptitude and energy of Catherine. Frederick's student shamed his teacher by the ineptitude of his defense. He abdicated docilely, according to the expression of the King of Prussia, "like a child being sent to his bed." Now Catherine II reigned and Peter III died miserably in the Rocha Villa.

The power resulting from the coup d'état initially seemed to want to be a government of reaction against all that had been done or projected by the late Emperor: in foreign politics as well as in the interior matters. The proclamation of advent denounced the King of Prussia as "the perfidious enemy"; the measures adopted in the province of East Prussia; the movements of the Russian armies in Pomerania, on the Vistula and in Poland, caused to fear that after having passed from the camp of the "great alliance" into the Prussian camp, they would take up again the fight against Frederick II with as much eagerness as at the time of Elisabeth.

The fears the King of Prussia could have answered those which he inspired at St Petersburg. At the first moment, it had been believed there that Frederick II would take up the cause of his unhappy friend; that he would make some attempt to deliver him or to avenge him. It was especially expected that he would retain Tchernychev's army and make it prisoner.

When it was seen that it was nothing and that Tchernychev had already passed over the Oder and quietly continued his march on Posen, they were reassured.

The news that all the Russian armies, even Brandt's flying corps, already engaged in Mecklenburg, had taken oath without incident, calmed all other concerns. Those concerns had been sharp enough as the Tsarina apparently thought that Rumyantsev was completely devoted to Peter III; her first concern had been to recall him, while enjoining to him to give his command to Panine. The young General had to justify himself a second time in front of a new regime. In his report of 19 July, where he informed Catherine that his army had taken the oath, he added:

> Permit the most submissive and humble slave of Your
> Imperial Majesty to solicit the continuation of her favor

and goodwill, and to assure her in all sincerity that I have
never placed my happiness and the safety of my homeland
anywhere but in the person of Your Imperial Majesty, the only
consolation and the only comfort in the extremes and already
long concerns which the past has caused me to conceive.

He immediately left for St Petersburg, where he barely had time to
justify himself there and then returned to resume command.

It was in his absence and during the interim command of Panine that
most of the dispositions relative to the return of the armies was taken. A badly
established power still found it dangerous for it to resume the war against
Frederick II, be it for the conservation of East Prussia, as to continue in liaison
with him against Austria or Denmark. It was necessary to liquidate at the same
time all this business and to ensure Russia this peace which she wished even
more than the maintenance of her conquests.

It was too evident that the Seven Years War was drawing to an end.
Sweden had, following the Russian example, abandoned the "great alliance"
and signed a peace at Hamburg, on 22 May 1762, returning to Frederick
everything that he occupied in Pomerania. The French saw themselves
almost completely chased out of Hesse by Ferdinand von Braunschweig. The
intervention of Spain had added noting but the ruin of its colonies and its navy
to the French Navy and colonies. Austria, concerned over the agitations of the
Ottomans, who had been roused up on their southern borders by Frederick's
politics, resigned itself to mourning for the loss of Silesia. Even if Russia
had returned to the arena with all its forces, it would not have succeeded in
raising the courage of its ancient allies. Perhaps Catherine II, worried over
Courland, Poland, Turkey, and Sweden, foresaw in the future, herself in an
agreement if not an alliance with Frederick II, with broad compensations for
the abandonment of East Prussia.

However, in the decisions taken by the Council of War held by Panine,
on 22 July, one still found a trace of sharp deviance towards their former ally,
and the enemy before that. They decided that th,ey would remain in their
camp before Kolberg, as long as Brandt had not brought his troops out of
Mecklenburg and while Tchernychev was not yet securely in Poland. Brandt
was under orders to retreat a bit to the right to Tempelburg, "in order to be
able to move to the assistance of Tchernychev, in the case where Frederick II
attempted to forcibly retain him." Remo was decided not to break the camp
under Kolberg until all the armies had concentrated beyond any threat. In
awaiting this, they already returned to Russia, by sea, all the heavy baggage,
the siege artillery, the sick and the wounded. Then, when all the forces were
concentrated, they began moving in the direction of the Vistula. Tchernychev
had orders to march on Dünaberg, Panine on the same point to then continue

on Smolensk, and Dolgorukov on Riga. Soon all the troops were in their winter quarters in the old provinces of the Empire. East Prussia was totally evacuated and the Russo-Prussian Peace of 5 May was executed completely in all its articles. Only the treaty of alliance, of 19 June, was not ratified, and was considered as null and void.

Furthermore, all of Europe suffered from the same war fatigue. The death of Elisabeth and the eccentricities of Peter III had torn apart the "great alliance" forever. On 3 November 1762 the preliminaries for a peace were signed at Fontainebleau between France, Spain, and England, which led to the Treaty of Paris, on 10 February. Almost at the same time, on 15 February 1763, the two great German powers sign the Peace of Hubertsburg.

No one, except England had gained anything from the Seven Years War. France had renounced its hopes with regards to Belgium as Austria had renounced the reconquest of Silesia, as Russia has renounced holding East Prussia. They could only console themselves that they had weakened the power of Frederick II, even though they had not reduced the size of his lands by a single inch. On the other hand, how much had his moral force and prestige grown! Prussia, from this point of view, had grown and not been defeated. The genius of its king had legitimized its intrusion into the ranks of the great powers of Europe.

Russia had renounced East Prussia, the only fruit of its victories, which would have assured it a most advantageous situation on the Baltic coast. Had it lost everything?

No, because the role that it had played in the Seven Years War had aggrandized it as well. Just as with Prussia, it had made its entry into the European theater.

Alone among the members of the Coalition, and almost the equal of England and Prussia, Russia, initially a simple auxiliary of Austria, gained the honors of the war. It had shown of what weight it could bring to bear on the European Continent, in spite of the weaknesses and the abrupt turns of its policy. Its accession to the Franco-Austrian coalition had been enough to counterbalance all the genius of Frederick II; it was enough for it to leave the Coalition for the Coalition to fall into dissolution.

From the military perspective, it is noted that, throughout the course of the Seven Years War, the Russian army had always arrived late to the principal theater of war. In July and August, it delivered some great blow; from October to November, it resumed its interminable marches that would take it to the Lower Vistula. Not once did it winter in Germany. This was generally the result of the uncertainty of its senior command and, more frequently, the difficulty of supplying such a numerous force, encumbered with so much cavalry and so many draft animals, in a land that was so poor and so frequently ravaged. The intervention of the Russian army, slow, delayed, and of short duration, was like a storm that overthrew in a moment all the theater of war, disconcerting the tactics of friends and foes, stacking up mounds of ruins and bodies, then, like a storm struck by a change of wind, moved away while thundering towards the northeast. The Russian army disappeared, the war, erudite, meticulous, and methodical, resumed between Frederick II and Daun, Prince Henry and Laudon; one picked up the pieces on the chessboard knocked down by the Muscovite storm, the pawns, the knights, the rooks, and the game of chess continued. Furthermore, Daun sometimes regretted the premature retirement of these frightening allies, because it is after their departure for the Vistula, on 3 November 1757, that Frederick inflicted the bloody defeat of Torgau to him.

Assuredly Russian tactics, during this period, were inferior to Frederickian tactics. This army only knew how to fight a war of positions, abandoning to the enemy the initiative of operations. In its victories at Gross-Jägersdorf, Paltzig, and Kunersdorf, in the glorious and indecisive battle of Zorndorf, the positions taken by the Russians assumed a preponderant role. This tradition, extremely dangerous, was not lost in subsequent wars: Austerlitz, Friedland, and Borodino were position battles for the Russians, and the victor, was the heir to the genius of Frederickian tactics.

However, it was the Seven Years War that reminded Europe of the existence of the Russian Army. Until then, during the reigns of Peter the Great and Anna Ivanovna, it had appeared in only some localized fights along the Baltic and North Sea. Or with Anna Ivanovna or Elizabeth, it had shown itself only in two military parades that coincided with the end of the two wars of succession, whose ends it hastened. The Russian Army had only fought against the Swedes, the Poles, the Tartars, the Turks, and the Persians. For the first time it descended into the great arena, emulating the French and Austrian armies, frequently victorious over the Prussian Army, and twice it had come face-to-face with Frederick II. These are very important pages of its history, names of such glorious battles embroidered its standards, that one is astonished that their memory could be obliterated by the wars of the long reign of Catherine II, where it was far from having an adversary worthy of it. All in all, Catherine II still had to fight only the Swedes, the Poles and the Turks. Considering everything, the campaigns of the Russian Army in the Seven Years War remain its military university during the 18th century. From the Northern War under Peter the Great to the wars in Italy and Switzerland with Suvorov and with the formidable Napoleonic Wars, the culminating point of the Russian record, is really Seven Years War. There is not a battle from the wars of Catherine II that can compare with Gross-Jägersdorf, Zorndorf, Paltzig, or Kunersdorf, because it was not only the bravery of the enemy, it was also the technical merits which give value to the victory. Before these battles, it is necessary to look back to Poltava; after these battles, it is necessary to go to Cassano, Trebbia, Novi, Austerlitz, Eylau, Friedland, Borodino, and Leipzig, to find its equivalent. Between Charles XII and the France of the Directory and Empire, the Russians met one serious adversary: That is Frederick II. It is however this enemy whom Elisabeth drove back, that Fermor held in check, and Saltykov crushed.

In this war, the Russian army practiced all the parts of the art of warfare such as one knew it in the 18th century; not only did it fight great battles, but, with Saltykov, it made erudite steps, followed the enemy or delayed his pursuit, crossed rivers in the enemy's presence, occupied positions where it could stop without combat. With Rumyantsev, before Kolberg, it found itself capable of executing a regular siege, forcing the enemy to evacuate his supporting camp, dispersing or blocking relief forces, combining the ground operations with those of the Navy, and finally ending the siege with an open breach and a capitulation.

From the first year of the war, it had not stopped perfecting every branch of its army. Its infantry had always shown itself superior to the Prussian infantry, be it by its tenacity in the defensive, or by its élan in the offensive, withstanding the most terrible artillery fire and withstanding, without its usual chevaux de frise, the charges of cavalry. Its regular cavalry, so mediocre at the beginning of the campaign, so badly mounted, so badly instructed, had finished by reaching a state where it could accept battle, on an equal basis, with that of the Prussians. The irregular cavalry got rid of some of its original vices, such as the excessive multitude of its pack horses. Under leaders such as Stoffeln, Tottleben, and Berg it had shown itself incomparable for its audacity and the speed of its raids, the rapidity with which it could cover immense spaces, cutting the enemy's communications, reducing Frederick II to blindness by eliminating his scouts, assuring the security of the army while marching and concealing its movements. From the beginning its artillery was revealed as having the best equipment in Europe, notably the Shuvalov howitzers, the equivalent of which was not possessed by either France or Prussia. It had reformed its limbers. It had given itself, by the creation of specialized regiments of cannoneers and artillery fusiliers, which were necessary to protect and provide for the good operation of the guns.

It is true that this coalition of four European powers, not including Saxony and the States of the Holy Roman Empire, could not triumph over Frederick II and force him to return his earlier conquests. Politics had a greater part in this failure than the insufficiency of the Allied armies. We have shown the causes of the weaknesses and divisions in the "great alliance," and what other issues in St. Petersburg even irritated the absolute will of the Tsarina. In each of the Allied courts, just as between them all, there was dissension, mistrust, and ulterior motives. In each one of their armies, there were conflicts between the generals, between Laudon and Daun, Broglie and Soubise. The best generals were shackled in their action by the Conference, the Aulic

Council, and court intrigues. There was only resolution in Frederick II's camp and the councils of the King of England.

In everything that concerns the government, diplomacy, and military customs of the 18th century, however, are the particularities and accidents of the time. We attach what is durable, permanent, deep, to what is due to the character of the nation and can only perish with it.

For the Russian Army, which is really national both at the time of the writing of this book and in 1757, which is found again in the wars of Peter the Great, in the wars of Elisabeth, in the wars of Suvorov, in the wars of Alexander against Napoleon, which we found at Sevastopol and Plevna, it is the really excellent composition of this army that makes it the image of the nation; it is its burning devotion to the Orthodox Religion, the tsar, and the fatherland; it is its selflessness in front of dangers, deprivations and fatigue; it is the solidity of these infantrymen who Napoleon, after Frederick II, said that it was not enough to kill them to defeat them; it is the inexhaustible flood of this light cavalry, which, in the 19th century, is irregular only in name; it is this mobility and this audacity which always makes it so frightening in the vast plains of the north; it is its tenacity, stoicism, and the sure eye of the gunners of 1759, of 1812, of 1854, of 1877. All qualities, all the military virtues that appeared in Seven Years War seem to be preserved intact at the end of the 19th century. At that time, it had only added the technical improvements that a 150 years of European culture and scientific progress made it possible for Russia to realize.

THE END.

Index

Look for more books from Winged Hussar Publishing, LLC – E-books, paperbacks and Limited-Edition hardcovers.

The best in history, science fiction and fantasy at:

https://www. wingedhussarpublishing.com

https://www.whpsupplyroom.com

or follow us on Facebook at:

Winged Hussar Publishing LLC

Or on twitter at:

WingHusPubLLC
For information and upcoming publications

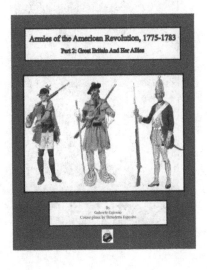

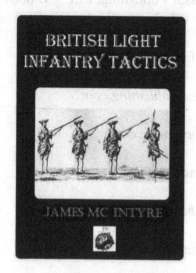

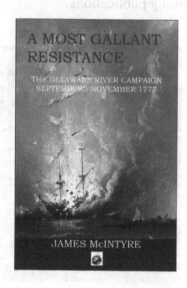

ABOUT THE AUTHOR

Alfred Nicolas Rambaud (2 July 1842 – 10 November 1905) was a French historian born in Besançon. After studying at the École Normale Supérieure, he completed his studies in Germany. He was appointed répétiteur at the École des Hautes Études on its foundation in 1868. At this time Russia was a growing power as a counterweight to Germany. He threw himself into the study of Russian history, staying in Russia in order to learn its language, institutions and customs. On his return, he published *La Russie épique*, a study of the dumas, *Ukrainian Epic Songs* (1876), a short but excellent *Histoire de la Russie depuis les origines jusqu'à l'année 1877* (1878; 5th ed., 1900), *Français et Russes, Moscou et Sévastopol 1812–1854* (1876; 2nd ed., 1881), and finally the two important volumes on Russian diplomatic history in the *Recueil des Instructions données aux ambassadeurs* (vols. vii. and ix., 1890 and 1891). He published his *Russes et Prussiens, guerre de Sept Ans* (1895), a popular work, though based on solid research. After teaching history in the Faculties of Arts at Caen (1871) and Nancy (1873), he was hired at the Sorbonne (1883), where he was the first to occupy the chair of contemporary history. He was elected a Senator later in life and he died at Paris in 1905.

ABOUT THE TRANSLATOR

George Nafziger is a translator of over 200 books and has long been considered one of the deans of military history.

Other Books from the Nafziger Collection

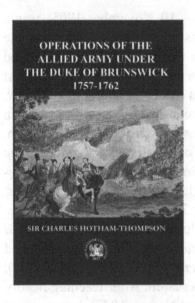

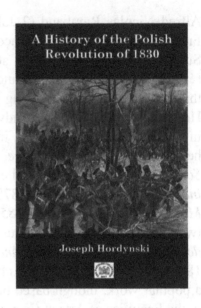

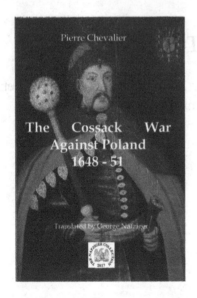

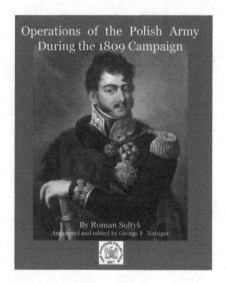

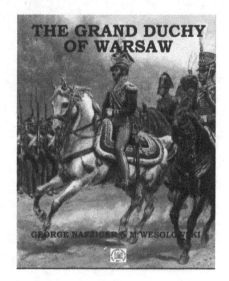